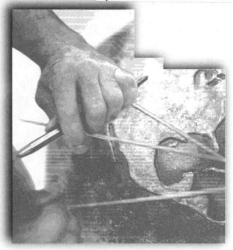

Cracking the New E-conomy™

Business Tools for Entrepreneurs

Gary McAvoy

EDITOR

Washington Software Alliance

Washington
Software Alliance

ASCENT
Partners, Inc.

Davis
Wright
Tremaine LLP

KPMG

Microsoft®

Silicon Valley Bank

▪ Disclaimer ▪

The views, opinions, and advice expressed by the contributing authors of *Cracking the New E-conomy*™ are those of the authors and not of the Washington Software Alliance. The Washington Software Alliance disclaims any responsibility with respect to this book or the accuracy of its contents. This book contains general information, including information regarding legal, accounting, and other matters of a technical nature, which may or may not apply to specific situations. Readers should contact their professional advisors to obtain individualized advice and should not consider the information contained herein as an adequate substitute for such advice.

Washington Software Alliance Publishing

Kathleen P. Wilcox, President and CEO

M. Craig Sanders, Publisher

Gary McAvoy, Editor
An Enterprise Technology Consultant based in Kirkland, Washington, McAvoy is fluent in all aspects of start-up growth management and leadership, with emphasis on strategic alliances, business development, marketing, and operations.

Randy Fisher, Interviewer
Fisher is a former business journalist. His company, iCentro Corporation provides marketing expertise to hi-tech companies and specializes in strategic coaching to sustain high performing work teams and business alliances.

Special Thanks to PhotoDisc, Inc. for cover images.   ISBN 1-887925-01-5

BK $75.00

Table of Contents

Section IV

Information for Mature Companies

Appendices

▪ Preface ▪

Ever since The Washington Software Alliance published *Beyond Code: Business Tools for Software Entrepreneurs* in 1992, we have had requests for a reissue.

The book in your hands today represents a major update of that earlier effort. Experts in a variety of disciplines that support and relate to software and digital media developers have contributed to this new effort.

Two years and major management have resulted in a book we feel confident will contribute significantly to the success not only of software entrepreneurs but entrepreneurs in many areas of high tech and manufacturing who discover the need for basic business information, who need additional information as they experience growth, and who need to know how to manage a mature endeavor.

We have received support not only from contributors of information but major sponsors without which this book could not materialize:

- Silicon Valley Bank
- KPMG LLP
- Davis Wright Tremaine LLP
- Ascent Partners, Inc.
- Microsoft Corporation

With their support and our good wishes, go forth and crack the New E-conomy.

Kathleen P. Wilcox
President and Chief Executive Officer
Washington Software Alliance

This compilation of advice and good practice for entrepreneurs forms three distinct sections:

- **Information for Start-Up and Young Companies**
- **Information for Expanding Companies**
- **Information for Mature Companies**

In addition, in Section One we have provided two provocative articles on the nature of work in the newly emerging information technology field. We suspect they describe work in the broader area of high technology—and perhaps describe the nature of work in the twenty-first-century.

Within these covers you will hear the voices of experience: in law, marketing, finance, sales, intelligence, and global commerce. Take heed—and succeed.

Gary McAvoy
Editor

▪ C h a p t e r   1 ▪

Virtual Construction Workers

Excerpted from *Joystick Nation*

—by J. C. Herz

Having grown up wandering through game worlds from Atari *Adventure* to *Castle Wolfenstein,* my generation of vidkids can appreciate the care and craftsmanship that goes into a high-quality virtual environment: artful dimensions, good doorway design, well-placed obstacles, easy-to-reach ammunition. Two decades of cartridge games breed a deep familiarity with the conventions of vector graphs, tile maps, and 3D-rendered polygons. And even if video games haven't prepared us to be fighter pilots, as Ronald Reagan liked to think they would, they have prepared us for high-paying jobs in the booming virtual construction industry. The manufacturing economy may be sputtering, but there are plenty of assembly jobs in the video game industry: computer-aided drafting, 3D model making, texture mapping, object design, puzzle building, landscaping, backgrounding, and polygon animation.

At this point, game worlds have become so immense and complicated that their construction requires crews of postcollegiate code carpenters and graphic design masons working 16-hour days for months or years, either as company employees or independent contractors. It's like building a skyscraper, or a cathedral, or some kind of fabulous gargantuan sea vessel.

"I do the carpeting for the *Titanic,*" drawls Billy Davenport, a 26-year-old graphic designer from Tullahoma, Tennessee. Billy drives a pickup truck, sports a red Co-Op Feeds gimme cap, and happens to bear a striking resemblance to Bo Duke from the *Dukes of Hazard.* Fifty years ago, he'd have taken a job that involved wood planes, sandpaper, circular saws, and lots of varnish. But in the age of interactive interiors, he does digital wainscoting and furniture finishing for CyberFlix, a CD-ROM developer in Knoxville. CyberFlix has produced a string of award-winning CD-ROM games—a space opera, a post-apocalyptic shoot-'em-up, a Western, a horror title—*Lunicus, Jump Raven, Dust,* and *Skullcracker,* respectively. The company is staffed by a squad of fresh-faced lads, and its principals have been written up in all the usual magazines for the sort of garage triumph that has long since become cliché.

Their current project is *Titanic,* a mystery adventure set aboard the notorious Edwardian luxury liner that, for the purposes of this game, has been painstakingly reconstructed as a perfect scale replica of the original. The doors swing the same way. The taps work. Every deck, cabin, corridor, and engine compartment corresponds to its actual counterpart rotting on the bottom of the North Atlantic. This process involves two construction crews. The 3D crew builds the skeleton and strutwork on high-end workstations from the original plans and blueprints. At this stage, the ship is architecturally complete, a schematic phantom floating in virtual dry dock.[1] Then the 2D guys come in and put the skin on it.

Essentially, what guys like Billy do is gild two-dimensional surfaces onto this transparent 3D structure. They shrink-wrap the frame with textures and interior details. Imagine walking through a house where every wall, ceiling, and floor was *trompe l'oeil*, where every texture, from the furniture upholstery to the play of light on the silverware, was painted on. This is how a CD-ROM environment is built. In this case, the visual shrink-wrap comprises the original fixtures and surfaces and provisions of the HMS *Titanic*. So for the past year, Billy has been coating the walls with authentic *Titanic* paint colors, hanging wallpaper duplicated from period photographs, putting in the domed skylights, laying seventeenth-century Arabian-style mosaics in the Turkish bath, and fashioning plaster moldings in the lounges and galleries.

Billy takes a craftsman's pride in his 2D design work. "We have a room where you start out in the game, and I've outfitted the desk with postcards that you can actually flip over and read, and magazines like *Brave New World* magazine, and I've designed the covers for 'em, so you can pick those up and look at 'em. There's a lot of detail in there that we don't even expect people to actually look at. It's like, if you were just tryin' to half-ass it and get through it, you might make a lamp, but you might not make the electric cord that goes *behind* the desk. We're tryin' to get all the detail in there. There's a lot of games that you look at today, and a lot of people don't take the time and energy to go in and really work with their maps to make 'em look real, so they end up coming out lookin' plastic or fake."

This is the sort of thing you don't think about in the real world, where, if you get closer to an object, you see it in more detail. In a game world, this isn't necessarily true. If there are cans in a cupboard, a graphic designer has to come up with the wood grain and vintage food labels so that the 3D guys can map them onto the planes and cylinders in some corner pantry of the *Titanic*. Every level of resolution is deliberate, to say nothing of all the dirt that must be strategically strewn and the corners that have to be ground down. Because in the end, what conveys reality is signs of deterioration. And all that scuffing and staining and denting requires endless hours of meticulous work. It's historical restoration in reverse. But it tends to attract the same kind of radical perfectionist. On the *Titanic* project, Billy's pride and joy is a scrapbook on the mantel in the opening scene. "I made it so that when you click on the scrapbook, it opens up, and then all the pages are just full of imagery, you know,

---

[1] In an eerie twist of fate, Paul Haskins, one of the 3D artists who spent two years digitally rebuilding the *Titanic* in cyberspace, is the direct descendant of an Irish shipyard worker employed by Harland and Wolff, the Belfast shipbuilder that assembled and launched the original *Titanic*. Reconstructing the behemoth vessel in cyberspace added a haunting sense of karmic return to the normal stress of the workday. The ship, he explains, was as long as three football fields and had nine decks. "Re-creating that digitally in 3D, we were working with data files of immense proportions and a huge amount of complexity. Naturally, it hit a chord with me—I'm working with mathematical calculations to re-create the kinds of things my grandfather helped craft out of iron and steel."

ephemera, things like that. So I go out and I find all the stuff to go in the scrapbook and put it in there. That's the fun job. I could spend a day or I could spend a month on that book."

As players, we have come to expect a certain level of realism and depth in videogames, and that level continues to rise. So now game companies have to employ people to crumple up the scenery. And this kind of work is incredibly labor-intensive. It is not a glamour job. That's the Silicon Valley fantasy of what it's like to work on videogames—this vision of a 30-something millionaire cruising down the Pacific Coast Highway with a cell phone in one hand and a fistful of stock options in his pocket. The reality is that most of the people who assemble videogames are just out of school. And they're not chin-scratching liberal arts majors from Ivy League universities hugging the track of an old boy network. They're fresh out of some technical institute. They're trade school graduates. And they're pulling double shifts six days a week. "I worked 36 hours in two days last week," Billy says with shrug. "But they try to make it as accommodating as possible. We've got showers, you know. And they stock the refrigerators with Cokes. Everybody gives you Cokes. They want you gettin' wired so you stay there all the time. And they got some couches. So I mean, you can stay here forever."

Indeed, CyberFlix HQ does possess that 24-hour Kinko's Copies atmosphere—full of equipment and overworked 20-somethings, simultaneously frenetic and oddly mellow. Because, as hard as everyone's working, there's no whistle at the end of the day. Because, well, there is no end of the day. In fact, there is no daylight to speak of, because the vertical blinds have been drawn to shut out the sun, leaving the downtown loft in complete darkness, save for the glow of computer monitors and a few lava lamps. CyberFlixers like it this way. They have showers. They have caffeinated beverages. They have Blow Pops, Pop-Tarts, and Atomic Fireballs and a Ping-Pong area. They can go for days. And at this point, they have lost all circadian perspective, because the beta deadline for *Titanic* is a week away. Along every wall, white boards outline the grid of work still to be done. Blueprints of the *Titanic* hang outside the testing room, where half a dozen 20-something programmers are rooting out the bugs in the latest draft of the game. From outside, you can hear them heckling the hell out of it.

"Knock-out gas? Who came up with *that* term. It's like some old *Batman* show or something."

"Just click the top one, stupid."

"I dunno how much longer I can play this game."

"Well you've been at it about six hours."

"You shoulda seen the redneck we had in here yesterday to test. He was like, 'Damn, do you mean to tell me you can't kill shit in this game?' He was just like, outraged."

It has been a very long day. It's been a long week. It's been a long month. But at six o'clock on a Friday, everyone is still here, fully engaged in the most labor-intensive facet of the game: puppet scripting. In the course of *Titanic's* espionage mystery drama, you have to converse with dozens of photorealistic characters aboard the ship. Each one of these characters has dialogue, and all of it has to be dubbed from recorded voice-overs onto the mouth movements of animated talking heads. Or rather, the mouth movements have to be manipulated to lip-synch the audio. This involves reducing words and phrases to their phonetic building blocks, which go into one end of a proprietary authoring tool and come out the other side matched with appropriate lip shapes. So, for instance, "I've no use for that" becomes "iv no os for that." This is not difficult—it requires roughly the same amount of technical expertise as macramé. But translating 500 pages of screenplay into phonics is like one of those absurdly tedious home crafts projects, knitting a car cover, say, or latch-hooking a wall-to-wall carpet. It is a nontrivial task. At this point, every spare computer in the office has been put to use as a scripting machine, and everyone, from the creative director to the receptionist, is frantically stitching together video and dialogue. The entire staff of CyberFlix has abandoned their official job descriptions to become digital assembly-line workers.

In this regard, working at a videogame company is pretty much the opposite of working at a Fortune 500 corporation, where it's important to arrive at a certain time and dress a certain way, to look as if you're working hard while cultivating a network of contacts by spending a lot of time on the phone. At CyberFlix, dress code is nonexistent. Schedules are brutal, but entirely flexible. And the concept of face time does not exist. Getting the work done is all that counts—sheer, unadulterated output.

On every bulletin board in the building, someone has scrawled a running countdown in capital letters: 6 DAYS LEFT.

"They're keeping us pumped up on amphetamines and cheap pornography," cracks a 3D model maker, the infamous Alex Tschetter, resplendent in his mohawk, earrings, and multiple tattoos. "Whatever it takes to keep us here, whatever we want. The best part about this time is that you can come in looking like a wreck, reeking of booze, whatever, and they're never gonna fire you for it, because they need you." Alex is a burly former construction worker from the flatlands of Florida who happens to be a gifted computer animator. He also has a lengthy criminal record. No one bothers him.

Alex does not respond well to Authority. He was, in fact, kicked out of computer design trade school for accosting an instructor before the director of the 3D design program interceded on his behalf, took him under her wing, and introduced him to the wonderful world of high-end workstations. Given sufficiently powerful equipment and enough personal space, Alex hauls like a sled dog. He comes in at an unspecified hour, usually before noon, and stays for marathon sessions, bolting together 3D models on his souped-up SGI workstation. He functions in his own personal time zone. But he's allowed, because his work is jaw-droppingly good, and he cranks it out at a prodigious rate, and because his personal demeanor engenders a healthy respect—the kind of respect you would accord a large, friendly pit bull.

"Luckily enough," he says, "they've been thoughtful not to force any kind of real schedule on us. Just get in when you can and do your shit. So I just go to work doing whatever I have to do, build sets and do props, little things here and there where it needs to fit in, do movies, and help. While I've got big jobs off running on the SGI, I just jump around and do little different things, 2D work or whatever. As long as it takes is as long as you've got to spend, and if you're here friggin' 18 hours a day, so be it. And it's kind of very strange for me," he says, "because up until I came here to do this, I was always working construction, my whole life, and I felt sorry for the poor bastards trapped in air-conditioned prisons all day, and I thought it was so much fun to be roaming around on the job site, getting sun and running around and hollering and screaming. And that's all well and good, but you ain't never gonna make shit. You're gonna die poor or you're gonna die pissing away your social security check in some stinking little bar, and that's no good. So I just decided to take the step and at least do this for a few years to say that I could do it, and make some money out of it. If something went horribly wrong here tomorrow and I got kicked out or fired or I had to leave, I would just throw some things in the truck, get out, and go someplace else and do it. Because this industry is just replicating itself at such a disgusting rate and everybody's got something to do. And sure, not everything is quality, but it doesn't matter. It's like, you got money? All right, pay me, I'll do it. Give it up. And then you just do it and move on again."

Digital construction workers are the most technologically sophisticated migrant labor force the world has ever seen. Demand for their skills is at an all-time high, and they go where the work is. And the jobs are everywhere, because demand for computer-enhanced entertainment is skyrocketing. Game jobs are plummy because they're artistically demanding. But they are dwarfed by the more mundane (yet lucrative) opportunities to create flying 3D logos for local television stations, animated cumulus clouds for national weather shows, snazzy zooming statistics in industrial videos, and adorable computer-generated mascots.

And, Silicon Valley notwithstanding, the crackerjack videogame jobs are increasingly happening in out-of-the-way places. Hit games have a way of germinating in left field, in places like Spokane, Washington *(Myst)*, and Mesquite, Texas *(Doom)*, and Knoxville, Tennessee, home of CyberFlix. Making a game isn't like making a movie, which requires lots of site-specific infrastructure and schmoozing. Games aren't tied to the Bay Area the way that movies are tied to L.A. The tools are mobile and so are the people who use them. So the work can happen anywhere. Increasingly, it doesn't matter where you are. It only matters where your imperial corporate partners are. In the CyberFlix lobby, there are three clocks, marked Tokyo, Orlando, and Knoxville. This is the underlying irony of "indie success" in the game industry. Once the code is finished, the spunky individualist phase comes to an abrupt halt and the media empire machinations begin.[2] Most "garage multi-media" outfits harboring any talent are affiliated with some multinational behemoth—a movie studio, a telecommunications company, or a global distribution octopus like Bertelsmann.

In the big picture, "rogue" game producers are less like indie record labels and more like punk rock bands. In their own self defined environment, they create a particular kind of thrilling experience, which ends up as a string of ones and zeroes on an optical disc distributed by some media giant. In this case, CyberFlix signed a three-disc deal with Paramount after their first disc's initial glimmer of success. Now they're distributed in North America by GTE (which, like every other telecom concern, is lurching into the entertainment arena). In Europe and Southeast Asia, CyberFlix games are distributed by BMG. In Japan, by a titanic toy company, Bandai. Of course, there are strings. CyberFlix's project roster also includes production work for GTE and a *Mighty Morphin' Power Rangers* title for Bandai. But it's a small price to pay for global distribution and a home base in Smoky Mountain trout-fishing country.

And in their own slightly deranged way, the 3D modelers, animators, and programmers of CyberFlix belong here in Knoxville, where the three largest employers are the University of Tennessee, the TVA, and Oak Ridge National Labs. The regional economy is already based on high tech make-work programs for gearheads and construction crews. And as it turns out, most of Knoxville's young codesmiths are the spawn of Atomic Age engineers. These are kids whose dads built missiles and dams. CyberFlix's president is the son of a Martin Marietta physicist. Half the people on the payroll are related to architects of the Cold War or the Tennessee hydroelectric power grid. And now that those jobs are gone, children of the Smoky Mountain military-industrial complex have nothing better to do than play in punk rock bands, become snowboard thrashers, and start new media companies. And somehow, it's fitting that they should make their living on machines whose technological great-grandparents number-crunched nuclear impact, and that they should use these machines to build videogames set in outer space, the post-apocalypse, and aboard a massive, sinking steel ship—and that they should do it here, in the cradle of the atomic bomb.

—From *Joystick Nation* by J.C. Herz. Copyright 1997 by J.C. Herz. By permission of Little, Brown and Company.

---

[2] A chart of media empire investments in the interactive entertainment industry looks like a billion-dollar game of Twister. Having lost hundreds of millions of dollars opening (then closing) multimedia divisions, the Jolly Green Giants of Hollywood have decided it's a better idea to buy pieces of independent companies that actually know what they're doing. In addition to the Tinseltown contingent, hardware manufacturers like Matsushita, Philips, Sony, Toshiba, phone companies like GTE and AT&T, cable companies like TCI, television networks, and finger-in-every-pie conglomerates like Disney and Dreamworks have twisted themselves into a tangled Web of mutual investments with the likes of Sega and Microsoft, Silicon Graphics and IBM, strategic software tool developers, indie game producers, and of course, each other.

■ Chapter 2 ■

Work

Excerpted from *Release 2.0:*
A Design for Living in the Digital Age

—by Esther Dyson
CEO, EDventure Holdings
Chairman, Electronic Frontier Foundation

It's five years from now, and you hate your job. Should you be looking for a new one on the Net? How will your skills be valued in the new online world? Where can you check out the opportunities available? Is it realistic to think you could telecommute to a job in another city, let alone one in another country? You're scared to post too many of these questions, in case your current employer may be out there looking, too.

What kind of job are you looking for? If you're a saleswoman, you may want to stay within your field because you know the territory, or you may want to leave the field because you don't want to compete with your current company. You may be moving to a new town and looking for a similar job (with a raise, of course!) in the new location. Or you may be looking for a new opportunity, as a sales manager.

In all of these cases, you can find opportunities on the Net. You can check out the Web sites of companies in your field, or you can explore other industries. You can also read news articles, industry analysts' reports, and other objective third-party appraisals of the companies you're considering. To attract interest from them, you can list yourself with an anonymous résumé service, using the equivalent of a box number for replies so that your current employer won't find out. Or you can send e-mail to the personnel department or to other executives whose names you can find. You can narrow your search to your own hometown or to your preferred new location.

If you're a writer, on the other hand, you may not be looking for a steady job but rather for interesting assignments. In that case, you may be competing with Steve Fenichell, the writer who helped to edit this book as a freelancer. He has written two books of his own (most recently *Plastic*), and edited or coauthored others. Between books, he writes articles. He gets some assignments through his agent at International Creative Management, who calls him on the phone with proposals, requests, and ideas. He also gets calls from magazine editors, very much at random, who think of him from time to time. Sometimes when he has free time and would like to work, his agent doesn't know of anything appealing. Sometimes he has more offers than he knows what to do with. Sometimes there's work to be had, but he and his agent don't know about it.

How will he be looking for work five years from now? Assuming he learns how to use his browser (just kidding, Steve!), he'll probably be finding a lot of work on the Net. He may scan daily listings of editing jobs available; he may also post his own qualifications in search of work. If he's interested in a particular topic, or he wants to justify a trip to, say, Portugal, he might go outside the writers' communities into, say, a Portuguese site and ask for tips on interesting tourist events that he could write up for a travel magazine. (Would that be spamming? It's up to that Portuguese community to decide.)

To demonstrate his qualifications, he may post some of his past articles on his own Web site, where he'll put links to BarnesandNoble.com and Amazon.com to sell copies of his books. There's a lot of competition out there, and he needs to distinguish himself from all the other candidates. But he's nervous about posting new story ideas for fear of losing them to someone else; leave that for a quiet conversation with a travel-magazine editor he can trust.

What will have happened to his agent? Many of her other clients will also be trolling the Net, along with lots of amateurs. But she'll probably still be working with her clients because her skills go further than just finding work; she can negotiate contracts, give them advice on which publishers to deal with, and the like. She may well do much of this by e-mail, but every once in a while she and Steve will go out for a drink. She knows a lot of inside gossip that never gets posted anywhere, although some of it gets e-mailed. (The people whose business will really be cut into is the messenger services, who will no longer be carrying heavy documents around town; those will all go by e-mail, and even the contracts will have digital signatures.)

While freelancing in almost every field is becoming increasingly prevalent in 2004, Steve is still not the norm. Despite the technical possibilities, most people still have steady jobs with a regular employer and a predictable salary. There are two reasons for this. One, many people prefer the relative security of a steady job, and the teamwork, community, and affiliations they build at work. Companies, for their part, prefer people who have experience and are integrated into the company, who know how things are done, who have so-called "community memory." There's a lot more to a job than just the formal work.

Second, even those who would rather freelance often find it too difficult and nerve-wracking to generate a steady stream of work. Even if they know that they could find the work, they don't enjoy looking for it, negotiating, and testing their worth every day. These activities constitute what economists call "transaction costs," the costs of finding and arranging work. The Net reduces them, but it doesn't eliminate the process or the emotional anxiety that comes with it for at least some people. They'd rather find a comfortable place to work, settle in, and focus on the job.

Looking for Work

The Net won't change people's innate preferences between security/familiarity and variety. But it will enable those who prefer variety to achieve it much more easily. Indeed, the Net will support people all along the spectrum, whether they are looking for the job of a lifetime or for a week's work.

The way this works will not be through clumsy search engines but through online communities and specific-market online employment classifieds. The difference is that such ads will be easier to use for both sides. Employers can post job descriptions and reach potential employees worldwide; employees can search—or post their résumés—and likewise reach a worldwide labor market. (Of course, they'll still have to deal with restrictive labor and immigration laws on occasion.) In a few years, the old notion of using paper classifieds—with no way of searching, no way of telling which are out of date, and limited geographical reach—will seem ludicrously archaic. Books may not be replaced very quickly, but time-sensitive, search-ready information simply works best on the Net.

Already, many résumé-exchange Web sites are popping up, many of them industry-specific. For example, Scala, an accounting software company that I have invested in, sponsors the Scala Job Bank, a free online résumé service targeting users of Scala. Accountants and software experts looking for jobs use it; so do clients, companies who already use Scala and need employees familiar with the software. It works as subtle advertising for Scala, but it also offers real benefits: customers are more likely to purchase Scala if they know they can find workers trained to use it, and software and accounting experts are eager to learn Scala because they know they will be able to find a job. The fluid marketplace around the software makes the software itself more attractive, and the whole thing feeds on itself, occasionally luring in users of other brands of software. And of course Scala itself occasionally hires people through the Job Bank.

Join a Network

But as any job-seeker knows, traditional channels are not always the most effective. Two others often work better, and fortunately they have online equivalents, too. The first is old-fashioned networking: join the community in which you wish to work, make friends, get your name known, and then look for a job. There is no better place to do that than in an online community. You can do it in a work-specific community—a food-marketing group, for example or in the traditional more social way—a religious group, a charitable group, and so on. The kicker added by the Net is that you have far more choice of which groups to join, raising the chance that you'll find a job that you like and that employers will find a suitable employee.

Of course, employers can and should play this game, too. Are they interested in finding subject experts, or general, well-rounded managers active outside their work community?

Don't Find Your Job; Define It!

The second neo-traditional way to find a job is to create it for yourself. Find a company with a problem and propose a solution that involves you. You can do this to sell your consulting or your company's services or to find a steady job. Again, the Net makes it easier. You may come across a company that you really like and see an opportunity for its products in a market it doesn't seem to be exploiting, whether it's your own geographical territory or a market segment.

In the case of Juan, an animal trainer and biologist, he might notice that a certain zoo had just expanded its monkey section—as described in the zoo's Web site, focused more on luring visitors than animal trainers. But that's the point. The Net plus a little imagination . . .

He sends the zoo's Web site an e-mail asking if it needs someone to mind the new monkeys.

Wait! Not so fast!

Now the other features of the Net come into play. Having found some interesting opportunities, both sides can check out their potential partners. Juan can poke through the zoo's Web site at leisure. More interesting, he can read reviews of it in a variety of city guides. Now the news is not so good. The zoo is known for sloppy upkeep, unhealthy animals, and messy walkways. A few problems might mean an opportunity to help fix the situation, but a lot of problems may mean that it's unfixable and not a place Juan wants to work.

Now he's concerned. He searches the Web for some older information on the zoo, and finds the names of a couple of people who used to work there but no longer do. Politely, he sends them e-mail explaining that he's thinking of working at the zoo and can they give him some insights?

Over at the zoo, the person who filters the nonroutine messages received at the zoo's Web site has forwarded Juan's e-mail to Alice, head of human resources. She is now conducting an investigation of her own. Has Juan written any scholarly papers based on his work as a biologist? Has he commented in any discussion groups? It's pretty easy to find out, through a search engine called DejaNews, which indexes not only Web sites but most discussion groups. Aha! Not only is Juan a biologist, he also seems to be active in animal photography circles. Fortunately, Alice likes that; she is an amateur photographer herself. But now she looks at some of his comments; pretty fatuous, she thinks at first. Then she notices the dates of the most awkward comments and sorts them to follow his development over time. From an outspoken, uninformed novice, he seems to have matured into a thoughtful, principled expert, with interesting insights on the interplay between an animal's behavior and its size compared to the rest of its litter. She writes him back a note inviting him for an interview and hits the send button.

Visible Reputations

Whether you're an employee checking out companies, an employer checking out people or even a potential visitor checking out zeros, the free flow of information engendered by the Net will highlight the distinctions between good and bad. (Alice's zoo is in a pretty good position because there's probably no other zoo nearby, but it will be competing with other ways for people to spend their time—whether online or in the physical world. And local people will be better able to compare it with zoos elsewhere based on information on the Net.)

It's all very well for Alice to check out Juan, but this also means that a lot of people will be able to check out you. You may feel different about your privacy after you've been on the Net for a while, but let's consider what it means for your job hunt—and your work life. First of all, anything official will probably be available. Where did you work? What did you say? If you had a notable success or a notable failure, people will be able to find out about it.

There will be so much information out there, both favorable and unfavorable, reliable and unreliable, that no one will pay attention to most of it until someone starts to consider you in particular for a job. The sheer volume of information will reduce the sting of sensitive items, but you'll need to recognize that they're there. Employers will become more forgiving of failure once it's clear it's so common; the best thing to do is to disclose everything—and explain what you learned from it. In my case, I presided over a disastrous flop in the mid-'80s, with an ill-fated experiment at producing a daily newspaper for the computer industry. It failed for a variety of reasons, including the absence of the reliable online delivery system we would have had today. I ended up having to fire 27 people. And I could tell a prospective employer that I learned a lot!

Now suppose I—or you—had somehow developed an enemy. People may be reading nasty comments about you from totally unreliable sources. As you go on your job search, you should probably take the time to do what your prospective employers are doing: find out what other people are saying about you. There may be misinformation you want to correct, from a well-meaning but mistaken person. Tell the person, or if it's a public forum, write a correction that links to the original comment.[3] There may be nasty comments from

---

[3] One problem with much of the Web is the asymmetry of links. That is, I can write my own rebuttal to a comment and point to the original comment, but I usually cannot annotate the comment itself. People need to take the initiative to hear my side of the story. This ultimately needs a technological fix—though a lot of Web site owners don't really want outsiders commenting all over them.

people who are just flat-out unreliable or mean; one way or another, it's up to you to prove them wrong. But any sensible employer will measure the proportion of favorable versus unfavorable remarks, and can probably distinguish malice from truth. Finally, there may be embarrassing truths that you're just going to have to deal with. You were younger then, weren't you? But the Net certainly will foster truth-telling, if only because you want them to hear your version of the story first. Personally, I think this is good overall. People may become more realistic in what they expect of others, and of themselves. Feedback isn't always pleasant, but it's healthier than illusion.

Of course, some kinds of information just don't get onto the Net. There are always cases where, for example, no one says anything about an incompetent son-in-law. Some truths are kept within closed circles or sent by e-mail rather than posted publicly. Nonetheless, there's usually an astonishing amount of information available for anyone who takes the trouble to look for it. More is being added every day.

More troublesome yet are questions about health and moral issues. Should you disclose that you have cancer in a chat group, given that the news might get back to an employer and companies are reluctant to hire people with health risks (despite laws against discrimination)? Should you disclose that you have a criminal record? Those are much tougher questions, and in many cases they're handled by law. All I can say is that in the long run more honesty could help erase the stigma of certain diseases and conditions—although not the medical costs. The more people reveal their frailties, the more clear it will become how productive people can be anyway.

Companies and Products Have Reputations, Too

The information flow that illuminates employees' reputations will also include companies, products, and services. Their quality and other features will become easier to determine and faster to have an impact. Better communications, Net versions of best-10 lists, consumer ratings, and overall visibility will cause investors, managers, employees, and customers to gravitate to good companies; they will flee from bad or ineffective ones. Just as the pace at which you live your individual work life will speed up, so will the pace at which companies are created, grow, and disappear. There will always be market anomalies, but the life span of each individual company is likely to become shorter unless it can maintain quality and transform itself regularly. The giant companies created through mergers over the past few years are likely to keep changing their structure—with further mergers, divestitures, and reorganizations—over the next few years. They will also be competing with and acquiring an increasing number of start ups, as the barriers to entry into many markets will be lower for newcomers.

Meanwhile, the barriers to a graceful exit will be higher for existing firms. Companies stuck with the wrong things—people, strategies, culture—will find it harder to change.

Companies that lose steam will fall behind more quickly, as competing companies keep speeding ahead. The good news is that this "Darwinism" applies more to companies than to people. Bad companies die or get absorbed, but with luck their employees learn something and move on to better companies.

The Shrinking Company

All this means a tendency toward smaller company size—even though most of what we hear about is mergers and industry consolidation as the media focus on giants. Little companies will find it easier to reach customers without massive marketing efforts even as they stay small, and they will be able to specialize in just one or two functions instead of facing constant pressure to grow to achieve economies of scale. Those economies of scale will diminish as even small companies get access to just the resources they need over the Net; the transaction costs of finding and negotiating work will drop for companies as well as for workers.

Most companies will find it easy to shrink or stay small by outsourcing—hiring outside firms to do tasks that were once done inside. For example, Microsoft Network's consumer technical support is done by outside firms. In my own little company, we don't have a data-entry person on staff; we hire one when we need her. Meanwhile, Scala is doing a booming business running clients' payrolls. It's a dull and boring job, but it's difficult, especially in Central and Eastern Europe where the tax laws keep changing all the time and there are deductions for everything from children to military status, and people may be paid in several currencies. In a regular company, this is an onerous task; for Scala, it's a specialty. In the near future Scala will also be getting companies' time sheets and delivering payment information to their banks over the Net. (In Eastern Europe, most people are moving directly from cash to bank cards and electronic banking, without having to go through the stage of paper checks.)

On the other hand, the division of Scala that translates its software could well become an independent company or perhaps merge with another translation firm, as it already has several outside customers. One of its competitors based in the Czech Republic, Moravia Translations, already does a substantial part of its business over the Net, receiving files from customers, translating them, and sending them back electronically. In this way, this little 52-person company operates successfully in several countries, mostly using freelancers with whom it communicates over the Net.

From Ignored Department to Respected Partner

The impact of outsourcing is often this: what was a secondary function in a large company becomes the core business in a smaller outsourcing company. A translator in a translation division doesn't have much hope of career growth or respect from the larger company, but in a company focused on translation that translator could rise to become a manager or at least feel that he's an integral part of the company.

Meanwhile, employees are less likely to stay put when companies try to grow larger. All those start ups that sell out to larger companies will get integrated into their buyers, yes, but the born entrepreneurs will leave to start new companies. Others will leave to work for them or find themselves in smaller, more comfortable environments.

Many people don't necessarily want to grow companies or make a killing; they simply want to work in a small-company environment. The Net will make it easier for non-entre-preneurs to strike out on their own, avoiding both the perils of company growth and the opposing perils of corporate stagnation. They can run a small business without the imperative of grow or die. Change—yes; but growth is optional when you can stay small and productive. Or you can disband and start over. Why stick around when the magic fades?

Silicon Valley Syndrome

Like employees, investors are not likely to be as patient in the future as they have been. Turnover will be faster in companies as well as in people.

Modern firms' primary edge will be creativity and innovation: the ability to come up with new products, new services, new business models, and new strategies. The innovations won't always make sense; existing products may work perfectly well even as they are super-seded by newer ones. Silicon Valley abounds with examples of companies built around a single product or idea; many of these companies are acquired, or they just wither away. Examples acquired by Microsoft include Vermeer, with the product FrontPage (a Web site design tool), Coopers & Peters, and DimensionX, all software companies, and WebTV. For its part, Netscape has acquired Collabra (groupware), InSoft, DigitalStyle, and Portola Software. The moment something works, someone else will be out there trying to improve on it. Many of these "improvements" will be cosmetic, but they will cascade through the marketplace.

As information flows faster and as innovations are easier to copy and implement, the ability to keep innovating consistently (or to acquire people who can) and time to market will provide primary competitive advantage.[4]

This won't necessarily be a comfortable world to live in. For better or worse, Silicon Valley is becoming a model emulated worldwide—and is a model for the future for all of

---

[4] This may sound glib and unrealistic if you have bought anything lately, especially at the corner coffee shop, which has a captive market because of its location, or at a tourist trap where the retailer has little hope of repeat business anyway.

us. Many foreign people, and especially foreign governments, visit Silicon Valley in the hope that some of the Valley's economic fecundity will rub off on them. Often, they look at the wrong features, focusing just on high tech rather than on the culture that makes the companies thrive. Malaysia and Hungary, for example, both want to create their own high tech zones and are focusing on high tech infrastructure, government subsidies, and the like. What they may be missing is the entrepreneurial spirit and the cross-fertilization as companies start, merge, break up, and unleash second- and third-time entrepreneurs into the mix.

The good aspects are an openness to change, excitement, teamwork, a willingness to admit to and learn from mistakes. The bad aspects are troubling: obsession with work and neglect of families and human values, impatience, preoccupation with money and stock prices. Many of these companies' founders are more interested in selling their companies to Netscape or Microsoft than in building robust, healthy organizations. Their stockholding employees are more interested in going public, selling stock, and starting their own start ups. Companies shouldn't live forever, nor are they simply vehicles for stockholders' or employees' portfolios.

Earning That Job

So, you're still looking for that job. . . . As employers check you out on the Net, the efficient market for employment will lead to a widening gap between star employees and adequate ones—or worse. But the skills needed are not just creative brilliance or intelligence; they also include attitude. To the extent that workers can find a culture or community that suits them, attitudes may get better. (Or at least all the complainers will deserve each other!) As you develop or market your skills, there are four broad attributes that will be especially valuable.

Creativity and Intelligence

The fundamental talent is creativity—whether artistic or intellectual. As the world becomes faster-moving, companies will stay ahead not with proprietary technology, but with a constant flow of new technology and ideas. Employees will be valued for what they can produce, not for what they have produced.

Most successful will be those who can design innovations to help the company get or stay ahead. The major business of business will be design—of new products, new processes, even new business models. It will be much harder for any company to gain a persistent competitive advantage other than with a strong company culture/community that both perpetuates and renews itself through new design.

Employees will increasingly need to be good at thinking, rather than blindly following routine. Routines can be automated or at least farmed out to specialist firms; those specialists, meanwhile, need to implement familiar tasks efficiently, but their core value is—you guessed it!—coming up with new ways of doing the old tasks better.

Those who are good at doing what they're told will be able to survive, but they won't excel in the increasingly competitive marketplace. Nonetheless, support people will be valued to the extent that they can adjust to change while maintaining the healthy corporate culture. They will implement the crazy ideas of the dreamers and risk takers. Even as the market becomes more efficient and the stars can move around more easily, both companies and coworkers will come to value loyalty and comfort as an antidote to this friction-free world.

Real-time Performance

The second key attribute is a performance personality, for want of a better phrase. People who can think quickly will prevail. Can you respond quickly (rather than think slowly)? In the age of the Net, there will be less time to think, more need for quick response—whether a speedy reaction to e-mail, or a real-time interaction in (electronic) print or a video conference. Real-time performance will outrank careful production. Editors and writers will continue to be necessary, but more valuable will be people who can write and think: in real-time, participating in and moderating real-time online forums. Of course, these same capabilities are what "playing" on the Net hones—just as soldiers, toy cars, dolls, and Play-Doh prepared children for the tasks of the previous century. What people do for leisure, they will also do for pay. (Consider tennis pros, for another example.)

As the Internet's "local loops" become broadband, there will be more need for people who can perform the equivalent of online or telephone interaction in video—in short, remote customer service. The people who used to work in stores will now work online, but customers will expect more than a hand wave and a snarled "Over there!" Highly trained people will interpret complex instructions or give advice to customers who prefer to deal with a person. Yes, I know things should become easier and easier to use, but people will still want customer service from people, not from expert systems. It's a lot more convincing to have a person tell you a particular sweater will go great with the skirt than to hear it from a machine. Who wants baby-care advice from a computer? Persuasion is still a personal art rather than a computer technique.

My favorite example of a real-time employee performance was by a quick-thinking Southwest Airlines stewardess, back in the days before the Net when they were still called stewardesses. The doors of the aircraft had closed, most of us had found our seats, and she took up the microphone: "Hey y'all!" she drawled. "We got a little problem up here. We don't have the peanuts. Now we can set right here for about 15 minutes, and catering promises we'll have those peanuts right away . . . but I can't guarantee it. Or, folks, we could leave right away without those peanuts. Now I'm just gonna take a little vote. . . . " Before she could even finish, she was drowned out with shouts and cries: "Let's just go!

Fergit the pea-nuts! As long as we got beer, who needs peanuts?" We left on schedule and no one complained about the missing peanuts. We had a choice, and we had chosen.

Self-marketing

Imagine a company as a physical object. The companies of the past were black boxes that produced products and had a small surface area, composed mostly of PR and investor-relations people, and perhaps a couple of outspoken top executives. Consumer companies had ads, but they rarely involved anyone from inside the company—with notable exceptions such as Perdue and his chickens, Lee Iacocca and Chrysler, and Richard Branson with his Virgin product du jour. Exceptions were service companies such as airlines, competing on the friendliness of their stewardesses, and at least some retailers competing on the helpfulness of their personnel. But most employees were focused internally, designing and building products or perhaps writing ads or documentation. The products and the advertising spoke for themselves.

In a service/information/Net world all that changes. A company's surface area expands in relation to its volume; it's almost all membrane with very little contained inside. And if you remember the physics you took in high school, the smaller an object is, the greater its surface area is proportional to its volume. (Or to put it another way: there are fewer people inside to talk to, so employees spend more time dealing with the outside.)

The surface that a business exposes needs to be more than just posted information—even specific, customized information such as Federal Express's track-your-own package service. Companies will need to have real personality online—which means *persons*.

Accordingly, there will be a premium on people who can market themselves. In a world where competitive advantage comes either from new design or from the attention of people, those who succeed will be those who are good at getting their new designs or themselves noticed.

The person is the living face a company presents to the world. For example, take Jennifer Warf, who has run a Barbie Web site for some years. Other Barbie fans came upon the site, and pretty quickly it became an active center for discussions about Barbie, trading costumes and even dolls. The site eventually attracted attention from Mattel itself, and an enthusiastic Warf hinted that she might like a job with Mattel when she graduated from Indiana University. But instead of hiring her, Mattel's legal department wrote her a letter with warnings about copyright infringement. She has redone the site to remove all Mattel's content; she is using photos of her own dolls instead.

Unaffiliated with Mattel, she is now doing this as a labor of unrequited love. Of course, Mattel's version of the story focuses on its need to protect its image and its intellectual property, but it seems to me they have missed an opportunity. Unless, of course, they're secretly hoping that she'll just continue to promote their products for free.

Most Likely to Succeed

I once asked an Italian executive who worked for AT&T what he did as a manager, and I have always remembered his answer: "I absorb uncertainty." As routine is sucked out of our daily work lives, people who can create stability from chaos will be key. This man, Vittorio Cassoni, took the uncertainty out of his employees' lives so that they could go ahead and do their best. He did not tell them what to do, so much as he provided balance in a rocking sea.

These kinds of personal qualities—management skill, leadership, judgment, collaborative skills, risk taking, evenness of temperament—are now called emotional intelligence. As change becomes constant, leaders must have the flexibility and vision to handle it. It's the skill it takes to run a meeting effectively, whether in a conference room or over a network, internally or with partners and customers—but you have to do it on a global basis and over the long term. You have to fire people up and calm them down, resolve disputes, uncover the key points in a conflict or a strategy, make firm decisions. All these traits and capabilities inspire confidence and lead a company forward. These traits are the least definable and their impact is the most visible.

What Makes Companies Appealing to Employees

When goods and machines are cheap and mass-producible, people with the talents described above are valuable. What does it take to attract them? Other people. It's the other people in a company that will be a key factor in keeping employees. Even though employees will achieve greater freedom to move around because of the fluid job market, few people actually want to get up every morning and find out what jobs are available on the Net. They want stability; they want friends; they want familiarity; they want to be part of a community. What keeps employees as well as customers is the emotional intelligence described above—the presence of people they like to work for and with. All but the most solitary employees prefer to work with people whose company they enjoy and whose contributions they respect. They want to work with people who can add value to their own work, or with skillful managers who can make mostly incompatible people work together happily and effectively. Indeed, a company is a community. A company's best strategy is to attract employees and then to get them to invest in the company's community—not just by paying them but by fostering an environment that lets them flourish. Great value is created by teams who work together effectively, whether as repair people sharing experiences with balky machines or creative types coming up with a new multimedia extravaganza.

That doesn't mean that all companies will become identical happy families. They will have distinct cultures—perhaps more distinct than now because people will be better able to find an environment that suits them, whether it's aggressive and sales-oriented, technical and reserved, formal or informal. But overall, companies with people enthusiastic about their work are likely to be the most successful. Many people join a company because of the money, but most contribute and stay after joining because of the community, they find there. Relationships develop and people get comfortable; relationships stagnate or deteriorate and people move on.

Since both companies and employees will have more options, dissatisfied employees and employers are less likely to stick with an unhappy situation—a company community that doesn't really meet their needs. Now, to be productive, it is usually necessary to affiliate oneself with a large organization; in the future, those who want freedom will be able to work on their own terms without sacrificing as much as they must today. People who aren't much fun to work with will be able to become more independent, operating as one-person bands and contracting out for services.

These two forces—independence and the need for affiliation with a community—often conflict. The way they are resolved will vary from person to person and company to company.

The Net on the Job

The Net also changes the experience on the job. First of all, it will change the pace at which everything happens within the company as well as in competing with other firms. It will make it much easier for everyone to keep in touch, and it will probably reduce the need for middle management; employees will be able to communicate among themselves, rather than up and down a chain of command.

For example, suppose you have that new job as a saleswoman that you were looking for. You'll be thrown into a world of new accounts and new products. To find out what's going on, you'll ask other employees, but you'll also start poking around the company intranet. What has the company previously sold to Wanton Widgets, an account you have a strong relationship with? What are the most effective ways of competing against product X? Is there a technical wizard who's especially valuable on sales calls? Your new manager may ask you to post a report on the intranet on the competitive situation as you see it from the vantage of your old job—but no trade secrets, please!

All these trends will place a premium on reporting into the corporate memory, since there may no longer be a sales manager who knows what's going on in all territories. Employees will have to fill out their sales reports in greater, richer detail than ever before. Good companies will build in incentives to encourage their employees to share information, because it takes time to do so. Technology will help you to find information on the company intranet, but it can't do much about helping you generate the sales report—other than perhaps convenient forms to fill out and voice-recognition technology that will allow you to dictate instead of type.

And once you've made the sale, you'll be using e-mail to coordinate with your company's customer-service group to make sure your customer stays happy. You may refer some ancillary business from its overseas territory to the international sales group.

To find out more about your new industry, you may join a number of industry trade associations. Soon, you find that your outspoken comments in the industry mailing list are generating interest. You get speaking invitations, offers of other jobs . . . Your future is assured!

Telecommuting

Now, can you telecommute? I'm not a big fan of the concept—especially for people-oriented work such as sales. What it does mean is that you can travel more easily to see customers and stay close to your office. In my own life, I have found that e-mail lets me run the office from the road, but it does not reduce the amount of time I have to spend away getting to know people, having dinner, having arguments, and just doing the kind of high-intensity communication you can't do any way other than face-to-face.

On the other hand, if you're a programmer, a writer, or some other kind of "knowledge worker," you can work from home much more easily. Many people will do so. You can also work from India or Hungary or any other country for employers in the United States—which means a lot more competition for those jobs. But overall, I think the value of telecommuting for most jobs is overrated. People who work from home are more likely to be independent contractors than permanent employees, since telecommuting reduces a major benefit to both sides of permanent employment, which is team membership. The worker misses the companionship, and the employer misses the productivity enhancement of a tight-knit group. The technology will enable people to communicate more effectively over distances, but the best approach will still be to spend enough time together physically to build that community.

The Work Community and Its Rules

Remote or local, when you take a job you're making a decision to join a particular community. That means that you have the ability and the responsibility to find out about the working conditions, and that employers have the obligation to disclose them honestly. "Working conditions" includes all the traditional workplace issues, plus a few new Net-oriented areas where employees' rights can conflict with those of employers—most notably, privacy in the use of e-mail and the Web, and freedom of speech.

Many employers now monitor employees' use of the Net, sometimes using software filters to keep employees from playing games, downloading pornography, or sending out secrets. Some of the same filters used to protect children from porn can be used with timers to keep employees from playing games except on lunch hours and after 6 P.M.

However, employers who treat their workers like children are likely to get employees who deserve to be treated like children. Free use of the Net can be a lure in attracting the best employees, even though it also lures the worst abusers. It's up to the employer to detect the difference.

In a free market, employers can read employees' e-mail and control where they go on the Net (during working hours), as long as they disclose these practices. Of course, defining behavior "at work" gets more difficult as employees start to work from home, at odd hours, or from remote locations. Perhaps it means only when using the corporate ID, or on company equipment, or on company time if you have defined working hours. Companies care because they may be held liable for their employees' behavior—ranging from harassing others or creating a "hostile atmosphere" by downloading pornography, to misrepresenting themselves online, defaming competitors' products, or otherwise acting badly. Companies also care for less legitimate reasons, including thin skin.

What happens if an employee gets on the Net on Saturday night and trashes his own company's products—or its competition, provoking a lawsuit? What control does and should a company exercise on its employees' behavior, given that they represent the company in "public" on the Net? "The opinions expressed are purely my own" may no longer be a sufficient disclaimer.

The Net erodes the separation between the work and the person. Employees are no longer judged only on the products they create or what they do inside the company, but also on the way they interact with the world around them on the Net. Their job is to represent the company, so how can they not be judged for how they do so?

In the old days, employers could sack you if they saw you getting drunk and disorderly in the pub on Saturday night, no matter how well you did your job during the week. Nowadays, that's considered undue interference with an employee's personal, life. In the old days, an employer might ask you about your family and might give extra money to the employee with a sick wife.

Now in the United States, we have increasing legal restrictions on whatever might be considered favoritism, and strict barriers between home and work. That's the now-old world of traditional government and increasing regulation of working conditions. (Unions have helped redress the balance of power in favor of employees, but many of them have spawned their own bureaucracies and power politics.) In other parts of the world, standard working conditions are still generally unfair toward employees.

Power on the Job

But the world of the Net is tending the other way: toward freedom of contract.

I don't have an answer to how this will work itself out. But by 2004, you will find that the balance of power between creators and managers, and between employees and business owners, has shifted in favor of individual contributors, even though you and others may personally be playing several roles. That will give employees the upper hand in negotiations with employers—although the employers may not realize it yet. Employees who don't like the working conditions can go elsewhere. Now individuals are starting to have power as individuals rather than collectively, at least in the world of the Net and of well-educated employees. Employers control the tangible resources, but employees have more control over their own lives, more options, and more ways to find out those options. Certainly, independence is a matter of attitude as well as opportunity, but now you can almost always find a work community to suit you if you take the trouble to explore.

—From *Release 2.0* by Esther Dyson. Copyright 1997 by Esther Dyson. Used by permission of Broadway Books, a division of Random House, Inc.

▪ Chapter 3 ▪

Forming an Organization

3.1 Ensuring a High-Performance Team

—by Gary Roshak
Wildfire Communications, Inc.

"Our keys to Success have been:
▪ Building the management team.
▪ Developing the business plan.
▪ Taking the financial piece and making it go away."
—John Ballantine, Managing Partner, Chairman & CEO, iStart Ventures

The Entrepreneurial Context

In a Start-up, the organization will necessarily be small, and everyone must function together as a team. All teams will have a scarcity of resources, and the participants must understand and expect this circumstance. Deadlines will be short, due to a variety of external pressures: market timing and windows of opportunity, limited funding and investor patience. Team motivation is built from the challenge of achieving dramatic results within a short time frame. Thus, the organization must run on all cylinders, and each member must be willing and able to stretch individually.

Each person on the team will do a variety of things, and all will be required to work long, hard hours.

But assembling a group of people and calling them a team doesn't mean that they'll function as a team, much less a high-performance team. During the early stages of development, It is normal for teams to thrash and churn; this will appear as chaos to observers and the team alike. In his book *Out of Control*, Kevin Kelly explains that organisms that thrive and succeed over time constantly stand teetering on the edge of disaster.

So how then does the entrepreneur forge a well-tuned machine out of the chaos around him or her? The required elements for creation of a team are:

- A common goal;
- Some number of individuals;
- Appropriate resources, including time, materials, space and money. (Appropriate in this context doesn't mean adequate, but rather, just enough. Resources will never be sufficient, and more will be said later about stretching the team.);
- Vision;
- and of course, an idea.

The idea is what starts this whole process in the first place. But an entrepreneur must have the vision to bring the idea to life and translate it into success in the marketplace.

This vision is what establishes the common goal. It also inspires passion, a critical ingredient in the success of any venture. Passion is what allows the team to bond and to work out the inevitable fights and *us vs. them* situations that inevitably occur.

To this mix the entrepreneur then adds a deadline. Deadlines drive a team to perform. Without them, teams will over-engineer their plans and solutions. High-performance teams are driven by the energy the team creates internally. Deadlines help to create this energy, serving as a lens to focus the team on the desired result and to help build a sense of commitment.

The Entrepreneur's Role

It is useful to think of a software company through the metaphor of filmmakers. In effect, the organization is a production company. And in this context, the software entrepreneur is the producer, assembling around him/her the necessary resources to bring the idea to the big screen of the marketplace.

Much like the making of a film, in building software today ad hoc teams will come together and disband in a fluid choreography of people and skills as development progresses toward the goal. However, in building a high-performance team, the entrepreneur will want to assemble a core team of dedicated resources who persist over time. These individuals serve as the organization's memory or brain trust to retain knowledge, institutionalize learning, and guide the efforts of various ad hoc players and hired guns that will appear in cameo roles. Thus, a critical skill is that of stage direction. How do you unleash the creative potential of the assembled cast, with the clock ticking and chaos swirling around you?

The entrepreneur must provide committed and focused leadership. High-performance organizations follow leaders who are evangelists, leading the team members in pursuit of performance and the common goal. These leaders exhibit a constant focus on where the company is headed, along with an unrelenting dedication to behaviors required to get there. Good people will be attracted to this energy and vision, but more importantly, will be attracted to the opportunity to learn. Thus, the management in a high-performance organization must be committed to transferring knowledge and expertise to those around them.

Positive leadership will translate into a positive valuation, by both the marketplace and the team. This in turn equates to future rewards. Poor leadership, however, translates into a low valuation and is a recipe for future failure. Thus, poor leaders can't, or shouldn't, start companies. People will join the team in a Start-up only if there is some future reward attached, usually perceived in monetary terms. They will stay with the team, however, if they can "own" some part of the vision. This ownership over time replaces dollars as the reason to stay.

An effective champion must have several characteristics. Bodwell describes these as influence, contact, and knowledge. The champion must have contact with the organization's realities, both internal and external, and must understand the issues, concerns, challenges, and aspirations of the people who make up the organization. Leaders must be both aware of, and able to effectively balance, the needs of the business as well as the needs of the people. In doing so, they must be able to influence the behavior of both internal and external resources towards achievement of the goal.

Designing the organization

Individuals and teams both grow and learn faster when they operate outside of their comfort zone. A high-performance team is at its best while pushing the collective envelope, when it either doesn't know how to achieve the desired results or it doesn't know how to accomplish them in the time frame allowed. Bodwell refers to this as the zone of concern, which lies somewhere between the team's comfort zone and its anxiety zone. A team operating here is most likely to perform better and, as a result, to both bond better and become stronger when results are achieved.

It is important therefore to set stretch goals. Experience has shown that people will not only surprise you but, more importantly, themselves in what they are capable of achieving. In a high-performance team the members encourage each other to stretch beyond their comfort zone, offering advice or assistance when asked (or when it becomes obvious that another member needs it).

Design the culture. In designing the organization, several key principles serve to support this idea of stretching the team. As the entrepreneur assembles the necessary resources, he/she should:

- stress teamwork and flexible organization structures
- define broad work roles and responsibilities
- emphasize shared authority and responsibility
- encourage the open sharing of information

Keep in mind, however, that a team must have members who are accountable. This is the fuel for the creative and emotional expenditures they will need to make in pursuit of the vision. The leader's responsibility throughout this process is to keep the big picture visible for everyone. As the organization grows and evolves, there should be one person with the power to make Go/No Go decisions (typically the President or founder). Do not allow this to be multiple individuals, for any area of the business.

Throughout this process, it is critical to remember you are ultimately trying to create a culture that is both fun and motivating. You can design the culture! The entrepreneur explicitly designs the culture with what he/she wants, and tacitly designs it with other actions one might not be aware of. Thus, take care to *act* your culture every day.

Design the environment. Along with the culture, it is important to design the environment. It is no accident that so many Start-ups devote some portion of their precious office real estate to game rooms and recreational diversions. You are actively creating a place where people are willing to spend more time than they would at home. Yes, the work is challenging, and this is appealing to the team. But of equal importance is creating a place where they want to hang around with each other. The right environment will foster the camaraderie so critical to the team's success.

A few Maxims

Herewith follows a quick snapshot of favorite maxims that have proven useful in organization design and recruiting for building a high-performance team.

Org charts are unimportant, if not irrelevant.

In fact, they are dangerous, because of what people read into them. In any organization they will be, at minimum, out of date. But in most cases they will also be inaccurate in terms of power structures and who really gets things done. The entrepreneur should focus on the management structure of activities and responsibility for results, not boxes and reporting relationships. At the same time, one needs to be both cognizant of, and careful with respect to, the "soft org chart." Informal lines of communication and relationship networks will form naturally. Attention must be paid to these so as not to subvert the intended management structure and accountability.

Titles are unimportant.

For many years I have told people when hiring that everyone joins the team as "janitor." This doesn't mean you are hiring them to sweep the floors; rather, it just means that you expect them to be willing to do so. On any team, leaders will naturally emerge. Power is assumed as leadership is demonstrated; it is tacitly granted by the team, not conferred from above. Individuals who come into the organization insistent upon very clear lines of authority or big titles won't be comfortable in a Start up and are thus unlikely to succeed.

Beware of the "Corporate Amex card."

An easy trap for the entrepreneur to fall into while assembling the "dream team" of resources is to cherry pick high-profile individuals, with just the right pedigree of previous companies and positions combined with "been there, done that before" experience. While some of this is both appropriate and necessary, it must be balanced against the risk of recruiting individuals who are either unfamiliar, or uncomfortable, with the realities of a Start-up. (See *janitor* above.) Too often, these individuals are used to having entire departments and armies of individuals available to help them solve a problem or find a desk. In a Start-up, that army (or department) is you, the individual.

One riot, one ranger.

As discussed earlier, resources will necessarily be constrained. Thus, assign a single individual (ranger) to a given challenge (riot). It is this ranger's responsibility to figure out how big the riot is or will become and to determine what reinforcements are necessary over time. A corollary to this is to hire strong individuals who are capable of becoming leaders and managers but who demonstrate that they are willing to roll up their sleeves and get dirty as individual contributors in the early stages.

Look for spring steel, not titanium.

Titanium is a unique metal, and some applications are not possible without it. But as NASA engineers can tell you, subjected to extremes of heat or cold, it becomes brittle. Spring steel, on the other hand, is a wonderful material. You can heat it, or cool it, and it still snaps back to its original shape without unnecessary weakening. Thus, in a Start up, you want to hire strong, flexible people, not narrow (brittle) specialists. Over time, the organization will play to everyone's strengths. Initially, however, it may not be clear what those strengths are, and there will not be sufficient resources to go around.

You are choosing up a crew for a blue water cruise.

And despite whatever you learned about the laws of physics, boats do become smaller over time. So choose your crew carefully. Be sure to leave the dock with the resources you need and want along for the duration of the cruise. Those team members already in the boat get a vote on who joins the crew; those considering joining the crew get to vote with their feet. In other words, hire carefully. You don't want to have to throw someone overboard, as replacements are difficult and costly to obtain once at sea.

However, if you discover you have made a mistake, fire quickly. A bad hire in a Start up is like a cancer. Caught quickly, you can save the patient. Left unchecked, however, the harm to the patient can be irreparable.

Make your mistakes early.

Mistakes will happen, and we all make them. Don't be afraid of them. As the adage goes, if you aren't making some you aren't trying hard enough. In a Start up, they are somewhat inevitable, so get them out of the way early. If you plant an oak, after a while moving it becomes impossible.

10 Essential Characteristics of High-Performance Teams

1. Members clearly understand the team's purpose
2. Members want to belong to the team and are proud to work on it
3. Members work hard to build and maintain trust within the team culture
4. Members have the willingness and skills to communicate openly
5. Members know that conflict is necessary, and they are able to use it constructively
6. Members put team interests first, but also work well independently, or in subteams
7. Members value creativity and proactively plan for change
8. Members acknowledge and celebrate individual and team accomplishments
9. Members problem solve efficiently, and set realistic goals with adequate timelines
10. Members challenge abilities by setting and surpassing high-performance standards

Source: Consulting Resource Group International

"For success in the Internet Age, you look for certain things that allow you to create momentum. Building a world-class management team who is able to execute in the space is a definite factor."
—John Ballantine, Managing Partner, Chairman & CEO, iStart Ventures

3.2 Cross-functional Teams

—by Randy Fisher
Randy Fisher Communications

As high tech firms increasingly seek ways of reducing cycle time and of maximizing market share and competitive advantage, their strategic focus broadens beyond aggressive employee recruitment to include actively developing and sustaining cross-functional work teams.

Indeed, extremely short windows of opportunity and the ever-rising threshold of customer expectations are forcing them to reexamine how they develop products and leverage their employees' capabilities.

But simply cobbling together different functional specialties and *calling* it a team is not really the ticket. Far more profound is staffing specific new product development (NPD) groups with the right mix of time, human, technical, and financial resources to make well-considered and binding decisions, decisions that will be directly felt in the marketplace.

Critical Success Factors

A number of critical success factors underpin the creation of effective and high performing cross-functional teams in NPD environments.

Corporate vision. From the very beginning, there must be a crystal-clear corporate vision with achievable performance targets and measurable goals, even in times of risk and ambiguity. The firm's business and product strategies should be transparent and shared with programmers and front line employees to help shape team direction and build cohesiveness and morale. If employees and contractors believe strongly in a firm's or division's business direction (and, in some cases, prospects for survival), it can serve as a significant motivator in developing and deploying a winning product suite and in maintaining high levels of morale, greater feelings of job security, and competitive drive.

Cross-functional teams. Proper development of cross-functional teams requires careful thought about team size (ideally 6 to 12 members) and composition, including key roles and personality types. At the very heart of any development team is a considerable range of critical functional inputs, each with its special perspective and limitations. Whether engineering, sales and marketing, human resources, or operations; or quality, testing and integration; each function has an important contribution that's worth knowing at the beginning of a project (e.g., at the kickoff stage) versus hearing it later from dissatisfied customers or a nervous industry analyst.

Speaks for the customer. A critical, often overlooked team member speaks with the customer's voice—whether it's marketing or actual customers and/or external users. This individual can alert the NPD effort to critical requirements, key milestones, and specific market adoption characteristics and preferences: information which could have an enormous impact on time-to-market, market share, and corporate profits.

Team personalities. In recognizing and understanding the role of personality type, the popular Myers-Briggs Type Inventory assesses 16 different personality types (i.e., combinations of Extroverts vs. Introverts; Sensing vs. Intuition; Thinking vs. Feeling; and Perceiving vs. Judging), each of which exhibits different problem-solving abilities, individual roles, and communications preferences. Thus, when all member personality types of a particular team are visibly mapped, certain types might be over- or under-represented: serving as clues for potential conflicts or blind spots that might occur; signaling staffing changes, modifications, or even training that might be required for optimum performance.

Team diversity. A successful team effort benefits from shared leadership values, whereby members can assume different roles other than what their position or prestige would suggest—and still receive support and encouragement. By becoming more sensitive about each others' perspectives, knowledge base, and contributions, team members can tap into their lateral thinking skills to generate value-added applications and comprehensive, relevant, and workable solutions. This is especially important in valuing, and leveraging diversity.

Multicultural teams. Indeed, given the current IT skills shortage, multiculturalism in traditional and virtual work environments is fast becoming commonplace, with its own set of unique challenges and rich opportunities. Consider the complexities of effective cross-cultural communication between two programmers on an NPD team—

- Andy, a brash 25-year-old white male programmer from Seattle
- Emily, an introverted 30-year-old female software engineer from China

—where differing cultural assumptions and behavioral styles might cause conflict and misunderstanding and could stall project completion.

In a different scenario, it is likely that team dynamics and individual behaviors would change. For example, were the NPD effort to focus on developing a product for initial launch in China and subsequent roll-out in Asia, U.S. team members would probably turn to Emily for guidance and expert advice—in matters from marketing and promotion to customer preferences, and the look and feel of design, graphics, and other variables.

Working agreements. For cross-functional teams to remain effective throughout their life cycle, members need clear ground rules and defined working agreements. Experimentation and mistakes should be considered okay with no repercussions, and learning must be incorporated into future prototype development. There should be a repository of project data (e.g., lessons learned, shortcuts, technical libraries, URLs and orientation procedures) that is indexed, searchable, and accessible to any team member, in real-time, 24 hours a day. There should also be clear reporting procedures, and electronic and face-to-face mechanisms to ensure frequent communication and information-sharing between all team members, departments, and the entire organization.

Team authority. There must also be a clear understanding of how decisions will be made and implemented. If, for example, a team has no real power and authority, its decisions can be reversed or ignored. This powerlessness can seriously jeopardize staff morale and sabotage development efforts. The effect can be much worse, given that many high tech firms and large projects (e.g., Boeing 777) have multiple teams with overlapping memberships and significant task interdependencies.

Bridging the Gaps

A vital link between the team and senior management, the team sponsor ensures that key resources are available when needed, monitors progress and identifies potential obstacles, and constantly scans the horizon for new challenges and opportunities. Without such a person, the team risks a rapid loss of enthusiasm and failure. A recent study by Andersen Consulting's Mergers, Acquisitions and Alliances Center of Excellence, found that 70% of alliances (essentially big teams) either fail outright or fall captive to shifting priorities or to achieving only initial goals. The study found "the symptoms associated with their alliance's demise resulted from shifts in strategic direction by one or both partners (87%), shifts in senior management's attention (83%), and alliance sponsors moving onto new positions or projects without being replaced (81%).

The study also reported that "successful alliances are characterized by formal governance systems with agreed-upon performance metrics, and a commitment by senior management to follow through on execution for the life of the agreement. Moreover, effective governance systems allow for inevitable management turnover by the use of joint steering committees which meet regularly, adopt standardized succession procedures and offer genuine career-path opportunities for its members."

First Step: Kickoff Meeting

In designing high performing cross-functional teams, the best value for a firm's money and future efforts come through project kickoff meetings that allow all team members to meet face-to-face. (For employees outside North America, video conferencing is another, although less desirable, option.) Such events allow new relationships to develop and potentially reduce conflict, misunderstanding, and technical gaps by virtue of personal and informal relationships.

These labor-intensive forums require attention to detail and interpersonal and intercultural sensitivity. But they pay off in spades, after the midpoint of NPD efforts, particularly in terms of time savings. Essentially, they help foster an environment where teams (and individuals) have the tools and power to work effectively together and to build trust and address critical assumptions, perceptions, and expectations about participating in a cross-functional team.

They provide an excellent forum to introduce project objectives and key milestones and explore process gaps. In the case of a large North American telecommunications firm, one of its divisions missed its delivery schedule to a consumer market because of an inability to provide products and information for a Christmas catalog. Unfortunately, a lack of planning, foresight, and coordination between the sales force and NPD development team conspired to sink the division's fortunes. Unrealistic deadlines, missed targets, poor communication, and Asian market volatility haven't helped either.

Further, kickoff meetings can identify specific training required to develop soft skills and technical competencies; identify project blockages, team, and technical integration issues and deadline killers; and locate missing competitive and market information. They can also set the stage for future team reviews and learning audits: important activities that help team members to learn from past mistakes and omissions and to move forward, in other projects, more confidently and more "big picture-oriented" than before.

3.3 Pick and Stick:
Am I Working on the Right Things?

—by Russ Mann
Onyx Software, Inc.

How do you know if you are working on the right things? At the corporate level, this refers to which market to attack or alliance to create. At the individual level, this might mean the difference between working on a new product or refining an old one, creating budgets versus thinking about the next round of financing.

At every level of the company, picking the right activities and sticking to them is critical, and nowhere is this more important than at a Start-up. At a Start-up, every activity must be perfectly chosen, planned, and executed: there is little margin for error. This article supplies the new entrepreneur with a framework and real-life examples for picking activities at the corporate and the individual level, as well as a way of thinking about how to stick with those plans.

Picking

A Start-up is like a boat leaving harbor with only the wide sea in front of it: the territory is uncharted, the depths are full of monsters, there are no landmarks ahead, and only the stars are guides. The sky, or the horizon at least, is literally the limit. How to choose a course?

The answer seems simple, but in practice it is difficult. The new entrepreneur should:

- Project forward where you want to be
- Use the data to plan how to get there
- Check your gut; and
- Consider the implications several steps ahead

Projecting Forward

The new entrepreneur, like the captain of the boat setting out, can choose just to follow the wind wherever it takes the boat or can actually envision the end of the journey and then figure out how to accomplish that end.

This is a lot like what I have seen from the product managers and program managers at many companies; take, for example, Microsoft. There seem to be two very distinct types who thrive there. On the one hand are those who assess exactly where they are, what options are available to them and how they can move forward. They eventually get somewhere in their product development and release, although even they couldn't have told you in the beginning how it would have happened. On the other are those who can clearly see and explain where they want to be five or ten steps later on. Using that vision, they create a plan to accomplish their goals. The following graphs depict these two methods:

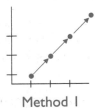

Method 1

Method 2

Another example comes from a Boston-based Internet Start up I once consulted for. This firm offered developing country information to corporate subscribers via the Web. They originally intended to focus on Eastern Europe. Based on Method 1, they could have attempted to maximize their business opportunities within those regions by pursuing as many data providers and subscribers as possible. Using a Method 2 approach and looking at where they wanted to be in five years, however, they realized they would need to pursue more dramatic strategies. Based on long-term growth objectives, this company made the major decision to invest in offices in China and India and to add industry-specific data providers that would appeal to major importers and exporters related to those two countries.

It may seem unfathomable, but you would not believe the number of businesses I have seen with no plans. Similarly, on a daily basis in any entrepreneurial company, projects and tasks are started with no real vision or plan—just a bunch of people running off to "get something done." Don't let the winds just take you—to quote Stephen Covey, "begin with the end in mind."

Using Data to Plan

The early '90s had the first wave of "broadband mania." Everyone was talking about 500 channels and the cable companies, the utilities and telcos, the media empires—all were figuring out how to play. There was "no question" that broadband would take off within two years and those poised with content would be kings. At least one state's public utilities commission took the time to gather some data.

We conducted over 15 focus groups with consumers and small business people. We supplemented this qualitative data with quantitative evidence of the rates of adoption of new technologies, the average current costs of broadband service substitutes, and the average incomes of households in their state: we found that there was no service or bundle of services that the public was willing to pay for to make the investment worthwhile. The quantitative evidence has so far proven correct, as it is now more than seven years later and a financially viable model of bundled broadband services has yet to be demonstrated.

Many new ventures are unfortunately founded on one visionary's belief that "if you build it, they will come." Countless Internet Start-ups funded in 1995–1997 are now being acquired or are closing their virtual storefronts because they believed in the hype and not the data.

Most projects at a Start-up are similarly pursued without any regard for numbers. This is interesting because a Start-up's cost of capital and the resulting necessary ROI are astronomical. Projects that yield only a 30% or 50% return may not be enough. This was clearly evident at a financial services software company I once worked with. They wanted to give away a free, Java-based tool over the Web because it seemed like it would drive market awareness and demand creation. A few conservative back-of-the-envelope calculations showed that the project would barely fund itself, much less drive the kind of demand necessary to spend the financial and human capital on the limited opportunity this marketing idea presented. Yet they still launched this site. Less than six months later, they were acquired by a larger competitor. Remember to think through the numbers before making big decisions at the strategic or the tactical level.

Checking Your Gut

By the same token, there are lies, damn lies, and statistics. Occasionally, the gut feel is the right feel. At ONYX, in fact, we now have a very successful product that was envisioned by the President but vetoed by none other than the author of this article. All the numbers indicated that the product would not yield the sales or impact to warrant the time spent. The President was convinced that it would be a winner, ignored the numbers, and created a small product that had a huge impact.

Consider the Implications

Finally, once you have projected forward, run the numbers, and then check your gut, remember to step back through the implications. Any action will most probably provoke a competitive or market reaction, for which many entrepreneurs fail to plan. Some argue, for example, that Netscape and Marimba did not adequately plan for the retaliation of Microsoft or that Amazon.com may or may not be ready for the onslaught of Barnes and Noble.

Similarly, consider the implications of *not* doing something. One online company I worked with in 1992 created a virtual community where local real-world companies could advertise their services. They based their entire platform around CompuServe. After playing with the concept for about six months and receiving little attention from CompuServe, the founding team abandoned the project. Had they pursued it, they would have preceded Microsoft's Sidewalk and the CitySearch product by almost four years. By the same token, they might have found themselves on a defunct platform and unnecessarily tied to a single Internet portal.

Thus, always remember to consider, as well, the opportunity cost of not moving.

Sticking

"Sticking," believe it or not, is actually more difficult than "picking." The biggest difficulty most Start-ups face is that they are presented with such an amazing array of activities but such a limited amount of resources and time that it becomes easy to be diverted from the primary strategy and tactics. There are ways, however, to overcome this problem and to stay the course.

Have a Plan: Communicate It Well

Most good navigators don't leave harbor without a charted route. Similarly, most good entrepreneurs and entrepreneurial managers begin with a plan, whether it is for the whole company or a given project. Having a plan and communicating it across the company makes it much easier to remember the primary goal and to have others reinforce the momentum to get there.

One of the worst offenders I have seen of this axiom was a CD-ROM gaming company in the Southwest. The President was a brilliant entrepreneur with over three entertainment successes under his belt. With his first software company, however, he went from interactive training to CD-ROM video games to computer-animated movies in the course of only three years. He hired my firm to help draft his business plan but then did not follow what he said were his intentions. Furthermore, he did not seem to communicate this to his harried senior managers, who were always left holding the bag and attempting to implement the last strategy. This made it very difficult for them to ascertain the best use of their time on even a daily level. Clearly, having a plan and communicating it well is the first step to "sticking."

Scan the Horizon, Tack When Appropriate

An important part of sticking is scanning the horizon. Competitive and market forces will always change like the wind, and you must be flexible enough to adapt to them. This does not mean changing course completely, however. Many companies find that even when using Method 2 described above, they still do a certain amount of tacking back and forth to reach the end goal (Method 3). This has been fairly apparent with Yahoo!, which began as a simple search index with advertising revenue. With changes in the market, they have gradually expanded their offerings to become more of a full-fledged Internet "portal."

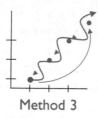

Method 3

Don't Divert: Send Out Side Expeditions

Often the entrepreneur is tempted by market conditions to go beyond just tacking to actually changing the entire business plan, as in the case of that Southwest video game developer. Tom Peters, in *Thriving on Chaos*, devotes an entire chapter to "investing in small starts." In effect, he is saying stick to your core strategy, and when you are tempted to divert, send out a side expedition instead.

Microsoft, Intel, many of the ERP vendors like SAP and Peoplesoft and even Adobe are well known for using this strategy. While "sticking to their knitting"—another Tom Peters axiom, they are making small financial or human resource investments in side projects. If these turn out to be successful, and as they are seen to impact the whole company strategy, they are gradually incorporated into the direction, rather than changing direction all at once.

I have seen this tactic work very effectively at the personal level as well. A certain colleague of mine had an idea for a new marketing campaign. Rather than immediately proposing that all her current activities be dropped and diverted to the new campaign, she spent a few extra hours on an evening and weekend developing the idea. She then tested the waters with colleagues and seniors. As her idea was generally supported, the project was naturally added to her responsibility set and incorporated into the activities of other dependent parties. Had she changed direction completely and quickly, she might have disrupted many other parts of the organization.

Plan for Plans to Fail

We all know that even the best laid plans fail, but we always assume that it won't happen to us. This did happen to several entrepreneurs I know, from an animation library house to a value-added cellular phone service Start-up. The best way to avoid this untimely end and to still stick to your strategy at the company or personal level is to do extensive risk management.

Risk management entails three activities: prevention planning, aversion tactics, and recovery actions.

- Prevention planning is about identifying risks and taking any steps necessary to ensure they do not occur. This could include securing additional financing or going over the demo that one more time.

- Aversion tactics occur when a trigger has been tripped but you still have time to react. At the macro level, I have seen companies say, "If we do not do one of these alliances, then we move to Plan B, which means releasing product faster." At the micro level, a tradeshow team I worked with knew that if there were any demo problems of a certain software at midnight the night before the show, they would swap to an older and more reliable demonstration.

- Finally, it makes sense to have *recovery actions* planned in case the worst does happen. What do you do if the demo crashes while you have Bill Gates in the room? What do you do if the financing doesn't go through? or if you have to close the doors of your fledgling company?

Remember Why You Set Sail

Remember, this article was about "picking" and "sticking" at the corporate and personal level. We went over some methods of picking and some ideas on how to keep sticking. At the end of the day, if you are about to pick something else, your last check should be another gut check—to remember why you set sail, your original vision.

In many cases, entrepreneurs and managers are presented with options that fall completely out of the realm of something they could run numbers on, something they have no gut feel for, something that was not covered by the plan or in any risk management activities. It is surprising how often this happens. On a daily basis at my current company, managers are presented with new technologies, partnership opportunities, exciting potential and under-served markets, and a host of other opportunities that could take up their time and resources—all things that were not in the annual operating plan.

Fortunately, our founders have articulated a very clear vision and the three tactics for this year by which we are approaching that vision. Any employee can determine whether any proposed activity or investment is going to help the whole team attain that vision through one of the three identified tactics. The vision has not changed since the founding of the company, and the tactics have changed only moderately over time.

This, then, may be the most valuable reason for picking and sticking—if you want to get synergies and leverage, you by definition cannot do it alone. Clearly picking and sticking will provide a model for your employees and your partners and will establish your company as one that consistently delivers predictable results. This is valued by your customers and by the market, and will ensure the success of your venture.

3.4 Establishing Facilities: Real Estate Planning and Lease Negotiations

—by Paul Suzman
Business Space Resources, Ltd.

The rapid changes and uncertainties that characterize the software industry make facilities planning difficult but nonetheless extremely important given the tight real estate market and escalating costs of occupancy. Large, well-established firms can better forecast their space needs five to ten years ahead. Young start-up companies, however, must guard against taking too much space too soon although the 1990s have seen extraordinary growth among many software companies nationally.

Lease arrangements can be made that offer built-in flexibility and help provide peace of mind to the most anxiety-ridden executive.

Ten Steps to Successful Real Estate Planning

Following are 10 basic steps that can lead you to a good space decision:

1. *Make space needs part of business planning.* The one thing we know about a business plan is that it is usually wrong. The same can be said for a real estate plan. However, it is important that you take the time to understand your requirements. The plan should change as facility circumstances require.

2. *Understand and quantify requirements.* Most software companies' spatial needs are not particularly technical and, at least during their start-up phase, they can adapt to most office configurations. Larger firms with more complex needs should, early in the process, hire a space planner/architect to establish specific space requirements and timing. Expensive items like data cabling and connection and telecommunications issues require early attention.

3. *Establish priorities and criteria.* Since small firms can adapt to most spaces, keep in mind that if you can take a space "as-is," the landlord has less money directly invested. That means you can usually negotiate an economical lease rate with the flexibility to cancel should you require more space or should you decide to discontinue your business. You might also consider subleasing a growing company's expansion space, especially if furniture systems and cabling is in place.

4. *Budget should be your bottom line.* Before considering alternative approaches, it might initially suit you to sublease space from another company and to share costs such as those for administrative services. Again, concentrate on short-term flexibility; don't let your space dictate your business plan.

5. *Thoroughly survey the market.* Be very open-minded in terms of locations. Remember, for most software companies, your clients care more about your product than your location. At the same time, if you can avoid commuting, you can spend more time doing what makes money for you. Unless you require your people to be present in the office for meetings and other collaborative work, consider a telecommuting policy. Telecommuting can reduce total square footage requirements and allow more flexible, efficient use of space.

6. *Analyze objectively.* Obviously, the larger you are, the greater the dollars involved in your real estate requirements, so the more time you should spend on the economic analysis of your alternatives.

7. *Plan for negotiations.* It is very important, whether considering a large or small space, that you have a "fallback" which will satisfy your needs. Never negotiate on just one space without an alternative(s). Even in a tight real estate market this is possible. And, be well prepared. Landlords are impressed by well organized business-like tenants of any size.

8. *Tailor the lease.* Because each company's needs are different, take time to ensure that the lease document presented to you will meet your objectives and that the intent of the business deal is faithfully translated into the content of a fair lease document.

9. *Monitor space build-out.* If your space requires demolition and build-out, ensure that your contract clearly designates responsibility for the work. For a larger project, name a project executive to represent the firm; then organize a team approach with the landlord/developer in building out the space. You also need to be aware of lead times and coordinate the purchase of equipment and furniture, telephone, and other amenities.

Plan move-in and follow-up. Again, time is of the essence. Be aware how time consuming move-in will be. The earlier you plan for your move-in, the more efficient the process will be.

The last and most important issue is timing. Invariably, the process takes more time than anticipated, so the earlier you start considering your alternatives, the better. We strongly advocate that you review your real estate plan on a regular basis so that, to the extent possible, you have contingencies for such occurrences as growth, shrinkage, merger, etc. For large firms, (i.e., those requiring more than 25,000 square feet), we sometimes start the process two years ahead of their current lease expiration. Firms over 100,000 square feet—which might consider a build-to-suit or build their own building—should start four years ahead.

A Glossary of Useful Terms for Tenants

People involved

Developer. Initiates and coordinates all the activities necessary for project development including design, financing, site acquisition, preparation, permitting, and lease-up. The developer's ownership role might be anywhere from 100% to 0%. Some work purely as "fee" developers with no equity.

Owner. If not the developer, ask who it is.

Lender. Will, to a great extent, dictate the terms and conditions of any significant deals that a developer or a developer's agent might negotiate. Preconditions for real estate lending are still tight. To finance a building, the sum of the percent of "real" money equity plus the percent of pre-leasing commitments by "bankable" tenants, must meet certain ratios. Lease rates have increased to the point where more speculative building is occurring than in the mid 1990s.

Leasing Agent. An independent contractor, usually working for a large commercial brokerage firm, represents the developer on a contingency or commission basis—no lease, no pay! The more space leased by the agent for the longest term at the highest rate will net the highest commission. Ask what the commission structure is. Ask if the agent has exclusive representation of the project.

Property Manager. Many developers do their own property management. Property managers are responsible for the care and upkeep of the premises and often coordinate leasing activities either directly or through the designated leasing agent. Be aware of the fees you are paying.

Tenant Representative. Specializing in planning and negotiating for tenants, the tenant representative's company should, preferably, not also be leasing agents representing the landlord. Reimbursement can be a flat fee or, if licensed by the state, the representative can share in the development's commission structure. Reimbursement should not, however, be based solely on the size or value of the deal. Working for the tenant, the tenant rep should provide the tenant the best possible counsel, including, where appropriate, discouraging the tenant from doing a particular deal.

Note: Other valuable players can include space planner/architect, attorney, project manager/cost estimator, move coordinator, etc.

Contract terms

Rates: Gross Vs. NNN. A rate quoted as "gross" includes all operating costs: utilities; heating, ventilation and air conditioning (HVAC); taxes; insurance; janitorial services; and maintenance charges. Rates currently range from $6.00 to $8.50 per square foot, depending on the type, location, and age of the building. The landlord pays gross rates.

A triple net or "NNN" lease includes none of these operating costs. All are paid for directly by the tenant.

Some leases are "net" or include partial payment of operating costs. Be certain that this is clearly spelled out. Real estate brokers often prefer a gross lease because, when calculated on a percentage basis, commissions are higher.

Base Year. The initial period during which a tenant on a gross lease will pay no pass-throughs, i.e., increases in operating costs over and above the base year, typically the first full calendar year of actual occupancy. If a tenant chooses to lease space in a new building, the calculation should be based on a minimum 90% occupancy rate, as high vacancy rates can unfairly weight a tenant's percentage of shared occupancy costs. Tax increases should only be above the year of full assessment, which probably is later than the base year.

Pass-Throughs. It is normal on a gross lease for the landlord to pass through to the tenant annual increases in operating costs. On a triple net (NNN) lease, this does not apply, as the tenant is paying all such expenses.

BOMA Standard. "Building Owners and Managers Association" standard for internal measurement of buildings.

Usable Square Feet. The space actually occupied by a tenant, including his internal hallways and elevator lobbies, if occupying an entire floor. Note that circulation can add up to 30%.

Rentable Square Feet. The usable square feet plus a load factor, i.e., a percentage (typically 7% to 12%, depending on the age, type and size of a building) of such common areas as the building lobby, common hallways, and restrooms. The load factor should not include vertical penetrations, i.e., elevator shafts and stairwells.

Gross Square Footage. The total square footage of the building, including machinery rooms, vertical penetrations, etc.

Most landlords quote on a rentable basis, but when the tenant is renting an entire floor or a whole building, rentable can equal usable. Be aware of the differential; it can be significant—5% to 10%.

Lease Term. Can be anything from one month to 20 years! Month-to-month leases are not common.

Tenant Improvements (TIs). First, determine what landlord-provided improvements are included in the space. There are two general bases.

- "Under ceiling" includes walls taped and ready for paint, HVAC system ready for specific distribution to offices, ceiling grid in place with lights and tile on the floor ready for placement, electric and plumbing stubbed off to the space and, often, window coverings.

- "Slab-to-slab" includes none of these. TIs are anything needed over and above these "basics."

Different landlords offer different base packages—be aware of the difference. As an example, the two bases noted above differ by approximately $15 per square foot! These figures will impact the rate quoted you.

Building Standards TIs. Merely indicate what level of TIs a landlord is willing to include as part of the TI package.

Amortization. The basis upon which the TIs are paid off over the period of the lease: "Financed" by the landlord or paid directly by the tenant. Do not confuse amortization with depreciation, which is the time over which buildings (31.5 years) or other equipment is written off. Amortization is usually calculated by mortgage payment tables providing constant monthly payments over the term.

Cost Segregation. Identifies circumstances where accelerated depreciation of certain building components is allowable.

Option. To extend the lease and/or to lease additional space, an option gives the tenant the right to extend or expand at his or her call at a certain point in time. May include pre-arranged lease rates or be negotiable at option time.

Right of First Offer. Landlords undertake to offer space to existing tenants prior to offering it to other potential tenants.

Right of First Refusal. Landlords undertake to offer space to existing tenants on the same terms and conditions as a bona fide offer they may have received for that space.

The many other terms and "rights" in a lease agreement all are negotiable. Your lease should always be reviewed by your attorney prior to signing, but the more you understand about the terminology and your rights as a tenant, the less chance there is that you will be unpleasantly surprised.

Commissions

Commissions are typically a percentage of the gross or NNN lease value over a fixed period. Example: On a 10-year lease, 4% to 5% of the value of the first 5 years of the lease and 2% to 2.5% of the next 5 years. Sometimes a commission is calculated not as a percentage but as a flat rate, e.g., $2.50 to $5.00 per square foot leased. Leasing agents will typically share the commission with an outside broker or tenant representative on a number of bases such as a 50%/50% split.

If you are considering several buildings, be certain your agent or tenant representative discloses the commission rates for each property. The rates payable to brokers can differ significantly.

▪ Chapter 4 ▪

Financing the Company

4.1 Forming Your Business

—by Peter Parsons
Davis Wright Tremaine LLP

Rarely does a great business suddenly spring to life complete with a mature technology, engineering, marketing, and management. It is not atypical for founders of a company to informally collaborate while developing a prototype or refining a business plan. During these formative stages of a venture, the founders can often sift through the relative contributions of their compatriots and develop a sense of the role they should take in the coming enterprise. Savvy entrepreneurs will be mindful of their cofounders' expectations and work to keep expectations realistic and in sync between team members. Putting a legal form to those expectations reduces the possibility of team dissention as the enterprise develops.

Consultation with an experienced lawyer early in the development process is essential. Initial issues that often need to be addressed before the new venture is formed include:

a. *Corporate Opportunity Doctrine.* This Common Law doctrine essentially holds that opportunities developed by officers or employees must first be offered to the employing corporation.

b. *Employee Invention Agreements.* Are any of the team members obligated under contract to reveal and assign inventions to their employers?

c. *Non-compete Agreements.* Are the team members free to pursue the proposed line of business?

d. *Technology Transfer.* Is the core technology to be transferred from an institution or founder? If so, how?

Individual Expectations

It is not uncommon for founders to work shoulder-to-shoulder for months without discussing their expectations on issues of ownership and leadership. Individuals know in their hearts what their contribution is really worth or the senior position they should assume in the new entity. Possibly chilled by a sense of reality, they fail to articulate these views until prodded by the routine organizational questions of the lawyer. When these expectations are finally brought forth and the parties' expectations of ownership exceed

100%, or there is more than one CEO, it falls to the lawyer to serve as a reluctant mediator in sorting out the relationships—if possible. As the lawyer usually represents the venture rather than a single party, the parties are often urged to seek their own individual counsel. The effects of dissention on an embryonic enterprise can be disastrous if not fatal. A room full of lawyers articulating their client's merit in the start-up venture is a poor substitute for good communications between founders.

Selection of the proper legal entity for the enterprise requires a careful examination of the probable future of the entity. Founders should view their future entity from at least four perspectives as (i) founders, (ii) key employees, (iii) initial investors and (iv) subsequent investors or acquirers. From those perspectives, they should ask themselves fundamental questions such as: Is the company likely to grow quickly? Are they prepared to share ownership with investors or employees? Will outside investors be required? Will the venture generate initial losses that might benefit investors? Are those outside investors likely to be wealthy individuals or venture capitalists? The answers to some of these questions invariably change as the enterprise matures. Nonetheless, having examined these issues, founders will be far better equipped to choose a form of business that best fits.

Lawyers representing technology-based companies tend to make several assumptions on formation of a new company. By the time the client and attorney have worked through the above issues, the alternatives of forming a general or limited partnership has been eliminated as unsuitable for high growth companies. Experienced counsel will guide the client toward organizing in the simplest manner possible. As the company grows, so does organizational complexity. In any entity, intricate organizational structures are a burden. In a young company, the founders should be focused on making the entity viable rather than playing shell games with legal entities.

Selecting an Entity

Invariably, the selection of entities comes down to three choices: (i) the Limited Liability Company, (ii) an "S" corporation or (iii) a "C" corporation. In a few instances, a company may begin as an LLC during product development, incorporate as an "S" corporation during the seed round, and finally convert to a "C" corporation when seeking venture or institutional funding.

LLC

Limited liability company (or "LLC") legislation in some form has been adopted in all 50 states and Washington, D.C. By statute an LLC's members are treated similarly to corporate shareholders for liability purposes. The LLC is treated under federal tax laws as a partnership. This flexible LLC allows members to create an entity closely tailored to their particular needs. Unlike an "S" corporation (see below), there are no limitations on the number or nature of members. In the technology arena, there are some instances where a

LLC is well suited for a new company. By way of example, consider a venture with a vertical software application that may be developed with the support of a few investors that would appreciate (and are able to use) a write-off of the early losses before profitability is reached. Assume further that the developed product is to be licensed to a limited number of end-users precluding the need for expensive marketing, support staff, and the financing associated with funding those needs. As the company becomes profitable, earnings flow directly to the members without taxation at the corporate level. Upon sale of the company or its liquidation, proceeds flow directly to the members without corporate taxation. A final benefit of the LLC is that it may be neatly rolled into the corporate form, usually without adverse tax consequences.

"S" corporation

The principal disadvantage of the LLC is that because it is relatively new, it does not benefit from the well-developed body of law that surrounds corporations. The "S" corporation sacrifices some flexibility for the advantage of the familiar corporate form of business. An "S" corporation is limited to 75 shareholders (rarely a problem) and may not have corporate, partnership, or foreign shareholders (often a problem). While limited to one class of shares, the "S" corporation is often the organization of choice for founders who desire the tax advantages of a pass-through entity. If there comes a point when the "S" corporation election has outlived its usefulness, the shareholders can revoke the election and be treated as a standard "C" corporation. Institutional and venture capital investors (often organized as LLCs themselves) are rarely interested in pass-through tax advantages for their institutional investors. Most new companies succeed in retaining the majority of its shares for the founders while giving up a minority interest to early investors. In most circumstances, the allocation of tax benefits to equity owners is then apportioned to the founders who often are not in a position to take advantage of them. While in a theoretical sense the members of an LLC or the shareholders of an "S" corporation may collectively pay less tax than a "C" corporation and its shareholders, nonetheless, the poor matching of tax benefits and the ability of investors to use those benefits preclude their long-term use by a growth company.

Most young technology companies expect to grow and grow quickly. In seeking financing, the founders wisely choose to promote the technology and the economic opportunity rather than short-term tax advantages. Absent special circumstances, the vast majority of young companies begin as "C" corporations. A point of clarification may be in order. Except as to the qualification for "S" corporation tax treatment (and agreements relating to that status), there is no difference between a "S" and a "C" corporation. Assuming all other issues to be equal, the documents filed with the state of incorporation are identical for both entities.

The great thing about corporations is that most issues have been thrashed out in the courts, and where the statutes do not provide an answer, the Common Law often does. In many states, an incorporator may obtain a one-page "Articles of Incorporation," pay filing fees, and—presto!—a new corporation has been formed. There is a place for these documents, but not as the foundation of a new high growth company. By way of example, if the articles are silent on the subject, the new shareholders will have both preemptive rights. Preemptive rights are the ability of an existing shareholder to maintain their proportional shareholdings by being entitled to participate in the subsequent issuance of stock. While similar rights may be granted by agreement, professional investors have no interest in dealing with the preemptive rights of an existing shareholder who may not be financially qualified to participate in a venture financing. The existence of cumulative voting and a lack of proper director indemnification provisions are often the shortcomings of the form book type of corporate documents. There is no excuse for improper incorporation. Doing it correctly is a relatively minor expense. At best poor corporate documents look inept when viewed by an investor in due diligence. At worst, the company could be held hostage by a shareholder faction reluctant to being diluted.

Founding your Corporation

When founding your corporation think big, but keep it simple. We often will incorporate a company with 50 million authorized shares of common stock. Of the authorized shares, 15–20 million will be issued to the founders. As a rule of thumb, stock option plans will constitute 10%–15% of the fully diluted outstanding shares. In this case, 1.5–3 million shares may be set aside for options. This leaves plenty of shares for the future common stock investors in a seed round and grants for warrants, if needed. (Wealthy and venture investors in later rounds will invariably demand, and receive, preferred stock that requires further amendment of the corporate articles.) There is no magic in the big numbers. If given a choice, most people would prefer 10,000 to 100 shares or options—even if the values are equivalent. It is not logical, but it is so.

At start-up, be sure to follow through with the organizational meeting, adoption of proper bylaws, formal transfers of technology, timely filing of the "S" corporation election (if appropriate), and the issuance of shares. Corporations are separate legal entities. To get the benefits of incorporation, the entity must be treated as such. Consider a shareholder's agreement that restricts the ability of the shareholders to sell their stock. A typical arrangement requires that shareholders offer their stock first to the company and then to other shareholders before they are allowed to sell to a third party.

Investors will often require the creation of sophisticated series of preferred stock issues. Accommodating those requirements necessitates amendment of the corporate documents. Unless your company is venture-backed from start-up, it is usually a waste of time to anticipate the form of these documents. If you have structured your entity properly from the beginning, the founders will be in a position to respond to the legitimate needs of outside investors.

Neglecting the Entity

It is not unusual for a neglected corporate entity to stand in the way of a financing deal. Investors are interested in opportunities, not other people's messes. During the early phases of your company's development, imagine a very fastidious corporate attorney who may represent an investor, acquirer, or underwriter. As he or she runs white gloves over your LLC or corporate records during a due diligence review, will he or she find a critical document missing? Is there an undocumented grant of options? Is it clear that the technology was properly transferred to the company? Most law firms have a maintenance program to assure the basics are accomplished. Subscribe to it. It is cheap insurance. When it comes time for financing or the realization of an exit strategy, your shareholders will be pleased that you did.

4.2 Creating That All-important Business Plan

—by Ron Kornfeld
Normandy Partners, LLC

Business plans are the method by which entrepreneurs communicate their vision and structure to their organizations, each other, and potential investors.

The discipline and focus required to document strategy and practices is an end in itself— a better business results from logical analysis and planning. A business plan fortifies a company's ability to identify its goals and plans to meet them in a format that is the accepted vernacular of all business professionals.

Generally, business plans fall into two categories: operational plans and plans designed to attract investors. Though they share many of the same data, their spin is different. Operational plans tend to target an internal audience and focus on a detailed "as-is" assessment of your company, warts and all. Plans for investors tend to focus on the "to-be" view of your firm and include more detailed forward-looking marketing strategy. They also demonstrate the enhancements that you envision for your business with the targeted investment.

All business plans are about the choices you have made, or will make, and about where you are going and how you will know it when you get there.

A good business plan:

- Establishes performance goals and objectives;
- Systematizes the evaluation of performance;
- Documents the company's message to management, employee prospects, and potential investors

The Five-Step Program

Like any undertaking of substance, the writing of a business plan takes planning and milestone-oriented execution. The five general steps to a successful business plan are:

Step 1—identify your audience

Who will read the plan will define how you choose to showcase the attributes of your company. A comprehensive vision of who will read the plan and what they may know about your company through previous contacts or media coverage will help you frame what you want to tell them in the plan. You should also have a clear view of how you want them to use the information that you will present them in the plan. Do you want them to come to work for you? Invest in you? Distribute your products?

There will always be conflicts between your perspective of what your target audience probably wants to know and what you want them to know; resolving these early will save you numerous revisions of the plan.

Step 2—outline the business plan

Almost all writers have found that a crisp outline for a business plan will help crystallize the flow of the content and, maybe more importantly, facilitate delegation of the creation of content to others inside your company. The last section of this article contains this critical process.

Once you have populated the outline based on what you know about your audience and your objectives for the plan, socialize it within your organization and among trusted advisors. It is much easier to modify content at this stage of development than later in the process.

Step 3—write the plan

Writing the plan includes three elements—above and beyond the basic drafting of the text:

- Information Collection
- Market Research
- Financial Documentation

Information Collection is the process of gathering all of the internal source materials you will need to prepare the plan. These materials can include previous plan iterations, business plans and prospectuses from other similar companies, résumés, and forecasts. Newer businesses will have less of this at their disposal while older businesses will have to distill a substantial data store into a useful baseline of information.

Market Research is an essential part of every plan. Internal and external readers will be very interested in your company and product positioning, competitors, and overall market strategy. This research is the cornerstone of all of your assumptions and strategies described in the plan, and you can count on the fact that your audience will review it. This effort can be performed in parallel with the internal data gathering task to shorten the duration of the writing effort.

Financial Documentation. When these elements are complete you can start the process of building the financial model for your business. A number of standard formats for the conveyance of this information are collectively referred to as *pro forma statements*. There is a distinct advantage in fine-tuning the math on the pro forma package before moving on: this exercise will give you an excellent idea which strategies will work from a financial perspective before you invest many hours in writing a detailed narrative description of them.

In order to insure that none of the subtleties of your reasoning are lost in this process, it is essential to keep detailed notes on the assumptions you make in building the model. These also form the basis of the footnotes that must accompany the pro forma statements. You are now ready to draft the plan. Note that the last element of a business plan to be prepared is always the Executive Summary. As a summary of the plan, its contents are contingent on the rest of the document; it just cannot be written properly until the other components of the plan are complete.

Step 4—review the plan

After you have arrived at a satisfactory draft of the plan, get some other opinions. The input of anyone familiar with managing or investing in a business similar to yours should be meaningful. Have them give you feedback on its comprehensiveness, objectivity, logic, format and presentation, and overall effectiveness in communicating your message.

How many reviewers should you have? A balance must be struck between broad input and the practicality of implementing potentially contradictory advice. Ultimately, it is your plan and you will have to execute it—make the changes that intuition tells you are important. Also, there's always . . .

Step 5—the update process

Like your business, your business plan is living; it must be periodically updated to reflect your growing and changing business and markets. Take the time to update the plan as part of the management oversight of your business.

It is also advisable that each copy of your plan be numbered and that you keep a record of who has received each numbered copy. This tracking will allow you to distribute updates and to more effectively follow up with recipients.

Each copy should also be marked with appropriate language that limits the ability of recipients to distribute or copy the plan without your consent. If the purpose of the plan is to secure a private placement, you may also need to include certain statutory disclaimers in the plan. Check with competent legal counsel on both of these matters prior to finalizing and distributing your plan.

Outline of a Basic Business Plan

I. Executive summary

This is arguably the most important component of your plan because it is the most likely to be read by a wide audience. The most critical meta-point to be communicated in the Executive Summary is why your company is uniquely qualified to execute the plan and why that execution is plausible, important, and financially compelling.

The best Executive Summaries are less than four pages in length and lure the reader into delving into the entire business plan. The Executive Summary should include a brief table of contents designed to assist readers in locating specific sections in the plan.

The specific content of the Executive Summary should be:

A. *The Purpose of the Plan*
    1. Generate Investor Interest; or
    2. Memialize an operational plan for optimizing the business

B. *Market Analysis*
    1. The complexion of your target market (demographic, geographic, etc.)
    2. The products or services you will deliver to meet those needs

C. *The Company*
    1. How your company is organized
    2. The unique role your company plays in meeting market needs

D. *Marketing and Sales Activities*
    1. Key elements of your marketing strategy
    2. Methodology of revenue generation through sales activity
    3. Success factors vs. your competition

E. *Product or Service Research and Development*
    1. Major deliverables and milestones in your product plan
    2. Release schedule and upgrade plans

F. *Organization and Personnel*
1. Summary of management team and their philosophy
2. Ownership structure
3. Other key employees and organizational strategy

G. *Financials*
1. Amount of funds desired and their use
2. Historical financials summary
3. Forecasted future financials summary (should show impact of desired funds, if applicable)

II. Market analysis

This section provides your opportunity to flex your muscles and demonstrate your knowledge of your industry and your ability to analyze your market research. If you want to present more granular market research data, attach them as appendices to your plan.

The Specific content should be:

A. *Overview*
1. Profile of your industry
2. Metrics of your industry
   a. Historical
   b. Current
   c. Three-year view
   d. Five-years view
3. Your company's role in the industry
   a. Historical
   b. Current
   c. Future

B. *Target Markets*
1. Market Characteristics and Segmentation
   a. Needs profile, your value proposition
   b. How those needs are being met now (without your product)
   c. Customer definition
   d. Physical distribution (geography or locality)
   e. How buyers make decisions—purchasing behaviors
   f. Cyclicality (seasonality or other)
2. Target Market Metrics
   a. Number of target customers
   b. Current purchase volumes of alternative solutions
   c. Growth forecast

3. Product Penetration Model
   a. Market share
   b. Customer count
   c. Geography, locality, or nationality
   d. Basis model for penetration
4. Pricing
   a. Arithmetic relationship of price to gross margins
   b. Net margin levels
   c. Pricing plans and discounts
5. Target Market Identification and Acquisition
   a. Directories and lists
   b. Publications
   c. Public records
6. Media Plan
   a. Print
   b. Radio/television
   c. Agency relationships, professional relationships
7. Secondary Target Market Metrics
   a. Number of target customers
   b. Current purchase volumes of alternative solutions
   c. Growth forecast

C. *Primary Market Research*
   1. Prospect contact strategy/survey structure
   2. Demo strategy
   3. Prospect responses
   4. Relevancy model/needs fulfillment
   5. Focus Groups and other information gathering techniques

D. *Competition*
   1. Calibration
      a. Participants
      b. Market share/revenues
      c. Potential competitors
      d. Direct competitors
      e. Indirect and adjacent products that may compete
   2. Competitive Assessment (for each)
      a. Needs fulfillment
      b. Comparative penetration
      c. Brand equity and media coverage
      d. Financial estimates
      e. Executives and organization
      f. Relevancy of your target market to their business model

3. Barriers to entry for each market entrant
   a. Financial cost
   b. Timeline or process
   c. Technology
   d. Personnel
   e. Brand loyalty and/or inertia
   f. Patents and trademarks issues

E. *Regulatory Restrictions (if applicable)*
   1. Regulatory constraints on you or your customers
   2. Process to address the constraints
   3. Regulatory timeline
   4. Forecast and change models

III. Company description

This section describes briefly how you are organized and how that positions you for success. Because many of these items are covered elsewhere in the plan, a summary approach is best.

A. *Nature of Your Business*
   1. Value proposition
   2. Needs fulfillment model
   3. Target customer profile

B. *Success Factors*
   1. Optimal needs fulfillment model
   2. Economies of scale or efficiencies of process
   3. Superior technology
   4. Management and/or personnel

IV. Sales and marketing strategies

Your pro forma financials describe your fiscal goals. This section shows how your sales and marketing strategies are architected to fulfill those plans.

A. *Sales Strategies*
   1. Sales force
      a. Staffing strategy employee vs. independent representatives
      b. Metrics
      c. How you find and develop sales professionals
      d. How they are motivated, compensated, and retained
   2. Sales process
      a. Prospect identification
      b. Prioritization
      c. Sales calls and productivity measures
      d. Sales cycle by task and timeline
      e. Revenue-per-sale metrics

B. *Marketing Strategy*
1. Overall direction
2. Growth model
   a. Direct sales
   b. Acquisition of base
   c. Franchise
   d. Horizontal tactics
   e. Vertical tactics
3. Channel strategy and distribution chain
   a. OEM
   b. Resellers
   c. Distributors
   d. Retail
4. Communication
   a. Promotion strategy
   b. Advertising
   c. PR
   d. Collateral and point of sale
   e. Web strategy/E-commerce

V. Products and services

This section describes your company's offerings in a summary form. Effective business plans are not product plans—they showcase only the most important insights about your product capabilities.

A. *Product/Service Summary*
1. Benefits of product/service
2. Competitive advantages
3. Development model

B. *Life Cycle*
1. Position within product life cycle
2. Change possibilities for life cycle
   a. Extension
   b. Contraction

C. *Copyrights, Patents, and Trade Secrets*
1. Existing or pending copyrights or patents
2. Copyright and patent filings
3. Unpatented or copyrighted components
4. Qualified trade secrets
5. Extant legal agreements
   a. Non-disclosure agreements
   b. Non-compete agreements
   c. Licensing agreements

D. *Research & Development*
   1. Project plan
   2. Release schedule and enhancements
   3. Product plan
      a. New products or services
      b. Test plan for each product
      c. Generational plan
      d. Complementary offerings
      e. Replacement offerings

VI. Operations

This section establishes the model by which you operate your business and the measures with which you will keep it progressing towards the plan's objectives.

A. *Production and Service Delivery*
   1. Procedures
   2. Resources
      a. Internal
      b. Subcontractors
   3. Capacity issues
      a. Investment requirements
      b. Cost components
      c. Timeline

B. *Unique Operating Advantages Vs. Competition*
   1. Processes
   2. Human capital
   3. Economies of scale and efficiency
   4. Lower costs

C. *Supplier Model*
   1. Suppliers of critical elements
      a. Primary
      b. Secondary
   2. Lead-time
   3. Risk assessment of component shortages
   4. Contractual relationships with suppliers

VII. Management and ownership

This section describes your human capital and its unique blend of skills and culture. Positioned properly, it becomes a competitive advantage. This section also reviews your **current** ownership structure. At the appropriate time, prospective investors will present you with terms and ownership conditions under which they will invest—these should not be included in the plan.

A. *Management Organization*
1. Mission and cultural outlook of the management team
2. Organization chart and description

B. *Management Profiles (for each)*
1. Name
2. Title
3. Brief position description
4. Primary responsibilities and authority
5. The individual's unique skills that contribute to your company's core Competencies (complete résumés should be in the appendix section).
6. Compensation structure

C. *Additions to the Management Team (for each)*
1. Title
2. Brief position description and timing of placement
3. Primary responsibilities and authority
4. Skills sought that will contribute to your company's core competencies
5. Compensation structure

D. *Legal Structure*
1. Corporation type
   a. C corporation
   b. S corporation
2. Partnership
   a. General
   b Limited
   c. LLC
   d. Sole proprietorship

E. *Owners (for each)*
1. Name
2. Percentage ownership
3. Involvement with the company
4. Form of ownership
   a. Common stock
   b. Preferred stock
   c. General partner
   d. Limited partner
5. Outstanding equity
   a. Options
   b. Warrants
   c. Convertible debt

6. Common stock
    a. Authorized
    b. Issued

F. Board of Directors (for each)
    1. Name
    2. Position on the board
    3. Extent of involvement with the company
    4. Background and representative accomplishments

VIII. Funding required and its uses

This section defines the amount of funds you are seeking and their use. It should reflect the assumptions outlined in your marketing strategies and pro forma financials.

A. Immediate Funding Requirements
    1. Amount
    2. Timing
    3. Type
        a. Equity
        b. Debt
        c. Mezzanine
    4. Optimal terms

B. Funding Requirements Over the Next Five Years
    1. Amount
    2. Timing
    3. Type
        a. Equity
        b. Debt
        c. Mezzanine
    4. Optimal terms

C. Use of Funds (choose all that are applicable)
    1. Capital expense
    2. Working capital
    3. Debt retirement
    4. Acquisition

D. Exit Strategy
    1. IPO
    2. LBO
    3. Acquisition
    4. Liquidation

IX. Financial data

This section presents the pro forma financial statements that support the other sections of your plan.

A. *Historical Financials (no more than three-year view)*
   1. Annual statements
      a. Income
      b. Balance sheet
      c. Cash flows
   2. CPA profile
      a. Audit
      b. Review
      c. Compilation

B. *Forecasted Financials (five-year view)*
   1. Month-month view of the next fiscal or calendar year
      a. Income
      b. Balance sheet
      c. Cash flows
      d. Capital expenditure budget
   2. Quarterly view of next four years
      a. Income
      b. Balance sheet
      c. Cash flows
      d. Capital expenditure budget
   3. Assumptions and narrative
   4. CPA profile
      a. Assembly
      b. Agreed-upon procedures
      c. Review
      d. Examination

C. *Analysis*
   1. Historical financials
      a. Ratio analysis
      b. Trend analysis with graphic presentation
   2. Prospective financials
      a. Ratio analysis
      b. Trend analysis with graphic presentation

X. Appendices or exhibits

A. *Résumés of Key Managers*

B. *References*

C. *Market Studies*

D. *Bibliography*
1. Magazine articles
2. Books
3. URLs

E. *Patents*

F. *Contracts*
1. Leases
2. Sales contracts
3. Purchase contracts
4. Partnership/ownership agreements
5. Stock option agreements
6. Employment/compensation agreements
7. Non-compete agreements
8. Insurance
   a. Product liability
   b. Officers' and directors' liability
   c. General liability

4.3 Making Sense Of Financing

—by A. Peter Parsons
Davis Wright Tremaine LLP

There is only one constant in raising capital for young companies: people invest in people. If you can integrate this maxim into your strategy, your chances of receiving funding will improve remarkably. By way of example, in the founding stages of a company, capital is often provided by friends and family. Are these people investing because of an algorithm or your marketing plans to dominate a market enrapture them? Heck no! In most cases, they have not a clue why the company's technology enjoys an unfair advantage over current products. One or more of the founders has earned their trust and confidence.

They invest because they believe the people in the company will get the job done. Even in the most sophisticated financings, when you pare away preliminary issues of valuation, due diligence, and technology assessment, generating investor confidence in the company's people remains the essential key to attracting capital.

Okay, so you have great people, a world-beating technology and a business plan that excites the savvy reader. Where do you go from here?

Raising Money

For some CEOs raising capital comes as second nature. These fortunate souls are few and far between. Most CEOs of young companies feel uncomfortable with the process. The CEO has the job, however, because he or she is capable of leading a team in developing a product and getting it to market. The CEO may be preeminent in his or her field, but rarely are technology CEOs trained as investment bankers. Most would prefer a root canal to pitching a business plan to investors. It is simply not what they are comfortable with doing.

Unfortunately, raising money is not a hobby to be done on the side. Like it or not, a majority of the CEO's time will be spent in the money raising process (often while putting in a full work week); there is simply no other way. Raising money is uncomfortable. After all, we are talking about the CEO's baby. Rejection of his or her vision can (and should be) taken very personally. On the other hand, professional investors did not get their jobs because they are uncritical. If they are venture investors, they are stewards of other people's money, and it is their job (and fiduciary duty) to wade through masses of business plans to find the few that meet their fund's investment requirements. If a CEO does not take criticism well, raising money can be a humiliating process. Conversely, those who take critical comments to heart can often refine their business plan and secure financing.

The time demands of a start-up are enormous. Because the CEO is often needed to keep product development on time or to do other pressing managerial tasks, why not delegate raising capital? Why not delegate the task to the CFO, a director, or other member of senior management? Why not retain an "investment banker" or money finder to bring in the investors? By choosing one of these paths, the CEO stays on target and the money will flow in.

If raising money were only that easy, there would be fewer ulcers in this world! Intermediaries such as investment bankers can be of great assistance and can open many doors for a CEO, but only the CEO can walk through them. In young, unproven companies, investors will accept no substitutes. They are investing in that CEO, not in some commissioned agent. Quite fairly, investors expect to be sold by the person that will be taking their money. Again, people invest in people.

Investment Banks

Investment banking is an elastic term. Both consummate professionals and charlatans use it. They are not easy to differentiate. Some respected professionals work out of their homes while some charlatans have fancy offices and even fancier letterhead. Some real jerks work (at least briefly) for reputable firms. Because start-up companies are easy targets for the unscrupulous and because the discomfort of senior management in raising money is an open secret, charlatans typically succeed because the CEO wants to believe in them. The CEO wants to believe that his or her company is worth every penny (and more!) that the business plan suggests. The CEO (and the company's board) wants to believe that paying a $25,000–$50,000 retainer will have investors clamoring to invest. Frankly, some of these "investment bankers" are not dishonest—they are simply self-delusional. In any event if an investment banker is to be relied upon for raising capital, a thorough reference check on the firm and the specific individual is far cheaper than a painful disaster.

A Financing Tale

For purposes of our financing narrative, let us mercifully skip the actual money-raising process. Let us assume the CEO has spent too many days on the road pitching investors while trying to keep the company on track at night by phone, fax, and e-mail. The road has been a long and tough one, but the end is in sight. Today, a group of investors has said that they have every faith that the management team is bound to succeed, the technology superior, the potential market enormous. In closing the meeting, the lead investor observes that while they intend to invest, they cannot accept the common stock structure suggested by the company. Nonetheless, they are sure the CEO will be pleased to accept the term sheet that will be faxed to her hotel in the afternoon. They will meet and discuss the term sheet over dinner. Elated and anxious, our CEO returns to her hotel.

Having done due diligence on these investors, the CEO believes these potential investors to be a great mix of talent and relevant industry experience. Our CEO suddenly realizes that during the past few months she has been pitching the company and a specific valuation. She has responded vaguely to investor inquiries about preferred stock and convertible debt but steered the conversation back to the company's offering of common stock. Our CEO realizes that she really does not have a working knowledge of the terms associated with these forms of investment. In a panic, she calls her trusted company counsel. The lawyer reminds her that in these negotiations she needs to balance the needs not only of her existing shareholders, the company, its board, and its management team but also the needs of future investors who will view this transaction in hindsight when making their own decisions.

Transaction terms

The attorney offers the following outline of transaction terms:

Convertible Debt. In business school, we are taught that debt is the cheapest form of financing. It carries a rate of interest and may be paid off. In technology-based companies (if all goes well), we expect exponential growth and a dynamic increase in shareholder equity. Unlike equity, debt does have to be paid back. While undoubtedly expensive, the interest that accrues to a lender is minimal when compared to an increase in shareholder value. If a company is capable of taking out and paying off loans, existing shareholders will be far better off than if the same money had been raised through the sale of stock. Unfortunately, investors have figured this out. If venture investors offer some debt financing, it will undoubtedly be convertible. Convertible debt allows them the best of both worlds. (These instruments are often known by the fancier term "convertible debenture.") Lenders can then partake in the upside by converting to common stock if things look good. If things do not go well, they can be the wolf at the door with other creditors.

All financing vehicles have infinite variations and convertible debt is no different. Some features to consider:

Bridge financing. If the convertible debt is being offered as a "*bridge*" to the company while a preferred equity deal is being put together, it may convert into that preferred security. The person who loans the money is usually referred to as the "*holder.*"

"Convertible" means that the debt (and usually accumulated interest) may be converted into common stock at an agreed price. Except in some circumstances, conversion is invariably at the option of the holder and may not be redeemed without the holder's being given an opportunity to convert.

Subordination. Most convertible debt is subordinated to institutional lenders. In short, the bank comes first.

Security interest. Investors may demand (like the bank) a security interest in the assets of the company. Be very careful here. If you cannot pay, the holders may foreclose on their debt and own the assets. This is not an academic issue: frustrated investors are usually not as patient as a bank; when things go wrong, they tend to get involved—for good or evil. If the company has obtained secured bank financing, the investor will be forced to take somewhat of a backseat to the bank.

Warrants. Warrants may be tagged on to convertible debt. A warrant is the right to buy a share of stock at a price certain for a limited period of time. Investors will often speak of *warrant coverage* in percentages. By way of example, if an investor loaned the company $100,000 when the common stock was currently valued at $1, 10% warrant coverage would allow the holder to buy 10,000 common shares at $1 until the warrant expired (usually two to five years).

Preferred stock

On Wall Street preferred stock is often a fairly innocuous security that enjoys a stated preferential dividend and priority over the common shares at liquidation. In young companies, preferred stock invariably has the preferential dividend and the priority at liquidation, but those are just a start. (In the context of venture investing, it is sometimes called "*participating preferred.*") Let me acquaint you with a few of the common "bells and whistles" associated with a venture-type preferred stock financing round:

Series. Preferred stock is issued in Series: hence, Series A, Series B, etc. Most series are a result of different rounds of financing and may vote as a series or as a class on certain issues.

Convertibility. Preferred stock is always convertible into common stock at the option of the shareholder but will automatically convert upon a public offering or sale of the company. The *conversion ratio* (usually in dollar terms) is set at the time of closing with an adjustment formula. The conversion formula then adjusts for various factors including accumulated dividends, stock splits, stock dividends, and antidilution adjustments. In some transactions, this formula is adjusted if the company does not meet certain financial benchmarks.

Dividends. Preferred stock will carry a dividend of approximately 6%–10% that may be paid in cash, but usually is applied to the conversion into common stock.

Ratchets. Every company believes that the value of its stock will continue to climb, and every investor hopes the company is correct. To hedge their bets, investors will request a "*full ratchet*" to protect themselves from a sale at a lower price. On the other hand, the company may offer a "*weighted ratchet*" for a limited period of time. By way of comparative example, under a full ratchet, if a company sells investors shares at $2 and later (before the ratchet expires) sells a single share for $1, then the conversion formula would automatically cause the number shares owned by the $2 investor to double, giving an effective price of $1. Assuming the same facts with a weighted-ratchet, the workings of the formula would proportionately adjust the shareholder's conversion formula. If the investor had purchased 100,000 shares, the adjustment for the sale of a single share would be miniscule. Invariably, stock options are addressed in the ratchet provisions and are usually excluded to a specified level. Obviously it is important to make sure enough options are available during the period that the ratchet is in force. Beware: some investors will insist that there be no time limitation on the ratchet. From the company's perspective, this is foolish because new investors will look askance at old ratchets diluting the value of their new cash.

Board position and information rights

In most transactions, investors may request one or more board positions. If a company has assembled an outstanding board, the preferred investors may not demand board representation. If no board position is expected, consider it a compliment. Board "*visitation*" rights allow a representative of the preferred shareholders to sit in, participate in discussions, but not vote in board meetings. Do not be fooled. Except when a dispute arises, boards work by consensus. A board visitor is the substantial equivalent of a board member. If you must (and usually you do) cede one or more board positions to the investor group, attempt to control who those persons will be. By way of example, "an industry CEO" acceptable to key founders may be highly desirable. A wet-behind-the-ears MBA from a venture fund may be worse than useless. Less intrusive are "*information rights*" that require the company to provide the investors with financial and managerial information. Because the investors do not know your company, their term sheet is likely to contain a laundry list of reports that you neither generate nor plan to generate. Be sure to agree to provide only the information that you currently do or "should" provide in the future. Board positions are often guaranteed to the investor through shareholder voting arrangements that may contain agreements to vote for certain persons by name or category (i.e., the representative nominated by more than 50% of the series holders).

Redemption rights. Sooner or later, investors want their money back. Their sense of timing may not coincide with that of the board of directors or the availability of a sale or public offering. Redemption is the right of the shareholders to put their stock back to the company. This is another of those "gun to the head" provisions. Rarely does the company have the liquidity to simply buy out a class of impatient investors. If you must agree to redemption rights, make sure that they are at least five years in the future.

Registration rights. Again, investors may not always agree with the board of directors on the timing of a public offering. Registration rights permit them to demand the company register their shares, In real life, investors most often use these redemption and registration rights to get management and the board seriously thinking about shareholder liquidity. Both can be effective prods. Also included in this section are "*piggyback*" rights. Simply put, this is the right to add the investor's securities to those being registered by the company. This is rarely an issue and commonly granted to the investor. Of interest to founders are "*lock-up*" arrangements that may lock up their stock for six to eighteen months after an initial public offering.

Co-sale rights. In most instances, the founders must agree that if they sell or transfer their shares (except for estate planning purposes), the investors may "*tag along*" and sell a proportionate amount of their shares to the purchaser. Investors do not want the founders "bailing out" or taking advantage of eager purchasers without their consent or participation. Less common are "*bring along*" rights, recognizing that sale of a minority interest is difficult. Bring along rights permit the investors to sell all the shares of the corporation. Obviously the timing of the sale of a company should be left to the board of directors and an appropriate majority of its shareholders, and this is therefore a right that the company should avoid granting if possible. If there are no other alternatives, these rights should be put far in the company's future.

Right of first refusal. Rights of first refusal to participate in subsequent rounds of financing are not uncommon. Far better (and equally common) are rights to maintain the investor's prorata interest in a subsequent series. Be on guard for a term that requires the consent of the series shareholders to undertake future financing. Let them participate in future rounds but not control the timing (or nature) of your financing.

Covenants and restrictions. Invariably, the term sheet will provide that no modification may be made to the articles or bylaws of the corporation without the consent of the series shareholders. Most of these items are usually covered by statute and are not a big deal. Also, investors will invariably tag on additional prohibitions such as limitations on salaries, borrowing, transfer of core business elements, departures from the approved business plan, increases in stock option pools, replacement of executives, and the like. If you are not careful, an investor may be able to hamstring your company's future with these provisions. Often the investor does have a legitimate concern when proposing these restrictions. A reasonable alternative in many cases is to provide for a super-majority vote of the board on many of these issues.

Common term sheet provisions

Regardless of the security, there are provisions that apply both to debt and equity, such as:

Fees and expenses. Most venture firms will require that you pay their legal, accounting, and due diligence fees. If they really like the deal, you may be able to negotiate this out of the agreement. If not, make sure that you have a maximum limitation inserted in the agreement. Expect the investors' fees to be equal to your own and in some cases you will be pleasantly surprised. In others where negotiations have been prolonged, you will be pleased with the limitation.

Confidentiality. This speaks for itself; nevertheless be cautious because the investor often does not want you to mention the pending financing to third parties until after closing. If the investor is a large corporation, it may not wish to have the deal made public at all!

No-shop and exclusivity. The investors have expressed faith in your company by extending a term sheet. They do not want you shopping it for better terms. Do not sign the agreement unless you are ready to deal exclusively. There is no harm in telling the investor that you are flattered but are waiting to see the term sheet of another investor. While it can be a risky game, simultaneously negotiating with several investors on deal terms can often both sweeten your valuation and strengthen your bargaining strength. In any event, do not sign any exclusivity provision unless it has a termination date (45–90 days). In a hot market, you do not want to be turning away potential investors while this one dithers in due diligence.

Break-up fees. Not common, but worth asking for, essentially a break-up fee provides that if a party breaks off negotiations for other than a material due diligence item, the other receives a payment or reimbursement of its expenses. While these are uncommon provisions and difficult as a evidentiary matter to establish, investors who back out of a transaction are often willing (even in the absence of an agreement—when nudged) to reimburse legal and accounting fees.

There are infinite variations of all of the above. Occasionally, an investor will give these provisions different names. None of these provisions exists in isolation and the interplay between them is subtle and complex. Omitted from the above term sheet features are matters such as indemnification, conditions precedent, legal opinions, accounting reviews, and other matters that counsel can assist the company with before the term sheet is signed. Keep in mind that a signed term sheet is not a deal. Except for certain provisions (i.e. exclusivity and confidentiality), it is not binding on either party. While the investor may have performed preliminary due diligence, the real inspection begins in earnest with an invasion of attorneys, accountants, and investor representatives. During this period, the terms will be reduced to definitive agreements to effect their terms.

Issues inevitably arise in the period between the term sheet and the final closing. You are betrothed but not yet married. Use these negotiations to take a good look at your investors: you are going to be with them a long time. While you are bound to negotiate in good faith, you are not required to commit suicide. As the deal goes forward, do not bet your company on the closing. Do not become dependent on those dollars until the deal closes. Listen to your gut. If, prior to closing, you realize that you have made a horrible mistake, get out of the deal! It is far better to swallow the lost time and expense in the short run than to have a jerk of an investor forever.

Most deals close! Once closed, make your investors feel part of the team. If a representative serves on your board, make sure the representative gets called between meetings and is kept up-to-date on company developments. If the representative is merely a shareholder, send out quarterly reports and make sure that all shareholders are on your press release list. These are the same investors that you will want to give you good marks in the next round of financing. Now that the financing is closed, you can get back to business—until the next time.

4.4 Developing Business: Basics

—by Ron Kornfeld
Normandy Partners, LLC

In a world of increasingly complex markets and regulatory structures, technology enterprises often seek to form relationships with other companies to increase their revenues and odds of success. The activities of licensing, distribution, co-branding, co-marketing, bundling, and alliance-building all fall into the broad category of Business Development—literally the art of effective deal-making with selected relationship targets.

It is easy to envision the practice of deal-making as one that revolves around tough negotiating and getting your counterparts to sign some sort of an agreement. Though these are essential elements of executing deals, experience has shown that the most successful and sustainable outcomes derive from a broader continuum of business development tasks. These tasks begin with the crafting of a clear market management vision and end long after a deal is signed.

Business development for technology companies begins with developing an understanding of two essential concepts about your own business:

- How to identify and get your target customers
- How you want a potential relationship to affect your business (financially, organizationally)

Identifying Customers

To ascertain the first concept, you need to perform the necessary research and analysis to define who your target customers are and why they buy your product. This definition is an essential element in selecting a target relationship. Understanding how a relationship can increase acquisition velocity or market share or reduce base churn or impact your tech support organization will help guide you in the process of narrowing the field of potential partners. Understanding how it will benefit your relationship target will help you create a win-win value proposition at the appropriate time.

Defining Relationship

The second concept requires you to evaluate your resources and business strategy to determine how a relationship may assist you in reaching your objectives. A relationship can provide a source of non-dilutive seed capital or a source for long-term cash in-flows, give you access to customer bases, make you a more desirable investment, make it easier to hire key talent, give you access to laboratory and test facilities, give you management expertise, and facilitate the development of additional relationships. However, any one relationship will probably not give you all of these benefits. Knowing which ones you want will help you further narrow the field of potential relationship target.

Narrowing the Field

You want to narrow the field because you want to limit the number of companies with whom you speak. Because you may inspire one that does not want to form a relationship with you to become a competitor, proactively narrowing your scope can limit your exposure to this risk.

In addition to understanding these two key concepts that represent your motivations, you must also have comprehensive information about potential relationship targets, their customers, the competitive landscape, and their key points of motivation. You'll use all of this information to form a value proposition with which the eventual deal will comply.

Having a Clear View

Most negotiations fail because the negotiating parties lack a clear view of what they hope to ultimately derive from a consummated deal. You have a unique opportunity to express your deal parameters in a clear value proposition—based on the research you have performed.

Once you have a firm grasp on your value proposition, your motivations and needs and your relationship targets, you're ready to build a contact database and start introducing yourself.

You can identify key contacts for small and medium size targets from their Web sites. Usually executives are identified as being in charge of Business Development. Feel free to call them; it's their job to evaluate potential relationships, and because you've already done sufficient research to be very specific about how a win-win relationship could be articulated, you should be of high interest.

Dealing with Larger Firms

For larger firms, you may need an introduction to get to the right person (once again, your research can help you define who the right person is). Here investors and other friends of your firm may come in handy to connect you and to lend you some of their credibility to facilitate a first conversation.

It is important to note that you should always keep a contact database in a format where you can easily assemble key information about your contacts, where you track your attempts to reach them, and where you subsequently document your conversations. The database will become one of your most valuable assets and should be accessible to your peers within your company should something happen to you. Active business development requires significant contact effort—the more organized you are, the more efficient you can be.

Use each conversation, whether it is networking inside or outside your relationship target, to understand the politics of the target organization and the role of the individuals you are contacting. This is the only way to avoid the perils of inertia and competition. Document all of your findings in your database.

Meeting with Prospective Partners

As your contact activity builds momentum, you'll start to have meetings with prospective relationship partners. Make sure that these meetings are bound by a reasonable Non-Disclosure Agreement (NDA). Work with your attorney to draft one for you to present. Never sign one presented by a relationship target without reading it thoroughly and having your attorney answer any questions you may have.

You should also be aware that expectation-setting about your needs and your value proposition begin at those first meetings (another good reason to have performed the research proactively). In essence, you lay the foundations of your negotiations very early in your communications and you should reinforce them all the way through the deal-development process.

Understanding Deal Types

Deal types generally fall into a number of categories ranging from simple licensing all the way to outright acquisition of your company. Wherever your deal and value proposition fall on this continuum, the stakes are extreme because you are likely to be able to negotiate and execute only a few deals in parallel. Your competitors will likely be striking deals with all the companies with whom you're not.

With risks like these, you want to be sure that whoever is performing your negotiations has substantial experience in crafting deals like the one you are seeking and is intimate with your value proposition. Ideally, this person is one of the principals of your company; if not, and you choose to use a consultant, always thoroughly check references. Always have an attorney review every document before signing it.

The work doesn't stop here, though. Most technology firms who enter into agreements fail to take into account the post signature randomization that often occurs within the organizations of their relationship partners. The deal's original champions may not have the time or inclination to establish a roll-out architecture poised for success, the principal reason that the life of most deals begins to wane after the press release.

Executing Audit Deals

It is wise to evaluate the relationship partner's roll-out plans within the context of the market modeling you performed earlier in this process and to be persistent in auditing (and even assisting in) their roll-out of your technology. Better still, audit their plans before you sign a deal and make the actions that accomplish your market model part of the terms of the deal.

Executed properly, Business Development can redefine your business's prospects and help you seize a sustainable hold on success. The art lies in proactively taking the steps to establish and enforce your value proposition.

4.5 Developing Software Costs

—by Paul Brajcich
KPMG LLP

Generally accepted accounting principles establish the rules as to how software development costs should be treated in a company's financial statements. This guidance is provided in Statement of Financial Accounting Standards No. 86 (Statement 86).

Statement 86

Statement 86 distinguishes between research and development activities and software development costs incurred subsequent to when technological feasibility of the software product has been established. Any software development costs capitalized will be recorded as an intangible asset on the company's balance sheet.

Technological feasibility, which is an accounting definition, appears under Statement 86, the point at which software development costs must be capitalized. This is achieved when "the enterprise has completed all planning, designing, coding and testing activities necessary to establish that the product can be produced to meet its design specifications, including functions, features and technical requirements." The accounting literature requires that the company will have completed a detailed program design or a working model of the software product. The accounting literature provides more specific guidance as to what must be included in a detailed program design or the extent of testing to be completed on the working model to conclude that technological feasibility of the product has been established.

The types of costs which should be capitalized once technological feasibility has been established include these:

- direct and indirect costs, such as programmer salaries, testing costs, allocated facility costs, and outside contractor costs.

- general and administrative costs, such as executive salaries, should not be capitalized unless it is clear that it is related to software production.

Amortization

The company must begin to amortize capitalized software development costs when the product is available for general release. The annual amortization charge is computed on a product-by-product basis and is the greater of an amount based upon a ratio of current period to total estimated revenues of the product, or straight-line amortization determined over the remaining estimated economic life of the product. The amortization charge is included in cost of revenues.

The unamortized portion of capitalized software development costs must be compared to the net realizable value of the product at each balance sheet date. The amount by which the unamortized capitalized software costs exceed the estimated future revenue from that product, reduced by costs of completing and disposing of that product, will be charged to expense. Since many early-stage software companies have no established distribution channels or prior sales experience, any costs which meet the criteria for capitalization will commonly be written off due to uncertain net realizable value.

The capitalization of software development costs is a complex area, and it is advisable to consult a CPA with significant experience in this area as you apply the guidance of Statement 86 to your company.

4.6 Debt Financing for Emerging Growth Companies

—by Kathleen Borie
Senior Vice President
Business Advisory Services
Silicon Valley Bank

Emerging growth companies often use a combination of equity and debt as part of their financial strategy to establish their businesses and accelerate growth.

An emerging growth company's first form of financing is usually in the form of equity, which can be raised from private individuals, angel investors, venture capitalists, and corporate investors. This equity can fund operations that initially focus on research and product development. Subsequent rounds of equity financing, usually negotiated upon completion of specified technological or financial milestones, are used to establish sales and marketing functions and/or to develop new products.

Once equity financing has been obtained, bank debt can also act as an important financing vehicle. Combining debt and equity in early stage technology companies is a relatively recent phenomenon. In the past, the risk was just too great for banks to make loans to companies that had no track record but that had capital expenditure and working capital needs. Today, some lenders are making debt available to young companies who have obtained equity financing.

The key to this shift has been the emerging relationships between lenders and equity sources. Long-term strategic relationships between lenders and investors have contributed to the development of successful lending programs. In addition, understanding equity trends in technology and life sciences markets has enabled these lenders to mitigate the risk factors associated with loans to emerging growth companies.

Debt financing provides a valuable tool for emerging growth companies who have received equity financing, for the following reasons:

- Debt financing is less expensive than equity
- Debt financing enables a company to "stretch" its equity dollars in order to meet product and financial milestones toward improving future valuations
- Like equity, debt finances asset growth (such as capital expenditures, accounts receivable, and business acquisitions)

Technology lenders consider a number of factors as they evaluate a company's sources of repayment. These include:

- Business Relationships (who's in the deal—management and equity partners)
- Validity of Business Plan (technology platform, market opportunity, competitive strategy, access to additional capital)
- Performance to Plan (financial covenants)
- Collateral Package (quality of assets, liquidity)

Consequently, it is important for prospective clients to provide their banks with adequate information to complete their due diligence. Technology lenders usually require the following:

- Business Plan
- Monthly Projections
- Historical Financial Statements (if available)
- Capitalization Tables
- Accounts Receivable/Accounts Payable agings (if available)
- Investor/Service Provider/Customer References

Once the bank has obtained this information, the process of business point negotiation begins. Negotiations involve discussions with the prospect on credit facility amounts, pricing, advance rates, covenants, and collateral. Once these have been agreed upon, the lender will obtain internal credit approval. Upon approval, legal documentation is completed and the credit facility is established.

The negotiation of credit facilities is often the "entry-way" into a long-term relationship. It is therefore important to consider the following criteria when selecting a banker:

- Industry commitment
- Length of commitment
- Willingness to lend
- Ability to provide introductions and references
- Financial advice
- Account Officer quality

In summary, bank debt can serve as a key component in an emerging growth company's capital structure. Understanding the bank's evaluation process and how the company fits their criteria is key to establishing good communication and choosing the best banking relationship. **Most importantly, look for a bank that will be your business partner.**

• Chapter 5 •

Accounting for the Company

5.1 Setting Up an Accounting System

—by Roger Clark
Clark & Associates

"Having too much cash without the right financial controls and budgeting process can put a company out of business quicker than a company without any cash."
—John Ballantine, Managing Partner, Chairman & CEO, iStart Ventures

If you intend to do your own accounting, selecting an accounting system that you can understand will prevent losing track of financial information and creating inexpensive messes that require an accountant to fix.

Manual systems such as an Economix check register (see an office supply store) can work well in keeping track of accounting on a cash basis. The software program, QuickBooks, has worked for some non-accountant entrepreneurs with a little coaching from a CPA. Finally, if you really need accrual basis financial statements, you need an automated general ledger system to be efficient.

Find a part-time accountant to help with record keeping. Generally, it is also a good idea to use a CPA to assist in the preparation of annual tax returns and to advise you on tax and accounting issues.

Using Financial Statements

Most well-managed software companies produce accrual basis financial statements on a monthly basis. Prepare these financial statements in a format that can be compared to the budget in your forecasted financial statements. Prepare a monthly comparison of budget to actual results, with significant differences investigated if the causes are not understood (for example, differences of at least 20% and $500, whichever is greater).

These comparisons will increase your understanding of your business, including its sources of revenue, average monthly operating costs, fixed expenses, and variable expenses. Such an understanding will help in setting product and service prices, controlling costs, and detecting accounting errors or employee theft.

Revenue Recognition

Although cash flow is the most important barometer for any business, the timing of revenue recognition has a big impact on how your company looks to investors, creditors, employees, and tax authorities. Significant changes in revenue recognition were recently made in the rules on how software companies recognize revenue. These changes have had a major impact on how public companies report their revenue, and may also affect how private companies recognize revenue.

If you license a prepackaged product and provide no maintenance or technical support to customers, or if you primarily do custom software development and get paid as you earn your money, these rules may have little impact on your company. Otherwise, it is advisable to obtain a copy of the rules or to consult with an accountant to obtain an understanding of how the new rules affect your company.

5.2 Tax Issues for Software Companies

—by Heather Mills
Tax Manager, KPMG LLP

The information here is general in nature and based on authorities that are subject to change. Particular situations require specific analysis in order to comprehensively determine all potential consequences.

Registering with the State and Cities

You should register your software company with the appropriate state, county, and city agencies. Generally, check with the Secretary of State's Office or Department of Commerce in your state about where and how to properly register your company. You may be required to register elsewhere, depending upon the location, nature, and scope of your business.

Registering with the Internal Revenue Service

You may obtain an Employer Identification Number (EIN) by completing Form SS-4, "Application for Employer Identification Number." You may mail this form to the address in the instructions or fax it to the Internal Revenue Service. If your principal business is located in the State of Washington, you may fax your form to (801) 620-7115. You may request to be notified of your EIN by a return fax. If you do not receive your EIN by return fax within five working days, you may call (801) 620-6755 to check on its status.

General Tax Issues

Filing Requirements. Your company will be required to file a federal income tax return annually. If you estimate your corporation's tax liability to be $500 or more, federal estimated tax payments will be required, in four installments. Other taxes that may be applicable to your corporation include alternative minimum tax, personal holding company tax, state franchise/income tax, state sales/use tax, gross receipts tax, and payroll tax.

Taxable Year. A *new* corporate taxpayer may adopt its tax year either on a calendar year or fiscal year basis. This election is made on the initial tax return filed. Special rules apply to non-corporate entities that may limit the use of fiscal years.

Method of Accounting. There are two overall methods of accounting: cash and accrual. Most software companies must use the accrual method of accounting due to inventory sales. If you use the cash method of accounting, you will generally recognize income in the year of actual or constructive receipt. Generally, you will deduct expenses in the year paid. If you use the accrual method of accounting, you will generally recognize income when all the events have occurred that fix the right to receive the income and that permit determining the amount with reasonable accuracy. You will deduct expenses when the liability is incurred, generally when you receive the services or the goods.

Start-up and Organizational Costs. Costs that are paid or incurred before you begin operating your business, which would otherwise be deductible, are considered start-up costs. Costs that relate to the creation of the entity are organizational costs. Instead of deducting these costs when paid, you must capitalize them and you may elect to deduct them equally over 60 months beginning in the month you begin your business.

Research Expenditures. There are three methods for deducting research expenditures:

- claim a current year deduction by taking that deduction on the tax return for the first year in which you incur expenses on a project
- elect instead to deduct them equally over at least 60 months
- elect an optional 10-year deduction. If you believe that your corporation will be incurring losses which may not be utilized, you may wish to delay the timing of the deductions (see *Net Operating Losses* below for determining when your losses will be limited or expire)

Current Year Deductions for Depreciable Property. You may elect to expense certain depreciable business assets up to a specified total in a given year. Your business must have taxable income to the extent of this deduction. A phase-out limitation will reduce your deduction if you have purchased more than $200,000 of qualified assets in the tax year.

Expensing of Package Design Costs. You may deduct package design costs using one of three permissible methods:

- Capitalization and amortizing over the useful life
- Design-by-design capitalization and 60-month amortization
- Pool-of-cost capitalization and 48-month amortization.

Depreciation Methods. Each year, you may elect the method of depreciation for each class of assets you placed in service during that tax year. Modified accelerated cost recovery system (MACRS) depreciation is the normal method of depreciation for tax purposes. However, you may elect straight-line depreciation.

Revenue Recognition. The year in which income is earned does not always determine the year in which it is taxable. In general, taxpayers report income received in the taxable year or when properly recognized under their tax method of accounting.

Sale of Goods. In a situation involving the sale of goods, a taxpayer generally earns income when the sale takes place.

Providing Services. In a situation involving the provision of services, a taxpayer generally earns income when it substantially performs the services, even if minor or ministerial tasks remain to be performed. Usually advance payments from customers for services or goods to be provided in the future are recognized upon receipt. Exceptions generally are available only to taxpayers using the accrual method of accounting.

Mixed-purpose Contracts. A mixed-purpose contract is one where both services and goods are provided under a single contract. The tax treatment of advance payments under mixed-purpose contracts is complicated. For more details on this and for comparison charts of differences between book and tax treatments, see the downloadable file posted on Washington Software Alliance's Web site (**http://www.wsa1.org**).

Stock Options. If you plan on using nonqualified stock options or ISOs as an incentive for your employees, some reporting requirements will relate to the issuance and exercise of those options. Nonqualified stock options create taxable compensation to your employees and a salary deduction for your company upon exercise. Incentive stock options (ISOs) create special tax consequences and reporting requirements depending upon the period they are held by the employee.

Net Operating Losses. If your corporation has losses, you may carry those losses back to the preceding two or three years in which tax was paid to obtain a refund, or you may carry the losses forward 15 to 20 years to offset future taxable income. However, if an ownership change of greater than 50% has occurred in a three-year period, you may be limited in your use of losses.

Research Credit. You may be eligible for a research tax credit. The credit calculation is based upon 20% of your eligible costs in excess of a base amount. Eligible costs include certain wages, supplies, amounts paid for computer use in qualified research, and 65% of contract research expenses. Various legislative proposals may be enacted to influence these credits.

State Franchise and Income Tax. If you have sufficient physical presence or "nexus" in a state, you may be subject to state franchise or income tax.

State Sales and Use Taxation. Most states impose a sales tax on the retail sale of tangible personal property. Typically, the seller is required to collect the sales tax on retail sales and remit it to the state. A use tax, designed to supplement the sales tax, is imposed either as a separate tax or as an extension of the base of taxes otherwise levied upon sales. Use taxes generally are imposed on the storage, use, or consumption in the state of tangible personal property so purchased, other than property upon which the sales tax has been paid.

The taxability of computer software for state sales/use tax purposes largely depends upon the characterization of the software—canned vs. custom. Most states currently treat canned (shrink-wrap or off-the-shelf) software as tangible property subject to sales/use tax. In addition, most states treat custom software as intangible property or service not subject to sales/use tax, although generally the medium of transfer (e.g., diskette) is subject to tax. The definitions of canned, custom, and various other types of software, vary from state to state.

- **Chapter 6** -

Human Relations

6.1 Building a Human Resources Department

—by Mark Berry
Davis Wright Tremaine LLP

As a new business begins, the human resources or personnel functions often are delegated to the founder deemed to have the best "people skills." This may work for a time. However, as the business grows, the human resource functions increasingly drain the founder's time and attention. Furthermore, the sophistication of the issues often easily outstrips the founder's knowledge, interest, and time.

As the business grows or anticipates significant growth, the company should consider hiring an experienced human resource professional to handle the human resource issues. Someone with a wide range of experiences—commonly known as a generalist—is ideal. At this early stage, an experienced professional can assist in the development of sound company policies and practices as well as attractive compensation and benefits packages. The experienced professional can also help identify trouble areas. Avoiding one lawsuit will more than pay for the cost of the professional's salary.

Alternatively, many businesses pass the human resource functions to an administrative manager, such as an office manager. This individual, perhaps having no particular knowledge or experience to justify being given these responsibilities, may seem a better fit than others whose background may be in product development or marketing. Unfortunately, the complexity of the issues—from understanding wage and hour requirements to handling accommodations for employees with disabilities—can overwhelm the novice. In this situation, the administrator must take advantage of every training and seminar opportunity as well as have full authority to use resources such as employment law attorneys and consultants.

Irrespective of background and experience, the individual with designated human resource responsibility should be the authority to propose policies and address issues as well as direct access to the top decision-makers in the organization. The person should then be consulted on all hiring, discipline, and termination issues. This ensures (1) that the decisions are sound and consistent and (2) that the company creates practices and precedents consistent with its overall management philosophy.

The company may choose to contract with third parties to handle payroll, benefits, unemployment, and workers' compensation. These services (particularly for payroll and benefits) can be invaluable and cost-effective, certainly less expensive than hiring extra employees.

The experienced human resource professional or a consultant can help determine when to add additional full- or part-time assistants to the growing demand for human resource personnel. One common rule of thumb is that the department should have one staff member for every 100 employees.

The issues within the organization often will determine who should be hired to assist the human resource professional. In businesses with high growth or significant turnover, a recruiting specialist may be appropriate. In others, a benefits specialist may be the best fit. In any event, it is important for the business to continually reaffirm its commitment to its employees by committing company resources to the human resource department and emphasizing its role and importance.

6.2 Essential Documents—Employee Handbooks

—by Jennifer Wright
Davis Wright Tremaine LLP

A well-drafted employee handbook can serve a number of important functions within an organization. It can communicate the organization's goals and values. It can put employees on notice of what behavior and performance is expected of them. It can promote fair and consistent application of the organization's policies. It can avoid claims of guaranteed employment. It can help avoid litigation. And, it can help protect an employer from union organizing.

At the same time, a poorly written or poorly applied handbook can create a number of problems for an organization. To be effective, handbooks must be clearly written and consistent with the law. In addition, the handbooks must be distributed to all employees and the policies contained in the handbook must be consistently enforced.

General Principles for Employee Handbooks

Do include appropriate disclaimer language. This includes statements that:
- The employee handbook is not a contract.
- The handbook can be revised at any time, and any revisions will supersede the earlier policies. Employment is at will.

- No one has any authority to enter into an agreement contrary to at-will employment (except in writing and signed by the President).

Don't use dangerous phrases. Examples:
- "Just cause?"
- "Permanent status?"
- "Like a member of the family?"

Do retain discretion and flexibility in management wherever possible. Use words like:
- "The company reserves the right to . . ."
- "In the sole discretion of the company . . ."
- "Unless circumstances require otherwise . . ."

Don't use absolutes unless **absolutely** *necessary.* Avoid words like "Always," "Must," "Never," or "Shall."

Do examine your handbook closely for clarity and consistency.
- Make sure that your handbook is internally consistent.
- Make sure that your handbook is consistent with other company documents, including application forms, supervisory manuals, and underlying policies.

Don't use someone else's handbook and just change the names.
- You are likely to end up with a handbook that is inconsistent with your internal policies and practices.
- Your handbook needs to reflect your corporate culture and policies.

Do evaluate the merits of your policies and procedures as you draft your handbook. Don't just write what sounds good; do what will *work* for your company.

Don't take the position that you are better off without any handbook at all. It is true that a bad handbook not followed may be worse than no handbook at all, but a well-written handbook, even if occasionally not followed, is infinitely better than no handbook at all.

Do use non-exhaustive lists. Use phrases like:
- "Including but not limited to . . ."
- "The following are some examples of . . ."

Don't assume that a good handbook is all you need.
- Verbal promises can give rise to implied contracts.
- Other company documents and memoranda can give rise to implied contracts.

Do cross-reference to other sources of information or documents where appropriate.
- The handbook is not the proper place to provide every detail of every policy and procedure, especially in the employee benefits arena.
- Consider whether you need both a personnel manual and an employee handbook.
- Refer employees to supervisors or Human Resources for further information.

Recommended Handbook Contents

- *Disclaimer.* The disclaimer should be a clear statement that the handbook is not a contract of employment, does not alter the at-will employment relationship, and can be modified at any time. From a litigation avoidance perspective, this may be the most important page in your handbook. Put your disclaimers in bold print near the front of the handbook. If they are not conspicuous, they may not be effective.

- *Introduction.* The introduction can welcome employees and communicate the important concepts of your corporate culture.

- *Company's History and Objectives.* This section can give your employees an appreciation of your business tradition and how it is important to carry it forward into the future. If your company is new, emphasize your goals for the future.

- *Basic Definitions.* Providing some basic definitions may help avoid later questions about how company policies should be applied. Terms that it is helpful to define include: Employment categories (orientation employee, regular employee, part-time employee, etc.); Orientation period; Workweek; and Breaks (type and length).

- *Compensation.* It is helpful for employees to have a good understanding of payroll basics. Introduce employees to your general pay practices. Explain your pay periods, payday, payroll deductions, and any special payroll programs. It is also helpful to explain your overtime policy to employees. This section could also emphasize your policy to maintain accurate time records by, for example, prohibiting removal of time records from the company and not allowing anyone to enter time for another employee. This section could also explain your organization's expense reimbursement policy.

- *Performance Appraisals.* The handbook can emphasize the importance of an effective evaluation system and educate your employees on the procedures that your organization follows in conducting evaluations.

- *Equal Employment Opportunity.* The handbook should include a statement of your equal employment opportunity policy. In addition, an effective statement of your sexual harassment policy can educate employees and protect the company against liability.

- *Employment of Relatives.* In drafting a policy limiting the employment of relatives, be careful not to draft a rule that discriminates improperly on the basis of marriage.

- *Personal Information and Personnel Records.* By state law, employees have annual access rights to files you maintain on them. You may want to explain this in your handbook. You may also want to inform employees about your policy for releasing personnel information. Your handbook can also help maintain current records by asking employees to notify the company when they move, change their telephone number, or have other changes in personal information.

- *Employee Responsibilities.* The handbook can set out your organization's standards of conduct, as well as your policies on attendance, personal appearance, smoking, and conflicts of interests.

- **Employee Discipline.** The handbook can explain the procedures the organization will generally follow in disciplining employees for violating company policies. This section should be carefully drafted to retain utmost flexibility in management.

- **Complaint Resolution.** A complaint resolution procedure can be an important aid to resolving problems before they create major human resource dilemmas or lawsuits. An effective procedure should also provide for feedback explaining the organization's reasons for its action (or inaction).

- **Employee Separation/Status Change.** This portion of the handbook should reiterate the employees' at-will status. It can also set forth guidelines for voluntary resignations and for layoffs or reductions-in-force. Any description of involuntary termination policies should be carefully examined to see that they are consistent with the organization's discipline policy. This portion of the handbook can also describe employees' COBRA rights and COBRA procedures and any procedures the organization has for separation pay. It can also be used to set forth the organization's policies with respect to transfers and promotions.

- **Communications.** Use the handbook to publicize your newsletter, public address system, interoffice memoranda, bulletin boards, and e-mail policies.

- **Company facilities.** The handbook can assure that employees are aware of the company facilities available to them, as well as any restrictions that may apply.

- **Safety.** The handbook should describe your organization's unique safety rules, special governmental safety rules that apply to your organization, and the OSHA general duty of safety, if applicable.

- **Selling and Solicitation.** Policies against selling and solicitation should stress the policy's legitimate safety purpose; policies should be consistently enforced.

- **Security.** The handbook can educate employees about the importance of security to your operations and can set forth any special security rules particular to your business, such as check-in or badges for guests and, in retail, shoplifting prevention.

- **Drug and Alcohol Policy.** Many contracts and governmental regulations require employers to have a written policy concerning drugs and alcohol. The handbook can educate employees about these policies. The policy should describe the acts that are prohibited, the consequences for violating the policy, the circumstances under which testing will be required, and the options for employee assistance.

- **Insurance and Retirement Benefits.** Generally, it is better to avoid elaborate handbook discussions of insurance coverage and retirement benefits because the details change too frequently. In the handbook, address general eligibility requirements, such as completion of the orientation period and whether benefit is company- or employee-paid. As a reminder to supervisors, it is also helpful to highlight COBRA continuation requirements in the handbook.

- *Holidays and Vacation.* The handbook should precisely explain the requirements for paid holiday eligibility. The handbook should also clearly explain how vacation is accrued and how it can be used.

- *Leave.* The handbook should explain the organization's policies for medical leave, parental leave, personal leave, bereavement leave, military leave, jury duty leave, and any other type of leave offered by the organization. The handbook should specify which leaves are paid and which are unpaid and should describe the eligibility requirements for each type of leave. This section of the handbook should be carefully examined to insure that the organization's policies comply with federal, state, and local laws regarding employee leaves.

- *Educational Assistance.* The handbook can describe any educational assistance program the organization might have and describe the procedures for qualifying for assistance.

- *Employee Assistance.* Although not required by law, an employee assistance program can be beneficial, especially if you have a substance abuse policy. The handbook should assure employees of confidentiality if they request employee assistance.

- *Statement of Receipt / Understanding.* A signed "understanding" statement verifies that the employee received the handbook, and verifies agreement to at-will employment, critical to litigation avoidance.

Other Potentially Important Documents

- *Benefit Plan Descriptions.* The Employee Retirement Income Security Act (ERISA) requires that employees receive a summary plan description of all benefit programs governed by ERISA. These would normally include any insurance benefits and pension or profit sharing plans.

- *Individual Employment Contracts.* Employers may want to consider entering into individual employment contracts with key employees. Typically these agreements would provide for a specific term or duration of employment, limit the employee's reasons for resignation, provide for a longer notice period before resignation, and clearly define the employee's compensation. The risk of these agreements is that they may lock in the employer as well as the employee.

- *Covenants Not to Compete.* These can limit an employee's ability to leave your organization to work for a competitor. Covenants not to compete are generally enforceable in most states if they are reasonable as to time, geographic scope, and nature of restrictions and if the employer has provided something of value to the employee in exchange for the agreement. If the covenant not to compete is agreed to at the time of hire, the position itself and accompanying training qualify as consideration. If the agreement is made after the employee has been hired, additional consideration, such as a bonus, promotion, or additional benefits, is needed.

- ***Confidentiality Agreements.*** Although employees are already prohibited from disclosing or using "trade secrets" under the Trade Secrets Act of many states, confidentiality agreements have the added benefit of allowing employers to define what information is "confidential." In addition, the employer can include a liquidated damages provision in these agreements and thereby avoid the difficult burden of having to prove the monetary cost of damage incurred as a result of a disclosure.

- ***Arbitration Agreements.*** Employers can use arbitration agreements to limit their employees' ability to bring employment disputes into court. Arbitration agreements are generally enforceable in most states if the employee has entered into them knowingly. However, some courts have yet to determine whether agreements to arbitrate employment discrimination claims are enforceable. Federal law, which is often followed by many state courts in discrimination cases, provides that agreements to arbitrate employment discrimination claims will be enforced if the employee voluntarily agreed to be bound by the agreement. In other words, the employer cannot force the employee to sign the agreement as a term and condition of employment.

• Chapter 7 •

Hiring and Retaining Employees

7.1 Recruiting and Search Firms

—by Jack McHale
McHale & Associates

Recruiting new employees is an essential part of the human resources function. The role of the executive search firm is to supplement the company's recruiting capabilities and facilitate the hiring process.

> "The key to the kind of people that you have to hire in the very beginning is that they have to do whatever it takes. They have to be self-starters, go-getters, multi-talented. When a company gets nice and big, that's when you have to hire the specialists."
> —Richard Richmond, Founder and Chairman of Active Voice

Why Hire a Search Firm?

Many companies hire search firms instead of conducting candidate searches themselves, especially at upper management levels. The reasons are numerous:

- A need for confidentiality in the hiring process: the company may not wish to divulge the fact it is seeking a new high-level executive.
- Senior management wants an objective, outsider's view of the executive job market.
- The position has unique requirements, outside the normal recruiting capabilities of the firm.
- An outside consultant's judgment is objective and free of political considerations within the company.
- The company desires to find a candidate who is not looking for a job.
- The demand for new hires exceeds the capacity of the human resource department to get the job done, for reasons of growth, start-ups, or market cycles.
- Many senior managers may lack experience doing recruiting, or may lack the time to do so.
- Companies find it difficult or impossible to recruit from competitor firms or industries. Search firms shelter the company from awkward situations when recruiting executives in allied or competitive firms.
- Start-up companies frequently need replacement or additional executives to move the company from the incubator phase to the next level of development and growth.
- To determine whether internal candidates are promotable, especially for high-level positions, management will hire a consultant to create a mix of internal and external candidates.
- A company needs to find a leader to change company culture or direction.

- Outsourcing part of the recruiting function can lower overhead costs by permitting wider search capability and speedier reaction times.

Contingency vs. Retained Search Firms

Generally, search firms are of two types: contingency and retained. Some search firms attempt to do both retained and contingency searches. Because the two types of search are quite different and require different levels of skill and experience, caution should be exercised in dealing with such firms.

Contingency search firms

Contingency search firms generally operate without a contract. They are paid a fee only if their candidate receives and accepts a job offer from the firm. They do not have an exclusive agreement with the client company, and they offer no guarantees. Fees are negotiable, but the fee range of most national contingency search firms is 25 to 30% of the first year's salary.

At lower to middle levels of an organization, a common recruiting method involves providing a job description to a number of contingency search firms. The search firms place ads, do some candidate screening, and submit résumés to the company, which in turn screens résumés, interviews candidates, check references, and selects a final candidate. Only the contingency firm whose candidate is hired earns a fee.

Contingency firms may have an incentive to submit a large number of résumés to maximize the chances of filling a position. But this practice causes a great deal of work for the client company: résumé screening, reference checking, and interviewing. But it does provide a large number of prescreened candidates and allows the company to outsource part of the recruiting function.

Retained executive search firms

Retained executive search firms operate under exclusive agreements that outline the course of the search, including individualized job description, time needed to complete the search, candidate screening, interviewing techniques, reference checks and confirmation of academic credentials, presentation of finalists, and final candidate selection.

Although fees vary, national search firms typically charge 33% of the first year's total annual remuneration (not just salary). In exchange for an exclusive contract, retained search firms offer a guarantee: if the initially presented candidates are not acceptable, or if the final candidate rejects the offer of employment, the search is continued until successfully completed. In addition, should the person hired be terminated for cause or resign within a year, a replacement search is typically conducted at no charge other than expenses.

Retained search firms usually work at higher executive levels in client companies. They may provide organizational analysis to assist in defining the position and conduct salary surveys to determine the appropriate compensation level. The recruitment process begins with strategic planning, progresses through strategic staffing, and takes into account the company's succession planning process and executive development program.

The retained search consultant writes a detailed position description to create a yardstick against which candidates are measured. The position description should provide an uniformly understood and agreed-upon description of the type of candidate being sought.

The retained firm networks with candidate sources, places advertising as needed, screens résumés, interviews candidates, keeps the client company informed of the progress of the search, and toward the end of the process presents three to five finalist candidates to the client. If the finalist candidates are unacceptable, the search continues until an acceptable candidate is found.

Most retained search consultants also assist clients by being flexible regarding the fee schedule, by suggesting interview techniques, and, if requested, by directly participating in the client's interviews with finalists.

Selecting a Retained Executive Search Firm

- Pay careful attention to the reputation of the firm. Look for a firm that values long-term relationships, similar to those of a good law firm or accounting firm.
- Even more importantly, look to the character, competence, judgment, and track record of the individual executive search consultant. The consultant must have good perceptions and judgment, abstractions that are difficult to measure; must be able to recognize leadership abilities in candidates; and must measure them against the culture of the company. Leadership, particularly in the software industry, is a product more of DNA than of MBA.
- Check references. Good search firms have long-term relationships with client companies. Talk to these companies and look for a search firm that receives repeat business from client companies.
- Search firms specializing in certain industries or specialties may be useful in recruiting for lower and middle level positions. For upper level positions, the personal and professional qualities of the individual consultant are more important than whether the firm specializes.

7.2 Your Worker: an Employee or an Independent Contractor?

—by Anne E. Denecke
Davis Wright Tremaine LLP

Both new and existing businesses are sometimes unclear whether certain individuals they employ are employees or independent contractors. Although the practical differences between an employee and an independent contractor may be relatively minor, the tax and legal implications are significant.

Further complicating the issue, the legal boundary line between employees and independent contractors varies from one law to the next. *Generally*, an independent contractor is one who is engaged in an independent occupation and who retains the right to control the manner in which he/she performs the assigned work. In contrast, in an employment relationship the employee does not engage in an independent business and the employer retains the right to control the manner in which the work is performed.

Many business are aware that, for tax purposes, independent contractors are responsible not only for payment of their own federal and state income taxes, they also generally must pay a self-employment tax. On the other hand, a business that employs employees is responsible for payment of federal and state income tax payments for each employee and applicable state unemployment taxes. Additionally, businesses must provide workers' compensation insurance for covered employees.

Depending upon the purpose for which a business is determining whether an individual is an employee or an independent contractor, the outcome often will be different. For instance, individuals generally considered to be independent contractors for workers' compensation purposes will not necessarily also be independent contractors for purposes of state and federal employment discrimination statutes because in many states workers' compensation laws define "employee" quite broadly. On the other hand, under Title VII of the Civil Rights Act of 1964 (as amended), the Rehabilitation Act of 1973, and the Age Discrimination in Employment Act, the definition of "employee" is more narrow and typically focuses on the employer's "right to control" the individual (i.e., the right to control the manner and means by which the work is accomplished).

For wage and hour purposes, courts typically analyze the following factors to determine the "economic realities" of the relationship: whether the individual is economically dependent on the employer:

- Integral part of the employer's business
- Investment in facilities and equipment
- Control exercised by employer
- Individual's opportunity for profit or loss
- Amount of skill, initiative, judgment, or foresight required
- Permanency or duration of relationship

Businesses are anxious to take advantage of the benefits of employing independent contractors as opposed to employees. Consequently, individuals sometimes are misclassified as independent contractors. The potential tax and legal consequences of misclassifying individuals is significant.

For example, state and federal tax agencies that determine that an individual should have been categorized as an employee can assess the employer past payroll taxes, interest, and penalties. Regarding employee benefits, one needs to look no further than the recent lawsuit involving Microsoft, in which the court determined that individuals incorrectly classified by the company as "freelancers" (independent contractors) actually should have been classified as employees for purposes of employee benefits. As a result, Microsoft was ordered to retroactively provide the individuals with employee benefits for the period they were misclassified. In this particular case, if the Washington Department of Labor and Industries determines that an individual is an employee rather than an independent contractor, the Department may assess numerous penalties against the employer. It is always prudent to check your own state's statutes regards the status of employees and independent contractors.

From the standpoint of an employer's liability for possible civil rights violations *against* independent contractors, Title VII of the Civil Rights Act does not protect independent contractors because they are considered "non-employees." Similarly, the National Labor Relations Act does not cover independent contractors. On the other hand, employers probably are liable for the unlawful actions of individuals who are incorrectly classified as an independent contractors but who are later determined to be employees. In addition, an individual who actually is an employee, but whom the employer incorrectly classified as an independent contractor, may have recourse against the employer for claims such as wrongful termination or discrimination.

It is worth an employer's effort to carefully analyze whether an individual who currently is considered an independent contractor, is actually an employee. Because there are different tests depending upon the reason for the inquiry, consultation with employment counsel is advised.

7.3 Guidelines for Keeping Software Developers on the Job

—by Stephen Elston
Advanced Interactive Systems

"The goal is to get them signed up and excited. There has to be exciting work for them in the Mother company, and people they want to work with. Change the perception that it's a 600-person company, but you're working with five people you like."
—Jeremy A. Jaech, Chief Executive Officer; President; Chairman of the Board, Visio Corporation

Software developers are in short supply in today's job market. The companies that hire and keep the best developers, companies who do not lose their "brain trust" at the critical 18 to 24 month period, have the best chance for survival. It is important to pay special attention to their needs. If the company is well managed most of the ingredients needed to have a happy and motivated team of software engineers will already be part of the culture. The management work required to have a successful company resembles the work required to have a happy work force who stays on the job.

Pay Scales Must Be Competitive

"One of the best resources is to understand that people want to be autonomous and take ownership of their work."
—Charles Crystle, Founder, CTO and Chairman of the Board, Chili!Soft

Legend in the software industry has it that in some bygone era all great programmers lived to write code and cared about nothing else. These types still exist today but usually in academic rather than commercial production environments. The work these people do has a tremendous effect on industry; the origins of the World Wide Web provide just one example. On the other hand, people in a commercial setting generally know what they are worth and expect to get it. In reality, most good—and even great—software engineers want to drive a decent car, pay the mortgage on their house, and buy the latest computer gear for their homes. These people want to maximize their income for the benefit of their families and themselves.

A company can sustain some pay imbalance if other conditions allow it. For example, if your company is growing at an amazing rate and employees have abundant stock options, beware the trap of thinking, "This project is so interesting, I am sure they will stay even though our pay is 20% or 30% below average"—or even worse, "our stock options are going to be so valuable, no one would leave." This is naïve thinking. Software engineers know what their friends and acquaintances are making and expect/need to be treated the same way. Since most viable companies offer stock options and believe they are going to be very valuable, providing them as a benefit for your company only levels the playing field; it does not distinguish your company.

Technical Work Must Be Interesting and Challenging

The best technical people cherish the opportunities to work on exciting projects at the cutting edge of technology. Make sure your company is a place where these projects happen and where developers at all levels are encouraged to learn new technologies and work on them. Top software engineers live in constant fear of falling behind the technology curve. They keep their careers on track by constantly diving into whatever is new and interesting. You are doing your people and your company a great service by encouraging this behavior. Having a technical library on site and encouraging continuing education, sending people to seminars and industry training sessions, user's group meetings, and SIGs can effectively demonstrate you care about their technical growth.

> "We look for intelligent people, and people with passion."
> —John Ballantine, Managing Partner, Chairman & CEO, iStart Ventures

The Company Must Have a Believable Plan

Technical people like to have a clear goal and purpose for what they are doing. If they feel the company is unfocused, they will leave to find a place where the goals are clear and the plan compelling. A clear and constant articulation of the mission/vision and business proposition goes a long way to alleviate anxiety.

Make sure all of the technical people in the company know what the short- and long-term goals are and how each project moves the company toward these goals. Perhaps the 4.3 release of the XYZ widget is not the most exciting thing, but there are good reasons to do it.

Good Software engineers are analytical; they make decisions based on data. They know that when they follow prescribed rules, they can predict the outcome. Your quality assurance professionals are also paid to be analytical and critical. Therefore, when sharing the plan or business proposition, include data to support your position. Be on the look out for probing questions that start with phrases like "If that is true, then why are we doing . . . ," "Given that such and such is the case how can you say that . . . ," and "But our competitors are doing . . . " Remember that good technical people know what others in the business, including competitors, are doing. If they see problems with the goals or the plans, you have reason to pause. Your people need to really believe in your plan. If they don't, treat this as your early warning. If your plan is flawed, it is better to find it out from your people now than from the market when it is too late.

The Work Environment Needs to Be Optimum

The best people want to be productive. They will not tolerate an environment that fails to support productive work. Little things can get in the way of productivity. Old computers, building environments that don't work, networks that crawl—all are enemies of productivity. The best people want to get things done "now" and will not put up with these situations for long. Recognize the underlying issue of status: every engineer wants the latest and greatest tools to work with. Acknowledge this even if you can't accommodate.

All of us want to receive due recognition for what we have done and what we are capable of doing. You greatly increase the chance that someone you value stays with your company if that person is made to feel valued and respected. Aside from department-wide and company-wide attribution, an occasional pizza party or gift certificate buys a lot of goodwill.

Engineering Practices Have to Be in Place

Experienced software professionals, and especially those with college degrees, understand the need for engineering process. Schedules need to be created with the input of the developers so they feel in charge of their own destiny. Using configuration management and version control tools assures that they will not have to do extraneous work. Design review sessions and postmortems give them opportunities to be heard, to learn from each other, and to prove their ideas in a safe environment. Most important: freeze the feature set. A collective groan can be heard every time a development team is asked to include a new feature while the schedule does not change.

Get Rid of the Deadwood

It may seem strange to discuss firing people in an article about retaining software engineers, but there is a reason to do so. Few things can spoil job satisfaction more than feeling someone is getting a free ride or that someone has to work twice as hard to make up for mistakes made by others. The performers recognize the deadwood and resent their presence. Most people want to feel pride in their organization. If they feel their peers are high caliber, and the company has a commitment to maintaining that standard, they are inclined to stay put.

Stock Options Help

The theory behind stock options is simple. Give people a stake in the company and they will work like crazy to make their share worth something. A great incentive, options can't be used as a substitute for the other ingredients required to have a successful company that holds on to its people. A clear exit strategy and business plan which defines the method to accomplish liquidity must be believable and understandable. If the technical people do not really believe in the plan, if the working environment is poor or the technical challenges limited, the best people will have no problem finding work at a company with a better plan, a great working environment, a really cool technology, a nice option package.

7.4 Developing and Sustaining Corporate Culture

—by Sally von Bargen
Co-President, PhotoDisc, Inc.

Corporate culture is, simply put, the "walk" not the "talk" of a company. It is how things really get done in an organization, how individuals are really treated, and what people really believe about where they work. A positive and proactively-managed culture is the difference between good companies and great companies.

Values, the cornerstones of any corporate culture, rest at the heart of achieving success. Values provide a sense of common ground and direction for all employees; they guide the day-to-day decisions and behavior. The things that a company values are propelled through the myths, stories, and "inside jokes" that serve as its oral history and, most importantly, through the day-to-day action of the leaders, managers, and through company policy. If you want to know what a company *is* committed to, look at what it does and how it does it.

Look at what it does when the going gets rough—then you see a company's culture in action. At our company we have five values—communication that is truthful, fair and constructive; teamwork; service to others; doing the whole job; and innovation. These values propel our business and orient how we work together.

Because a company's culture directly impacts employee productivity, morale, and retention, it would serve executives well to attend to cultural issues and development. A corporate culture that supports innovation, constructive communication, teamwork, and results can go a long way toward improving the bottom line. Employees who care, who feel part of a team, and who have fun at their work are more creative and more dedicated, and their attitude often becomes visible in customer communications. A culture that mandates a strong customer service ethic provides a distinct competitive advantage—customers respond to sales staff who have good attitudes and are positive about their products and about their employer. So you may wonder how a company develops a strong corporate culture. Culture is built in many ways.

Driven by Leadership

A company's management plays a vital role, intentionally or not, in developing, sustaining, and championing an effective corporate culture. The behavior example set by managers is reflected in the behavior of staff—good and bad.

> "We need to rethink the way HR is approached in the marketplace. How do we build a great Internet culture? At Online Interactive, we built a place that empowered individuals and created that dream and job right from the get-go. We created a whole new culture."
> —John Ballantine, *Managing Partner, Chairman & CEO, iStart Ventures*

"I admire Leonardo da Vinci because he was someone who had an incredible ability and intelligence to go to so many places. He had no boundaries."
—John Ballantine,
Managing Partner,
Chairman & CEO,
iStart Ventures

Linked to brand

The values a company sets for its brand affect the values of the organization internally, as well. Corporate culture becomes part of a company's brand personality as its staff interact with customers. It can become an important tool to advance a brand and ensure that customers have a consistent experience with an organization.

Connected by Traditions, Rituals and Habit

Long-standing traditions often become part of a corporate culture, simply by virtue of "we've always done it this way" mentality. For instance, if the staff has developed a habit of knocking off early on Friday, over time that becomes part of the "culture" at the company. In the same way, positive traditions such as a regular recognition of "the person who solved the most difficult problem this month" can become a cultural ritual that celebrates success and achievement.

Resulting from legacy

A company's culture can also be influenced by contact with cultures you absorb through mergers/acquisitions or through the influx of new management and staff hired from other companies. Strong new leaders bring cultures of their own to a division or to a group. Finding ways to integrate these new influences into existing culture can strengthen the sense of community in the organization.

Culture can be intentionally designed or left to develop. Whether corporate culture is built by design, by accident, or by osmosis, it is built nonetheless, and smart company leaders pay attention to it. During the early founding days of PhotoDisc in 1991, we were very clear about the type of culture we wanted to build, and we had long conversations about what was important to us and what values we wanted to reflect within our company.

We told each other horror stories about company cultures that bred distrust and back-stabbing competition, or those with fairy tale cultures—kiss a prince, wake up married to a frog!

We wanted to build a company that we would want to work at for a very long time and would "jump us out of bed each morning." Our ideal then, and the ideal that supports our management philosophy today, is that any person who works for our company will "grow personally, professionally, and financially." From the beginning we have tried to communicate this ideal to employees, explaining the values and encouraging employees to be accountable for caring for and cultivating our company's culture.

Those companies that don't proactively work on developing a corporate culture are often surprised to find that they end up with one anyway. Cultures do spring up organically—but cultures developed this way can often conflict with a company's brand personality or reflect the negative attributes that take on a life of their own, attributes that become ingrained and are very hard to change. Companies with weak cultures often lack strategic clarity; where there is clarity, they may lack the organizational competencies to sustain innovation or manage change. Companies with poor cultures often do well at managing wasteful and costly employee churn and brain drain.

Good business

A strong and positive corporate culture is good business; it can be measured in significant gains in efficiencies and employee retention. We know that our culture is a significant reason why our employees stick with our company—through good times and tough. Because our rate of employee turnover is well below standard rates, we enjoy tremendous cost savings in hiring and training of new employees. Our employee satisfaction rating in a recent *Inc.*/Gallup poll put us in the 98% percentile nationwide. Great culture has great impact!

Companies successful at developing and sustaining great cultures recognize several common themes that link to success. By no means the definitive list, we attend, monitor, and manage the following aspects of culture; all companies with strong positive cultures purposefully manage to do a good job in these areas.

- *Communication.* For my company this means "Truthful, fair and constructive communications" at all levels of the company, particularly top down. Employees need to trust in a company's leadership and be assured of proactive communications in order to develop a culture that values communication. We strive to make sure that employee ideas, feelings, and concerns are heard and acted on.

- *Culture Keepers.* Companies that set up a formal group to look after the company's culture, comprising management and staff, tend to find that their cultures develop more quickly and positively. Leadership involvement in culture is crucial to maintaining the link to brand and to company values and goals.

- *Traditions and Rituals.* Foster those traditions that link new employees to the organization, that allow employees to remember and celebrate past successes, and that reinforce company values. Don't underestimate the power of public recognition of something to make it "official" in the eyes of staff.

- *Respect for Diversity.* Embrace ideas that are new, welcome people whose attitudes, experiences, and culture may be different, and ensure that everyone throughout the organization is treated with respect and appreciated for individuality.

- *Agility—High Tolerance for Change.* Culture is an important way of preparing the organization for the kinds of changes common to growing companies—the link to past successes, the comfort of familiar traditions, and the common understanding of goals and values all make a company more tolerant of change. We focus on rapid evolution—change that ensures our company will thrive in dynamic times.

- *Tradition vs. Habit.* Management needs to clearly understand when a beneficial habit can be turned into a tradition (by formally recognizing it as part of the "culture") and when a bad habit needs to be stopped before it turns into tradition.

These areas of focus can help guide a company in developing great cultures that both support the organization's values and drive real bottom-line benefits.

I see our strong culture as a strategic asset, as a tool we must use to successfully manage and thrive in a business environment defined by rapid innovation, aggressive competition, and shrinking talent pools. When times are tough, we can reach deeply into our shared values and our commonly held beliefs; there we will find the truth and strength to roll up our sleeves and keep working on making the right things happen—together.

▪ Chapter 8 ▪

Partnerships with Third Parties

Growing the Developer Community: A Roadmap

—by Diana Reid
Microsoft Corporation

"We reached out
to a potential
partner by going
out and visiting
them. We did some
convincing that
[the alliance]
would work.
It made the
difference."
*—Bard Richmond,
Founder and
Chairman of Active
Voice*

Although decisions about selecting an operating system depend largely on the functionality offered by the operating system itself, they depend also on the availability of a wide variety of third-party applications that fully exploit its capabilities. With a wide range of supporting applications, users can benefit from powerful operating system functionality, such as 3-D graphics or multimedia support; built-in access to printers, scanners and fax machines; Internet support; support for audio and video files and devices; and much more. This is why vibrant third-party applications and partnerships with developers are so important to Microsoft Corporation.

It is also the reason for the success of the Microsoft® Windows® operating system. Today, about 100,000 software applications run on Windows. However, this self-fueling market growth is neither automatic nor inevitable. An operating system vendor remains competitive only if its current offering is feature-rich and attracts application developers. In very little time, an operating system that loses application support can go from popularity to irrelevance. Other operating system vendors are also seeking new applications and users, and new vendors and platforms spring up, providing further competition and innovation. To remain competitive and to ensure that a growing number of top-quality third-party applications are available for its computing platforms, Microsoft has, for nearly two decades, been evangelizing its platform technologies to the developer community, including independent software vendors (ISVs), independent hardware vendors, solution developers, value-added providers, Web site builders, consultants, and custom application developers. These third parties are integral to the success of Microsoft and certainly to the growth of the overall software industry.

Microsoft's long-standing commitment to supporting the developer community began in 1975 when Microsoft was founded to develop languages and tools for PC applications developers. As software developers themselves, Microsoft's early employees understood firsthand the difficulties of supporting products on the multiplicity of operating systems that existed in the late 1970s and early 1980s. One of Microsoft's key interests in the MS-DOS® operating system was to create a broadly popular platform that would greatly simplify its own internal development work. In recognizing this need, Microsoft also realized that it must gain the support of other third party software developers—as well as that of hardware developers—to help create a critical mass of support for MS-DOS.

To strengthen its developer support efforts, the developer relations group (DRG) was formed in 1984. The mission and charter of this group was to "drive the success of Microsoft's strategic platforms by creating a critical mass of third-party applications." Initially, the DRG focused on generating application support for Windows version 1.0, which was to be released the following year. Four people were hired that year to carry out this important mission.

This modest beginning has given way to a thriving developer support organization that encompasses a growing number of groups within Microsoft. Today, Microsoft employs more than 2,000 people worldwide who are dedicated to developer relations, and it spends over $600 million annually on developer-related activities, including evangelism, research, events, marketing assistance, training programs, product support, publications and more— all in a continued effort to foster the growth of, and ensure the success of, the worldwide developer community.

The Evangelism Process: Information Early and Often

Microsoft's DRG evangelism process helps developers identify important technology initiatives that may impact their own development efforts and brings them to the attention of developers early, while the technologies are still in the planning and development process. In doing so, the process gives developers these advantages:

- A head start on creating applications that take advantage of emerging Microsoft platform technologies.
- An avenue for providing input on and influencing the development of these new platform technologies.

DRG evangelists work one-on-one with third-party developers to ensure they are successful in developing or updating their products to take advantage of these new technologies. Additionally, DRG conducts a number of other activities and events, such as technical labs and training, provides beta software and software development kits, and more, to ensure that third-party developers have timely access to information on new and emerging platform technologies, as well as an opportunity to meet and work with Microsoft technical personnel and provide feedback.

This evangelism process provides far-reaching benefits. Benefiting from the input of developers who will be building applications with or for the new technology, Microsoft can strengthen and enhance emerging technology specifications to best meet developer and customer needs. Third-party developers, in turn, benefit by gaining an advance look at where the technology is headed and get a jump-start on using it in their development efforts, as well as influence the design and implementation of key new platform technologies, and ultimately, end users benefit from wide variety of robust software applications and devices to meet their computing needs.

Building Partnerships with Developers

In addition to its work with selected independent software or commercial developers on emerging platform technologies via the DRG evangelism process, Microsoft also partners with individual developers and the development community at large via MSDN™, the Microsoft Developer Network. MSDN is a comprehensive set of information and support offerings from Microsoft, delivering essential resources for developers. MSDN offers developers early access to key Microsoft platform tools and technologies, the latest product information, a broad range of regional, national and international training events and seminars, as well as co-marketing and business development programs. Through its membership programs, events and the MSDN Online Web site, MSDN provides an environment where developers can meet partners, share best practices, network with one another, gain access to potential investors, and spread the word about their products and services.

Below is an overview of MSDN program offerings and where to find more details on events or resources to match your growing company's technology and information needs:

CD and DVD-ROM subscriptions

MSDN subscriptions provide to core set of tools and information on CD-ROM or DVD-ROM that allows developers convenient, timely, and comprehensive access to all Microsoft products and technologies. The three levels, designed to meet any developer needs, are:

- *The MSDN Library Subscription* offers the most comprehensive programming information available on Microsoft applications, tools, and technologies, and is a fundamental reference for developers using Microsoft development tools or targeting any architecture that includes Windows.

- *The MSDN Professional Subscription* provides all the information in the MSDN Library, plus access to the latest Microsoft operating systems and development kits (including the latest SDKs and DDKs).

- *The Universal Subscription* provides the most comprehensive information, testing platforms, and Microsoft developer tools for anyone creating distributed systems using Microsoft technologies. Universal subscribers get everything in the Professional Subscription, along with all other Microsoft tools and development platforms.

See **http://msdn.microsoft.com/subscriptions/** for more information.

"As a newly-minted entrepreneur, you've got to rely on outside resources to help recognize and evaluate potential. My advice is that people ask others they trust, to evaluate the competence of a potential hire."
—Jeremy A. Jaech, Chief Executive Officer; President; Chairman of the Board, Visio Corporation

Online information

MSDN online information is designed to provide developers with a quick, easy path to important new information via the Internet. Online resources include:

- **MSDN Online Web site.** The MSDN Web site is the first destination for anyone interested in Windows development and serves as the gateway to a host of information about tools, programs, and the other resources available through MSDN. **http://msdn.microsoft.com/**

- **MSDN Flash.** MSDN Flash is a biweekly e-mail newsletter featuring developer news, announcements, events, and resources. **http://www.msdn.microsoft.com/developer/news/flash.htm**

- **MSDN Training** offers in-depth resources and training content for Windows developers to help them quickly locate training information, gain new skills and maximize their training investment. **http://msdn.microsoft.com/training/**

Membership programs

MSDN membership programs offer a deeper level of resources that are geared to the specific needs of individual developers or companies. The programs, which MSDN members can use to tailor a wealth of information to their particular needs, include:

- **MSDN Online Membership Program.** This free membership provides access to an international community of more than 2 million developers. Benefits include free downloadable tools; online special-interest groups (OSIGs), a Members Helping Members area for sharing development solutions; and discounts on software, magazines and books. **http://msdn.microsoft.com/community/**

- **The MSDN ISV Program** is designed for independent software vendors (ISVs) that produce shrink-wrapped or downloadable software that supports or runs on Microsoft products, technologies, and platforms. Members receive timely technical and business information as well as marketing opportunities to help their business grow. **http://msdn.microsoft.com/msdnisv/**

- **MSDN ISV Start up Program.** A key component of the MSDN ISV Start up Program is specifically aimed at newly established or start-up companies in the computer industry—those companies with less than 40 employees or are less than 4 years old. It provides marketing and promotional opportunities, such as events that expose a business to the larger development community, investors, the press, and potential partners. Microsoft also helps start-up companies by introducing them to venture capitalists through a newsletter and Web site provided for the investment community. **http://msdn.microsoft.com/msdnisv/startups/**

- **The MSDN User Group Program** provides over 550 developer-specific user groups with the information and resources they need to insure their local community of developers is getting the most out of technology. **http://msdn. microsoft.com/community/usergroup/**

Events and Regional Developer Centers

MSDN-sponsored events provide these opportunities and more via a variety of national and international conferences, and more than 2,000 other regional and local events, designed to help developers learn the latest on Microsoft development tools and technologies, interact with their peers, and meet industry experts. These events are designed to fit a wide range of budgets, information needs, and skills levels and are offered over a broad geographical area—enabling developers of any budget or skill the opportunity to gain in-depth knowledge about Microsoft technologies and platforms. **http://msdn.microsoft.com/resources/events.asp**

MSDN-sponsored events

- *Professional Developers Conference (PDC).* This multiday event provides the general developer community with a detailed articulation of Microsoft's future platform directions, including APIs, SDKs, alpha and beta versions of code, white papers and demos. Open to all developers, the event usually draws some 6,000 attendees and encompasses more than 200 in-depth, technical presentations.

- *Tech-Ed.* This annual developer conference provides education and training on current technology offerings from Microsoft, giving attendees in-depth information on how to integrate various technologies into their solutions. Tech-Ed currently attracts over 10,000 Solution Providers, consultants, and corporate developers each year.

- *Developer Days.* An annual, one-day technical event delivered to the developer community by regional technology experts in a local setting, and provides information on new platform and tools technologies such as Visual Studio, Windows NT, Internet Explorer and more. Held in more than 130 cities, in 50+ countries, Developer Days draws more than 70,000 attendees worldwide, making it the largest one-day developer event in the industry.

- *MSDN Regional Events.* Microsoft offers more than 2,000 local events worldwide, designed to provide an easy, cost and time-effective way for developers to learn about the latest products and technologies in their local area.

- *Silicon Valley Developer Center (SVDC).* Located in the heart of Silicon Valley, the SVDC provides assistance and resources to many of the more than 1,200 Windows ISVs and Start up companies in the high-tech centric Silicon Valley region. The SVDC hosts technical labs on development topics, conducts business roundtables and hosts a wide array of other developer community events, as well as provides inroads with the local investment community and other local high tech associations for its partners. **http://msdn.microsoft.com/svdevcenter/**. In addition, Microsoft will open a similar facility in the Boston area in late 1999 to serve the needs of developers in this growing high-tech community.

Get Plugged In—Personalize Your Roadmap

Because there are a variety of business models in the technology marketplace, in addition to the MSDN programs and events mentioned above, Microsoft offers additional programs, information and Web sites for its many partners. Each is designed to provide information and resources for a specific business or partner type—or to help you meet the needs of your specific customer segment or audience.

The table offers a list of resources to help software companies find the right Microsoft programs for their business. Some programs, Web sites and resources are developed exclusively for ISVs, some are for partners across multiple business models (e.g., custom application developers, solution providers, service providers.). Use this chart to help guide you to more information on programs, Web sites, and resources to help you in partnering with Microsoft.

If your company does this:	You should join this program:	URL	And get these benefits:
Builds pre-packaged applications	(ISV) MSDN® ISV Program, MSDN ISV Start up Program	msdn.microsoft.com/msdnisv msdn.microsoft.com/msdnisv/ startups/	Co-marketing opportunities, product and service discounts, and business development benefits for ISVs and Start up companies
Builds pre-packaged applications, customized solutions or value added services	MSDN , the Microsoft Developer Network	msdn.microsoft.com	Everything individual developers need to be successful, including tools, technologies, education, information, and technical events
Offers value added services or customized solutions	Microsoft Certified Solution Provider	www.microsoft.com/mcsp	Co-marketing opportunities and early access to product information
Embeds Microsoft products into your solution	Product Integration Program	www.microsoft.com/enterprise/ licensing/general/pip1.htm	A structured agreement which allows you to offer an integrated solution to your customers

Develops pre-packaged or customized applications, sells computer-related hardware or software, or provides consulting that leverages Microsoft products	Microsoft® Direct Access	**www.microsoft.com/ directaccess**	Product information and discounts, events, newsgroups and community activities, marketing and sales tools and training, and more
Wants to use the Microsoft Windows logo on your product packaging and participate in Windows marketing events	Microsoft Windows® Logo Program	**www.microsoft.com/windows/ compatible/default.asp**	Logo usage on your product packaging and co-marketing opportunities with Microsoft Windows
Wants to use the Microsoft BackOffice logo on your product packaging and participate in BackOffice marketing events	Microsoft BackOffice® Logo Program	**www.microsoft.com/backoffice/ designed**	Logo usage on your product packaging and co-marketing opportunities with Microsoft BackOffice
Wants to use the Microsoft Windows CE logo on product packaging and participate in Windows CE marketing events	Windows CE Logo Program	**www.microsoft.com/windowsce/ developer/programs/logo.asp**	Logo usage on your product packaging and co-marketing opportunities with Microsoft Windows CE
Develops add-ins for any of the Microsoft Office family of products	Office Update Vendor Program	**http://officeupdate.microsoft. com/Articles/ouvendorprogram. htm**	Co-marketing opportunities with Microsoft Office
Builds PCs or distributes hard disks or motherboards	OEM System Builder Program	**www.microsoft.com/oem/main. htm**	Technical support, product information, and special deals for Systems Builders
Wants to provide your customers with Visual Basic for Applications for their application customization and integration	Visual Basic® for Applications Program	**msdn.Microsoft.com/vba/partner/ benefits.asp**	Technical and marketing support to easily integrate VBA into your products and promote your VBA-enabled applications
Wants to provide development tools to your large corporate customers	Enterprise Developer Partner	**http://msdnisv.microsoft.com/ epp/**	Invitation only program to receive co-marketing and support
Wants to display your customer success story as a case study on Microsoft.com	Customer Solutions Directory	**http://www.microsoft.com/ customers/home.asp**	Exposure for your success story on a Microsoft.com customer search directory

Your Success is Our Success

Platform and partnering decisions are amongst the most important you can make in growing a new technology company. The information provided here is only the tip of the iceberg in evaluating and selecting technologies and partners that are right for your needs, but it is our hope that it, along with the wealth of information provided in this book, will give you some food for thought, and help your young company begin to achieve the tremendous success you're striving for.

At Microsoft, we never lose sight of the fact that our company's success results largely from the work we do in helping developers succeed in their endeavors, and we look forward to the opportunity to work with you.

▪ Chapter 9 ▪

Attending to Basic Legal Matters

9.1 Intellectual Property

—by Marshall Nelson
Davis Wright Tremaine LLP

Overview

Intellectual property is not "property" at all, in the traditional sense. It refers to the combination of laws and legal rights that protect inventions and other intangible works. In common practice, the term intellectual property is also used to describe the intangible works themselves, but it is important to recognize that the value, even the existence, of intellectual property depends entirely on whether and to what extent the law will protect the owner's *exclusive* rights to it.

Exclusive rights—the right to "exclude" others—are the commercial foundation of the entire software industry. The owner of an exclusive right has the ability to charge others who want to exercise that right and to place limits on how it can be used. All licenses, from the simplest shrink-wrap to the most sophisticated joint development agreements, are nothing more than contracts defining the terms on which the owner will allow someone else to exercise his or her exclusive intellectual property rights.

Software and content are almost pure intellectual property. Even marketing materials describing the products are virtually useless without trademark rights to prevent imitation of the names and symbols that identify the company and its products. Yet very few start-up companies invest the effort to understand the intellectual property rights they have and to develop an informed strategy for protecting and exploiting those rights. Instead, what often happens is a haphazard (and expensive) pursuit of hastily chosen trademarks and marginal patents and an uninformed reliance on copyrights and boilerplate licenses that may or may not provide the protection they need.

Basic principles

This section summarizes only the most basic principles of intellectual property law, concentrating instead on practical suggestions for protecting whatever rights the business may have. There are volumes of legal treatises and comprehensive Internet resources in each area listed below for those who are interested in more detail.

Intellectual property laws generally fall into four traditional categories. In simplest terms, they are:

Copyright automatically protects the form of expression (but *not* the ideas, methods, and concepts) in any "work of authorship" that is originated by the author and fixed in a tangible medium. The code in computer programs is protected by copyright.

Patent protects inventions (including ideas, methods, and concepts) that are reduced to practice and that rise to the level of a novel advancement over prior art in the area. Some aspects of computer programs may be eligible for patent protection.

Trademark protects any name, word, or symbol that identifies the goods or services of a business and that can distinguish them from the goods or services of others. The first user of a trademark is entitled to prevent others from adopting a similar trademark that is likely to cause confusion or, if the first trademark becomes "famous," is likely to dilute its effectiveness as a trademark.

Trade Secret (Proprietary Information) protects information that derives value from the fact that it is unknown to competitors and to the general public, where the owner takes reasonable steps to protect it against unauthorized disclosure. Protection for most software combines copyright and trade secret, reflected in license terms that restrict disclosure and other unauthorized uses.

The exclusive rights recognized under each of these categories are not absolute and are subject to many restrictions spelled out in statutes or developed through judicial interpretation. The limitations usually reflect complex compromises between the needs of intellectual property owners and the public interest in the free exchange of information. In the area of intellectual property, therefore, it is dangerous to trust what appears to be a common sense answer without a clear understanding of the rights and legal restrictions involved.

Ownership of intellectual property

Ownership of intellectual property, which can be a confusing puzzle, depends on the kind of intellectual property and the business and employment relationship of the parties. The only general rule with any certainty is that merely registering or applying for a copyright, trademark, or patent does *not* establish ownership. In fact, such a claim without a legal right to ownership may be considered a fraudulent application.

Unless it is clearly agreed and well documented at the outset, the issue of ownership can create major problems for a business. Unresolved ownership claims may prevent or delay product releases; they will almost certainly interfere with financing and investment in the company; and if a product is successful, conflicting claims may surface as legal demands for a share of the profits. The solution calls for a clear understanding of who owns what under which law, and then clear documentation of the parties' agreement.

Copyright. Under copyright law, the "author" of a copyrightable work owns the copyright. If he or she is an employee of someone else and the work is within the scope of employment, the employer owns the copyright as a "work made for hire" unless the parties agree otherwise in writing signed by both. (*See* "A Note on Work for Hire" below.) Copyright may be assigned, but only by writing signed by the copyright owner.

Patent. The right to patent an invention belongs to the individual inventor but may be assigned under certain circumstances. The right of an employer to require assignment of an employee's patent rights may also be restricted by state law

Trademark. A trademark cannot be owned in the abstract. Trademark rights are tied to the ongoing business that produces or controls the goods or services identified by the trademark. Thus, an artist or consultant who creates a trademark has no claim to it unless the artwork rises to the level of a copyrightable work or the parties agree to limitations on use. Trademarks can be assigned only with the goodwill of the portion of the business identified by the trademark.

Trade secrets. Trade secrets are owned by the business that develops and protects them. Employees have a legal duty not to disclose or use them except for the benefit of the employer, even if there is no written nondisclosure agreement.

A note on "work for hire"

Many businesses blindly demand "work for hire" agreements from every employee and independent contractor, without understanding what that means. The work for hire doctrine relates to copyrightable "works," not work in the sense of effort or services. Under Sections 101 and 201(b) of the Copyright Act, the employer for hire is treated as the "author" of the work for all purposes and owns the copyright from the moment the work is created.

A work created by an employee within the scope of employment is automatically a work made for hire, without the need for any written agreement. If the creator of the work is not an employee, but is an independent contractor, the parties may agree, *in certain limited circumstances*, that any copyrightable works will be considered works made for hire, but only if specifically agreed in writing signed by both parties. To be eligible for this agreed work for hire status, the work must be a contribution to a collective work (defined as an assembly of contributions that are "separate and independent works in themselves") or part of an audiovisual work or certain other specific categories.

Much of the work done by independent contractors may not meet the requirements for work-for-hire treatment. It is therefore important to couple any work-for-hire language with a backup assignment language, something like:

If any work created by Contractor under this Agreement is not eligible for treatment as a work made for hire, Contractor hereby assigns and agrees to assign all rights, including all copyright, in such work to Company and agrees to execute any documentation necessary to evidence this assignment.

As a practical matter, assignment of copyright accomplishes virtually the same thing as work-for-hire language unless the work is likely to have value after 35 years, at which point an assignment may be terminated and/or renegotiated.

A note on joint ownership

Joint ownership is a problem unless there is a clear agreement as to how and by whom decisions will be made concerning exploitation of the joint work. Under U.S. law, the default position for both copyrights and patents is that each joint owner usually has the right to use and exploit the work without the consent of the others, subject only to a possible duty to account for a share of the profits. In many other countries the opposite is true; the work may not be exploited without the consent of all joint owners unless otherwise agreed. In the case of joint efforts it is often better practice to recognize ownership by one party, with broad license rights granted to the other(s), but in any event, there should be agreement in advance as to how the property is to be managed.

Joint ownership of a trademark is an even bigger problem. The U.S. Trademark Office takes the position that joint ownership is inconsistent with the legal duty of a trademark owner to control the quality of the trademarked goods or services, and it may reject registration of a jointly-owned trademark without proof of unitary control.

Copyright

Under Section 102(a) of the Copyright Act, protection exists for all "original works of authorship fixed in any tangible medium of expression . . . from which they can be perceived, reproduced, or otherwise communicated, either directly or with the aid of a machine or device." *Original* in this context does not mean unique or novel, but only that the work was originated by the author. According to the Supreme Court this involves something more than the mere "sweat equity" involved in compiling information, but requires only "some minimal degree of creativity."

Computer programs are specifically recognized as works of authorship entitled to copyright protection, but that protection is limited. Section 102(b) of the Copyright Act states:

> In no case does copyright protection for an original work of authorship extend to any idea, procedure, process, system, method of operation, concept, principle, or discovery, regardless of the form in which it is described, explained, illustrated, or embodied in such work.

In other words, much of what is valuable in computer programs—the underlying concepts and methods of operation—are *not* protected by copyright. Unless they rise to the rare level of patented inventions or, as in most cases, are protected as trade secrets under careful license restrictions, these underlying ideas may be freely used, as long as the particular form of expression is not copied. Most of the significant copyright litigation in the software industry has centered on this "idea/expression" dichotomy.

If the minimal threshold of creativity is met, copyright protection is automatic, regardless of whether a copyright notice is used or the copyright is registered. Complying with these formalities has definite benefits when it comes time to enforcing copyrights, but the absence of either a notice or registration should never be read as an indication that a work is in the public domain and free for the taking.

Adding a proper copyright notice to a work accomplishes two things: first, it puts others on notice as to who claims ownership; and second, it avoids possible defenses that an infringer was misled by the absence of a notice. In most cases, a proper copyright notice must have three elements: (1) the international copyright symbol © (or the word "Copyright" or the abbreviation "Copr."); (2) the year of first publication of the particular version or edition (publication years of prior versions is optional); and (3) the name of the copyright owner. If any one of these elements is missing, the notice may be defective and therefore useless, no matter how much legalese appears around it. The words "all rights reserved" are often added to cover an earlier international treaty requirement that may still survive.

Copyright may be registered with the U.S. Copyright Office by depositing two copies (or specified excerpts) of the work with the required application form and filing fee. Forms with instructions are available from the Copyright Office or at its Web site, http://lcWeb.loc.gov/copyright/. Remember that the facts stated on this form and the resulting registration will form the basis for any infringement action and will be subject to legal challenge by the infringer. A copyright application is not simply a form to be filled out; it is a statement of the owner's legal position with regard to ownership and the scope of copyright for that work and should be completed with the help of qualified legal counsel.

Registration is not essential to secure copyright protection, but it is required before suit can be filed for infringement. In addition, if registration is made within three months after publication (or before infringement, in the case of unpublished works), the copyright owner may be able to recover its attorneys fees in an infringement action and may be eligible for statutory damages in an amount fixed by the judge without proof of actual damages. In any case, if infringement is established, the copyright owner may be entitled to an injunction against further infringement, recovery of the infringer's profits, and any additional damages that can be proved, among other civil and criminal remedies.

International copyright protection is generally available under the Universal Copyright Convention without need of additional registration in foreign countries. In the case of specific localized versions of a product, there may be strategic reasons for additional registration, but these should be carefully considered on a case-by-case basis.

Trademarks

Any name, word, symbol, or combination of those—that identifies a person's goods or services and distinguishes them from the goods and services of another—is entitled to protection as a trademark. This principle applies equally to corporate names, trade names, advertising slogans, service marks, and traditional trademarks. (The term "trademark" or "mark" is often used to refer to all names or symbols that identify goods and services. Technically, a trademark identifies goods, a service mark identifies services, a trade name is an assumed name (or "d/b/a") that identifies a business. A single name or mark can easily serve all these functions and be the corporate name as well. In this section, "trademark" is usually used in this generic sense. A trademark need have no distinctive typeface or logo; nor does it have to be registered.

Choosing a trademark

Choosing a business name or trademark involves a combination of marketing and legal concerns that boil down to two questions: (1) Will the new name or trademark conflict with another one already in use? (2) How difficult will it be to register and protect? The key is to gather enough information about similar product and business names in use in the same general industry to answer these questions. Merely searching trademark filings for an identical trademark may be a waste of time and money. Worse yet, inadequate research can create a dangerous false sense of security.

The question of whether two trademarks will conflict depends on many factors, including the nature and similarities of the marks, their relative strength or weakness under trademark law, how they are used, the marketing environment, the nature of the products or services, the likely purchasers, and other facts that affect how the trademarks are likely to be perceived by the public. A trademark search, no matter how thorough, will not by itself answer these questions. The answers depend on knowledge of the specific business and knowledge of trademark law.

However, it is important to recognize that no one, not even the U.S. Patent & Trademark Office, can guarantee that a new name or trademark is "clear" of all obstacles. Even when all available information is in, there is still no guarantee that a conflicting unregistered trademark is not in use or in the same early stages of development as the proposed trademark. Until the trademark is well established, there will always be some degree of risk.

As a rule of thumb, the more common or descriptive the trademark is, the more difficult it will be to register and protect against similar trademarks in the future. Under the law, the greatest protection is reserved for what are called "fanciful" or "arbitrary" marks, such as Kodak and Exxon. A highly descriptive trademark may acquire strength through extensive advertising and efforts to protect it against encroachment by other similar marks, but until public recognition is established, trademark protection will be weak. If the mark is nothing more than a generic description of the product or service, there may be no protection.

Federal trademark registration

The right to use a trademark does not depend on registration; the person who first uses a trademark in connection with given goods or services has a right, under laws addressing unfair competition, to prevent others from using the same or a similar trademark in a manner that is likely to confuse the public. However, there are distinct advantages to federal trademark registration with the U.S. Patent & Trademark Office (PTO) if the mark qualifies, including a presumption of nationwide rights and possible incontestability after five years. Registration also confers the right to use the federal registration symbol ® and the deterrent effect it has on potential infringement. Without it, notice is limited to the informal ™ symbol, which indicates nothing more than the owner's unexamined claim of common law rights. State registration is also available, but it provides relatively little protection and does not carry the right to use the ® symbol.

There are also sound business reasons for federal trademark registration. Registration adds value to the name, and thus to the company, in the eyes of potential investors, lenders, and corporate partners. In many businesses the goodwill associated with a product name may be the company's most valuable asset, and the registration is seen as some degree of insurance for that asset and the ability to exploit it.

Federal trademark registration requires proof of actual use of the trademark in connection with the offering of goods or services in interstate commerce. However, it is possible to apply in advance on the basis of a bona fide intent to use a trademark, and if registration is granted upon proof of later use within statutory deadlines, the earlier date of application establishes the trademark owner's priority as though first use had occurred on that date. It is therefore good practice to apply for registration as soon as the trademark is selected, even if the product will be delayed. Early application may also provide advance warning of problems with the trademark before there is a substantial investment in marketing and packaging.

An Examining Attorney at the PTO reviews each application to determine whether the trademark meets statutory requirements, is distinctive enough to warrant registration, and does not conflict with an existing registration or application. This process usually takes months and may involve one or more "office actions" refusing registration unless the application is amended and/or additional information is provided. This process may involve limiting the registration or transferring it to the Supplemental Register without the benefits of a full registration. In some cases, if the examiner's objections cannot be overcome, the application may simply be abandoned without affecting the owner's right to use the trademark.

If the examiner approves the application, it is "published for opposition" for 30 days, during which any person who can claim to be damaged by the registration may oppose it. The usual practice is to request a series of extensions while the parties attempt to negotiate a compromise. If a formal opposition is filed, it is conducted before the Trademark Trial and

Appeal Board under essentially the same procedures as federal litigation and can be both expensive and time-consuming.

If registration is granted, it is still subject to cancellation during the first five years under essentially the same procedures as an opposition. It may also be cancelled by the PTO if the owner does not file proof of continuing use during the sixth year of registration. At that time, if the trademark has not been successfully challenged, it is also possible to file an Affidavit of Incontestability, cutting off all but a few grounds for challenging the trademark. This is one of the primary benefits of federal registration.

International trademark registration

Unlike copyright, no international treaty automatically enforces a U.S. trademark registration in foreign countries. However, it is possible to register in other countries on the basis of the U.S. registration if the trademark is otherwise eligible under local law. Moreover, if the foreign application is filed within six months after filing an application in the U.S., the foreign registration will have priority as of the date of the U.S. application if the U.S. registration is granted. This opportunity for priority must be weighed carefully against the considerable cost of country-by-country application. Even the much-touted European Community registration process, which allows for a single filing for member countries, can be very expensive and carries with it some substantial risks. An international registration strategy should be carefully analyzed with an eye to the practical needs and expansion plans of the business over the several years that will invariably be involved in the registration process.

Trademarks and domain names

The legal relationship between trademarks and Internet domain names is currently in a state of confusion. All that can be said safely at this time is that courts will enforce trademark rights against some infringing domain names; the PTO will register some domain names as trademarks *if* it can be shown that they are actually used as trademarks. However, registration of a trademark does not automatically secure the right to register a domain name, and vice versa. The two registers are completely separate for now, and both should be researched in the process of choosing a new trademark and/or domain name.

Trade Secrets (Proprietary Information)

Trade secret protection is largely a matter of common sense. There is neither formal procedure for registration at either the state or federal level nor specific restrictions as to what may qualify as a trade secret. Under the Uniform Trade Secrets Act, adopted as state law by many states, all that is required is that it be "information . . . that (1) derives independent economic value, actual or potential, from not being generally known to, and not being readily ascertainable by proper means by, other persons who can obtain economic value from its disclosure or use; and (2) is the subject of efforts that are reasonable under the circumstances to maintain its secrecy."

The concepts, methods, and algorithms embodied in computer programs arc obviously trade secrets under the first part of this definition. The dilemma is how to distribute copies of the programs without negating the second requirement. Unlike secret formulae used in the manufacture of other products, a computer program is, in a very real sense, the trade secret itself. The answer lies in the traditional software license agreement, under which the licensee agrees not to use, copy, disclose, distribute, or reverse engineer the software and is usually denied access to source code except under certain circumstances. This not only restricts the licensee's use but also establishes the licensor's reasonable efforts to restrict disclosure of the embodied trade secrets.

Other steps can and should be taken to protect trade secrets, including written employment agreements with nondisclosure provisions and acknowledgement of the employer's ownership; nondisclosure/confidentiality agreements with independent contractors and potential business partners; and simple common sense workplace procedures to restrict access to work in progress.

In the case of key personnel, consider employment or contractor agreements with reasonable restrictions on subsequent work for competitors, to avoid disclosure of general proprietary information. Exit interviews and debriefing to emphasize confidentiality obligations and to insure return of all proprietary materials are also helpful. In some cases it may be appropriate to put a subsequent employer on notice as to general areas of proprietary information that should be off limits, but this should be done carefully, to avoid the appearance of overreaching interference with the new employment/contractor relationship.

As a general rule of thumb in all cases, recognize that the defendant in an infringement action will be trying to prove that reasonable steps were *not* taken to maintain secrecy. It is therefore important to adopt and enforce procedures that will stand up to this cross-examination. The more sensitive and valuable the secret, the more restrictions should be in place.

Licensing

A license is nothing more than permission to use one or more intellectual property rights that belong to the licensor, usually subject to certain terms and conditions. There is no "standard" form license agreement. Often, the grant of a license appears as part of a broader business agreement, but it may also take the form of a shrink-wrap or break-seal notice on consumer software, a "click-here" acceptance of online terms, or a simple letter granting permission to use an excerpt of a copyrighted work. In some cases a license may even be implied from the dealings of the parties.

No matter what form the license may take or what type of intellectual property is involved, a license usually addresses certain basic considerations. Treating these as business decisions before they are ever reduced to legalese will save a lot of time, legal expense, and misunderstanding in the long run.

General checklist

The following is a general checklist of some of the substantive areas that may need to be covered:

Licensed Property. What is the licensee authorized to use? The more precise the definition, the less misunderstanding or overreaching there will be.

Scope of License. What is the licensee authorized to do with the licensed property? Are there limits on time, territory, the kind of products, or manner in which it can be used? Are the licensee's rights exclusive or nonexclusive? (If exclusive, do they exclude even the owner from exercising the licensed rights during the term of the license? Often overlooked.)

Restrictions. What does the licensee affirmatively agree *not* to do as a condition of using the licensed property?

Ownership. This usually reaffirms and acknowledges the licensor's ownership and the fact that the licensee acquires no rights in the underlying property, but if the licensed property is to be created or modified in the course of a consulting arrangement, ownership of the resulting product may be an issue.

Confidentiality. Is specific nondisclosure language needed? (If the licensee has already signed a nondisclosure agreement, is this language consistent? Which agreement takes precedence?)

Quality Control . This is an essential element of a trademark license. Unless the trademark owner exercises control over the quality of goods and services associated with the trademark, the license may be invalid and, in extreme cases, may result in abandonment of trademark rights. Control extends to more than just how the trademark is used; it requires control over the goods and services themselves.

Third-Party Infringement. Who has the responsibility/right to enforce intellectual property rights against third-party infringers? What if the parties can't agree?

Warranties and Indemnities. Will the licensor guarantee the licensed property? To what extent? For how long? What will the licensor do if the property does not conform to the warranties given? (Many software licenses adopt the "no warranties/as is" language of traditional shrink-wrap licenses, but this seldom survives negotiation. Consider including a limited warranty at the outset with a reasonable form of remedy.)

Limitation of Liabilities. This fixes the top end financial exposure of the parties in the event of loss or damage relating to activities under the license agreement. It is especially important in software licenses because of unpredictability as to how the software may be used in the licensee's business.

Termination. Under what circumstances may the license be terminated? When and by whom? More importantly, what happens to the licensee's products upon termination? Is a transition period necessary?

Dispute Resolution. What happens if there is a violation of the agreement? Is mandatory mediation and/or arbitration workable? Are there specific issues that may need immediate court action, such as disclosure or infringement of intellectual property?

Many other terms may be covered, especially if payment involves royalties based on sales or if the licensor provides ongoing support services. There may be restrictions on sub-licensing, additional licenses and restrictions relating to enhancements and modifications, and specific restrictions on further assignment of rights. In most cases, however, addressing some or all of these basic considerations will help to insure that the license matches the business needs of the company.

A Final Note on Online Issues

There is no question that the Internet and online commerce have changed the landscape of intellectual property. The ready availability, ease of copying, and practical impossibility of monitoring all uses affect how and to what extent intellectual property rights can be enforced. But it is important to recognize that the law does not change when it goes online. The same basic principles outlined in this section continue to apply and continue to be applied by the courts, in the online context. Until there are definitive changes, the only safe course is to assume that use of intellectual property will continue to be governed by the same rules, no matter where it appears.

9.2 Patents

—by Brian Deagle
Davis Wright Tremaine LLP

"Get your own patents. Make the investment and make sure you have your own portfolio."
—Bard Richmond, Founder and Chairman of Active Voice

A patent, a government granted right, *precludes* others from (1) making, (2) using, (3) selling, (4) offering for sale, or (5) importing the claimed invention. Notice, however, that a patent does not grant the patent owner the right to make, use or sell—that is, "practice"—

the claimed invention. In fact, many patent owners cannot practice their invention because doing so would infringe the claims of a patent owned by another party.

The right to seek patent protection is based expressly on the *U.S. Constitution*. Article I, Section 8 of the *U.S. Constitution* states that "The congress shall have the power . . . to promote the progress of . . . [the] useful arts, by securing for limited time to . . . inventors the exclusive rights to their discoveries." Patent law essentially embodies the government's legal bargain with inventors that in exchange for teaching the world about the invention, the government will grant the inventor exclusive rights to the invention for a limited time.

There are two main types of patents: utility patents and design patents. Utility patents protect the useful aspects of a product or discovery, while design patents protect the ornamental, versus functional, appearance of a product. For software inventions, utility patents can claim, for example, the method or process achieved by the software, the hardware with embedded software apparatus, the software product itself, the data structure achieved by the software and the business model achieved with the software. For software inventions, design patents can claim the ornamental appearance of fonts, typefaces, and icons on a computer screen.

"Novel" and "Best Mode"

Patent requirements are broken into issues involving the invention itself and issues involving the patent application disclosure. The basic requirements for obtaining a patent are (1) that the invention is "novel" and "non-obvious" compared to the "prior art," and (2) that the patent disclosure describe both how to make and use the invention, and the "best mode" of the invention.

Prior art

What constitutes "prior art" can be highly detailed; it depends generally on the date when the invention was conceived and reduced to practice and on the date of filing the patent application. Generally, prior art is the state of the applicable science as shown, for instance, in printed publications and issued patents. Researching the prior art for software patents can be difficult at best, because the search vehicles are word-based and software developers do not use uniform terms. Traditional searching methods, therefore, cannot completely uncover previously issued patents on software inventions.

Because the Patent & Trademark Office (the "PTO") encounters this same difficulty, some people consider that many patented software inventions will not survive the close scrutiny of a patent infringement lawsuit. Not that software patents have no or little value because in the coming battle over patent rights the market players without a patent will have little, if any, negotiating leverage. (Note: an inventor need not search for prior art before filing a patent application. The inventor is required, however, to disclose to the PTO known relevant references, such as articles and issued patents).

Novelty. Novelty means that the entire invention has not previously been described in the prior art. "Nonobviousness" is a highly technical term that depends on many factors, but it essentially means that the improvements in the invention as compared to the prior art would not have been clear, or "obvious," to someone "skilled in the art," such as a software programmer for a software patent.

The patent application (and, therefore, the patent upon issuance) must describe the invention in sufficient detail to teach one skilled in the art how to make and use the invention. Also, the patent must disclose the "best mode" of the invention, that is, the variation of the invention that the inventor believes (at the time the application is filed) works the best.

Obtaining a Patent

The process of obtaining a patent is not as mysterious as it may appear. The inventor must prepare (or have an attorney prepare) an application and file it with the PTO. The PTO requires a nontrivial fee for filing. (Note: The PTO is essentially self-funded and almost every document filed requires an accompanying fee, although the fee amounts are generally reduced for certain parties, such as individuals and small companies.) The "prosecution" of a patent is essentially between the inventor (and his or her attorney) and the PTO. The prosecution is confidential, and no person except the inventor can obtain the patent application file. (When the patent issues, however, the prosecution file history is open to the public.) During prosecution, the PTO examiner conducts a search of the prior art and examines the claims in the patent application. Usually, the examiner requests revisions to the claims and disclosure (both substantive revisions and revisions of form), and the applicant must comply with the examiner's request or appeal the rejection or objection. After the successful resolution of all rejections and objections, the patent is issued.

The patent owner has the right to bring suit in the federal court system to enforce his or her patent rights and to collect damages for infringement. The patent owner should carefully plan—well in advance of the actual date the patent issues—how to address potential infringement. For example, an aggressive letter asserting infringement may result in having to appear in federal court miles from home to defend a suit seeking to invalidate a patent. On the other hand, failing to enforce a patent against known infringement may mean that one gives up the right to enforce it against other parties. A person accused of infringing on another party's patent should seek legal counsel immediately. Patent infringement is a serious and fact-specific allegation and requires careful analysis.

Once issued, the patent is enforceable until 20 years from the date of the original patent application filing. This time period reflects a relatively recent change in patent law: the prior term of enforcement was 17 years from the date the patent issued. For all patents which were either pending applications or in force on June 8, 1995, the term of enforcement ends on the date which is the longer of 17 years from issuance or 20 years from the earliest filing date. The actual term for software patents has little significance because rapid technological changes often render obsolete the patented invention before the actual expiration of the term.

Claims to software inventions can be in a multitude of forms, including method claims or software product claims. Patent-claiming strategy must consider specific product applications, and the patent claim structure should be designed to protect the commercial product, or at least deter competitors from entering the market.

Patents can be extremely valuable to a company. It is imperative, however, to have patent counsel that understand the applicable business and market, so that one protects commercial products rather than just "neat ideas." With the right strategy, the patent can provide a way to exert leverage over competitors, gain a higher valuation in financing transactions, increase the company's appeal as a strategic partner, and contribute to a company's reputation as an innovator. A patent is a potentially valuable property right that can be sold for a single lump sum, licensed for a continuous revenue stream, or used to increase company valuation. In a highly competitive field, a strategic patent portfolio can prevent competitors from adopting the company's practices. Seeking patent protection without a carefully constructed strategy, however, can waste money and may result in obtaining mere "wall plaques" versus valuable property rights.

Software or software-related patents are proliferating rapidly (some have labeled it an "arms race"). Many of these patents likely cover similar inventions, creating a "sorting" out of rights through a combination of litigation, negotiation, and cross licensing arrangements. Only players with a patent "card" will participate in this sorting game. In evaluating intellectual property, one should carefully consider patent protection as a vehicle for achieving the maximum company valuation.

• Chapter 10 •

Marketing the Product

10.1 Design for Marketing

—by John Burgess
Werkhaus Design

"People get caught in the idea of building a product. Meet with customers and compare their product specs with five or six other customers. If you don't listen to your customer, then you have feature groups that people don't use."
—*Charles Crystle, Founder, CTO and Chairman of the Board, Chili!Soft*

Design Is an Asset

You've got a new product idea, a solid business plan, competent executive teams in place, and enough financing to get your company off the ground. Now it's time to package it and take it to market.

First, design is important. It should not be overlooked. It can provide the cornerstone for your company's marketing efforts and provide consistency and clarity to your messages in a crowded, often confusing industry. Your new company's design program can provide a visual and messaging foundation for all communication efforts to follow. You will spend valuable resources and time creating it. Think of it as an asset, a valuable driver of marketing communications and sales. Your successful use of design will help provide clarity to your messages, establish credibility, and break through the clutter.

Remember, your business will survive on its sales, and sales are supported by your marketing. Although creative and marketing disciplines are full of jargon and taste varies widely, never underestimate the power of design in establishing the message.

Brand, identity, visual systems, leveraged design, creative programs: the first step is recognizing its importance. With the right consultants and designers, you can develop a "look and feel" for your company and its products that will position it appropriately, maximize your marketing budget, and support sales the way the textbooks say it should. No single right approach exists, but one fact is true: identity requires thoughtful reflection, insight from experienced marketing professionals, and a creative design team that can translate your marketing objectives into an effective visual and messaging campaign.

Selecting a Creative Firm

Like most professional services, your search begins with your peers. Ask around. Referrals provide the best source of information. Spend some time on this one. Your creative team can be as important to your marketing success as your financial or legal counsel is to general business. A successful creative program can help separate you from the pack and positively affect sales.

Ask a lot of questions. Check your gut instinct. You will have to work with these people for quite awhile, entrusting them to make important decisions on behalf of your company. What is their philosophy and their approach to design? Can they provide strategic direction? What is their relevant experience? Will they provide all services or just part of the whole? There is no single model. Educate yourself through this process. When reviewing portfolios, look beyond the surface. Explore the reasons why something is the way it is. Become familiar with how this team thinks. Ask how they will approach your scope of work. Speak frankly about your concerns, budgets, schedules, challenges. Designers and creative professionals are problem solvers. Listen carefully to their responses. This will tell you a lot about what it will be like if you retain them.

Build Rapport

When used appropriately, your design and creative team will become extremely valuable to you and your company. They are experts in marketing communications. Bring them in early on in your process. Use their experience and expertise to your benefit. They will bring a different perspective and will have valuable insight that can positively impact the strategy, concept, cost-effectiveness and eventual success of your design program. Establish the scope together. Allow them to help you build an appropriate budget. Be open with them. Their passion is to help you succeed—so help them help you. Once you have established a good rapport, open up and let them into your business world. The more a design professional knows about you, your company, its product and market—the better. Input— equals output. Ideas do not come out of thin air. They come from a clear understanding of your business and marketing challenges.

Establish Objectives

In essence, you want your design program to be a visual and written translation of your core marketing objectives. Your overall look, feel, and messaging should somehow resonate with the position and personality you wish to own in the marketplace. Together, your creative team can help you to clarify the primary objectives that will infuse your marketing programs and they should then own the responsibility to achieve those objectives.

The three most important things to consider will be: (1) your key messages, (2) the competitive landscape, (3) future product and marketing plans—and how these areas may influence the design choices you make today. Before asking your creative team to begin sketching ideas, you should be clear on all the above. The final creative choices should reflect your marketing communication objectives and drive your messaging. If the final idea and its creative execution communicates effectively, you are on your way.

Know Your Competition—Know Your Customers

Bottom line is this, you must provide your customers with a compelling reason to buy your products over others. Everything you do in your communications program should keep this in mind. Differentiate. Differentiate. Differentiate. Your key messages should resonate in everything you do—in the story that a logo tells, the colors you choose to associate with your product, a product's name and theme line, the narrative of a brochure. This visual language and messaging, brought to life in both words and design, should then be consistently used in all communications. The methodology is quite straightforward. Have a clear idea of what differentiates your product and company, then apply strong creative that puts these messages in the foreground, making your customers aware of your position and key points of difference.

Of course, this requires that you have a thorough understanding of your competition. Do a creative audit of their marketing materials. What are their messages? What works? What seems to be the same? Can you build a program that will project a different set of messages into the marketplace? Or do you want a parity approach? Think it through with your creative team, and be clear on where it is you want your design program to go, prior to asking it to go somewhere.

Judging Solutions

Your creative team will undoubtedly conduct a creative 'study' to explore various design ideas and words that achieve your communication objectives. This is an important part of the process. Through this study, your objectives should become even clearer, with new ideas informing preexisting ones. A creative strategy should be uncovered that delivers your messages and compels your audience to care about and understand your company and products. It is likely that there are several good ways to solve your objectives, so stay open-minded. Try your best to put personal tastes aside. Think objectively. If part of your key messaging is urgency (for example), then perhaps red is the perfect color—even if you had a traumatic accident on your red bicycle as a child.

Go back to your objectives. Do the ideas proposed provide clarity to your position? Help to differentiate? Compel interest? Establish credibility? Do they keep in mind your plans for future growth? Are they appropriate for the intended audience? Design is not only about the surface, but about a way of communicating.

Good Design Is Good Business

If you look at design as a tactical business tool, asking it to help position and to differentiate your company and its products, you will be one step ahead of the next-guy-with-an-idea. Design can make things look cool, look timeless, look trendy or look conservative—but what should it do for your company? This is the question to keep in mind.

Several marketing cycles or years down the road, when products and technologies have changed but your audience remains, your design program is what they may recall. It may be the core of their relationship with your company. It can be the asset that resonates most powerfully.

"The companies that serve customers the best are going to win. That's it. End of story."
—*Charles Crystle, Founder, CTO and Chairman of the Board, Chili!Soft*

10.2 Taking Names: Why Customer Registration Is Vital

—by Gary McAvoy and Colleen Byrum

Most companies underestimate the value and importance of one of their most significant marketing tools: product registration. Leave that oversight to your competition.

Whether you collect data via the Internet or by a registration card enclosed with a packaged product, product registration is the key element in building customer database that will provide you with an ongoing revenue stream from upgrades and cross-selling your products. Registration can also deliver key information about how your customer uses your product and what influenced their decision to purchase your product.

Registration Card

For packaged products, start by considering how to get customers to fill out the registration card and return it. Consider design, placement in the product box, and ease of pulling out the card. This piece should be distinctive, easy to find, and hard to misplace or throw away accidentally. It should be linked in some way to your service message and support policies: requiring customers to register in order to receive support is a key incentive to return the registration card.

Whatever you invent as a way of drawing attention to the registration card, do not let it become lost in the product box among a sea of other marketing collateral, notices, updates, Read Me's, and so on. As anyone who has ever purchased a Microsoft product knows that the company has cleverly included a large, bright yellow card that reads on one side, "Want the name and address of the most important person at Microsoft?" If you were hoping to get Bill's address you may be disappointed or amused to find, "So do we. You're our most important partner" followed by space to fill out your name and address. Another company makes filling out the registration card part of the installation process. While the software is installing, a screen appears where the customer fills out his name and address information. The registration card is automatically printed to the available printer and an envelope is provided for mailing the registration card.

Incentives

You may want to consider offering incentive items to the customers for returning their registration cards, although this gets you into the fulfillment business. Investigate the possibility of outsourcing registration card data entry and any fulfillment that goes along with it.

If you choose to provide incentives for customers to return their registration cards, the incentive should relate meaningfully to your product. Is there an add-on product, desk accessory, subscription to a publication or service that would be of use to your customers? Subscriptions are particularly convenient because often the third party handles the fulfillment.

Technical support

A standard incentive requires customers to be registered in order to receive technical support. This means you must define your technical support policies before you ship your product. If you do not establish policies before you ship your product and have to change policies in midstream, you face the risks associated with trying to re-set customer expectation for service after those expectations are set.

Registration Required for Product Download

Providing the opportunity for customers to download your product off a Web site offers a nearly foolproof way to ensure 100% registration (assuming the customer provides honest and accurate responses).

Since the registration page will precede the download page, it must be determined beforehand which questions require a response and which are optional; that depends entirely on what kind of information you feel you need to develop a worthwhile database. Given the growing emphasis on privacy issues, your particular information requests need to be given careful consideration.

For either registration method, if you require customers to register in order to receive technical support, the support policies should be stated somewhere near the registration card or process.

Product registration is an opportunity to collect key marketing data from your customer, but it is possible to overdo it. If you ask too many questions or place too many check boxes,

> "Always focus on the customer. Our competitive position is to save the customer time and eliminate a chore. We've picked a breadth of products that are typically in, or near the medicine cabinet."
> —Peter Neupert, CEO, Drugstore.com

customers may not want to bother with it. As a good check and balance, only collect data you have a specific, current need for and only collect data you have the database to manage.

The database

The data from registration forms the basis of the technical support database. For most start-up companies it is prudent to write this database in-house, though many fine and simple database products on the market today can serve the purpose. Recognize that it will have limitations and a limited life span, but also recognize that you face a steep learning curve in the first year or so of business. It is a better investment of your time and money to develop or acquire a higher end database when you have had time to learn what you really need in the way of information support.

When designing this initial database, ask your technical support manager or whoever is writing it, to work with the marketing staff to integrate registration card data with database features and reports that will be useful for your particular marketing efforts. For example, your future product development efforts may require the purchase of additional hardware. In the registration process, ask if purchasers anticipate buying this piece of hardware ever, in one to six months, or in six to twelve months. You will then be able to generate reports that profile your installed base with respect to key hardware decisions.

When thinking through the purpose and usefulness of product registration, it is easy to see how this modest but essential process can have a significant effect on profitability. A well designed registration process that entices customers to register provides an extremely welltargeted audience for your company's direct mail or e-mail marketing programs.

10.3 Answering Questions About Marketing:

Marketing and Pricing

—by Barry Briggs
Barry Briggs and Company

Marketing Software Products

This section will help you answer fundamental questions about marketing software products. By working through this section, you should gain a basic understanding of the questions software marketers must address. And, you should gain a methodology for answering those questions yourself.

Keep in mind that Information Technology manufacturers develop and market the broadest possible range of software products, from vertical market mainframe products to horizontal market commodity microcomputer products; from applications to utilities to development tools; from products intended for the home to products intended for business; from shareware to commercial products. The discussion of marketing is necessarily broad and directional in nature; it's unlikely to address all of your questions.

Therefore, before you invest in a marketing program, seek experienced marketing counsel, either by hiring a permanent marketing manager or by contracting for the services of a professional software marketing firm.

Definitions

Marketing is the process of causing consumers to want a product. There are typically three stages to this process.

In the first stage, the product marketer defines a marketplace and researches that marketplace to understand what product opportunities might exist.

Once it has been determined that opportunities for a product or service exist, the marketer works with research and development to create an appropriate product or service, one that will meet consumer needs.

Finally, the product marketer creates programs that build consumer awareness and interest in the product or service. These marketing and communications programs may range from developing a retail distribution plan to developing an advertising program. Marketing and sales are closely related but different disciplines. Where marketing builds consumer demand for a product or service, sales fulfills that demand by selling the product or service to the consumer. For example, a product manager might create an advertising campaign to generate leads from interested customers. These leads would then be handed to a sales manager who would be responsible for making the sale.

Pricing Products

The optimum price for a product is based on the goals of the product and of the company.

A. *Can you specify a goal for your product?* (for example, a targeted market share, a per unit targeted return objective, a profit maximization objective.)
- If yes, go to B, below.
- If no, determine the goal for the product based on the market and the long-term objectives of the company.

B. *Do you know the prices of similar products in the market?* (Have you done secondary market research?)

- If yes, go to C.
- If no, gather market information on competitive products through secondary or, if necessary, primary market research. (See "Market Research" section.)

C. *Does your product / company offer extra value to the market?* (That is, does your product offer features and capabilities, or does your company have a positive image that your audience would be willing to pay a premium for?)

- If yes, go to D.
- If no, go to E.

D. *Can you quantify this perceived value?*

- If yes, go to E.
- If no, go to "Market Research" section.

E. *Do you have a good idea of the future of the market, such as new products and market factors?*

- If yes, you have the information you need to determine the price for your product: the objective for your product, the pricing of competitive products, the perceived value of your product, and the future market dynamics that will impact the various competitors and the pricing of your product market.
- If no, go to "Market Research" section.

10.4 Branding for Start-Ups and Small Companies

—by Joe LePla
Parker LePla

Many start-up companies feel like they don't have the time and resources to do branding. They think branding is something that takes a lot of marketing dollars and would divert the attention of their company from their primary mission of making a product and capturing market share.

Integrated brand development should be as central a part of the start-up process as shopping for the right venture capitalist. Integrated branding helps a company:

- put in a place a method for consistently focusing on its core strengths

- create a compass for product development
- jump-start its teambuilding efforts
- develop the right capabilities to capture and retain market share

It accomplishes all of this by focusing young companies on core strengths in relationship to what customers or potential customers value.

Integrated branding is so powerful because it models human behavior in a way that allows companies and products to form deep relationships with customers. The starting point of this process is focusing staff around a company's unique approach to its marketplace that customers value, and then retaining the discipline of that focus year in and year out.

Branding to Avoid Potential Pitfalls

By creating this discipline from the start, a company can effectively retain its focus as it grows and avoid costly pitfalls that a "we're just developing a product" mentality can cause.

For instance, without a strong brand direction, a company that develops software for IT department management might typically develop a grab bag of product features that didn't meet the needs of any specific IT customer segment. With a strong brand in place that defined a company's brand approach as "an IT guide for large enterprises," product features would be developed that strengthened the product's ability to act as an IT guide. The first company could easily find itself falling behind on key features for this large enterprise IT market as it tried to develop all features equally; or worse, it might develop features that obstructed the ability of IT to run the enterprise.

As companies grow beyond one product, they tend to either continue using the same name as their successful initial product or they go to the other extreme and create new names for everything. Using the same name risks confusion and dilution of a brand's strength if the new product is not in the same business category as the first product. Naming everything differently means creating many brands—a strategy that requires a huge investment of time and money to keep afloat. The brand process can create the most effective path between these two extremes.

How Brand Helps in Raising Capital

A strong brand can directly affect the valuation of a company doing its first initial public offering (IPO). Strong brand translates into the ability to charge a 15 to 20% price premium over market average even in a highly competitive market. This price protection results in predictable higher margins on future sales and, hence, a potential higher initial evaluation of the stock. Strong brands also have less turnover in their installed base resulting in lower cost of sales through higher repeat sales. They also add elements to the company story that analysts probe for such as management focus and vision.

Finally, a strong brand is sexy. It creates a buzz factor on the street that translates into higher demand for the IPO.

▪ Chapter 11 ▪

Growing an Organization

11.1 Getting Your Board Onboard

—by Peter Parsons
Davis Wright Tremaine LLP

Are your shareholders interested in shareholder liquidity? Are you considering going public or selling your company? If so, before receiving the letter of intent it is time to take a good look at your board of directors.

Boards of directors are the most overlooked potential resource in young companies. Entrepreneurs are too busy doing business to mess with developing a real board of directors. The image of a sailor in a rowboat in a stormy sea comes to mind. The person at the oars is looking aft and rowing like hell to stay alive. By being so focused on staying afloat, the rower may miss a safe harbor or a rescue. An alert and seasoned crew in the rowboat may be able to guide the rower through shoals and to navigate unseen hazards.

A competent board of directors is not a panacea but does offer the company a relatively inexpensive method of tapping top leadership talent not otherwise available to it. Undeniably, a natural tension exists between management and its board. Entrepreneurs often see little value in placing strangers in authority over themselves. Having a real board of directors requires a lot of extra energy. The board may ask hard questions and demand responsive answers. Why do it?

Board as Value

If you are exploring shareholder liquidity alternatives, the answer is easy. A truly good board of directors brings real economic value to your company. Very often, the acquirer is introduced to your organization through a board member. In any acquisition, management is a component of value that has to stand on its own merits. Nonetheless, the fact that your board contains solid experienced members gives you—as an acquisition candidate—and your management team added credibility and perceived value. Your board is an unknown to an acquirer and may be used for leverage to achieve a higher price. (You can dicker with a CEO, not with a board.) Experience and logic suggest that an acquirer will offer a better price if it appears that its offer will require the approval of a seasoned board.

Looking for money in an IPO or financing? Put yourself in the investor's shoes. Are you

"I get a lot of help. We use our board for key hires because so much of time is spent with the people we work with. What I look for is for (1) competence (people who "know the job cold" and who have a successful track record; (2) an ability to communicate and lead others; and (3) good character and a straight shooter."
—Jeremy A. Jaech, Chief Executive Officer; President; Chairman of the Board, Visio Corporation

more likely to put your faith in a company guided by a stellar board, or one populated by founders? If you are at the venture stage, will a company with a great outside board be more able to resist demands for board positions by a venture investor? You bet! If you have troublesome investors on your board, will adding seasoned members ameliorate their influence? Right again! Regardless of your inestimable merits as a CEO, a strong board communicates to the world that these people believe in you and your company.

Never Too Early

It is never too early to start developing your board. My favorite example is a client who started with a strong board at the business plan stage. A few months later (on very favorable terms), it had to turn away investors when it reached 115% of its funding goal. While proud of their achievements, the founders will readily point to the board as the reason for their remarkable fundraising success.

A great board will not save a loser of a company. It may help revive a troubled one. A great board can lead a good management team to outstanding success. How do you know a good management team? They have a great board!

---

11. 2 Defining Your Company's Vision, Mission, and Goals

—by Casey Ward
FutureWorks, Inc.

Establishing and adhering to a clear, concise, and compelling set of vision, mission, and goals for your company is a crucial factor to its becoming what you want it to be—and to its achieving ongoing success. Operating a company without them would be like driving a car blindfolded to an unknown destination! Or like operating a sailboat without a rudder and without a clue about where you want to go. It is true that one could actually achieve some level of success in one form or another without these, but the chances of effectively and efficiently achieving your desired end result without them is next to impossible.

Some important benefits of having and following clear, concise and compelling vision, mission and goals include:[5]

- They communicate the desired end results to everyone in the company—thus giving direction to and guiding all company personnel toward achieving the company's desired results.

- They inspire and energize the individuals on their day-to-day journey (which is especially helpful during the difficult times).

- They create structural tension necessary for achieving the desired end result.

- They build community and camaraderie within the company.

- They create synergy among the colleagues (where the whole achievement is greater than the sum of the individual efforts).

- They eliminate chaos, confusion, and waste; rather, they promote order, clarity, effectiveness, and efficiency.

- They serve as a measuring stick to see how the company is performing, to enable the leadership to make whatever adjustments are necessary to keep the company on track.

All of these will increase your company's effectiveness (quality and excellence) and efficiency (productivity) while increasing the probability of achieving the desired end results for your company—thus increasing the likelihood of its success.

As the terms vision, mission, and goals are often variously defined, a definition of each follows for this discussion. Simply put, your company *vision* is the clear *mental image, or visualization,* that you have of it: precisely what it is you *imagine* it to be, what it looks like when it is "completed," and how it appears along the way. Your company *mission* is the special task(s) or duty(s) that your company sets out to perform for the purpose of realizing the company vision. And your company *goals* are specific measurable achievements (results) to be realized at particular points along the way—serving as necessary contributions to the creation of your desired end result (vision).

In using the analogy of creating a new house, an architect begins with a specific *vision* of the house to be built. She would start with a picture in mind of the structure, size, and look, including that of the landscape surrounding it—perhaps imagined in full or obtained from other existing similar structures (or some combination of the two). She would draw a clear and detailed picture of the house and landscape including both internal and external views. Her *mission* might be to create this home using redwood and stone with state-of-the-art computer-aided processes. Some *goals* might be:

1. trees cleared and landscape shaped by March 15

---

[5] A necessary component is understanding and holding a clear picture of the current reality along with a clear picture of the desired result. See Robert Fritz in his book *The Path of Least Resistance* (Stillpoint Publishing Fawcett Books, 1989).

2. foundation in place according to specification by April 1

3. frame established by April 20

Anything created materially is first created in one's mind—that is, imagined. Sometimes a created thing was initially imagined for some other purpose, but in the end it served some very different purpose (imagined later!). Take Post-it® Notes by 3M® Corporation for instance. 3M set out to create a special glue for the purpose of attaching labels sufficiently to surfaces but not too tightly (not too difficult to remove when no longer needed—for example, price tags). The product didn't work as designed and planned because the glue was not sticky enough for the purpose. It turns out that an employee at 3M found the pads useful for posting little notes and reminder messages where they could be easily attached, seen, and removed. The idea caught on and the amazing success story is history! Perhaps Post-It Notes would never have been invented if 3M didn't courageously march forward toward the attainment of its initial (and different) vision; and then have the creativity, flexibility, and open-mindedness along the way to reinvent a new purpose for its creation.

Values, Beliefs, and Guiding Principles

Your company's vision, mission and goals plus any basic beliefs or guiding principles should always reflect its core values. If you or your employees do not truly believe in what the company is attempting to do and create—if deep down it really doesn't matter and is not important to those delivering the product or service—it will be difficult if not impossible to deliver the products and/or services with high quality and excellence and to remain competitive in the long run.

IBM has been one of the most successful and profitable companies in world history and has greatly influenced the shaping of the world in the twentieth century. Thomas Watson attributes the incredible success story of IBM to core values or, as IBM called them, its *Basic Beliefs*. They are: 1) Respect for the individual, 2) Superior customer service, 3) Excellence in everything we do.

It's important to give careful thought and attention to the core values of the company and write them down. Be sure to make them clear and memorable. Once established you are ready to move on to the vision statement.

Vision Statement

Your company vision serves as the picture of what your company is to become, the positive difference it will make in the world and what it stands for. Your company's vision statement should be authentic and reflect the core values and beliefs of its people. A well articulated, believed, and supported vision across the company is a key factor in determining its success. Much like having a clear and detailed blueprint for a new house doesn't guarantee that the house will be built according to the design or in a cost-effective and timely manner. But try building a house without the blueprint or other such architectural diagrams! It's important that your company effectively carry out its mission and attain its goals (*vision pieces* or steps) along the way that together bring your company vision to life.

Your vision statement should be a clear, written description of the *ideal* end result you want to create. At its best it is the end result or desire you are *passionate* about bringing into existence. Here are nine key guidelines to consider when designing and communicating your company's vision statement: "It is written down."

1. It should be based on your core values, beliefs and convictions.

2. It should contain sufficient, descriptive detail for its readers and listeners to clearly picture.

3. It should be inspiring and compelling.

4. Its realization should contribute to the well-being of others.

5. It should be clearly documented and posted for everyone in the company to see.

6. It should be regularly discussed, referenced, and assumed by the company leadership and ideally by all personnel.

7. It should lead to personal character growth for all contributors as they perform the company mission to bring the vision to existence.

8. It should be written as if already accomplished (e.g., avoid "to become").

9. It should not limit the methods, activities, paths, services, products, or time necessary to achieve it

Mission Statement

While the vision statement is a clear written description of the end result you desire to create, the mission statement defines the process or path your company will follow for the purpose of bringing your vision into existence. It is a brief description of what the company does daily.

Here are seven key guidelines to consider when designing and communicating your company mission statement:

1. It should be a single sentence in length.

2. It should contain *at least* one verb to specify the actions(s) your company will be taking.

3. It should reflect (directly or indirectly) the company's core value(s) (e.g., what value your company will be providing its customers).

4. It should identify (directly or indirectly) the customer(s) your company is serving.

5. It should be a path such that if followed and carried out with excellence will lead the company to the attainment of its goals and vision.

6. It should be clearly and easily understood by everyone in the company and anyone else who is related to the company in any way (e.g., customers, potential investors, vendors).

7. It should be able to *easily* be recited from memory by *everyone* in the company at any time.

For example, Amazon.com, Inc.'s mission statement is: "To use the Internet to offer products that educate, inform, and inspire." Amazon clearly and simply describes their primary actions: *use the Internet* and *offer products* (of a specific type); their values: *educate*, *inform*, and *inspire* (other implied values by their use of the Internet may be *cost effectiveness*, *speed/high performance*, *technology/innovation*, *simplicity/ease*, and/or *efficiency*); and customer they are serving: anyone with access to the Internet with an interest in the values offered (implied).

Some other examples, each with slightly different styles, may be:

- Company X frees single parents to work at home by creating and providing advanced telecommunications products.

- We broaden the availability of effective cancer-reducing drugs to those who otherwise could not afford them.

- Our mission is to increase fuel efficiency and restore the environment through computer controlled emission systems.

- To advance learning retention and courseware availability to the software industry via multimedia and Internet technology.

Goals

Your major company goals are like stepping stones toward your end destination (vision). They are the specific, measurable, secondary results that lead your company to its primary desired result—what it sets out to become or create—its vision. Goals should *always* have a specific target date for attainment.

James Collins and Jerry Porras talk about setting BHAGs (Big Hairy Audacious Goals!) in their book, *Built to Last*. "A BHAG engages people—it reaches out and grabs them in the gut. It is tangible, energized, highly focused. People 'get it' right away; it takes little or no explanation."

Like your mission statement, your goals should be simply and plainly stated, clearly understood, memorable, and inspiring. Your company goals keep your company focused in the right direction and on the right path (mission) toward your desired creation (vision).

Goal-setting

Your goals can be categorized as primary and secondary. Primary goals are the largest objectives or milestones such that the total attainment of them leads to the attainment of your company vision. Secondary goals are the subgoals that make up (or are necessary to achieve in order to realize) each primary goal (i.e., each primary goal may be broken down into smaller, more easily attainable objectives that we will call secondary goals). Here are some guidelines for setting your company's goals.

General goal-setting guidelines

1. All company goals should be clear, specific, easily understood and measurable.
2. They should be realistic and attainable.
3. Each goal should in some way contribute to the realization of the company vision (e.g., if the vision is a picture puzzle, each goal is a puzzle piece).
4. They generally should cause employees to stretch outside their comfort zone in order to attain them.
5. They should describe what is *really* desired (i.e., not something made up because it "sounds good" or what is "supposed to be" according to someone else's standards or desires).
6. Each goal should be assigned a target attainment date.
7. Each goal should be stated as a positive, current accomplishment.
8. Ideally, each primary goal should be emotionally appealing—exciting.

Goal attainment process

There are four general steps involved in effectively setting and attaining your company goals. The individual(s) or group(s) responsible for attaining the company goals should be involved in both the setting and the attainment of the goals. In attaining these goals, your company should be moving along a path as described in the company mission statement, toward the destination described in the company vision statement.

1. *Set all primary goals first.* It's important to keep in mind the company vision while setting all primary goals. These goals may spread over a period of years, possibly three to five years. (It's quite possible and very likely that your long-range goals will change periodically. That's okay—it's important to set them anyway. The industry, economy, customers, employees, investors, vendors, interests, needs, and all aspects of life are in a continuous state of change. When you revisit your long-range primary goals periodically you can change them at that time, and thus modify your course of direction accordingly. Your company at all times should have a current set of goals in which it is striving to attain based on the state of affairs and known information at the time.)

2. *For each primary goal (i.e., desired end result), break it down into smaller, more easily attainable secondary goals.* One way to do this is to begin with the primary goal and work backwards. Write down one clear and separate objective that has to happen just prior to reaching your primary goal. Then identify and write down another

objective that has to be achieved just prior to reaching that goal, and so on. Continue to do this until you arrive at where you are today. These secondary goals are like stepping stones toward your primary goal. It's very important to have a clear and accurate understanding of current reality (i.e., where your company is today in relation to the desired end result or goal). This understanding will help generate the energy necessary to propel you toward your desired goals and will help you to know what actions you need to take and changes you need to make to move in the direction toward attaining your goals. Also, make sure your secondary goals are attainable in the near term (small daily and weekly accomplishments and other accomplishments not more than six months away). It is important to feel the success in attaining your goals and to generate momentum and confidence to continue forward; especially through the difficult periods.

3. *Once your primary and secondary goals have been written down you can then design a plan of action steps to take.* For each nearest scheduled secondary goal, make a prioritized list of specific actions you need to take to attain each desired outcome. Also, try to identify one or more activities you can do consistently which would bring a goal into being. For example, call 10 prospective clients from the "leads" database each morning to inform them of the company's new Web Development Services Program. This may lead to the attainment of your goal of signing on three new clients by September 30.

4. *Finally, take action!* Go through your list one by one and complete each task, focusing on one thing at a time. Cross off each task as it is completed.

With your company values, vision, mission and goals firmly in place, always remember that your company is essentially all about people—no matter what your products and/or services may be. It's about people serving other people and meeting their wants and needs in some way. The best companies will do so with courage, conviction, compassion, respect, and excellence.

11.3 Hiring an Accountant

—by Roger Clark
Clark & Associates

An accountant should be a key professional advisor to your company. Depending on the type of accountant that you select, he or she can help you in the areas of accounting, financial reporting, federal and state tax preparation and planning, mergers and acquisitions, valuation, business planning, and operations.

In general terms, an "accountant" is someone whose primary business is the provision of accounting and related services to businesses and/or individuals. An accountant who has passed a fairly difficult exam administered by the American Institute of Certified Public Accountants is called a certified public accountant, or "CPA." Some accountants are CPAs and some are not. Due to the complexity of tax and accounting rules that are specific to the software industry, it is wise to require that your accountant be a CPA.

What CPAs Do

CPAs work in various business structures that help indicate the size and scope of their CPA practice and services. A "sole practitioner" works alone or with a few employees; a local CPA firm usually has one or two offices and five to 60 people. A regional CPA firm has offices in a region, like the West Coast; national or international firms have offices all over; and the "Big 5 Firms" are the five largest accounting firms in the world with offices internationally.

Finding a Good Accountant

Because there are so many CPAs in Washington, finding an accountant is easy. Finding a good accountant for your business is harder and will require from two to twenty hours depending on the magnitude of your needs and how wide a CPA search you conduct. Most smaller software businesses spend about six hours selecting an accountant, while larger businesses whose accounting fees and needs are greater will spend much more time in their search.

Whether you have experience in working with a CPA or not, start your search by talking with friends and business associates that use CPAs for their software businesses. Find contacts whose businesses are about your size and larger so that you get a good sample of similar situations. Record their responses to the following questions:

1. What CPA firm have they used in the last five years?
2. Who was the CPA partner on their account and the primary service provider at the CPA firm?
3. What services did the CPA firm offer, and what services did they use?
4. Did the CPA firm understand their business and the software industry?
5. How did the CPA firm bill for their services, and do they think the fees were high, low, or reasonable given the services that they received?
6. Would they recommend their CPA for your business?

Also contact your attorney, banker, and other advisors for their recommendations for a CPA.

After the above conversations, you probably have developed or improved your understanding of what your business should expect from an accountant. List the factors that you will consider in selecting a CPA, which may include the following:

1. What is the reputation and quality of service of the firm, and can you validate the reputation by checking references?
2. Is the CPA firm experienced in serving the software industry?
3. Does the size of the CPA firm fit your business, and can it handle the reasonably foreseeable needs of your business for the next two to three years?
4. Is the range of services broad enough for your business?
5. Who will be your primary contact at the firm, and will that work for you?

Select two or three of the CPAs from your research that seem to meet your requirements. Generally, it is a good idea to get some diversity by selecting smaller and larger CPA firms to get a broader range of service approaches.

Contact one of the individuals who is an owner at the firm and set up a one-hour complimentary appointment to obtain information on the above questions. Make sure that you will also meet with the individuals that will be your primary contact, if different. Have a list of questions on the issues that you are facing and take notes regarding the approach, knowledge, and expertise of the CPA. Ask if the CPA provides any special billing or payment terms that might apply to your situation.

Evaluate the results, make a decision, and hire your accountant!

11.4 Electronic Risk Control: A Necessity

—by Joan E. Feldman

Computer Forensics

Why Is an Electronic Risk Control Plan Necessary?

The ease with which computers create, distribute, and store information has produced new risks not prevalent when documents existed only in printed form. The goal of an Electronic Risk Control (ERC) plan should be (1) to establish an efficient organizational framework for all documents created within the establishment; (2) to safeguard the preservation of important information while periodically destroying data whose usefulness has expired; and (3) to reduce litigation exposure through proper system management.

The goal of an ERC plan is to facilitate easy retention and retrieval of electronic information. With respect to possible legal claims, an ERC plan will enable an organization to locate documents that can be used offensively in a legal proceeding and avoid the staggering costs associated with data retrieval when the exact location of information is unknown. Such procedures can range in cost from $1500 for a single computer to $100,000 to examine an entire computer system. Additionally, the ability to access and retrieve information will lessen the chances of being assessed discovery sanctions. Recently, Prudential Insurance Company was sanctioned $1 million dollars and was forced to reimburse a substantial portion of the plaintiffs' attorneys' fees due to the unintentional destruction of electronic evidence. Prudential was said to have failed to preserve evidence. See *Prudential Ins. Co. of Am. Sales Practices Lit.*, 169 F.R.D. 598 (1997).

Formative Stage of an ERC Plan

In order to ensure that a newly developed ERC plan meets the needs of all members of a given company, it is important that all levels of the organization are represented during the planning stages. An ERC team should comprise personnel from the information systems, records management, human resources, accounting, and legal departments, as well as representatives of the operational departments of sales and production. The goal of the newly established team should be to identify all types of data generated by the organization, to address legal, statutory and organizational record keeping and access requirements, and ultimately to facilitate the implementation of the newly created plan.

System overview

To develop a comprehensive ERC system requires a clear understanding of the existing infrastructure. The team should assess the total number of users, the hardware and software components, and the networking software and hardware configuration. Additionally, there should be a thorough analysis of the software and database packages used by the various departments, the e-mail provider and Internet interface, and whether any of the employees telecommute.

User interaction with system

Once the team has a clear understanding of the system's configuration, it will need to analyze user interaction with the system and the existing relationships among the different endusers in the organization. The team should consider how departments create, access, manipulate, and save data. Specifically, the team will need to know what applications are used and the current naming conventions for saving data. With respect to databases, the team should understand control of access to the databases, the type of data entered, the manner in which data is entered and retrieved, and the reports generated.

Security measures

With a clear understanding of the system's configuration coupled with the user interface, the team must consider the methods of data retention that are currently in place. A determination of which documents constitute the organization's official business records should follow. Such records should receive special consideration: their retention is of paramount importance. Taking into account all that has been learned during the investigative stage, the team will then be able to develop protocols that will determine appropriate back-up schedules, including rotation schedules for backup media and the physical storage location. Additionally, the team should give special thought to the hardware and software programs that will be used to create the backup tapes. As hardware and software is frequently upgraded, they must develop that will ensure backup tapes are accessible in the future. This could be accomplished through hardware retention or by periodically converting the backup tapes to make them compatible with changes in hardware.

Developing the ERC Plan

It is critical to remember that the ERC plan needs to account for every document that is generated and stored in the organization's computer system. To develop a comprehensive ERC plan, our firm uses its "PROTECT" approach. This approach incorporates seven essential elements:

Policies. Clearly defined and disseminated policies, including style guidelines, are enacted to allow an organization to define the organization's expectation with respect to users' rights.

Retention Schedules. Retention schedules that serve legal, regulatory and organizational needs are created.

Organization of Data. Uniform naming conventions and directory allocations are established to standardize file retention. Additionally, access control audits and distribution lists ensure that information is not disseminated to unauthorized parties.

Trade Secret, Proprietary and Confidential Information. Information is categorized to ensure that the ERC provides methods for identifying and safeguarding privileged and proprietary information such as trade secrets. This type of information may not be discoverable in legal actions and should be segregated from all other retained data.

E-Mail and Voice Mail. E-mail often proves to be the most challenging part of a risk control plan. E-mail is difficult to delete and is easily copied and forwarded. Additionally, users are often far more candid in an e-mail, presenting legitimate litigation concerns for the organization. To ensure consistency in the e-mail sent from the organization, specific stylistic guidelines are enacted. Additionally, employees are advised that as users of the organization's computer system, e-mail sent from and received by the organization is the property of the organization. In this manner, employees are advised that they do not have an expectation of privacy. Similar guidelines are established for voice mail.

Compliance. No system, regardless of how precise, will be of any benefit to a company unless there is strict compliance. Regularly scheduled audits, both automated and user defined, are scheduled to assure adherence to the system. The audits serve to identify unanticipated problems and facilitate resolutions.

Training. Seminars are conducted (1) to educate users about the risks associated with uncontrolled use of electronic data; (2) to advise users of the policies and stylistic guidelines that have been adopted; and (3) to teach users about aspects of the ERC plan that have been tailored to their respective departments.

Conclusion

With the ever-increasing number of documents that are never reduced to printed form, every organization must develop an easy electronic record retention and retrieval system. A good ERC plan can keep problems from occurring, and when a problem does arise, an ERC plan can help limit the potential liability exposure. While an ERC plan will necessarily be a dynamic process, establishing the initial plan will be the hardest aspect. Once the system is in place, changes can be made on an ongoing basis as the need arises.

11.5 Planning for Facilities Growth:

How Expanding Software Firms Can Plan for Rapid Growth in an Inflexible Commercial Real Estate Environment

—by Richard Peterson and Eric Postle
Puget Sound Properties Commercial Real Estate Services, LLC

Our area has experienced an explosive growth in local software companies. Successful companies are finding that in order to adapt their business to exploit the opportunities presented by today's dynamic business environment, they must be able to grow rapidly with relatively little notice.

Rapid growth leads to relatively short facility plans. In most cases, it is difficult to predict growth beyond 12 to 24 months out. The commercial real estate environment has a difficult time responding to these short-term needs. Most landlords will require a company to commit for a minimum of three- to five-year lease terms or longer if new construction is involved.

Several ways outlined below can ensure that your company can meet its growth needs in this relatively inflexible commercial real estate environment. The starting point is to determine what your facility needs are.

Questions to Consider in Expanding Your Facility

- Where are my customers and in what proximity do I need them to be located?
- Where do my current and future key employees reside?
- Where is the right type of building space for my business? a suburban office park, or a downtown high-rise?
- How much parking do I need? (Parking constraints may determine where you locate.)
- Do my employees utilize transit? How convenient is transit in my planning?
- What type of amenities are important to the company operation (hotels, airport access, etc.) and employees (good access, restaurants, parking, transit, entertainment)?
- What in our new facility is important for making a statement to our customers? attracting new employees? providing an important image for our business?

How Much Space Do You Need?

Most tenants determine the amount of space they'll need in the future by looking at the current square footage they occupy, dividing it by the number of employees they have, and then multiplying it by the number of employees they plan to hire. This approach, however, doesn't account for the potential change in how the space will be used.

Outlined below is an example of a space programming exercise that will help you get a better handle on your company's future space needs. This way of calculating space takes the actual area of the items used, such as a 6' x 8' workstation being 48 square feet, or a 10' x 12' office being 120 square feet. You calculate the types of spaces that you need, as well as special use rooms such as conference rooms, war rooms, computer rooms, mail and copy centers, reception. Once you calculate the net area for these functions, add a circulation factor. This circulation factor takes into consideration the corridors and other areas needed to make these spaces functional. The circulation factor is generally 25% to 30%.

This calculation gives you a net usable area. Multiply the net usable area by a load factor for each building. Generally, load factors run between 12% and 18%. So, if 10,000 square feet of net usable area have a building load factor of 15% then the net rentable area would be 11,500 square feet. That's right, you're paying a rate that reflects 1,500 square feet that is not inside the space you use: for the building corridors, restrooms, elevators and common areas.

Space Programming Matrix Example

PROPOSED SPACE NEEDS

Quantity	Description	Dimensions	Total SF	# of Employees
1	Reception Area	12 x 20 ft.	240	1
5	Executive Offices	12 x 14 ft.	840	5
8	Administrative Offices	10 x 12 ft.		8
40	Work Stations	8 x 7 ft.	2240	40
1	Computer Rooms	12 x 16 ft.	192	1
1	Main Conference Room	16 x 24 ft.	384	0
2	Small Conference Room	12 x 14 ft.	336	0
1	Recreation Rooms	12 x 20 ft.	240	0
2	Storage Rooms	12 x 12 ft.	288	0
1	Copy Centers	10 x 16 ft.	160	0
1	Coffee Stations	5 x 6 ft.	30	0
1	Lunchroom	16 x 14 ft.	224	0
3	Small Work Stations	5 x 6 ft.	90	3
0	Special Equipment Room			
1	Telephone Room (addnl.)	8 x 10 ft.	80	0
2	Internal Restrooms	8 x 16 ft.	256	0
1	Configuration Room	10 x 16 ft.	160	2
TOTALS				**60**

Square Footage Above:	6,720
Multiply by 25% for Corridor Factor:	1,680
Net Usable Area:	8,400
Multiply Net Usable by 115% for Net Rentable Area:	9,960
SF/Employee:	170

*Special Features or Needs:*_____

FUTURE GROWTH - OFFICE

Year	Addnl. Employees	x Ratio	Addnl. = SF
1	10	170	1,700
2	15	170	2,550
3	20	170	3,400

Efficient Floor Plans Can Save You Big Money

An efficient floor plate with minimal angles and the proper bay depths for your type of workstations can make a difference of 10% to 20% in how many people you can actually fit into a particular space. This type of efficiency can make a big difference in your budget. Don't assume all square footages are the same. They are not.

What type of space do you need for your employees?

- Open Office Concept
- Semi-private Cubicles
- Private Offices

Companies competing for employees, software developers especially, often say that Microsoft sets the standard. They generally provide their programmers private offices and utilize open cubicle concepts for customer service and other areas of their business. This "standard," however, is changing. Many software developers feel the "team concept" and the open communication of the cubicle workstations can contribute to productivity. Certainly the open work environment offers a substantial advantage in costs of tenant improvement and in flexibility—allowing for more growth and general reusability of the space.

So, don't jump to the conclusion that a private office environment is the only way to go. Limiting these areas to managers or key functions can often be effective and make a much more pleasant and productive workplace for those who don't have the private office with a nice window to the outside. Look at all the factors, including corporate communication, flexibility, and cost. Generally, your tenant improvement build out can cost 30% to 50% more for a complete private office environment than for open space (with a mix of private offices and open space).

Short-Term Leases

It may be possible to obtain short-term leases through looking at subleases that have one to two years remaining. Or, you could commit to a landlord for a short-term—knowing that you will have to move at the end of that term because the space you occupy is committed to another larger tenant after your short-term lease expires. The advantage to a short-term lease is the limited commitment that your company has to the space. The disadvantage is your lack of control. Nonetheless, companies that expect rapid growth in the near future and emerging growth companies can benefit from short-term leases.

Buy Out Clauses

It's better to negotiate a way out of the lease early up front. A "buy out" or early termination agreement should specify not only the right to terminate but also the notification time frames and termination costs. If things have gone well and you're "busting at the seams," having a fixed dollar amount you can pay to vacate the space will often be your best and most effective alternative.

Sublease Rights

Make certain that the lease you negotiate today allows you to be flexible in subleasing it to other tenants in the future. This arrangement will allow you to move on to bigger space, or in the unfortunate event business plans reverse themselves, then you're also able to cover your exposure on the lease.

Subleasing rights may include passing on any additional profit to the landlord, but of course subleasing has costs involved—commissions and possible re-tenant improvements or free rent. These items should be negotiated as costs of subleasing and not characterized as additional rent that you have to pay back to the landlord.

Expansion Pockets

Expansion pockets offer an effective way to control the space that you anticipate growing into. They normally take two forms:

1. *Space Pocket.* This is space that you commit to today that you will have to pay rent on in the future, say 12 months down the road. This option requires you to grow and incur those costs,

2. *First Right of Refusal on Adjacent Space.* Locating your business next to existing tenants with leases that terminate one or two years down the road may provide opportunities to take their space and grow without having to relocate your business.

Growth Expansion Options

Some landlords will permit you to move within their complex if you outgrow your space. This advantage could become more difficult to get as markets tighten.

Equipment

Relocating often requires the investment in new equipment. One should look closely at the systems available and their capacities. Quite often you can buy a phone system that will take you far into the future for your growth needs for only an initial investment of a few thousand dollars more. Such more technically advanced phone systems can accommodate growth through the purchase of additional equipment. Some smaller systems for handling up to 12 to 20 employees often cannot grow beyond that number and therefore must be discarded. The same holds true for voice mail systems.

Looking at the capacity and expansion potential of each of these items can save considerable dollars in the future as well as the inconvenience of complete replacement.

Furniture

Companies often select furniture based on what type of working environment they want rather than for growth. Be aware, however, that elements of the furniture you choose can affect how you grow.

In open configuration settings, for example, integrated systems furniture provides a means of running cable and electrical conduit for the workstations. These systems can easily expand as your company continues to grow. Selecting standard rather than custom features can often reduce the lead time and provide more available options to expand in the future. Custom systems can have a lead time of up to six months whereas standard systems are generally readily available in 30 days.

Freestanding furniture is much less expensive to relocate, both in assembly and total move time. If your company is in the early stages, freestanding furniture can often be acquired inexpensively, especially used.

Moving

Most companies will end up moving over a weekend or a few days before the weekend depending on their size. It is possible to relocate a company of 250 to 300 people in a 3-day period—even relocating systems furniture and other large items. The proper planning of a move, however, can take several weeks.

The cost of moving offices and relocating machines will depend on the type of furniture you have—whether it's freestanding or systems furniture. Relocating systems furniture generally costs about $500 per person; moving freestanding furniture costs $300 per person. Setting up network systems for a large installation costs approximately $100 per person. These rates allow for the employees to pack personal items, leave on Friday, come back on Monday and turn on the computer terminal—and away they go! Cabling for network and phones usually runs about $2.50 to $3.00 per square foot.

Timing

Planning an effective relocation generally takes more time than generally expected. The larger the company, the less emphasis they put on their real estate needs, it seems, and when they have a need it's always immediate. The best way to plan and satisfy customers is to emphasize to management and key managers the time involved in the relocation process. The table below shows how long it generally takes to plan an effective relocation for these companies:

How long does it take to relocate?		
Size	Minimum	Normal*
0 to 10,000 SF	60 days	90 to 120 days
10,000 to 25, 000 SF	120 days	180 days
25,000 SF and up	150 days	240 days

*Variances can depend on building permits for tenant improvements and build outs for various municipalities.

Facility managers in larger companies have a challenge in responding quickly to their internal customers, the employee, and their managers. Internal customers often get approval for expansion plans for employees or other items and need space quickly. The best way to respond quickly is to keep an awareness of the market and to assemble a team of vendors who can quickly assemble a new space: your furniture vendor, phone consultant, and real estate advisors.

In today's business environment rarely are software firms given much advanced notice of the need to expand. Unfortunately, the commercial real estate market, by its nature, does not respond positively to sudden changes. It is important for your firm to deploy strategies to give your firm maximum flexibility.

"Half of the equation was building the technology; the other half is distribution, and we have some very big distribution partners."
—Bard Richmond, Founder and Chairman of Active Voice

• Chapter 12 •

Financing the Company

12.1 Partnering: When Not to Go It Alone

—by Byron B. McCann and Theodore Feierstein
Ascent Partners, Inc.

Make sure you include "partnering" as part of your business model as well as strategy and tactics.

Introduction

Rarely can a technology company "go it alone" today. Winning companies view strategic partnering as a vital and widespread practice for success. Partnering is a critical weapon in one's competitive arsenal because in today's complex business environment, no single company can do it all. Partnering is also size-independent. Monster companies as well as new start-ups partner aggressively—and should.

Much has been spoken of the "virtual corporation" in recent years. The virtual corporation is based upon strong alliances with many constituents, even with employees. There is no end to how alliances and partnering can be used to configure resources to meet a market need effectively; the virtual corporation concept shows how far it can be taken.

Advisors have probably suggested that you must have "focus, focus, focus" in what your company does. We believe the need to focus on one's business mission *forces* partnering. A successful company will typically exhibit excellent focus on the one thing it does well and does uniquely, its *core competence*. If all companies are focusing on their particular mission, who is going to do the things that they don't do well? For example, your company may have invented a complex, enabling technology for Internet security. Is it more important for you to package the technology into a complete security application or license it to others to embed into existing applications with well-established distribution channels? Others will have excellent marketing and distribution established and/or an installed base that fits your target market.

Given harsh competitive realities, think about leveraging your valuable technology asset by partnering with vendors with access to resources that you do not control, but with the long-run exit strategy in mind. Do not enter an alliance that prevents you from doing a more significant one down the road. When negotiating any agreement, think about how you can unwind it gracefully if things don't work out as expected. Often exit strategy becomes the most important element of the agreement.

Partnering compresses time in a competitive environment, and as you are aware, no other industry has shorter windows of opportunity than Information Technology. As a result, no other industry rewards vendors that are quick-to-market as much as the IT industry. Time is so critical that any technique to reduce "time-to-market" can lead to success. Additionally, since less time consumes less capital and brings revenue faster, the financial impact can be enormous to you and your investors.

If you are not partnering or planning to partner, look in the mirror and ask yourself why not? Your investors probably will. And while you're contemplating partnering, keep in mind that your competitors are, at this very moment, in discussions with larger partners plotting ways to grab market share at your expense.

Partnering Forms Relationships

Partnering is the act of forming valuable relationships aimed at furthering your business mission to achieve your ultimate vision. Naturally, your partner must benefit as well. The more ways you find to benefit your partners, the more value they will help you derive from that partnership. Understanding your needs will help you identify partner candidates. Understanding their needs will help you derive value from them. Therefore it is most important to know what your partner is trying to achieve and to leverage that for your benefit.

Computer Associates International (CA), is an interesting example. When they released the first, completely object-oriented database called *Jasmine*™, they needed to establish it in the marketplace against the other, well-entrenched database companies such as Oracle, IBM, Informix, Sybase, and now Microsoft. Any technologies that would help CA add value to their database (e.g., new functionality that leverages off of their unique object capability), would enhance its value to potential customers and help them compete. Also, if you have an Internet, E-commerce, multimedia application that runs on *Jasmine*, CA will likely help you gain access to customers since they will be able to sell the underlying database platform that supports your application. As expected, CA has an aggressive partnering program for third parties.

Partnering can help:
- Fund product development
- Promote products
- Reduce marketing costs
- Gain access to customers or channels
- Enter international markets cost-effectively
- Reduce time-to-market

- Acquire needed technology or application functionality
- Gain expertise
- Reduce risk
- Secure "non-dilutive" financial resources
- Sell capital
- Attract investors
- Attract key employees

Partnering can come in many forms with various benefits. Some are listed below:

Type	Structure	Benefit
Promotional	Joint endorsement in marketing materials and press releases	- Amplifies voice in market-place
Marketing	Joint marketing of each other's products	- Reduced cost - Customer access - Market credibility
Cross-Selling and Up-Selling	Selling complementary products into your and your partners installed base	- More sales - More registered users
Technology	OEM license of technology—up-front payment and/or royalty on sales	- Non-dilutive financial - Rapid time-to-market - Endorsement of technology
Financial	Loan; equity investment in exchange for favorable business terms for product or technology	- Needed working capital - Sale of equity

Note that revenue-driven items appear at the top of the table. While all of the items are important, revenue acceleration tends to be the most important market validation metric. Companies are often valued by the stock market or acquirers based on multiples of trailing or future expected revenue instead of operating profit. Emerging companies are often profit-delayed. Amazon.com is an excellent example of a company that the equity market values on its market leadership, brand establishment, and future growth, not profit because it doesn't yet or is not planned to exist for the foreseeable future.

Be creative in the range of possibilities for the many forms of partnering. Build a "partnering portfolio" to cover various needed elements in your business. Remember to keep your future options open when doing so.

12.2 Strategic Equity Investments

—by Byron McCann and Theodore Feierstein
Ascent Partners, Inc.

Your company needs financial capital from some source. Strategic equity comes from parties that may offer more than money. Often those extras are more valuable than the money itself. When seeking capital, consider strategic partners as investors along with financial investors. The financial ones can be more motivated by the strategic ones.

Often an entrepreneur can raise capital by virtue of its strategic value as perceived by a larger company. Importantly, a *strategic* investor, unlike a *financial* investor, is willing to pay a higher valuation and, hence, less dilution to the founders or existing investors. They can do this because they will gain from the relationship in various other ways. Most importantly, a strategic investor signals acceptance or validation of the "value-proposition" your company is offering to the market. Such market-driven credibility is immeasurable and highly leverageable. A strategic investment by a large company in a relatively new one enhances the new company's value. The established company benefits as well since it is seen as adopting new technology. For example, Microsoft's investment in RealNetworks, Inc. and licensing contract helped validate RealNetworks as the Internet audio standard and enhanced its value for a subsequent initial public offering, even though the two companies can also be seen as competitors!

Often today's strategic equity investment can lead to tomorrow's acquisition or liquidity event. This often offers the most desired exit strategy for you to cash in on your hard work and to get a return on investment for your investor's capital. More than 10 acquisitions occur for each initial public offering. Knowing this makes the often heard "we plan to go public" ring somewhat hollow. Tremendous valuations coming from acquisitions may be the way you cash in!

Strategic equity partners can pay more for your equity and can often be your exit partner upon the sale of the business. They add value to your business and can reduce risk. Look for corporate investors today and negotiate flexibility to accommodate your future exit.

When Alliances and Partnerships Are Strategic

Strategic means your mission is being supported to help you reach your vision. Be clear about the difference between your vision and mission and those of your potential partners.

"When raising money, you are selling both the software and the team. Raising money lets you figure out what problems there are with the plan. To protect your idea, talk to only a few reputable VC funds. You have to be willing to network to sell your ideas —you need to sell yourself and your ideas—you get money by believing that 'you can do it.'"
—Jeremy A. Jaech, *Chief Executive Officer; President; Chairman of the Board, Visio Corporation*

Most alliances and partnerships are strategic because they help gain some form of market advantage, some form of leverage. Oracle, Sun Microsystems, and IBM formed strategic alliances with the Java language to gain leverage against Microsoft, each for a different reason. Whenever there is leverage, an alliance or partnership is strategic.

Some alliances may be considered tactical where you will see "business partner," increasingly common where large platform vendors will have active business partner programs to help solidify the platform's acceptance. Pretty much tactical, this often does not have terrific leverage for the non-platform vendor. That is not to say that it isn't important. Tactical things such as trade show presence, early product release information, and inclusion in catalogs are helpful but not as vital as a strategic relationship which catapults you into your target market to increase your chances of attaining a leadership position.

Know how to distinguish between strategic and tactical. If you are trying to play the standards or platform game, you need to be engaging others to amplify your standard. When your strategy is to be the standard, strategic relationships come from other technology standards companies. In tactical alliances, others implement your standards, and you offer support and marketing.

Corporate Examples of Partnering

CrossRoute Software

A great example of a relatively new venture that excels at partnering, CrossRoute Software is a leader in cross-enterprise electronic commerce solutions that address one of a company's biggest challenges: how to streamline processes with suppliers, distributors, and customers.

Its product, appropriately named *Alliance*™, provides a complete solution for automating a wide variety of cross-enterprise processes, such as distributor ordering, supply chain integration, inventory replenishment, and logistics coordination. Below is their partnering statement:

Partnering For Successs

Partnerships are an important part of CrossRoute Software's extended enterprise solutions. We work closely with industry leaders—including application vendors, consulting firms, platform vendors and technology providers—to create and deploy world-class customer solutions.

Current relationships include:

- SAP   - Oracle Corporation   - PeopleSoft   - Cap Gemini   - Microsoft

---

CrossRoute even segments their partners into different program categories to emphasize the distinct roles for a complete solution that they play:

- Application Partner Program
- Consulting Partner Program
- Platform Partner Program
- Technology Partner Program

A young company, CrossRoute has experienced management who understand the power of alliances.

PeopleSoft

PeopleSoft, another example of a savvy partnering company, is a leader in enterprise-scale applications including human resources, financials, materials management, distribution, manufacturing, and industry specific solutions. Their partnering portfolio, as promoted in their Web site, appears below:

Meet PeopleSoft Partners

The many software, service, and platform organizations worldwide who are our global alliance partners are all industry leaders dedicated to providing outstanding service and delivering exceptional value to our customers. Each and every one of them supports our mission to provide innovative software solutions to meet the changing business demands of enterprises worldwide.

- Service Partners
- Software Partners
- Platform Partners

They then go into detail about each group of partners and who they are. This creates a perception of killer momentum. If this many companies are signed on, this must be a "for real" type of attitude.

As you can observe, partnering on several, concurrent levels can become quite extensive. For the early stage entrepreneur, probably two or three key alliances will help accelerate you to rapid evolution and success. Concentrate on those, first; then get some help internally or externally to go after the rest.

With any deal, try to keep it simple, have both parties "win," and plan for an exit if things don't work, requiring something else that better supports your mission.

Because each deal is unique, "typical" is more a guideline for ideas than a blueprint for a deal. In the context of each party's needs, the structure of a deal will emerge naturally. Both sides must consider how to most efficiently meet their immediate needs yet keep their options open. We list and summarize below the many forms of deals.

One deal's appearance can be another's reality. In a merger or acquisition process, we sometimes see a major, worldwide, exclusive technology license as the same as a full acquisition if it is functionally equivalent. An exclusive distribution agreement can have the same effect, offering a way to get around some other constraint such as the burden of writing off goodwill (excess of deal value over book value) or the inability to do a "pooling" form of merger. (Pooling is a merger where the accounting treatment allows both companies to combine financial statements as though they had always been one company. Pooling provides an attractive way to avoid write-offs of goodwill, but many conditions can make it difficult to accomplish.)

Summary of various forms of deals:

- Technology license
- Distribution agreement
- Joint marketing agreement
- Original Equipment Manufacturer (OEM agreement)
- Private label
- Joint venture
- Equity investment (minority or majority)
- Full acquisition

Often one of these will lead to another, more involved relationship. Depending upon where you are in your company's life cycle, several of these relationships can operate concurrently. A potential corporate investor or buyer may want to "try before they buy," enter into a licensing agreement, and later make an acquisition.

Technology License

A technology license is often most appropriately granted for a specific market or product category that matches the partner's strengths. Typically, one is allowing another to use its technology in a product as an enabling or more complete solution. Too broad a technology license could dilute its value if it makes sense to have more than one licensee for other market segments. Branding can be important here: we advise that your brand be named on your partner's product to extend your company's recognition. Intel is a master at that strategy with their *Intel Inside*™ program.

Distribution Agreement

This agreement may be considered more tactical but exerts tremendous leverage to gain access to distribution and customers. Because distribution can be expensive in terms of time and cost, Internet commerce distribution models eliminate (disintermediate) middle distribution tiers and enable more profit margin as well as more cost savings to customers. These agreements can be extremely valuable for both parties, but depending upon the level of commitment, exercise caution in structuring them.

Joint Marketing Agreement

These agreements, the most lightweight of the list, nevertheless can be a valuable and critical component in an entrepreneur's mix of tools when combined with other deals. JMAs can serve just to demonstrate market acceptance. But don't rely on this because many people can see through these agreements if the commitment levels are low. We recommend that these agreements be used aggressively and keep your options open if someone might want to acquire you.

OEM Agreement

Making OEM agreements has become a verb like "fedexing" a package. Microsoft OEMs Windows to Compaq, Dell, Gateway, IBM, and others. US Robotics OEMs modems to the PC manufacturers. INSO OEMs International CorrectSpell™ spellchecker to word processing vendors such as Microsoft. OEM means your product is sold and incorporated into someone's product. It resembles a technology license because a technology license component is included in most software OEM deals. However, OEM deals typically involve more complete products whereas a technology license may not.

Private Label Agreement

Private label is similar to OEM and can be the same in many cases. In a private label deal, you sell your product to another company who will apply their brand name to it. Private labeling does not help your brand identity but does give you revenue and customer credibility. It may be an excellent source of "capital" or revenue when you sell to a customer who is not a competitor. You may want to open up market segments you probably would not have prioritized highly, anyway.

Joint Venture Agreement

Joint venture agreements can be complex because two or more parties form a new corporate entity and jointly own it. This can be appropriate when trying to accomplish a complex task or to set up an organization in a foreign country. Joint ventures pose difficulty in an exit because the parties' objectives at exit time may have changed. On the other hand, joint ventures can go public and take on a life of their own.

Equity Investment

In equity investment, you sell stock in your company to an investor who will have (typically) a minority ownership and voting position. Equity provides critical "risk" capital to help the company establish viability. Strategic investors will want to make equity investments to help ensure the viability of the firm, establish a voting position to make sure its interests are served, or to set up a option to buy out the company in the future. Equity is important to the entrepreneur because it does not have to be paid back like a loan. Moreover, a strategic investor can provide invaluable help in many forms beyond its investment. Because strategic equity capital is so important, we focus our clients on searching for it.

Full Acquisition

An acquisition occurs because buyers want to control the destiny of your business as part of theirs. Not that they diverge in strategy or focus from yours; they just need to make you part of their company so their customers see it as one complete value proposition.

Acquisition takes the form of an asset sale—a purchase of your stock. A stock deal can be a "purchase" or a "pooling." The difference is that a pooling allows you to avoid goodwill arising on the buyer's balance sheet but it does not allow for any contingent payouts. A purchase can incorporate an "earnout" contingent on sales, profits, or some other metric. An earnout typically is layered on top of up-front consideration (cash, stock, royalty or distribution advances) to provide an incentive for the sellers to keep driving the business to success for both parties to win.

Summary

As we mentioned, strive for simplicity in agreements so that each party has a clear understanding of what is expected. Try to make the terms measurable so performance can easily be measured and communicated. Perhaps most importantly, seek out the counsel of an experienced corporate deal attorney who has done many of these deals for firms like yours. A good attorney will give you many useful ideas to help you structure your transaction; an experienced one will suggest the appropriate ones to keep the momentum of the deal going forward. Because international agreements can have an entirely different set of "rules" you have to play by, an experienced attorney will be invaluable in arranging them.

To see how graceful unwinding a deal might be, always simulate termination scenarios before signing an agreement. If you go public or are acquired, think how difficult this agreement may be to change when you want to accomplish that important milestone. Consider time limits to the agreement and be cautious when granting exclusivity of any kind. Finally, save substantial time by looking to investment bankers who focus on your industry; they can be valuable advisors since they often have initiated and negotiated many of these arrangements and will yield value many times their fees. Because you do not do these deals everyday, you should consider assembling a team of experienced advisors to help you. Investment bankers, corporate attorneys, market consultants, and others can offer invaluable advice in transactions that can make or break your company.

Knowing When to Back Out of an Alliance

Keep communication open. Identify any problems or issues early on in order to resolve them. Keep a written record to support your position on issues. Be creative to make it work, but realistically evaluate your business model needs. Be vigilant to stay on track with alliances that support those needs.

It is difficult at times to back out of an alliance because of either adverse public perceptions or elimination of valuable benefits. However, trust your intuition: if the deal does not feel right to you, there must be a flaw somewhere and you should not enter into it without substantial analysis.

Some reasons why backing out of an existing deal is necessary:

- The partner is not performing
- The partner is not effective in delivering the intended benefits
- A new, third party provides a significantly better proposition worth switching to
- A new, third party offers a deal which simply conflicts or is mutually exclusive in some way with your existing deal and forces a switch
- Your strategy changes either in technology, business model, or distribution; prior arrangements may become constraints to your future evolution

Should you need to back out of an alliance, to avoid bad faith make sure communication with your partner is open and honest . . . . Letting your partner know early in the process that things are not working well or as anticipated and documenting the process can help avoid surprises and ill feelings. Generally, a good agreement structure will enable you to "legally" exit. Your attorney may help here. However, this is a small world and if you have to end a relationship, do it in a fashion that preserves your ability to use the former partner as a reference, often a good test of how successful you have managed a relationship.

Transactions for Growth and Funding

Several ways to structure a deal

While each deal is different to accommodate the particular circumstance, consider a few guiding principles:

- A deal is an opportunity to get up-front cash to help you grow
- Nonrefundable royalty advances look like cost free capital to you and your investors
- The other party is a source of hard and soft assets to help you succeed
- Technical support and its costs can be the responsibility of the other party if the margins are not there for you to do it
- Deals with credible parties enhance your business in the eyes of investors
- Business risk can be shared between the parties so the Start up is not so heavily burdened

Phases of growth funding

Seed Funding. Seed funding is useful for financing your existence to prove your business concept. Typically, a milestone is a working prototype or successful first customer validation that they will purchase if you deliver a final product. This is the riskiest and most "expensive" capital to raise because the value of your business is the lowest it will be, assuming success.

Early Stage. Often called First Round financing, this stage finances the completion of your product and gets it to market in order to generate customers and revenue. A common mistake is to under-finance this phase. You may have heard the old saw, "It takes twice as long and three times as much money than we thought." You don't want a hiccup in this phase to force you to raise additional capital on weakness, at lower valuations. Depending upon where their stock option exercise prices sit, this can de-motivate your management team.

Consider business deals as early stage capital, as well. These can provide cash without selling equity (a percentage of your company). Early in your company's life, you may be more willing to cut any business deal just to survive. But keep in mind that what you want is probably achievable within reason without giving away the store. Sometimes you have to give something up to live to fight another day. Decent business people understand that you have to win as well. Because the character of the parties you are dealing with is paramount, always try to get references from other companies they have done transactions with to get a sense for how they support their "partners." Doing deals with strategic partners is important in funding your early stage growth in concert with equity funding.

When seeking equity capital at this phase, it is often wise to get more than one large investor so you can tap into a broader business network. Look at your investors as the most likely source of expansion capital. Because raising capital is often like a "full-time business" in itself to CEOs, having able and willing investors ready to go saves an immense amount of your precious time.

Expansion Capital. As your company matures and its cash flow become more predictable, you will have access to other forms of lower cost capital. Equity capital is the most expensive form of capital unless you are one of the fortunate few to be valued at astronomical "Internet" valuations. In that case, raising equity capital "while you can" at those high valuations should be a first priority because equity market conditions can change faster than one can react to them.

An expansion round of equity capital typifies many venture-backed companies who are still on a strong growth track and are net consumers of cash. Expansion capital generally focuses on cementing a market position relative to the competition and on driving revenues to a critical mass, the point generally where profitability kicks in.

Non-equity forms of expansion capital include:

- Bank lines of credit to finance receivables and inventories
- Equipment leases to finance office equipment and production equipment
- Long-term debt to finance growth assuming sufficient debt coverage (ability to pay the interest and principal) exists

Non-financing sources of operating capital are extremely beneficial because your revenue model can finance the company in whole or part and avoid equity dilution or interest charges. Royalty or license fee advances against future sales provide operating cash up front and reduce the need for other forms of financing. Alliances with larger partners can be structured so that initial payments help finance development. An important financing benefit comes from understanding how cash flows will work in your company and from being creative with contract structures.

Late Stage or Mezzanine Round. This final stage is typically designed to strengthen the balance sheet to give the company financial strength to continue its growth trajectory. Importantly, mezzanine rounds give the appearance that the company can operate for a long time with this capital base and that they don't really "need" to go public. This strength can help boost valuations for public offerings or acquisitions, which come after mezzanine rounds.

When to Take Outside Funding

If you have immediate growth requirements that internally developed cash flow or alliance deals can't fund, consider outside capital. Taking on financial partners is a large incremental responsibility, but they can help you achieve your market objectives faster with less risk and add significant value from experience and contacts.

If you remember the mantra "Never run out of capital," then always have enough to get to the next major milestone if you can. Financing milestones gets you to success faster and more predictably than struggling bit by bit on internal funds. Once you fall short in capital, and often it comes as a surprise, you limit flexibility and raise the cost of fixing the problem.

Investors, aware of this, can tell you many stories of how it took twice as much money and three times as long as planned to reach profitability or some metric of success. Outside capital can be useful not only for milestone financing but for retaining financial partners for the next round who can give invaluable business advice and contacts. Because raising capital takes an enormous amount of time away from running the business and working with customers, anything you can do to minimize capital-raising time is valuable.

One of the strongest reasons to take outside capital is simply to seize a competitive market position before someone else does. Since time is a critical success factor, outside capital can help compress time and arrive faster at your next milestone—as seen in the mega-venture deals happening in the late 1990s. Large venture funds need to deploy reasonably large amounts of capital per deal. And because they tend to invest together, the size of a financing can add up quickly depending on what the venture needs. Substantial capital enables large venture deals that can put a company on the map and into revenue producing position quickly before the competition. While megadeals are in the minority, they illustrate how entrepreneurs and investors look at growing enterprises in competitive environments.

12.3 Capital Ideas: Preparing for Venture Capital

—by Byron McCann and Theodore Feierstein
Ascent Partners, Inc.

Securing venture capital is effectively a sales process. You are selling your understanding of acute market need: meeting that need with a series of solutions leading to future, reasonably predictable cash flows. Investors want to understand how this works and how you are going to accomplish it. You want to know how the investor can help you achieve your goals as well.

But whether you actually raise venture capital, the discipline of preparing to do so will impose a powerful reality check on the adrenalized excitement of your new venture.

Preparing for a Business Plan

Raising capital is a communications process. The first step is usually providing a business plan unless you have some exceptional contacts and proven track record. Writing a business plan is a difficult but invaluable process. The process can also build excitement as you learn more about your market and what it needs. Should you learn that there are more competitors who are better funded than you were aware of, it can also be highly discouraging. Never deny a critical, negative market factor because you are too excited about being your own boss and getting rich.

To keep you on target, there is usually a way around that negative market factor that needs implementing before it is too late. On the other hand, preparing for capital but stopping the process if it does not look promising could prevent a tremendous waste of your time and career. You are probably creative enough to find a better idea if this one doesn't pencil out.

Planning for Venture Capital

You will hear that the top three reasons that a business failed is due to 1) lack of planning, 2) lack of planning, and 3) lack of planning. The best way to prepare for venture capital is to create a plan and know it cold. Investors will feel the confidence that emerges as you describe your venture. High confidence can be infectious and exciting to investors.

Writing a Business Plan

There are many resources for how to write business plans. A simple first source is your local university's school of business or the Small Business Administration. They have outlines and examples to review. You'll also find an excellent example in "Creating That All-important Business Plan" (Chapter 4.2). Or, seek out entrepreneurs who have successfully funded a business and ask them how they did it and how they addressed the business plan.

Business plans vary, so choose what is best for your enterprise. It's always a good idea to have several people review your plan to get various perspectives. Make sure your idea, the problem you are solving, and your product offering are easily understood. Investors, constantly reading plans, look for the essence as fast as possible.

Understanding Your Market

Investors want to see clearly that you know your market, what it needs, and how it is solving its problems today. This is all about meeting some form of need or want. It is not just reducing costs but meeting some need that the market "must" solve to evolve to the

"If someone gives you a term sheet, never accept 'standard' conditions. If the VCs got away with something in the previous deal, they'll pass it on as 'standard.' Be very careful on retaining any law firm that does a lot of business with VCs. Find one that will work in the best interest of the clients. For many law firms, entrepreneurs come and go. VCs remain the same. And, there's always another deal coming along."
—*Charles Crystle, Founder, CTO and Chairman of the Board, Chili!Soft*

next step in the business process. To the extent management has that nailed, investors will show enormous confidence in the team and will fund the solution at a good valuation. If they question whether you "get" your market's dynamic, its competitors, or products, they will not fund you—unless they are unsophisticated investors who can't effectively help you build an enterprise.

Getting Great People

Besides his own brilliance, Bill Gates excelled at building Microsoft by hiring great people. Knowing personal strengths and weaknesses, an entrepreneur can build a management team that rounds out an enterprise's capabilities—essential for success. Professional marketing, sales, finance, operations, and development talent are key. If you are the visionary type who has a good technical knowledge of the solution and has identified a market opportunity you are passionate about, you will probably need a good sales executive to drive the revenue side of the business and a detail-oriented operations person to help with day-to-day issues including finance.

Knowing Your Competitors

We frequently see good business plans and companies, but surprisingly they have little information at their fingertips on their competitors. Certainly a small company has to focus on delivering one thing well and let the competitors make the mistakes; however, lack of top-of-mind knowledge of your competitors is fertile ground for not optimizing your value proposition to the market.

Running a Tight Ship

Nothing contributes more to generating a sense of trust and professionalism than a well-run organization. How the receptionist answers the phone, how well you maintain financial and other records, and how organized you appear: these all give a sense you are on top of the situation and can be relied upon. Investors know that market conditions change and they don't fault management for it. However, they don't make bets on a management team they don't think understands market dynamics and can't respond quickly. You may hear the saying that investors "bet on the jockey more than the horse."

Keep appointments, stay organized, present information in a succinct and clear fashion, and clearly communicate your company's vision, mission, and needs. Investors should be impressed by your straightforwardness.

Keep in mind that investors will perform "due diligence" on you and your company.

Make this process as easy as possible for them and yourself by keeping up-to-date accurate legal, financial, personnel, customer, market, and product/technology documentation.

Being Fallible

Arrogance will turn off investors and much as confidence will turn them on. Because no one knows everything, remain intellectually open to others' ideas while holding on to your beliefs. Arrogance often translates into some form of blind spot, which will get the business into trouble somewhere down the road.

Investors are trained to find problems. While management is trained to find a way to make things happen or the "yes" in a deal, investors try to find the "no" in the deal. They try to understand risk and know something will go wrong. Those with entrepreneurial experience know this. They just don't know what will go wrong.

- Chapter 13 -

Manufacturing the Product

13.1 Software Manufacturing

—by Mark W. Meyer and Robert Unfug
PAC Services, Inc.

In-house vs. Outsourcing Considerations

Now that you have a product ready for market, you will need to decide where and how to produce it into a retail product. You will need to decide whether to produce it yourself or have it made by someone else. Many available suppliers can provide the complete range of services required should you decide to go that way.

You need to determine what the expected volume and duration will be for your product: how many you expect to sell and how long you will be able to maintain that volume. Experience shows that initial releases of new products are normally higher than the run rate.

You will need to fill the distribution pipeline as well as meet the initial demand: how long you have to get the product built and delivered from the time your software and raw materials are available. If you plan on using your existing employees to do the duplication and assembly, determine if they have the skills and time available to do so. You may want to hire someone to oversee the manufacturing operation and use temporary employees to do your work.

Outsourced manufacturing

The off-site companies may be a good choice to get started, or even for the long run. They have the facilities and resources available immediately to adapt to large swings in production needs. Whether you hire yourself or use Outsourcing or off-sites, you will want to evaluate their basic manufacturing skills. Besides the obvious assembly work, you should make sure that some type of quality assurance program exists to insure that your customers are receiving exactly the product you intended them to receive.

If you use a subcontractor (commonly called Outsourcing or off-site) to do all or some of your manufacturing, many companies can do just duplication, or assembly, or both for you. Additionally, some are capable of doing the purchasing and distribution functions. You should select the vendor that offers the combination of services that make the most sense to your company.

In-house manufacturing

If you decide to have your own production facility, one of the first concerns will be where to locate it. Software manufacturing requires a relatively large amount of space for the storage of raw materials and finished goods. It would be a good idea to talk with other established manufacturers to get an idea of space requirements before leasing. It may be possible to start in your garage, but at some point you will need to expand into commercial space.

Most software companies have a production cycle that starts with a large volume to meet initial demand and to fill the distribution pipeline. This is then followed by a decreasing run rate until a new update or version is available and then the cycle starts over again. Software development is notorious for slipping on its release to manufacturing dates. The slips can and will create large amounts of raw material problems as well as make labor planning difficult.

You may need to consider using temporary services to supply most of your assembly labor. If you do use temporaries you will still want to have a full-time person, or staff, that works for your company that will ultimately be in charge of your manufacturing operations. This person can also perform other functions such as purchasing, if you wish, but your product really needs to have a person who is protecting your interests. The best balance is to hire as many people as you will be able to keep busy year-round and then use temporaries to meet peak demand.

Equipment. If you have decided to start operations internally, you will need to get the appropriate equipment; you will need something more than a PC with disk drives for duplication. Only a couple of major manufacturers make quality media duplication equipment. After doing your research among other software vendors and manufacturers, you should arrange a meeting with the representatives of each supplier to find the model or size that will best suit your needs. Because this equipment can be very costly, you will need to consider various lease or purchase options (as offered by your bank or the manufacturer of the equipment).

You will also need equipment to analyze how the manufacturing equipment is performing as well as test equipment to do maintenance and repairs. Finding someone who understands and can maintain this equipment is vital to your business. If your product is delivered to your customers on duplicated diskettes, you will want to be sure they are duplicated accurately.

For an assembly surface, you can really use something as simple as a good strong table. You will want to make sure the work surface is at the correct height to prevent muscular strain or fatigue. Cushioned mats to stand on are a good idea also. If you plan on shrink-wrapping your product, you will need to find equipment suitable to your needs. This can range from a simple "L-bar" with a heat gun (for low volume production) to complete large scale "L-Bars" with heat tunnels and conveyer belts. The shrink-wrapping equipment can easily be leased from the vendors of the shrink-wrap itself. However, it does take quite a bit of time to get it in once it's ordered.

Warehousing. Your warehouse will probably benefit from a racking system (especially once your volume picks up) to store your raw materials and finished goods. The high cost of warehouse space nowadays makes it sensible to store as much as possible vertically. Once you have everything stored, you will also need to consider a lift truck (forklift) to retrieve and move materials. Of course all this can be sized to meet your individual needs. You may only need a small space for everything when you start. As your company grows, you can then keep adding on to it.

Purchasing

Your product may be as simple as a diskette in a shipping envelope or as complicated as many diskettes (and sizes), several manuals, collateral materials, templates, and a retail carton. Many of the subcontractors offer these "turnkey" services, but at some point in time you may decide to do your own purchasing. Either way, you need to manage the procurement of your raw materials in a way that will insure that you have the correct materials on hand, in the proper quantities, at the correct time, and at a fair cost.

You will need to set up a process that handles the administrative functions of purchase orders, receiving, inventory hacking, accounts payable, and rejects/returns. Many available PC-based software packages will do an excellent job of handling these functions. You can also easily do all of this manually, but for low expense a computer-based system would be desirable as soon as your company can support it.

13.2 Printing and Publishing

Printing

—by Mark W. Meyer and Robert Unfug
PAC Services, Inc.

It is important to understand the printing process since your product likely will include documentation and other printed materials. The process really starts with the creation of the text and artwork images that will be inside your manual or be part of your packaging or covers. These images (either camera ready artwork or electronic images) are stripped into film, the printing plates made from the film. Proofs made from the film can verify text and placement of images. Once these proofs, called "bluelines," have been approved, the plates are then attached to the printing presses and the densities of the inks are adjusted until the color and images are as desired. The desired number of impressions are printed, collated, bound, and trimmed to specifications.

The nature of offset printing requires a large amount of time preparing the plates and adjusting the equipment. Because of this, whether you want 100 or 10,000 copies, you face a large "fixed" cost to print something. For a "typical" manual, you could pay $125 each for 100 manuals, $30 each for 1,000 manuals or $3 each for 10,000 manuals. This price curve often forces you to purchase as many as possible to get the lower cost per unit, but don't let this be your only consideration when determining how many to buy. Many hidden costs, as well—such as storage, obsolescence, damaged materials—may add significantly to your printing costs.

If you feel your printing needs are in the 100 (or even fewer) copies range, don't despair. A recent innovation in printing manuals allows for "short-runs" of manuals at a cost-effective price. You may still have to print your covers in larger quantities (500 to 1,000), but the bulk of the text in your manual can be printed "on-demand" or "short-run." You order your covers separately and then order your manuals which will be bound in them. In the "short-run" system, you are limited to black text on white paper stock, but you can still apply screens and bleeds to dress up your documentation.

Please keep in mind that all these cost approximations reflect only the actual printing costs of the manuals. There are many "pre-press" costs associated with the film, places, and even the artwork. While many of these costs are difficult to estimate, they are real and do exist. It would be wise to do a complete budget and then have an outside "expert" go over it to make sure nothing is missing before committing to a printing job.

The approximate lead times for printed materials are listed:

- Manuals 4 to 6 weeks
- Corrugated products 2 to 4 weeks
- Templates 4 to 8 weeks
- Retail boxes 4 to 8 weeks
- Labels 1 to 2 weeks

These lead times count from the time you hand off your artwork to your printer. Establishing a good working relationship with your suppliers will enable you to reduce the lead times as well as to allow them to give you many good ideas for improving your printed materials.

Demand Publishing

—by Tina Charbonneau
First Image Demand Publishing

Demand publishing is a system of creating, maintaining, and distributing certain types of publications in the most cost-effective way. Demand publishing permits flexibility to produce short-runs, text changes on-the-fly, stress-free handling of unpredictable production loads, and inventory management. It utilizes a "Just-In-Time" delivery process for printed documents, best defined as "producing the smallest possible quantity at the latest possible time, eliminating inventory." When full-service demand publishing is in place, companies reduce costs, improve operating cash flow, and dramatically cut response time.

At a minimum, one should receive "print-on-demand" services. True demand print means output of original pages generally produced on high-speed laser printers. The industry standard for print resolution is now 600 d.p.i. This method offers several benefits over the old process of duplicating hard-copy "masters." It minimizes quality through higher resolution in both text and graphics, it eliminates damage to the master, and it provides more efficient revisions and faster turnaround. In order to take advantage of this service, you will need to provide electronic files in a format acceptable to the publisher. As an alternative, the publisher can scan existing hard copy documents to create electronic files.

On the basis of growing requirements in the industry, totally automated systems are available. From full-service demand publishers, you should expect value-added capabilities such as online electronic order entry and inventory, production and storage of component parts, full assembly, bindery, kitting, fulfillment, and worldwide distribution. Management reports tailored to your needs are a by-product of the best automated systems. Look for acceptance of your electronic media in a number of formats, such as data transmission, tape, or floppy disks. Once a document is in the system, you should be able to reorder it electronically, specifying the number of books and different locations to receive copies. Such systems mean faster turnaround and higher accuracy. They virtually eliminate the coordination of manual steps that most frequently produce errors.

Demand publishing eliminates problems—the high cost of short-runs, unpredictable print requirements, frequently changing text, too many vendors to manage, slow turnarounds, complex distribution, and delays to market. See it as a possible solution for your beta tests, new product documentation, training materials, technical bulletins, and directories.

13.3 Choosing Media

—by Mark W. Meyer
PAC Services, Inc.

Nothing spoils a good product like having inferior quality media fail while the user is installing it. To avoid this you will need a steady supply of high quality diskettes to put your software on. Of the many manufacturers of media to choose from, usually each manufacturer has identified a portion of the market to fulfill, so a little shopping around will enable you to find one willing to work with you.

Selecting Quality

Because all disks are not made the same, make sure that you are getting the quality level that you need for your product. There are ANSI standards for media, but many of the largest users don't rely on these standards alone. They usually upgrade to what is referred in the industry as "OEM Grade" media (with a 65%, or better clip rate). Those bargain diskettes you may be tempted to buy may not perform well in the long run, and it is your software that you are putting on them!

You will also need to determine the sizes and densities of diskettes to use by performing a market analysis. Due to demands by their distribution channels, some companies include both 3.5" and 5.25" media in their packages, while others include only a single media size. Your channel, or resellers, can help you in determining what size and densities are appropriate.

While many companies incorporate no copy protection schemes in their software anymore, you may want to consider using them. Serialization offers another way to verify authorized users for your product and may help your product support people in identifying licensed users while solving users' problems.

Nothing scares a software company more than hearing the word "virus." This simple item can destroy years and years worth of data as well as kill a market for a product that has been infected. Your entire company will want to be aware of viruses and to use good preventive practices. Virus checkers are available commercially as well as by shareware.

Quality Control as an Integrated Process

Whereas in older production manufacturing environments it was common to find quality control as a separate function, the notion of quality control as a separate function in today's manufacturing environment is archaic and often counter-productive. Separate quality control measures are often applied ad hoc to counteract difficulties found in manufacturing processes already underway. Even in situations where planning and foresight have been calculated, the role of QC is often seen as a secondary one, production's necessary evil. These attitudes and situations focus attention away from quality concerns rather than towards them; problems become a concern for QC to deal with rather that the production individual; errors are seen as personal attacks.

On the other hand it is possible to imagine an ideal group of highly cooperative and responsible workers, where the need for a separate quality process is minimal to non-existent. Somewhere between the two extremes lies the state of quality for any process:

High Cooperation	Low Cooperation
Integrated Quality Control	Separate Quality Control

The obvious goal, integration of QC into the process, is the basic idea behind all the "new" quality control plans (CWQC, TQC, etc.) coming out of Japan and found in modern industry. It invariably starts in production (Integrated QC) and ideally spreads outwards through the company (Company Wide QC), into the vendors (Total QC) and the economy.

A successful manufacturing environment will have incorporated elements of Integrated QC as an active component of the production process. Duplication operators, for example, must cross-check their work in entirely different computer environments. In addition to the normal verification percentage that is run concurrently, the software should also be checked, again concurrently, on host machines (IBMs, Macintosh, UNIX, etc.) This concurrent checking insures independent QC while allowing the job responsibility to remain with the duplication operator. It should be noted that Integrated QC in no way substitutes for or replaces other necessary and traditional quality assurance checks like those that take place in final inspection. It provides immediate and intimate error response to the person needing it the most: the employee directly involved in the process.

The industry needs Integrated QC as a building block to a more valuable product. Using the concept of Integrated QC, a company can assure itself of putting out the highest quality products possible.

13.4 Manufacturing Operations

—by Mark W. Meyer
PAC Services, Inc.

Staffing For Operations

While the Human Resources section of this book gives excellent insight into the hiring and staffing process, we will go into detail of the type of employees needed to competently staff your operations.

Unlike hiring on the technical side of your business, it is really hard to look at schooling background as a determining factor in hiring employees for the operations side. It is impossible to tell if that accounting major will work out or whether you should hire a more technically oriented person. Ideally you would want to bring on people able to grow with the tasks at hand.

Some of these criteria should apply in hiring operations staff:

Will you do most production in-house or outsource it? The person(s) you hire for production should either be able to manage an outside source or be knowledgeable to set up the systems needed to accommodate the growth you project for your company,

What will your production runs consist of? If your product is heavily oriented towards documentation, then that should be a strength you look for during the interview process. Determine what your product will consist of and then look for areas of needed expertise.

How much authority are you willing to let go of? This step will indicate the level of employee you need to bring in. Senior-level persons will get frustrated quite quickly in junior-level positions unless they see a chance for rapid growth.

Obviously you need to consider other criteria based on your particular products and situation. These concepts are provided only to point you in the right direction.

Note: Even the largest duplication and assembly operations use temporary workers. If you wish to consider this source please interview "temp" agencies carefully to make sure they understand your requirements thoroughly.

Leasing vs. Buying Equipment

Outside of financial and cash flow considerations, you should weigh other factors when deciding on leasing vs. buying equipment: obsolescence, expected usage of the equipment, type of lease, maintenance costs, as well as replacement costs.

Obsolescence plays a factor in the decision when the equipment is outdated and you're stuck in a lease for it still—or even when it isn't yet outdated and the lease runs out. Your decision is to terminate the lease (usually at a penalty to you) in the first case and, in the second, to purchase or re-lease the equipment. For example: PCs are usually out of date within months of purchasing them. Their useful life, however, can be years and years if assigned to the proper tasks in your organization and updated through hardware and software enhancements.

Consider the factor of expected usage of the equipment: if you are going to use the equipment heavily for a few months and then either sporadically or never after that, then you may consider renting the equipment you need for the short time you need it. Aside from the cash standpoint, you will also have the space and storage considerations once you are done with the equipment.

Maintenance can be rolled into a lease agreement quite easily. Then once equipment breaks down, you don't have the additional cost of repairs (unless the breakage comes as a result of misuse or abuse). If it is an electro-mechanical device (such as a copier for example), you may want to consider leasing with a maintenance contract rolled in.

The type of lease will influence your decision as well. One thing you should look for is an "out" should you need to upgrade the equipment, or even return it before the end of the lease. If you are upgrading equipment, most leasing companies will show flexibility if they are going to enhance their agreement with you.

Obviously buying all equipment is straightforward. Do talk with your accountant about the implications and tax issues before deciding on either leases or purchases of equipment.

Warehousing and Order Fulfillment

There are many options to consider when planning for warehousing and order fulfillment facilities:

- Do you handle it yourself?
- Do you work with a service provider that can handle it for you?
- How do you handle the volume of calls generated by your marketing campaign?
- What if your orders ramp up quite quickly?

These are among the many questions you will face when considering warehousing your product and fulfilling orders.

When doing it yourself, you complicate the task of leasing space. Not only do you have to have offices (and room for expansion), but you also have to plan for storage of your raw goods and finished goods. Then your success compounds the problem. As you sell more product, you have to order larger quantities of raw goods and also have to arrange for more room for finished goods.

Companies have successfully negotiated these waters before, making arrangements with landlords that accommodate growth without severely penalizing the tenant. Arrangements such as pocket space, set-asides, and larger facilities are pretty much standard among landlords that understand the software company's need.

Another alternative is to contract with a service provider for the warehousing and fulfillment services. Many companies in diskette duplication, printing, assembly, and packaging are more than willing to provide these services at a reasonable cost. Actually, some of them can build this into the contracts for their services.

Order fulfillment can be as simple as an account with UPS to a complete inbound order-taking department that processes the order through to completion. Be sure to be aware of the processes needed to handle customer orders. This function will start out simple at first: taking the orders and handling the shipping. But soon name capture as well as a demographic survey of your customers will become crucial to your marketing efforts. There is no better time to get this information than at the time the customer places an order.

So whether you decide to use a service provider or to do it yourself, keep a few basics in mind: make sure the systems are in place ahead of time to handle the volume (large or small); use the opportunity to capture customer names and demographic information to a marketing advantage; and plan ahead.

13.5 Checklists for Producing a Software Product

Quick Checklist for Producing a Software Product: Packaging

Does my product require a retail box? If your product is going to be distributed mainly outside of retail channels, then you may be able to get away with less than a standard SBS folding. Corrugated paper boxes may suit you well. Anything from 200 B flute Kraft to 175 F flute #1 white has been used.

However, if you are going into the retail channel, then you'd be better off going to a software outlet and looking at packages. Most retail companies do not like deviations too far from the norm in packaging. Standard in the retail channel is a multicolor SBS folding carton or a laminated corrugated product.

Do I need filler in the box? Most companies opt for something in the box to keep the parts (disks, manuals, registration cards) from sliding around. Filler also keeps the box from being crushed during shrink-wrapping or shipping. The most common filler is gray RJ33-100-800 open cell foam. The more ecologically conscious might use corrugated inserts. Styrene plastic trays may also be used: they fall into category #6 for recycling purposes.

Masterpack cartons. If you expect to have multiple sales to the same location and wonder how will you ship your product, you could combine the shipper box and the product box into one quality corrugated piece. If your volume warrants it, you may want to have a couple of sizes of shippers. A custom look will cost very little extra: to have your company name or product name or even a logo printed on two sides of your shipper box.

Quick Checklist for Producing a Software Product: Printed Materials

Determine how many copies of your manual you are going to need over a period of time. Then, depending on how often you update your manual and how big the print runs are, you need to decide between offset printing (cheaper in larger runs) and high speed copying

(can easily accommodate changes). You also need to decide how to do the cover. Anything from simple one or two colors to four-color process is possible, depending on what your market expects.

Quick Checklist for Producing A Software Product: The Diskset

What kind of disks will you need? The marketplace will determine floppy or CD-ROM and format (DOS, MAC, UNIX, Apple, etc.) of the disks for your product. However, you must determine the types of disks prevalent in your market and plan appropriately.

How are you going to package the disks? The traditional way is in a "Licensed Disk Package" (LDP) using a preprinted license envelope. The trend is away from this and to a sealed polybag. For larger volumes, this will make financial sense since the bags are purchased in rolls of 1,000 or more per roll. A sealed polybag should also cost less overall than the traditional LDP.

Printed labels on disks? Obviously one needs to label the disks in the diskset. If your volume justifies them, use preprinted. However, laser-produced labels will work as well. A number of disk duplication houses will produce printed labels on a pinfeed laser printer that look really good. For smaller runs of labels or for keeping the label SKUs to a minimum, laser printing should work well.

Quick Checklist for Producing a Software Product: Miscellaneous Printed Matter

If you add a registration card, thank you letter, catalog, or any other printed material to your product, you also need to identify the quantity as well as the printing method best suited to produce these items. Since anything you add increases the assembly cost as well, consider including some of these items in the manual itself.

Chapter 14

Making Use of Your Web Site

14.1 Internet Strategy and Building Your First Web Site

—by Mary Korman & and Bart Preecs
Sitewerks, A Bowne Company

Since the dawn of online commerce, software has consistently been one of the most popular products sold online. As a software startup, your company will be expected from day one to have both a presence on the Internet and a business plan to take advantage of the numerous opportunities presented by the net. The question you face is not *whether* to go online but how to approach it strategically and what to do once you get there.

Keep in mind that the process of building a Web site is very similar to building a software application. The same steps—research, plan, build, test, revise, repeat—are essential in both arenas. Use your knowledge of product development to guide you through the approach of building your first site.

The key concept is that your Web site should support your business, and not the other way around. Build the site to complement your business needs. Create an Internet strategy before you build a Web site. It is imperative to your success.

This section outlines the specific opportunities the Web presents to software entrepreneurs, components of Internet strategy development, process for planning development of your first site, criteria for choosing a Web development partner, and issues surrounding the build process and ongoing maintenance. It will offer a high-level approach to get you asking the right questions—of yourself, your audience and your development partners—in order to define what the Web will do for you.

For software startup companies, the Web offers many key opportunities:

- Researching customer needs
- Researching your current and future competition
- Selling and distributing products directly to customers
- Reaching new markets
- Serving and supporting existing customers

- Informing key audience (media, job candidates, investors, etc.)
- Managing partner relationships
- Forming strategic alliances

Remember, the Internet is more than just the World Wide Web. Your Internet strategy should cover how you use e-mail, documentation, or updates delivered by FTP or other creative tools. With this much effect on your operations and the software industry in general, your Internet strategy needs to be an integral part of your business plan.

Developing a strategy for the Web, we will focus on five steps to this process: setting strategic goals, analyzing your audience, and the answering the questions of selling direct, online support, and outsourcing.

Strategic Goals

For most software companies, the strategic goals of their Web sites could include things like:

- Increase sales through online commerce
- Control distribution through online downloads and registration
- Improve communication with resellers
- Enhance customer service with online technical support, surveys, loyalty programs
- Create a positive image for your companies among potential investors, employees, or other influential audiences

If you need help defining your goals, look at what your competitors—or companies you admire—are doing with their sites and decide whether it is appropriate for you. Don't think about tactics, yet; focus on what you want to get out of the site and not how you will do it.

With these high-level goals in mind, the next step in strategy development is to thoroughly analyze your target audience and any information you can gather about their online browsing habits.

While the general profile of the online buyer is already looking more like the general population at large, what matters most is what **your** target audience is doing. The more varied your audience is in terms of what they use—browsers, monitors, fonts, servers, connection speed, and color palettes—the more complicated your planning will be. The better you know your target audience, the fewer variables you will face, and the more likely you will be able to design and build a site your users will enjoy and will return to often.

Consider focus groups to learn what your target users really want. Follow up first with usability testing at the beta stage to find improvements before the site is launched. Later, more testing or focus groups can verify how well your site does with your audience.

Web-based Sales

The next key question to ask, a question that will not only affect your Web site but also your marketing strategy and your entire business plan, is whether or not you will sell your software directly on the Web. Even if you don't offer direct sales to customers at the start of your business, there are some related online marketing options that might be helpful to software startups:

- Offering downloads of trial versions
- Offering partially functional versions
- Offering some of your products for free

The issues surrounding Web-based sales and distribution are addressed in detail in other chapters (see Ch. 22.12, "Web-based Sales Strategies").

Selling direct via the Web raises a related question: How will you use the Web to support your customers and/or resellers? The post-sales support of customers and the ongoing support of resellers may be integral functions of your Web site. There is tremendous opportunity not only to leverage the interactive capabilities of the Internet to improve service but also to cut down on costs used by traditional means.

The last question in developing an Internet strategy is, what is the best way to get the job done? Will you develop your site internally or will you outsource? As Web site developers ourselves, we know we have an inherent bias on this question. Not surprisingly, we think you should build great software products and let us build you a great Web site.

You will probably have some very talented people working in your new company. But since the skills required to build a successful site are quite varied, you may not have all the skills needed. The list of required capabilities includes:

- internet graphic design
- user interface design
- multimedia
- usability testing
- programming (a host of languages including HTML, DHTML, Java, PERL, C++.... depending on your site's functionality)
- database development

- system integration
- quality assurance or testing
- project management
- hosting

Even if you already have these skills in-house, these talented people may already have more important product development responsibilities than developing or maintaining your Web site. Out-of-the-box HTML editor tools may help you build a small site, but they won't be much help if you decide you need a more complex site to meet your customers' needs.

But the choice needn't be all or nothing. A sophisticated development firm that has successfully tackled challenges similar to yours can work closely with your internal Internet team. An experienced team of Web site developers will know the best way to work with your internal people on your site's development, and they will know how to hand-off maintenance or further development responsibilities to your internal team in ways that make the transition as seamless as possible.

Even after you've worked out your strategy and chosen the people to do the work, you now need to develop a project plan. Does that sound familiar? Good Web site development requires lots of planning, just like good software development.

We worked on a project that was in the final stage of development when the team discovered that the particular kind of HTML they planned to use, Active Server Pages, was not allowed on the hosting environment. The site was not large and it took only a weekend's worth of work to recover from this oversight, but the failure to nail down this technical requirement could have been disastrous on a larger project.

We don't advise learning the hard way, as we did in this case. We see these as the main components of a Web site project plan:

- Determine your project goals and Critical Success Factors
- Pick a partner (if necessary)
- Develop design specifications
- Write navigation specifications
- Write technical specifications
- Develop functional specifications
- Test the plan
- Make hosting arrangements
- Promote the site
- Maintain the site

Site Building

The project plan is the first step in the site building process. If you have contracted an outside development firm, their work should start here. A Web site project plan lays out your site's architecture, look and feel, functionality, technical back-end, data model, timeline for development, roles and responsibilities of client and developer, detailed budget break-down, build specifications and transition plan. The entire development and hand-off process is designed and documented before the first line of code is ever written. No matter how large your site is, no matter who is building it, your Web site project is more likely to succeed if you take the time, at the outset, to ensure there are no surprises.

In contrast to your high level, Internet strategy goals, your site project plan must determine how you will measure success of the site. These goals are measured by metrics, or Critical Success Factors, and might include:

- number of downloads
- online sales
- use of traditional means of customer interaction such as 1-800 support service
- VAR relationship building
- brand recognition
- audience development

By identifying the metrics by which you will judge the results, you will be better able to determine whether you have reached goals to your satinfaction and to calculate the Return on Investment. Not only that, it will truly integrate the Web site with your business operations.

Define goals

If your Internet strategy includes hiring an outside firm to develop your site, don't choose that partner until you have defined the goals and scope of your project. It will be easier to choose the appropriate partner if you have your own set of criteria based on your defined needs. How you weigh different criteria such as stability, capabilities, culture, and cost, depends on your own business position, your priorities, and your project. Experienced, professional development firms offer a complete range of services and capabilities, along with strategic consulting to ensure you've thought of everything in your long term plans. As a general rule, look for a company with the following:

- Long term client references (check them)
- Specific experience in developing for your vertical market (look for software, hardware and other high-tech experience—and see if you like their style)
- Strategic consulting to complement and further develop your internet strategy

Be sure that they have all the expertise to develop your site within their office and that those resources are available. If they don't offer a particular service, or they have limited resources in one area, then beware—you could be charged extra for contractor services.

Of the many resources for finding Web development firms, online directories can be a good start, but you have to trust the source. Some "best of" listings are really advertisements, where firms have paid for their spot. The best solution is to ask around for referrals. Take a site you like and find out who built it by asking the company whose site it is. Interview several firms, check their references, and request proposals from the top three or four. Write a Request for Proposals (RFP) using what you already know—your goals, your audience profile, your criteria for development partners—along with any specific desired functionality, content requirements, internal resources, schedule, budget—to further define the project. Be prepared to offer some face time for each firm that is bidding on the project—it will add to the quality of the proposals you receive and ultimately to the quality of your project.

Write specifications

Next up is to write the specifications that detail the functional, design, navigation, and technical aspects of your site. The functional specification describes, in detail, the interactive features of the site. The navigational and design documents specify how to implement the functionality described in the functional specification document—the information architecture and graphical guidelines. The technical specifications summarize the back end. The test plan dictates how you will measure the site's performance before it is ready to launch—it will guide quality assurance testers with minimum browser and platform requirements and can also detail a usability test for beta development. These principles drawn from software development should be familiar to you.

The next part of the project plan should address the hosting arrangements required for your site. As a small, growing company, you may not want to host your site yourselves. Again, think about your core competencies. Choose an ISP the same way you chose a development firm—ask for references, interview several options, and put it out for bid. Make your decision based on your future traffic and technical needs—the last thing you need to do when your software becomes a roaring success is worry that your hosting arrangement is not adequate.

The project plan should also cover your post launch promotion efforts, including both traditional and online marketing. Having designed and implemented a highly interactive Web site doesn't mean much if no one knows you're out there. In order to get interconnected with your audience, you need to consider all the ways to incorporate your URL into your marketing efforts: make sure everywhere your brand touches, your site's address is referenced. In addition you will want to look at the specialized tools of online marketing.

The very last step in your project plan is to design a program for maintenance. Again, your options are internal or external resources, and costs relate to how often you plan to go through the evaluation and revision loop.

The actual process of building a Web site is the subject of shelves full of books at your nearest bookstore, not to mention a few silicon shopping carts online. Our favorites include "Creating Killer Web Sites," by David S. Siegel and "Click Here – Web Communication Design," by Robert Pirouz and Lynda Weinman. The steps below briefly outline the actual production process.

Assemble copy

Gather the text you want to include in you site. It's already written and of course it's been edited and proofed by a competent editor, right? What about multilingual needs?

Develop design, navigation, UI, templates, database (if necessary)

These are the key building blocks and your team will execute these steps in accordance with your plan, which will have covered everything that could go wrong in the production process. Right?

Test

In another parallel with software development, it's a good idea to set aside plenty of time for testing: test both multi-platform and browser, but also look for bugs, spelling mistakes, and broken links. It will be worth your while to test the individual components of the site as they are produced, even if you are testing on a local environment or a different server than you expect to use.

Assemble

As soon as the components are ready, you can start assembling.

Test again

Now you can really start testing. This time it's for real, and final testing should take place on the server that will host the site.

Launch

The key step here is the coordination between your development team and the people responsible for the server on which the site will run. With good planning and a bit of testing, there should be no surprises here.

Post launch

Although site launches are sometimes synonymous with quitting time, the time card isn't punched until a Post Mortem or Development Review is completed. Meet with the project team to discuss what worked well and what needs improvement. No need to make the same mistakes twice.

Evaluation

Research, reporting and metrics are integral measurements for the effectiveness of your site. If your server does not log the data you need, consider some tracking software. You should be able to get the following data about your site's visitors: where they are coming from, how long they stay, how they navigate, where they go, whether they follow a clear path, where they go when they leave. Seed the site with options like surveys and contests to entice users to supply valuable marketing data in exchange for a shot at a prize. Using this data, you can better understand your audience and fine-tune your site to more effectively reach the customers you want.

Maintenance/Revision

The data you gain is powerless if you don't use it. Maintenance includes not only keeping content relevant but also using the ongoing analysis of visitor data and structuring your future improvements around it.

Using log analysis, determine what's working and what's not, and make your changes accordingly. If banner ads are working, beef up on them. Clear up navigation if you find users don't take straight paths. Bring up popular areas closer to the home page. Most importantly, follow up on comments and questions that users have taken the time to write. By actively responding to the desires of your visitors, you can build your Web site into a productive information source.

Follow the common steps of software and Web site development—research your audience, plan before you build, test thoroughly, revise accordingly. When you approach the creation of your company's first Web site with the same strategic planning and disciplined execution that you bring to your product planning, your site will be a powerful tool to launch and support your business.

14.2 Total Customer Management:

Leveraging the Internet to Integrate Marketing, Sales, Service, and Support

—by Brian Janssen
Co-founder, Onyx Software

—by Brian Janssen
Co-founder, Onyx Software

Introduction

A key strategic objective of most software companies is to become closer to their customers, to take better care of customers in all departments, to create customers for life. Over the past decade, software companies have invested heavily in customer service systems, marketing systems, sales systems, and personnel. Despite these investments, most are still unable to maximize the value of their customer relationships.

To date, most software companies have attempted to better manage their customer relationships by automating existing departmental processes. The sales force is "automated" with laptops and contact management software. Technical Support implements its own system and database. Salespeople resell "blindly" to existing customers without being aware of their current service issues. Leads are not passed from service to sales because of the information system barriers. Product defect requests are lost in a chasm between service and engineering. Marketers struggle to gather customer information from various "islands" of data in incompatible information systems. Customers and revenue opportunities fall through system cracks.

Enter the Internet. For many companies, an immediate impact of the Internet was the creation of additional islands of disparate data deposited from a Web site, combined with ever-increasing customer expectations for immediate fulfillment. When combined as part of a holistic, customer-centric IT infrastructure, however, the Internet promises the progressive software company a rare opportunity to effectively and efficiently manage the entire customer lifecycle. At ONYX, we look at the customer lifecycle as a holistic, horizontal process (see Diagram 1). From this perspective, each department is a critical component of an integrated customer management process with responsibility for the whole— recognized and shared by the corporation. Each step in the process fosters the seamless transition from marketing to sales to service **and back again**. Each step in the process is clearly defined and related to corporate customer care objectives: to acquire low-cost, highly qualified customers to achieve marketshare objectives; to retain profitable customers; and to expand the business we do with current customers ("customer share").

"The Internet is a paradigm shift. A very real industrial revolution is occurring. It's a worldwide shift and companies have to make the transition to the Internet. There's a lot of issues that an executive team has to figure out."
—John Ballantine, Managing Partner, Chairman & CEO, iStart Ventures

Each step is managed within an integrated, customer information management system. Each interaction between ONYX and a customer provides an opportunity to add value to the customer relationship. The Internet enables us to deliver greater value to the most critical interactions we share with our customers.

Customer Acquisition

More than 30 percent of current ONYX customers first heard of the company through the Internet. In addition to being a major source of sales leads, the Web offers tremendous customer acquisition economies. For example, at a large industry trade show we typically gather about 500 qualified leads at a cost of $100,000, or $200 per qualified lead. Or consider direct mail, which traditionalists view as inexpensive lead generation. For ONYX, a recent $3 mailing to 2,000 targeted suspects yielded 30 qualified leads, again at a cost of approximately $200 per qualified lead. By contrast, the ONYX Web site (**www.onyx-software.com**) delivers at least 600 qualified leads per month, at a fully burdened cost of about $10,000 per month (less than $20 per qualified lead).

Prospects who first discover ONYX via the Internet are our best leads, our number-one priority. Not only are they low-cost, but within a properly designed process they are self-qualifying, the highest quality, and available in virtually unlimited abundance. To best describe our Web-based customer acquisition efforts, we separate them as follows:

- As a separate, distinct marketing program, to attract high-quality prospects;
- To support traditional marketing efforts such as database marketing, seminars, trade shows, alliances, public relations, and advertising; and
- As a sales-support tool, to reduce the length of the sales cycle, educate prospects, and bolster the effectiveness of the sales force by increasing close rates

The Web as a Separate Marketing Program

Many companies build their Web sites with little thought to first defining the target Internet audience and determining how to drive prospects to their Homepage. The only measurable success metric for many companies is the number of hits their sites receive. While that benchmark may make sense for a consumer-based business focused on branding, in a business-to-business selling model a random, nonmeasurable visit does little to ensure the effectiveness of a Web site. If we can attract prospects to the ONYX Web site, we feel that we can keep their interest with a compelling value proposition. Then, with an immediate, integrated process for rapid qualification, we can exceed the expectations of qualified prospects by providing what they want, when and how they want it.

Knowing Prospects

The first step in Web marketing is knowing your Internet prospects and anticipating how they will find you. It is a brave new world. The special audience of Web users are not "brandable." They don't respond to typical mass-marketing methods. They are very technology savvy, often falling into the "visionary" or early-adopter phases of the technology-adoption curve.

Attracting this type of prospect to a Web site is like waging guerrilla warfare. The Web marketer must anticipate where and how Web prospects will be searching. By listing ONYX product and company information in applicable search engines and solution directories using a variety of possible terms, we ensure that our site listing bubbles to the top of major search engines such as Excite, Yahoo!, Infoseek, Lycos, and Alta Vista. We try to understand each search engine algorithm and cater to it.

In addition, we try to anticipate a prospect's search patterns for similar products, including the names of competitors. Why not draft off the big marketing spending of your competitors by figuring out how to appear on the results list when they are found? Re-registering your URL with major search engines can be as easy as providing your URL or Web address. Their search "spiders" then visit your Web site and retrieve its text into their terabytes of indexed data. (If your Web site contains only graphics, the spider will be unable to index any meaningful content from your site.) Other sites such as Yahoo! invite you to supply the keywords that will link to your site. Buzzword-compliant descriptions attract far more people than making your positioning statement searchable to the masses. We constantly ask people, "What search sites and keywords were you using? How can we make it easier for you to find us?"

Identifying Prospects

After we lure prospects to the Web site, the second step in the Internet marketing program is to identify them. The challenge is to determine who they are and what they are looking for in what time frame. When a prospect takes the time to visit the ONYX site, it is our responsibility to present them with a compelling value proposition—to offer them something in exchange for the information they provide.

We believe that if a prospect is truly interested in our product, they will provide this data in exchange for educational value. To this end, we provide white papers, case studies, and links to industry research. In exchange, we ask the prospect to spend one minute and complete information contained on a three-part Web form. The first page of this form contains common demographic information (name, address, title, company name, phone, fax, e-mail, and Web site URL). The second page of the form presents the prospect with a list of collateral materials which they can have mailed, faxed, or e-mailed to them. The final page contains ten important identification questions which constitute the basis of our prospect quality rating, including:

- company information (number of employees, annual revenue, industry classification)
- which systems they use to manage customer information
- whether or not they are actively searching for customer management software
- which departments need a system and how many users exist in each department
- where they first learned of ONYX

Upon completion of this final page, the prospect is asked to submit the request to ONYX.

Gathering data on visitors to a Web site is common. But some companies ask for (and often receive) a host of information from prospects yet do little if anything to follow up promptly. The instant a qualified prospect interacts with your Web site, your company is presented with an opportunity to exceed their expectations.

Once a prospect "submits" Web information to ONYX, the real fun begins. The information is immediately populated in our customer database, and we instantly process requested faxes, e-mails, and literature. Based on the prospect's recently entered survey and demographic data, we generate a sales opportunity and a "pop-up" message for the internal sales team. For example, if a prospect is looking for 50 or more seats within the next 12 months, we instantly route a message to the regional telesales person. This telesales representative, having complete access to all of the data just entered on the forms, then calls the prospect and offers further assistance. In most cases the prospect is still browsing our Web site when this occurs.

In an independent test of Web responsiveness, Matterhorn Consulting, a customer management consulting firm in San Francisco, visited over 3,500 consumer and business-to-business Web sites asking for information through the vehicle provided by the site. None of the requests were in the form of unsolicited mail. After requesting the information, Matterhorn measured the speed, appropriateness, and completeness of the response. ONYX had the fastest response of the 3,500 companies tested, responding to the inquiry in 90 seconds.

"The average company surveyed responded in 15 days," said Barry Goldberg, president of Matterhorn Consulting. "There were only four same-day responses, and only two of those within an hour of the request. ONYX was on the phone before we were off their site. This kind of instant response should be the standard for companies who see themselves as customer centered."

Enhancing Traditional Marketing Programs

The Web has been instrumental in supporting and enhancing most traditional customer acquisition efforts. For programs such as alliances, advertising, public relations, and database marketing, the Web is an effective call to action, encouraging prospects to learn more at their convenience. For seminars and trade shows, the Web dramatically improves program execution and effectiveness.

Like many companies, pre-Internet ONYX struggled with high training seminar attrition rates. While response rates were encouraging (in excess of five percent), it was challenging to confirm, reconfirm, and follow through on all responses. With the Internet, most of that is automated. First and foremost, direct marketing efforts are now supported by making the call to action a visit to our Web site. While we still provide phone and fax numbers, as well as business reply cards, the focus is getting prospects to visit the Web site. There a prospect can learn much more about the seminar than can be presented on the mailer. Once at the seminar page, prospects are encouraged to register. As soon as prospects submit their registration, attendance is confirmed and confirmation materials and directions are faxed. If they indicate an interest but do not confirm, their response is used to prioritize telemarketing follow-up.

The next step is a completely "virtual seminar" model. Virtual seminars will enable us to "take control" of any computer in the world, educating people at their desktops with a complete multimedia presentation. These are supplemented by having current customers and industry experts "attend." Such virtual seminars offer great benefit to both ONYX (reduced cost and increased attendance of potential buyers) and prospects (eliminates travel).

Trade shows are the bane of existence for many software marketeers. Tremendous energies and resources are spent conducting the event; yet all too frequently a company's post-show response is less than energetic. Most companies scribble notes on business cards or card-scanner receipts. At best they manually import card reader output or enter leads in a prospect database, resulting in a delayed response often measured in weeks.

At trade shows we establish a direct link to our Web site. We swipe the cards of attendees and their card information immediately populates the first page of our standard Web lead form. Prospects are qualified as they talk with booth representatives and complete the remainder of the Web form (literature requests, notes, or specific instructions) in person. Their information is transmitted instantly via the Internet to our corporate customer database in Bellevue, WA. With real-time processing, requested literature is on the way to the prospects' offices from our corporate headquarters before the prospects leave the booth. It is also first on the prospects' desks when they return. Immediate qualification also guarantees that qualified prospects are automatically scheduled for immediate contact by their local ONYX sales representative.

Using the Web to Streamline the Sales Process

The Web streamlines the sales process in two main areas. First, self-qualified Web leads shorten the sales cycle and improve the close rate. Second, increased remote access capabilities via the Internet aid selling.

Traditional lead sources such as direct mail and telephone inquiries require significant qualification time by sales representatives, but Web leads are self-qualified and automatically delivered deeper into the sales pipeline. Telesales skips the qualification step and starts assessing the prospect's needs immediately. As a result, Web leads produce higher close rates and shorter sales cycles. Once we started receiving leads via the Web in 1996, our sales cycle was reduced from six months to four months.

As an example, Geir Ramleth, president of Genuity (a Bechtel company) in San Francisco, needed a sales force automation solution for his Start-up. Searching the Internet for suppliers, he came across the ONYX Web site. He registered as an online guest, requested additional product information, and provided contact information, number of employees, sales volume, and buying timeline. While he continued to explore the site, his assistant brought him a fax of the ONYX customer case study he had just requested online. Moments later, he received a phone call from ONYX's regional sales representative to explore his specific requirements for a solution. Impressed by this Internet-enabled responsiveness, Ramleth moved quickly through the sales process, becoming an ONYX customer eight days later.

The advent of cellular-based Internet access provides companies with even more leeway in accessing sales information at anytime and anywhere. For example, through a partnership with AT&T Wireless Data Services, marketing, sales, and service information is accessed via a cellular phone Internet browser. As an example, our most qualified Web leads are also sent to the cellular phone of the local sales executive. The ultimate level of sales responsiveness is achieved when a prospect self-qualifies via the Web, and while still browsing the Web site receives a "page" from their reception desk stating that "a sales representative is here to see you about your recent interest in their products."

The Internet also provides important interactive communication capabilities at all points in the ONYX sales process. For example, salespeople can perform "live" initial product demonstrations remotely with Microsoft's NetMeeting. This tool helps shorten each step in the process. This tool is also used to finalize contract agreements online, eliminating "fax volleyball" between ONYX and a prospect. Such interactivity reduces the sales cycle, decreases travel and communications expenses, and most importantly provides increased convenience to the potential customer.

Customer Retention

Once we have turned prospects into customers, we provide them with exceptional customer support to ensure that we keep their business for life. Effective delivery of customer support via the Internet can yield significant benefits:

- a reduction in the number of incoming telephone calls, often the most expensive way software companies provide support
- reduced staffing and overall support infrastructure
- increased customer satisfaction and retention because customers can get support problems diagnosed and solved quickly, at any time, and from any location

To realize these benefits we need to know our customers so well that we can anticipate their support needs with information and tools on our Web site. The Web-based support experience should be no less satisfying to the customer and no less effective than speaking directly with a customer service representative (CSR). At ONYX, more than 40 percent of current support issues are managed via the Internet.

Our efforts at continuing to grow this rate include:

Online Incident Creation and Management. The typical software support cycle involves incident creation, diagnosis, and solution. The customer will normally call customer support by telephone, wait in a queue to be connected to a CSR, and explain the problem while the CSR logs the problem. If the issue is complex, the CSR will research the problem and call the customer back later. In the meantime, if the customer wants to know the status of the issue or wants to add additional information regarding the issue, he or she will need to call again and wait in the queue again to be connected to the CSR—who may or may not be available.

ONYX customers can log a support incident directly from the ONYX Web site, eliminating the need to call to speak with a CSR directly. This capability not only saves the customer time, but it makes it convenient to interact with our CSRs at any time and from any location. Customers are also able to read work notes on their support incidents (if made customer-viewable by the CSR) and even add comments or information directly to a support incident.

Online Diagnostics and Problem Resolution. A key differentiation between effective and ineffective Internet support is the ability of a customer to use the Internet to quickly and properly diagnose and solve the problem. To provide volumes of information is not enough—to exceed customers' expectations, you must provide them with the tools and information they need to solve their problems and get back to work quickly. This requires not only technical information and KnowledgeBase articles but also an easy-to-use structure and diagnostic tools. The support choices or information an ONYX customer sees are based on the customer's unique registration profile. Using information in the customer's profile, diagnostic "wizards" help the customers quickly navigate through available information sources to diagnose and solve their current issues. These and subsequent product enhancements are driven by the goal of reducing the number of steps in the problem diagnosis and resolution process.

Product Enhancement Requests and Quality Assurance Issues. In many software companies, enhancement requests and QA issues drop into a black hole. When we receive these requests, we automatically attach them to the customer's record in our customer management application so that we can respond to them directly. When action is taken on the request or if the status changes, we automatically send an e-mail update. If a fix is made available, we either send it automatically to the customer, or we send a notification and a hyperlink to a download section on our Web site. In addition, we publish current enhancement requests and bug reports in a "customers only" section of our Web site so that customers know that their feedback is important and have continual visibility to our progress with it.

Customer Expansion

The third and final way ONYX uses the Internet and the Web is in marketing new products and services to existing customers to expand customer share. Our products have been purchased by many hyper-growth companies and our goal is to grow proportionally.

A private area of **www.onyxsoftware.com** is maintained only for ONYX customers. There, customers can catch up on company news, upcoming user events, product release schedules, new product features, and session notes from past customer conferences. The information is filtered based on the customer's record to ensure its relevance. For example, when logging in to our user's page, a customer from the United Kingdom is notified of our upcoming International Customer Feedback Roundtable meeting. Other customers can access a download area for fixes, patches, and templates, and discuss implementation options and best practices on dedicated newsgroups.

A problem many software companies face is identifying a customer's right to support. ONYX uses the Web to ensure complete and accurate product and customer registration. When customers log into the Web support site, we first verify that their companies have up-to-date maintenance contracts. If their maintenance contracts are current, they proceed directly to their support page. If not, we inform them that their support policy has expired and provide instructions for renewal.

We seek to avoid situations where customers need support but are unaware their support contracts have expired. On the individual customer's support page we post reminders of the soon-to-expire maintenance contract and we e-mail the primary support contact 60 days before the end date. By being proactive, we have kept a 100 percent maintenance renewal rate.

The Internet offers plenty of cross-selling and up-selling opportunities. ONYX's goal is to have all customers use our products in all departments. Based on the detailed profile information we capture on customers, we can recommend new or additional products. For example, if an ONYX user has more than three support incidents of type "user error," we recognize this as an opportunity for training, and we e-mail the customer a list of training classes (or make this information available on the Web support page) and send an alert to the ONYX account manager for the customer. Our continued efforts in this area will be the smartest and most efficient way to meet the company's expansion goals.

Referrals for new business from existing customers have also been an effective part of the Web-based marketing mix. We actively promote a customer-referral incentive program to our customer base and utilize an easy, Web-based form to capture not only the prospect's information but also the referring individual's information. This is promoted on our user Web page.

ONYX Software has invested significantly in our customer acquisition, retention and expansion efforts. It is hard work, requiring continual process analysis, refinement, and investment, but it pays off. Technology, however, is no panacea. Applying technology to poorly defined marketing programs may result in generating fewer qualified leads, or worse yet, more unqualified leads.

If your company delivers poor customer service, Internet enabling may do nothing more than allow you to deliver terrible service faster. If your company, however, is committed to providing Total Customer Management by integrating all marketing, sales, and service efforts around customers, the Web can greatly enhance customer interactions.

14.3   Web-based Marketing: Getting Started

—by Jim Shanklin
Ryan-Shanklin Ltd.

"Web-based marketing"—the term seems to epitomize the New Age of marketing: global customers from the start-up software business. But the phrase begs for some perspective on the wide range of businesses that it encompasses. Does it apply equally to software developers, media and entertainment companies, retailers, and Web developers; or do some aspects apply to some businesses and not to others? This section will attempt to identify some similarities, define some differences, and offer a basic overview for young companies involved in all aspects of software and Web-based businesses.

The Web Marketing Context

Internet journals and publications describe a growing understanding and acceptance of three concepts for doing business successfully on the Web: Content, Community, and Commerce. These linked concepts apply to Web-based marketing, irrespective of the type of product or service a company offers. Further, these terms help define some of the challenges, pitfalls, and potential successes possible through the application of good marketing practices to the unique environment of the Web.

Content. How do we make the content on the company Web site relevant; frequently updated; succinctly presented; and most importantly, of value to the user?

Community. How do we recognize our audiences as a community? How do we recognize the exponentially increasing micro-segments of interest around ever-tighter community identities? How do we foster community around prospects, customers, channel partners, and other visitors who will return benefits to a Web business?

Commerce. How do we create the sense of security among customers so critical to allowing commercial activity? How can we initiate E-commerce on the low budgets of a start-up company? How can we provide sufficient information or samples to prospects without allowing competitors in the door?

One-to-One Marketing

This is no cliché. Successful Web-based marketing requires an understanding that the customer is king; not only king, but also judge, jury, and executioner for Web businesses that refuse or are slow to recognize this fact.

Unlike any marketing context to date, the Web puts all decisions in the hands of the customer. The customer:

- chooses to come to the site
- decides to stay at the site, based upon its Content
- decides to engage in Commerce
- voluntarily goes through the steps required to make the purchase
- decides whether it is worth the effort to return for a second purchase, or for customer service information, or for a sense of Community

It's Still Marketing Basics

Ironically, because the Web is changing so rapidly, and customer expectations are changing with it, the basic blocking and tackling of marketing is more important today than before. Success in Web-based marketing ventures depends upon an understanding and a consistent execution of basic marketing steps.

Plan

Decide why you're doing this. Be sure you have a clear answer to the "Why?" before launching into Web-based marketing.

- Is your business Web-dependent?
- Are you providing a value-added service for your channel relationships?
- Are you setting up a customer service site to allow "ultimate feedback" from customers?
- Are you setting up a retail business?
- Are you a media company, seeking to tap the growing need for entertainment, travel and leisure content?

If the answer is not crystal clear, you may not have a compelling reason to adjust your business to the demands of the Web.

Identify your audience. Who is the customer? Web-based marketing demands that the customer, and the customer's customer, be identified and provided for on the Web site. A two-step distribution channel offline becomes one-step online. One-to-One marketing rapidly takes on new meaning for companies beginning to market on the Web.

Set objectives. What does the Web-based business intend to achieve? What milestones have you set to measure achievement? The answers may define the site itself, let alone how the site looks and feels and what services are available on the site.

Define your strategy. How will you achieve your objectives? If you have offline distribution partners, how will you overcome their inevitable territorial reactions?

On the Web, evolution is a daily process. How will the strategy evolve from early stage, to mid-stage, to the mature company you hope to create?

Execute

Once your plan makes sense, implement it. The work you put in on the marketing plan will pay off now in a big way. The Web is a place of consummate action, and "Ready, Fire, Aim" is too prevalent. With the advantage of a good plan, you can fire at will, with strength and certainty. Make adjustments as you continue to execute. You'll find customers and channel partners surprisingly patient at small setbacks on your part, if you communicate with them quickly and candidly.

Evaluate and apply what's learned

Marketing on the Web is like building the bicycle while you're riding it. As you learn what doesn't work, make changes on the fly, communicate the changes to your customers and channel partners, and move on to the next stage. Once on the Web and doing business, your prospects, customers, and channel partners will reward action and punish inaction. So don't delay in changing what doesn't work.

Avoiding Pitfalls

Marketing on the Web is so much about the customer that your customers and potential customers may provide the best help you could ask for in avoiding pitfalls. Ask them for their opinions. Ask before you launch the Web site. Ask after the site is launched. Ask when they place an order. Ask when the order is delivered.

If your business uses the customer or channel partner as a reference, you can avoid problems like the examples below, or remedy them very quickly.

The Web site that talks to itself

A surprising number of sites make it difficult for customers to find what they want. The site is not "About Us"; it's not "Our Philosophy"; it's not about the myriad number of other self-talking site segments that too often play a prominent role on the index page and other pages of a site.

Test your site structure with customers, close suppliers, or relatives before you launch.

A difficult ordering process

If your objective is to sell products, services, or merchandise, make it an easy process. Too many Web businesses make the process difficult whether by providing or requiring too much information, by putting in too many products, or by complicating the navigation path from product selection to purchase. The customer lost through a frustrating purchase process is a very tough loss.

Test your order process with customers and channel partners. Let them tell you it's easy or difficult. If it's difficult, make it easy.

Poor customer communication

Most surprising of the many research reports available from the Web are those that detail the many instances of nonresponse by Web businesses to customer inquiries through e-mail, or even through forms provided on the business's Web site.

You won't find a more receptive potential customer than one who takes the time to ask directly about a product or service you offer. An immediate, candid response can create not only a customer but also referrals to other potential customers.

Poor customer service

Even more surprising, in a large number of documented cases a Web marketer provides little to no effective customer service on the Web site. An 800-number can support direct e-mail customer service; it cannot substitute. Designate a specific individual for customer service in your company. Identify the customer service resource on your Web business by name, even if it's only a first name.

Great customer service creates new business; poor customer service kills existing business. It seems an easy choice.

Getting Started

If you're planning an E-commerce Web site, or converting an informational site to E-commerce, here are a few ideas to help make your Web marketing experience a good one.

Get help

If your site is up, ask people to critique it for usability and incorporate their suggestions into the site or its revision. Repeat the review process for your E-commerce section.

If you're about to build a site, consider outside help. A great software developer is not necessarily a great Web site designer. You might be able to trade product, consulting, or other services for assistance from a Web developer who will bring your business a dispassionate third party view.

Promote your business

Don't stop with search engine promotion. Use mutual linking, alliances, affiliations, and online and offline public relations to get your story out onto the Web. With 1 million URLs registered, the Web is not waiting for the next one. Give your best efforts to making your site and your story a memorable one.

Listen to customers and channel partners

Your best sources for improvement are the people who buy your products and services, both in the channel and beyond it. Nothing creates more loyal customers or distributors than asking their opinions and then making changes based upon their input. It's a timeless strategy for building business.

Identify who will be the customer service contact

This point can't be overemphasized. Prepare for more business than you'll get in the short-term by having excellent customer service, even one person, in place and trained when your Web marketing efforts are launched.

Summary

We hope that you take away one or more helpful ideas from this section. We've intentionally offered a broad overview of concepts and ideas that have been useful to us in marketing our own business. The three closing thoughts we'll leave with you are basic to the marketing process, on the Web or off the Web: Make your plan; work your plan; remember that the focus is customer, customer, and customer.

(See also Chapter 22.12 — "Web-based Sales Strategies")

■ **Chapter 15** ■

Hiring Employees

15.1 People Development

—by Mark Berry
Davis Wright Tremaine LLP

For most businesses in today's economy, the greatest resource is the employees, the human resources. This is particularly true in good economic times where the supply of qualified workers cannot meet the demand.

Studies often demonstrate that one of the most frequent reasons employees leave an organization is their sense of being at a "dead end" or of not being challenged or motivated by an ineffective manager. Therefore, to maintain a stable, qualified and productive work force, businesses must place a priority on their "people development."

Innovative "people development" must focus in two directions. First, businesses must help individual employees to develop new skills or enhance existing ones. This keeps employees challenged and able to adapt as the company's products and services change. It also readies them for promotion away from a "dead end" for their careers. Second, businesses must create work environments that are stimulating and filled with mutual respect and admiration. The sense of teamwork and that one's work is appreciated helps the employee to remain motivated toward the company's goals and interests.

Advancing Individual Skills

A business can help develop an employee's personal skills in a number of ways. These include (1) in-house or vendor training programs; (2) industry seminars and classes; (3) courses or degree programs at local colleges. Initially, managers must discuss skill development with each employee as part of the evaluation and goal-setting process. The company and managers can then identify useful training or education programs and provide the time and money to attend the training. An education reimbursement plan is often a valuable benefit.

At the conclusion of any course of study or seminar, the company should then work with the employee to apply the course materials in the work setting. In this way, the company receives a benefit of the new knowledge or skill and further cements the relationship between employee and employer.

Creating a Stimulating Work Environment

Creating an environment in which employees want to work begins with ensuring that business has an overall philosophy about its human resources. Consider describing the company's ideal workplace as part of the company's overall mission and vision. Involvement of the employees in this process improves its chances of success.

Managers should be trained to understand and strive to meet the ideal work environment described in company goals. The company should then evaluate manager performance against the philosophy. Individual managers must be well trained in delegating, providing feedback, setting performance standards, and encouraging teamwork. Even where individuals have been promoted to supervisor or managerial positions because of their technical proficiencies and not their management abilities, solid management training can smooth some of the edges.

Furthermore, managers need the tools to develop the teamwork and camaraderie necessary to achieve the company goals. Common approaches include departmental or company retreats and social events. Managers should also consider involving employees in other company activities, including new product ideas, recruiting, and retention. For these efforts, a stable, committed, and productive workforce will be the reward.

15.2 Conducting Effective Interviews

—by Jack McHale
McHale & Associates

In the hiring process, it is important to develop a foundation of facts supporting a candidate's experience, abilities, and intelligence.

Résumé

The process usually begins with the résumé. A chronologically arranged résumé is preferable as it allows the interviewer to gain understanding of the candidate's career in a logical, time-sequenced manner. The résumé should be concise and well written, in the third person, contain a job objective, an explanation for each position of size of budget, number of people reporting, supervisor, clarification of technical skills, educational information, and, if the candidate wishes, some personal information. The content of the résumé helps set the agenda for the interview.

Job Description

Further structure for the interview is provided by a well written and detailed job description, which provides the yardstick against which candidates are measured. Many job descriptions unfortunately contain superfluous and generalized information. A good description should include reporting relationships, remuneration information, brief profile of the organization, span of management, major areas of responsibility, required experience and skills, education requirements, and personal characteristics and management style.

Interviews

The two basic types of candidate interviews—screening interviews and selection interviews—may be directive, characterized by a series of structured questions with the intention to precipitate factual answers; or nondirective, characterized by a series of open-ended questions intended to draw out the candidate's subjective responses. Good interviewers use both techniques.

After initial screening, the interviewer should determine whether the candidate fits the "culture" of the organization. A vague concept, understanding corporate culture determines whether the candidate is likely to fit the organization. Meshing with company culture contributes to maintaining employee morale and low turnover rates.

Establishing the Facts

The interviewer should look specifically for responses that reflect a work history predictive of success in the new position, exploring academic preparation and preferred work environment and gaps in work history. Management style and training should blend with the company's style. The candidate's career goals should match the position. Leadership abilities, although sometimes difficult to measure, should be assessed. Communications ability, interpersonal skills, work ethic, and technical abilities should be analyzed and compared with those of other candidates for the position. The candidate's salary requirements should be known.

Qualifying for the Position

The interviewer should observe the candidate's speaking and listening abilities, intelligence, enthusiasm, attitude, demeanor, attire, confidence, knowledge of the organization, logic in answering questions, and demonstrated ability to ask insightful questions. The manner in which a question is answered may provide more insight than the content of the answer.

Technical Skills

If the position is intrinsically technical, the interviewer should qualify a candidate on general criteria and permit a technical person to qualify the candidate on technical skills. Interviewers should be objective and aware of their own limitations.

Pitfalls

Anyone who interviews a job candidate should know federal and state laws governing hiring practices. The prudent interviewer will avoid personal questions, as well as questions concerning race, religion, national origin, marital status, sex preference, and physical disability. The potential liabilities are significant for breaching these laws.

15.3 Preparing for Questions Asked by Applicants

—by Jack McHale
McHale & Associates

A good interviewer knows the history of the organization, the hiring practices, and benefit packages and has a significant understanding of information contained in the annual report and other company publications. Interviewers should be prepared to answer questions such as the following:

Regarding this position:
- What are some of the characteristics needed to succeed in this position?
- To whom does this position report and who reports to this position?
- What are the peer positions?
- How will my performance be evaluated?
- What are the opportunities for advancement?
- What is the salary range for this position?

- Who held this position previously and where is he/she now?
- How much travel is there with this position?
- Could one have a home office in this position?
- Are there any skills I am lacking to perform this job?
- Are there many other candidates for this job?

Regarding company policies:

- What are the company rules for the use of alcohol, drugs, and smoking?
- What is the company vacation policy?
- Will the company pay for further education?
- What is the company's relocation policy?
- Could you explain the stock option plan to me?
- What is the ethnic makeup of the work force?
- What is the expectation for attire?
- What is the company sexual harassment policy?
- Do you have a day care center?
- Is there an executive development program?
- Is there a succession planning policy in the company?

Regarding the company:

- What are the greatest challenges the company faces in the near future?
- Who is the company's strongest competitor and why?
- Could you describe the culture of this company?
- What is the financial condition of the company?
- What is the best thing about working for this company?
- Who is the largest single stockholder?
- Does the company have a community outreach program?
- Does the company have an investor relations department?
- Is this company unionized?
- Has the price of the stock fluctuated much during the past few years?
- How profitable was the company last year?
- What is the worst crisis the company has faced?
- What goals has the company set for itself and how does it plan to achieve them?

15.4 Hiring the Right Person for the Right Job

—by Jana Steffen
Amazon.com

Today's job market is tough for employers, especially those who are looking for high tech talent. Sourcing for positions alone can seem like looking for a needle in a haystack. After finding those scarce candidates, one must then decide which to hire. This gamble is often more art than science. Yet, some guidelines for you to follow will increase your odds and help you hire the right person.

Know What You Are Looking For

Identify the skills, qualifications, education, qualities, and attributes that will enable the person to be successful in the job. Identify the main responsibilities, the type and scope of decisions, the critical activities of the position, and the percentage of time spent on each activity. Determine the minimum skill set, depth of knowledge, and experience needed to meet these responsibilities. Develop a complete profile of the ideal candidate; distinguish between the minimum level of experience and skills necessary and the ideal. Then specify the top three qualities and attributes that will fit well with the culture of the work group and the company. For example an individual who is highly adaptable, flexible, and likes working with short timelines would thrive in a fast paced environment.

Think Twice Before Compromising

Once it is clear what you are looking for, be careful not to compromise on those aspects critical for the success of the position. When you are pressed to fill a position quickly, it can be tempting to settle for less experience, fewer skills, or fewer critical attributes. Bringing in someone with the right attitude but not enough experience may work if there is time and the staff to train the new hire.

The most common compromise often concerns not the skill set but the qualities and attributes. The candidate is an ace on the technical skills but lacks some of the attributes that you are looking for (e.g., team player, interpersonal skills). Unfortunately, these areas you are least able to change. You can always train new skills but find it difficult to modify core behavioral characteristics. Adding a person to your staff who is not going to work well with the team can cause tremendous strife and may even result in the loss of other good employees.

Allow Appropriate Time to Find Your Candidates

Finding good people can take time—be prepared. If you are trying to fill a senior-level position or a highly skilled technical position, be prepared to search for at least four to six months, if not longer. Searches for senior-level positions can often stretch into a year. If time is not on your side, consider filling the position temporarily through a subcontractor or a consultant, thus allowing the time to find the right person.

Take the Candidates Through a Comprehensive Hiring Process

Conduct solid interviews that identify past accomplishments, the scope and depth of past job responsibilities. Include behavioral questions that focus on how they have resolved past issues. Ask for specific examples and how they handled the situations. Have several people interview the candidate to give you additional perspective and insight. Be sure to provide the other interviewers the proper set of questions; be sure they've been coached on how to conduct an interview.

Give the Candidate All the Details

When we find our ideal candidates, we may be tempted to downplay the less glamorous aspects or the tough challenges of the job for fear of losing them. This information is necessary both for the candidates and for you to assess if it is a good match. While describing the less glamorous aspects, carefully watch the candidates' body language; if they are still leaning forward and demonstrating excitement, you know they are up for the mission. If they are disengaging, leaning back, or giving you a look of trepidation, then the position is probably not for them.

Identify the limitations of the job. Is there room for growth within the position and the company? If growth is important to the candidate, this will be an issue. If the position requires relocation, is the candidate really prepared to move? Is the new location similar to the candidate's current situation? Being clear on the details will help both parties determine if it is a good match.

Don't Let First Impressions Fool You

The book can have a great cover, but what's inside counts the most. Remain objective when making your decision. It is easy to "fall in love" with a candidate and overlook the red flags. Whatever your first impression, spend the time during the interview to disprove that impression. For example, if your first impression is favorable, look for weakness in skills, experience, or any factors that may place candidates out of the running. If your first

"There are three waves of employee growth: the first wavers work on the cool stuff. The second wavers expand on the vision, and the third wavers maintain it and keep the company running smoothly. It takes all kinds to make it work. It's important to keep the first and second wavers actively engaged. In some companies, the first wavers leave. Our strategy has been to keep them, to put them to work on cool projects."
—*Bill Baxter, President & CEO, BSQUARE*

impression is unfavorable, look for strengths, good qualities, and any factors that keep them in the running. Soon the candidates' strengths and weaknesses will unfold, making your decision easier.

Conduct Thorough References

Candidates should be able to supply the names of past supervisors and team members. Confirm the candidates' information. Find out how they did their job and how they interacted with others. Listen carefully to the responses to the questions. It is not so much what people say but how they say it. If you are not able to get a reference, leave a message stating that you are considering an individual for a position. Ask the reference to call you back if they enjoyed working with the candidate and would like to work with them again. Most people will call you back if the candidate did a good job.

Listen to Your Intuition

If you are deciding between several candidates and you feel one of them is perfect but there is a reservation that you can't quite put your finger on—listen to your intuition. Go back and review all of the candidate's information. Double-check for red flags. Ask the candidate more questions in the areas you are uncertain about. More often than not, you will identify something that was overlooked, confirming or disproving your gut feeling.

Pay Attention to the Red Flags

As you go through the hiring process, pay attention to the red flags. Some common red flags are:

- Gaps in employment without sufficient reason
- Negative attitudes toward past employers, supervisors, and coworkers
- Incomplete, circular, or verbose answers to questions
- Incomplete applications and inconsistent information between the application and the résumé or the reference
- Lack of accomplishments in positions, especially management positions
- Resignation without giving two weeks notice
- Getting fired from a job (explore as much as possible in these cases)
- Discrepancy between the candidate's ideal work environment/culture and your work environment/culture
- Difficulty in providing references, especially past supervisors

We never really know how candidates will perform until they actually start working. But you can make some very good, educated decisions that will increase your probability in hiring the right people. Set your standards high and hire the best, because outstanding people build outstanding companies.

(See also Chapter 22.3— "Sales Recruiting")

---

15. 5 Exempt vs. Non-Exempt

—by Jennifer Wright
Davis Wright Tremaine LLP

Though each state has different statutes dealing with minimum wage provisions, many employers must comply with the minimum pay, equal pay, and overtime provisions of the federal Fair Labor Standards Act (FLSA).

Each act, however, categorizes certain classes of employees as exempt from the requirements of the act. Because each exemption is narrowly defined under the law, an employer should carefully check an exemption's exact terms and conditions before applying it. In addition, under federal law, employers must comply with state or local law if that statute in ordinance is more favorable to employees. Consequently, although an employee may be exempt under the FLSA, the employer may still be required to pay overtime or minimum wage under their state's applicable Minimum Wage Act.

Exemptions under the FLSA

Several classes of employees are exempt from FLSA rules: executives, professionals, administrators.

Executives

Employees whose primary duty is to manage an enterprise or department or subdivision thereof and who customarily and regularly direct the work of two or more employees are exempt as executives. Bona fide executives must also have the authority to hire or fire or recommend hiring or firing and must customarily and regularly exercise discretionary powers.

Bona fide executives must also receive a salary of at least $155 per week and must spend more than 20% of their time on nonexempt work. If the executives work in the retail or service industry, they may spend up to 40% of their time in nonexempt work and still retain the exemption.

Additionally, if executives receive $250 a week or more in salary, then it must only be shown that their primary duty is to manage an enterprise or department or subdivision thereof and they customarily and regularly direct the work of two or more employees are exempt as executives. This is referred to as the "short test" for high salaried executives.

Professionals

Five basic categories of professionals are considered exempt under the FLSA:

- Employees who perform work that requires knowledge of an advance type in a field of science or learning, customarily obtained by a prolonged course of specialized instruction and study
- Employees who perform work that is original and creative in character in a recognized field of artistic endeavor and the result of which depends primarily on the employee's invention, imagination or talent
- Employees who teach, tutor, instruct, or lecture in the activity of imparting knowledge and are employed in this activity as a teacher either by certification or recognition from the institution at which he or she is employed
- Employees who perform work that requires theoretical and practical application of highly specialized knowledge in computer systems
- Employees who perform work that is predominantly intellectual and varied which cannot be standardized in point of time

Bona fide professional employees must also consistently exercise discretion and judgment. Additionally they must spend less than 20% of their time each week in nonexempt work and generally must be paid at least $170 a week. However, if the employee is paid more than $250 a week, then the 20% rule does not apply, and you need only show that the employee's primary duty is professional work requiring discretion and independent judgment.

Administrators

Employees in the four basic categories of exempt administrative must all regularly exercise discretion and independent judgment and must have authority to make important decisions. They must also be paid more than $155 per week and spend less than 20% of their weekly hours in nonexempt work, unless they work in a retail or service establishment, in which case they are allowed to spend 40% of their time in nonexempt work.

As with executives and professionals, if the employees are paid more than $250 a week, then the percentage limitations do not apply. The four general categories of exempt administrative employees are employees who are primarily (50% or more) engaged in work of the following type:

- Office or nonmanual work relating to management policies or general business operations of the employer or the employer's customers
- Regular and direct assistance of a proprietor or an executive or administrative employee
- Work under only general supervision along specialized or technical lines, requiring special training, experience or knowledge
- Special assignments and tasks under only general supervision

Management Trainees Are Not Exempt. The exemption for executive, administrative, and professional employees does not extend to workers in training for those capacities and not actually performing the duties of a full-fledged executive, administrative or professional employee. However, a full-fledged employee does not lose his or her exempt status merely by undergoing further training.

Outside Salespersons. Employees who regularly sell or obtain orders for goods or services wholly off the employer's premises are exempt from the minimum wage and overtime pay requirements of the FLSA. The exemption applies only to salespeople who are customarily and regularly engaged away from the employer's place of business in making sales of goods or services, the services to be performed by others. The time that can be spent by salespersons on the type of work performed by nonexempt employees is limited to 20 percent of the hours worked in the workweek, except for the work that is incidental to his or her sales or solicitations, such as clerical duties, deliveries, collections, travel or attending sales conferences. Trainees not actually performing the duties of outside salespersons are not exempt.

Other exemptions under the FLSA

A number of other exemptions and special provisions apply to certain employees. A list of such employees follows; however, employers with employees in these categories are advised to check the details of the provisions:

- Certain employees in computer-related occupations that receive at least $33.48 per hour or perform certain specified work
- Employees of seasonal amusement or recreational establishments that do not operate more than seven months in a calendar year or during the preceding calendar year, and whose average receipts for any six months of such a year were not more than 331/3 percent of its average receipts for the other six months of the year. (This exemption does not include persons employed in a National Park or Forest under a contract with the Secretary of the Interior or the Secretary of Agriculture.)
- Employees of weekly, semiweekly or daily newspapers with a circulation of less than 4,000, where the major part of its circulation is within the county where the newspaper is published or in the counties contiguous to it
- Switchboard operators employed by an independently owned public telephone company that has not more than 750 stations

- Seamen employed on foreign vessels; employees engaged in fishing operations; farm workers employed by anyone who used no more than 500 man days of farm labor in any calendar quarter of the preceding calendar year
- Casual babysitters and persons employed as companions to the elderly or infirm
- Certain criminal investigators
- Any employees exempted, pursuant to a U.S. Department of Labor regulation order or certificate

Exemptions From Overtime Provisions Only. Some employees are required to follow the minimum wage provisions of the FLSA, but are exempt from the overtime provisions. These include:

- Certain highly-paid, commissioned employees of retail or service establishments; auto, truck trailer, farm implement, boat or aircraft sales workers, or parts employees and mechanics servicing autos, trucks or farm implements, and who are employed by nonmanufacturing establishments primarily engaged in selling to ultimate purchasers
- Employees of railroads and air carriers, taxi drivers, certain employees of motor carriers, seamen on American vessels and local delivery employees paid on approved trip rate plan
- Announcers, news editors and chief engineers of nonmetropolitan broadcasting stations
- Domestic service workers residing in the employer's residences
- Employees of motion picture theaters
- Agricultural workers
- Outside buyers of poultry, eggs, cream, or milk in their raw or natural state
- Employees engaged in the processing of maple sap into sugar or syrup
- Employees engaged in transportation of fruits and vegetables
- Certain employees of public agencies
- Foster parents
- Certain forestry workers
- Certain national park employees
- Certain criminal investigators

Tacking Two or More Exemptions. As a general rule, FLSA exemptions for individual employees are figured on a workweek basis. An employee covered by the statute must be exempt during a whole workweek or he or she will have to be paid the wages specified in the statute for all of the hours worked, including those devoted to exempt work. If an employee spends the whole week on exempt work, but does work falling under two or more exemptions, government enforcement officials permit "tacking" the exempt work so as to form a combination exemption.

NOTE: The following section applies to laws governing the State of Washington to give the reader an idea of other relevant provisions on the state level; consequently, it would be prudent to check your own state's handling of these provisions.

Exemptions under the Washington Minimum Wage Act

Washington State generally follows the FLSA exemptions for executive, administrative and professional employees and outside salespeople for both minimum wage and overtime. Washington law regarding the "outside sales" exemption, however, expressly requires employers to advise such employees of their status as outside salespeople.

Other Exemptions to Washington's Minimum Wage Requirements Include:

- Individuals employed as hand-harvest laborers and paid on a piece-rate basis who commute from a permanent residence to a farm and who have been employed in agriculture less than 13 weeks during the preceding calendar year
- Individuals employed in casual labor in or about a private home, unless performed in the course of the employer's trade, business, or profession
- Individuals employed in activities of an educational, charitable, religious, state or local government body or agency or nonprofit organization where the employer-employee relationship does not in fact exist or where the services are rendered to the organization gratuitously
- Volunteers
- Newspaper vendors or carriers
- Carriers subject to regulation by Part 1 of the Interstate Commerce Act
- Individuals engaged in forest protection and fire prevention activities
- Individuals employed by charitable institutions charged with child care responsibilities engaged primarily in the development of character or citizenship or promoting health or physical fitness or providing or sponsoring recreational opportunities or facilities for young people or members of the United States armed forces
- Individuals whose duties require that they sleep or reside at their places of employment or who otherwise spend a substantial portion of their work time subject to call and not engaged in the performance of active duties
- Residents, inmates or patients of a state, county or municipal correctional, detention, treatment or rehabilitative institution
- Individuals who hold public elective or appointive office of the state or a county, city, town, municipal corporation or quasi-municipal corporation, political subdivision or any instrumentality thereof, or any employee of the State Legislature
- Vessel operating crews of the Washington State Ferries operated by the Department of Transportation
- Individuals employed as seamen on vessels other than American vessels
- Learners, apprentices, messengers employed primarily in delivering letters and messages and the physically or mentally disabled, if, for these groups, the Director of the Department of Labor and Industries issues a special certificate

Other Exemptions to the Overtime Payment Provisions in Washington Minimum Wage Act:

- Certain highly paid retail commission employees who earn at least 50 percent of their earnings from commissions and who earn at least time and a half minimum wage for *all hours worked*
- Seamen on American vessels
- Seasonal employees employed at concessions and recreational establishments at agricultural fairs if the period of employment does not exceed 14 working days per year
- Motion picture projectionists, if covered by a contract or a collective bargaining agreement which regulates hours of work and overtime pay
- Truck or bus drivers subject to the Federal Motor Carrier Act, if the compensation system under which the individuals are employed includes overtime pay reasonably equivalent to that required by the Washington Minimum Wage Act
- Individuals employed on a farm in connection with soil cultivation, raising or harvesting agricultural or horticultural commodities, including raising, shearing, feeding, caring for, training and managing livestock, bees, poultry, and fur bearing animals or wildlife, or in connection with the operation, management, conservation, improvement or maintenance of the farm, its tools and equipment
- Individuals employed in packing, packaging, grading, storing, or delivering to storage or market or to a carrier for transportation to market any agricultural or horticultural commodity
- Individuals employed in commercial canning, commercial freezing or any other commercial processing, or with respect to services performed in connection with the cultivation, raising, harvesting, and processing of oysters on or in connection with any agricultural or horticultural commodity after its delivery to a terminal market for distribution for consumption
- Any industry in which federal law provides overtime payment based on a workweek other than 40 hours
- Employees who request compensatory time off in lieu of overtime pay

- Chapter 16 -

Retaining Employees

16.1 Training and Continuing Education

—by Karina Miller
WASSER, Inc.

Bleeding-edge, fast-paced, highly competitive . . . how does a company succeed in this environment?

The market for customers and employees is as competitive as ever. If you want the best products, business strategies, and customer service, your company needs the ability to learn fast. If you want the best people, your company needs to offer the opportunity for people to learn. Salary and stock options may snag top performers, but what they can learn while working for you will give you the edge in hiring, ensure that people perform to their maximum ability, and let you hang on to them.[6]

Successful companies like Bay Networks, Xerox, 3Com, and Texas Instruments provide 10 to 20 days per year of training to their employees and spend between $1000 and $20,000 per employee.[7] That's a lot of time and money. Maximize your investment in training and development by following eight steps to designing a winning learning strategy.

Make a Commitment to Learning

Learning happens all the time, but effective learning takes energy, time, money, and commitment. Most people are just too busy. In almost every organization, human resources are the most expensive resources. The return on the investment in human resources will depend largely on your company's level of commitment to learning.

Create Alignment

Vision, values, mission, and goals—providing the best ways to make sure everyone in the organization is rowing in the same direction—are the most important things to teach your organization. Your commitment to learning should also be incorporated into your vision, values, mission, and goals. Create team and individual goals that map to the overall goals of the company. Or, as Stephen Covey would say, "Begin with the end in mind."[8]

---

6 William J. Smith, William J., "Winning the Battle for Key Talent,", *Washington CEO Magazine*, (February 1998).
7 Fawn Fitter,, Fawn, "Annual Training Survey", *Computerworld, Inc.*, (1998).
8 Steven Covey, Steven, *The 7 Habits of Highly Effective People: Powerful Lessons in Personal Change*, (1990).

Create a Learning Environment

Think of your biggest learning experience. Chances are it involved a mistake that you made. Some of our best learning comes from mistakes. Organizations tend to make the same mistakes over and over again because people are afraid to admit their mistakes and point out the mistakes of others. An effective learning environment values listening over talking, questions over answers, mistakes over perfection, and learning over knowing. Peter Senge has pioneered an entire movement to create a "learning culture" in the business arena.[9] Top companies such as Hewlett-Packard, Coca-Cola, and Proctor & Gamble create learning cultures that give them an edge over their competition.

Identify Core Competencies

The core competencies of your company form the foundation of your product or service: how you meet your customers needs and how you make money. The people who contribute to your organization need to have the competencies that will support the overall competencies and goals of the company. Identifying your company's unique core competencies constitute the first step in designing a training and development plan tailored to your company's needs.

Do a SWOT Analysis

Just as companies need to identify strengths, weaknesses, opportunities, and threats, so do teams and individuals. Identify team and individual Strengths, Weaknesses, Opportunities, and Threats in relation to the goals and core competencies needed. This needs assessment should take place during recruiting, interviewing, and reviewing— projects, peers, performance—market analysis, and obtaining feedback from customers. Individuals and teams should track areas for improvement on a continual basis and use this information to create and update effective development plans.

Create Effective Development Plans

Each team member should have a personal development plan that will contribute to personal career growth as well as meeting the goals of the company. Personal development plans can include brown-bag lunches, computer-based training, video training, reading books and magazines, attending professional association meetings and seminars, volunteer work, working with mentors, teaching others, and taking on new projects that will require learning.

---

[9] Peter Senge, Peter, *The Fifth Discipline: The Art and Practice of the Learning Organization*, (1994).

Track the Results

To ensure that your investment of time and money is getting the results you need, be sure to carefully track training and the associated costs in time and money. Then determine the net gain in individual and company performance and results. For example, by providing 132,000 employees 40 hours of training per year, Motorola saw a 139% rise in productivity in five years.[10] Track how your training and development efforts specifically contribute to each of your company's goals.

Be a Leader

Teach and inspire others by being a true leader. Share your personal development plan with the people on your team. Tell stories about you, your company, and where you want to go.[11] Be willing to admit your mistakes live-time and ask questions to learn from those around you. Be willing to learn from everyone in your organization, not have all the answers. There's no better way to get what you want from others than to set the example.

Any company faces the challenges of keeping up with rapidly changing markets, technologies, and competition. Exercising your learning strategy gives your organization the muscle needed to beat the competition. So, be sure to "sharpen the saw" by taking time for learning.

16.2 Employee Retention and Motivation

—by Rita Ashley
Rigel Executive Search

We are tempted to look for easy answers when it comes to employee retention and motivation. We want to know what perks, benefits, or rewards motivate our staff and encourage them to stay. In one sense, the answer is simple, but the implementation of the solution is comprehensive. *Employee retention begins with hiring the right people and setting reasonable expectations.* Retention is strengthened when employees are treated with respect and allowed to

"We have built an environment where people feel valued and respected. Apart from the financial, it's got to be the corporate culture that keeps people interested. Our core value is: respect is deserved and disrespect is earned."
—Bill Baxter, President & CEO, BSQUARE

---

10 Christina Novicki, Christina, "Best Outreach: Homegrown Mindware," *Fast Company*, Issue 5.
11 Elizabeth Weil, Elizabeth, "Every Leader Tells a Story,", *Fast Company*, Issue 15.

succeed. Employee motivation comes from the feeling of being a valued part of the success of the company. Perks, benefits, and special programs are secondary. People do not stay with a company based on its "trash and treasures." The following ideas are a compilation of input from CEOs of companies with low turnover and decades-long experience working for and with leaders in high technology as well as 12 years recruiting for high tech companies.

Hiring

Companies with low turnover tend to have a long hiring process. They are willing to spend the time and the money to recruit good people who will add to their corporate culture as well as their bottom line. They involve people from various parts of the company in the interviews, and they court serious candidates over meals where all can let their hair down, where first impressions have a chance to give way to data and chemistry.

Once hired, the employees are greeted by already familiar faces and they begin their job with support from many who have a vested interest in their success. While hiring is covered in depth elsewhere, these things have a strong bearing on retention and motivation.

1. Make sure objectives (not the "how" just the "what") and priorities for the position are clear to both candidates and interviewers.
2. Be clear on who makes what decisions and what resources are available.
3. Establish a metric by which success will be measured.
4. Convey the company mission statement and corporate culture.
5. With senior or executive candidates, involve the significant other.
6. Review compensation, bonuses, stock options and profit sharing in-depth, setting expectations of what is reasonable for the future. Discuss company exit strategy and company financing (VC, bootstrapped, angels).

Respect

People want to feel proud of the company they work for. Establishing a corporate culture known for treating its people with respect and encouraging creativity go a long way to retaining employees when the chips are down. As any young company will experience a bump in the road, loyalty established as a covenant makes it easier for employees to "just say no" to other opportunities. Demonstrating your company has a real commitment to each employee and her/his career serves as valuable currency in retention. While individual management styles may vary, the suggestions that follow have been shown to keep turnover low.

1. Keep employees informed to discourage gossip and anxiety. Hold company-wide meetings, including remote sites, discussing company successes, challenges, and programs for removing roadblocks. Talk consistently about company mission, business strategies,

and goals. Make sure employees understand they are the keepers of the culture.

2. Stock in the company provides a "we" feeling that *every* person in the company should share. Make sure everyone knows how stocks work and what drives tech stock pricing. "High stock price = high growth = rapid change = discomfort at work" is an equation everyone needs to understand. Since most high tech companies provide no retirement plan, providing stock options, stock purchase, profit sharing, and matching 401k plans is critical. Companies that give stock options as compensation *and* bonus are viewed as valuing their staff.

3. Make efforts to educate employees, a clear indication employees are valued.

4. Acknowledge accomplishments of teams and individuals company-wide.

5. Provide business cards for every person in the company. This small gesture goes a long way to promote "ownership" of their responsibility and of their pride in the company. Each person becomes a PR professional for your company if they understand the mission statement, your business, and their role.

6. Put in place and use a mechanism for dealing in a constructive way with failure. Get rid of "bad apples" quickly. The other employees will appreciate it. Show compassion for those having a difficult patch.

7. Establish a contract with each employee for long-term career growth with milestones, rewards for success, and objective measures.

8. Involve all employees in the solutions to the hard problems. Listen to their ideas. One VC Start up presented the issue of tight budgeting. The staff decided to restrict raises to 5% until profitability. Make certain everyone has a voice, but also make certain to base decisions on fact, not emotion.

9. Share with every person in the company the opportunity to meet the customers. Engineers frequently complain that they are kept away from the people they create for. Seminars, training sessions, user group meetings, and industry shows provide opportunities for exposure to your customers. Each employee can talk about "my" company.

Ownership is not just stock options. Since most companies provide them, they are less a "gating" item than we would like to believe. Ownership in the project, solutions, and company are also important: if employees feel valued, they will stay. Communicating value extends from clean bathrooms to well-lighted parking lots. It is less important to have baby nursing rooms and video games than to have reasonable work schedules and ownership.

People Want to be Successful in Their Work

The more your company provides resources for success, the stronger your retention rate will be. Work together to create solutions, goals, and priorities. Make clear what resources are available, what milestones will be rewarded, and what role each person has in the overall success of the product/company. Establish from the outset the part they "own."

The single biggest reason technical professionals change jobs is because they do not feel appreciated, do not feel that their work is valued. Projects are cancelled, reorganization occurs without consulting the employees; they are spread too thin so they can't do a terrific job on any one project; they feel no one is listening; they are not made privy to why decisions which affect them are made and commitments are not kept. For developers, add to this list that the feature set or product options are increased with no change to the schedule, no participation in creating the schedule, and no influence on the resulting unreasonable expectations. They also complain that when the feature set is not frozen early on, the quality of the product suffers, and they are not proud to be associated with the project.

It is not uncommon for high tech employees to feel the grueling schedules and unreasonable deadlines are due to understaffing whereas the founders feel it is because they are a start-up. The company feels they can't afford more staff. Meanwhile, the employees burn out and quit the company, leaving the company with the horrendous expense of finding qualified candidates, the loss of those individuals' work, and the ramp-up time and drain on the organization when new people start.

This pattern puts pressure on other employees to pick up the slack. Since they are already overstressed, the problem expands. Simply put, it is far less expensive to hire the right number of people than to replace them at critical points. Budgeting for recruiting and hiring adequate staff during funding not only easily remedies this problem, it effectively shows people your company cares about their success.

Most complaints can be eradicated with good communication, planning, and clear expectations. Bottom line: people want to be included, to know what is shaping the corporate destiny, and to know that the part they play is valued. The secret to retaining and motivating employees can be reduced to a bumper sticker: Value them and they will stay.

16.3 Planning Compensation

—by Joe Vershueren
Image X.com

There is certainly no more complex and sensitive issue in recruiting, motivating, and retaining quality employees than compensation. Many companies are penny-wise and pound-foolish when it comes to compensating their employees. Salespeople are reputed to be greedy, motivated only by money. The fact is, as several studies have shown, salespeople may differ from other employees in the amount of risk they are willing to take, but they are like every other type of employee in wanting more than just dollars as a reward for hard work.

Compensation takes many forms and has many different ways of being calculated. How you structure the compensation for a salesperson will be largely dictated by the type of job performance and behavior you are looking for. Keep in mind that this salesperson you are hiring, a key addition to your team, generates new revenues: the lifeblood of your company's survival.

If you plan that these people will develop and implement your sales strategy, you may want to have them take a cut at developing their own compensation program. If you determine that it is a win/win situation for them and your company, then they have already begun to do what they were hired for—relieve you of having to manage the sales area and free you to get back to where you should be spending your time in strategic planning, raising capital, or new product development.

As a general rule any sales compensation package should have four elements: a base salary, a performance package, equity participation, and benefits. How much weight you put into each of these will depend on what your company can afford, what you are trying to motivate this person to do on a day-to-day basis, and what long-term goals you and this person have set for them within the company.

We won't attempt to be too specific, but here are a few comments on each element:

- Base salary will be based in large measure on a person's experience and how the performance package is structured. Most salespeople look at their targeted yearly earnings. They will take a low base if the upside potential looks good.

- The amount of weight placed on a performance package is driven by the way you want to motivate your salesperson, the economics of your business, the length of your sales cycle, and the amount of experience your company has in selling your product. Performance packages, in the form of commissions or bonuses vary greatly in how they are calculated and how often they are paid varies: the closest thing to "rocket science" in American business. The uniqueness of your business will almost certainly assure that you can't use someone else's formula.

- Equity participation can have many forms. If this salesperson is going to help you grow the sales organization in your company, consider making growth a strong part of the compensation package, helping you to recruit someone with the type of experience you need but can't afford. For salespeople whose main responsibility it is to sell, equity will be less of a motivator.

- Benefits mean as much to salespeople as they do to you. Benefits may mean more if you are trying to attract a mature candidate than it will for attracting younger candidates who have no family responsibilities. Don't overlook the attractiveness of alternative work styles: telecommuting; flex hours; flexible workweeks. Many salespeople are more productive in a less structured environment.

Don't be misled by myths about salespeople who spend time playing golf instead of working. If you structure the compensation package that bases the weight of salespeople's income on revenue generation, you don't have to worry about how much they apply themselves. You can add additional motivation with an unconventional work environment, making your company a fun place to work. No employees like to work for a company where they are made to feel that they have to punch the clock.

■ Chapter 17 ■

Disciplining Employees

17.1 Managing Difficult Employees

—by Mary Drobka
Davis Wright Tremaine LLP

Most "difficult employees" present a supervisor or manager with either performance or misconduct problems (and sometimes both).

Regular performance appraisals and progressive discipline are a supervisor's or manager's most effective tools for dealing with difficult employees. Progressive discipline, up to and including discharge, should also be considered when addressing misconduct.

Performance Appraisals

Written performance appraisals or evaluations are one of the most important tools for addressing performance strengths and weaknesses. All too often, however, supervisors are not candid in either the grades or narrative comments given on performance evaluations. They also tend to delay or avoid completing the evaluation forms.

Open, timely communication is the goal of any good performance appraisal system. Remember, few employees are all bad or all good. An evaluation should deal with all aspects of an employee's performance. The evaluation can be the first step or further documentation of continuing attempts to deal with a difficult employee's work performance problems. If an evaluation is intended to become part of the progressive discipline process, make sure that this fact is clearly documented on the evaluation form.

Essential job functions. To be effective, the evaluation form should reflect the essential functions of the employee's job and should require the supervisor or manager to evaluate the employee's work performance against these functions. The best forms not only require a supervisor to grade the employee's performance but also provide narrative comments or explanations to justify the grade given. The narrative comments also provide a good place to document that the employee has been advised of what needs to be improved and the consequence of not improving (e.g., no pay increase, no promotion, further discipline, or discharge).

The difficult employee often challenges his or her performance evaluation. Thus, the more objective the supervisor or manager's evaluation can be, the less likely the employee can excuse away shortcomings. A supervisor or manager who expects such a challenge can also plan ahead by attaching documentation to the evaluation form which confirms the deadlines which were missed, the coding errors that were uncovered, the sales figure which fell below target, or similar performance problems.

Prepare carefully. Careful preparation can also significantly help the supervisor or manager through the evaluation session, especially with a difficult employee. Know the employee's job description and evaluate performance against the essential job functions, not personality. Evaluate the person's performance during the entire review period, not just the last few weeks or months. Have someone in higher management review the form before it is shared with the difficult employee, not only protecting against later attempts to appeal the grades to a higher level of management but also reassuring the evaluator that he or she is not being too hard or too soft on the employee.

The supervisor or manager should schedule enough time to do the evaluation session. When evaluating a difficult employee, choose a neutral location like a conference room, or if the employee has a private office, use the employee's office. The supervisor or manager should also have a plan and stick to it. Do not argue with the difficult employee over your decisions and do not agree to change grades (at least during the evaluation session). Give specific examples to support the grades given and seek the difficult employee's input as to why his or her performance problems are occurring. If the employee disagrees with your assessment, encourage the employee to put his or her comments on the section of the form that is designated for employee comments. If the employee refuses to sign the evaluation, simply note that on the form and conclude the evaluation session.

Progressive Discipline

Along with regular performance evaluations, progressive discipline provides an important tool for addressing both performance and misconduct problems. The basic purpose of progressive discipline is to inform employees about how their job performance is unsatisfactory or how their conduct in the workplace does not meet employer's standards or expectations. It is important that a supervisor or manager not delay disciplinary action. Prompt notice to the employee demonstrates that the employer is trying to give the employee a chance to change before performance or conduct problems become more serious. Remember, if a supervisor or manager fails to tell an employee that the level of performance or certain conduct is unacceptable, the employee will assume it is acceptable.

Progressive discipline needs to be applied equally among all employees, preferably in a positive way. Its elements generally include:

- Specific notice about what the problem is and how the employee needs to improve
- A reasonable time period to demonstrate improvement
- A clear statement as to the consequences of not improving
- A written documentation of the discipline
- Regular monitoring of the employee's progress after he or she has been disciplined

Special Considerations When Dealing With Misconduct

A supervisor or manager should carefully and thoroughly investigate the facts before deciding upon and sharing a disciplinary decision (like a written warning, suspension, or discharge) with the employee. Have a higher level manager review the investigation and proposed disciplinary action before the decision is implemented. When meeting with the employee, summarize the facts as you know them and give the employee the opportunity to tell his or her side of the story. If necessary, delay discipline if further investigation is necessary. Whenever nonemployees are involved (like customers), try to obtain written and signed statements. If a company rule is violated, attached a copy of the rule to the disciplinary documentation. Make sure that the discipline chosen fits the "crime" and that other employees who have done the same thing or similar things have been disciplined in the same or similar ways.

Serious misconduct (like theft, quid pro quo, sexual harassment, dishonesty, violence in the workplace) may merit discharge without prior warnings. Nevertheless, remember that attorneys, judges, and juries will look at the following factors when evaluating whether the discipline imposed was appropriate:

- What was the offense and how severe was it?
- Did the employer conduct a fair and thorough investigation?
- Had the employee had a good record prior to this incident?
- How long had the employee worked for the company?
- Was the employee told the company's rules or expectations, or was the employee previously warned for the same behavior?
- Were the company's rules reasonable?
- Are the rules uniformly or laxly enforced?
- Is there unequal or discriminatory treatment?
- Was the supervisor or manager also at fault?
- Has the employee's story or explanation changed over the course of the investigation?

One final word regarding documentation: spend the necessary time to do it right. Documentation helps an employer think through the reasons for a disciplinary decision. Documenting progressive discipline will prevent an employee from claiming he or she was never warned.

If memories fade, documentation can also refresh a supervisor or manager's recollection. Judges or juries also find documentation persuasive and reassuring—it helps prove that the reasons for discipline were not concocted after the fact.

17.2   At-will vs. Just Cause

by Holly Hearn
Davis Wright Tremaine LLP

Legal Framework

Employment "at-will" is the notion that employees can quit whenever they want and that the employer can fire them whenever it wants, unless there exists some contract or agreement to the contrary. Employment at-will allows employers to make employment decisions without having to justify them to the courts. In most states, employees typically work at the "will" of the employer.

On the other hand, if an employee is only terminable for "just cause" because of an employment contract or collective bargaining agreement, the employer must show a specific act or omission by the employee to warrant discipline or discharge. An employee can claim he is employed under an employment contract in two ways: (1) An express oral or written contract for a specified term usually containing specific provisions regarding termination, or (2) an implied contract—from statements made in policy manuals or handbooks or from job offers—that an employee will be able to work until retirement, and from statements that create a reasonable expectation that an employee will be treated in certain ways under certain circumstances.

"Wrongful discharge" lawsuits arise when an employee contends he or she was discharged without cause, or in breach of an alleged contract or contravention of a public policy (e.g., in retaliation for whistle-blowing).

Preserving At-will Employment

In light of recent decisions limiting the employment at-will doctrine, employers should develop an action plan to minimize the risk of a wrongful discharge suit. The following steps are generally recommended:

Adopt disclaimers establishing that employment is at-will.

- Revise employment documents to establish at-will employment, including employment applications, offer letters, written employment agreements, employee handbooks, and personnel policy manuals.

- Disclaimer language should include statements that the employment is at-will and that the document is not a contract; that policies and procedures can be modified at any time; and that no one in the company has the authority to agree to anything different from at-will employment. Write disclaimers in bold type and keep them simple.

- Documents should ask the employee to sign a statement acknowledging that he has read the disclaimer and understands employment is at-will. If the disclaimer is explained in a meeting, provide a sign-in sheet to prove employees were present at the meeting. Retain a copy of this sign-in sheet and an outline of what was covered in the meeting.

Implement policies designed to support at-will employment arguments.

- Preserve flexibility by writing policies describing disciplinary procedures in non-mandatory language, retaining discretion for management to decide appropriate action based on the circumstances.

- Offer lists of rules or actions that may lead to discipline as examples and not as exhaustive lists.

- If you choose to use an orientation period during which the employee may be terminated for any reason, include a provision stating that the employee remains employed at-will after the orientation period has ended. Without such a statement, a "for cause" requirement may be implied after the probationary period ends.

Train managers and supervisors to maintain at-will employment by avoiding representations regarding the permanence or length of employment, by avoiding listing reasons for which employees can be terminated, and by not promising that specific procedures or steps will be followed in disciplinary procedures.

Prepare written performance standards and job descriptions to ensure that employees know and understand what is expected of them. These will also assist the employer in establishing that the employee had notice to of what he or she was expected to do in the event the employee is discharged for performance problems.

Conduct employee relations as if "just cause" were required. Although this seems contradictory, firing people arbitrarily wastes employee talent, erodes employee confidence, and causes morale problems. If the disclaimers do not hold up in court, the company will be forced to prove that it had cause for the discharge decision. Also, arbitrary discharges may also result in claims of employment discrimination or violation of public policy, to which disclaimers provide no defense.

Just Cause for Discharge

The following summarizes the factors considered by labor arbitrators and courts when assessing whether there is cause for discharge.

Factors in establishing just cause

- How serious was the offense?

- Did management make a reasonable inquiry or investigation before deciding on a penalty?

- Has the company already been disciplined for the incident (double jeopardy)?

- What is the employee's past work record (single incident within a long good past work record vs. long pattern of unsatisfactory conduct and performance)?

- How long has the employee worked for the employer?

- Did the employee know or was he or she informed or warned of the rules and the employer's expectations?

- Has the employer enforced its rules or expectations uniformly?

- Has the employer treated the employee unequally or discriminatorily when compared to other employees with similar problems?

- Is management also at fault?

Establishing just cause for discharge

- Use candid employee evaluations that provide objective and specific statements about an employee's performance. Do not avoid negative statements if they apply. The absence of earlier references to problems in an employee's evaluations will be used to argue that the employer was not terminated for cause.

- Implement and use a system of progressive discipline to inform the employee that improvement or change is necessary and to encourage that improvement. Don't delay or the employee may think that this level of performance of conduct is acceptable. Delay also makes it more difficult for employees to stop making errors or violating work rules. Give the employee notice of the problem, an opportunity to improve, and let the employee know what consequences will follow if she or he fails to do so. Document all discipline in writing.

- Investigate all facts before disciplining an employee. The supervisor and human resources should conduct the investigation in an objective manner, allowing the employee to tell his or her side of the story. If a nonemployee is involved, try to obtain a written statement. Carefully document all of the facts and rules violated. Attach copies of all relevant documents to your report.

- If discipline appears appropriate, make sure the rules are being applied uniformly to all employees. Have upper management review the decision.

- When presenting the discipline, review the situation with the employee and present written documentation for the employee to sign. Note on the form if the employee refuses to do so.

17.3 How to Legally Terminate an Employee

by Holly Hearn
Davis Wright Tremaine LLP

Your operating assumption when terminating any employee should be that the termination has the potential to create litigation and significant liability for your company.

Avoid Getting In the Position Where Termination is Necessary

Pay increased attention to the employee selection processes and hire the best qualified person for the position.

Use "orientation" periods effectively. If you choose to use an orientation period which specifies that the employee can be terminated for any reason during this period, make sure to evaluate the performance of the employee before the period ends to determine whether he is meeting the company's standards.

Deal with performance problems sooner rather than later. Trust your instincts.

Utilize a progressive discipline approach to counsel employees about their problems. Along with candid performance evaluations, progressive discipline is the employer's chief means of documenting cause for discharge.

Document employee problems and counseling sessions. Even if an employee is counseled only verbally, make a note of when and where the conversation took place and summarize the substance of the conversation.

Make certain that employees have clear understanding of job requirements and company expectations by using job descriptions and regular feedback from supervisors.

Implement an employee evaluation system and use it on a regular basis. Train your supervisors in how to conduct evaluations and provide them guidance as to appropriate standards of performance. Be honest in identifying areas of poor performance in written evaluations. The absence of references to problems in evaluations can later be used to argue that the employee was a good performer. Effective employee evaluations include positive feedback, constructive criticism, guidance as to how the employee can improve (employer expectations and setting particular goals), notice to the employer of the consequences of failure to improve, and an opportunity for the employee to provide feedback.

Implementing Appropriate Personnel Procedures and Policies

Employment applications, employee handbooks, and policies and procedures manuals should all contain disclaimers regarding at-will employment. If you have an employee handbook, have the employee sign an acknowledgement that he or she has received a copy of the handbook and understands that it is not a contract of employment and that he or she is employed at-will.

Supervisors should be trained in personnel matters, including interviews, hiring, orientation, performance appraisals, discipline, and termination. Consider using a checklist to ensure that supervisors have been fully trained in each of these areas.

Implement a progressive discipline system to inform employees that improvement or change is necessary and to encourage that improvement. Whenever discipline is administered, it should contain the following elements: notice of performance problems and opportunities to improve; a reasonable time for improvement; the consequences that will follow if improvement does not occur; and documentation of all discipline in writing with a copy to the employee and the personnel file.

Performance evaluations should be objective and candid. Do not exaggerate the positive qualities of an employee's performance and avoid negative aspects. Later discipline for poor performance that has not been identified in earlier evaluations is often assumed by an employee to be unmeritorious or discriminatory. Consider using standard forms when conducting evaluations, and make sure to conduct them on a regular basis.

Implement procedures for reviewing proposed terminations and conducting termination interviews.

Evaluating Proposed Terminations

Obtain a "second opinion" evaluating the basis for an employee's discharge.

Carefully review the employee's personnel file, (official and unofficial) and check records of counseling, performance evaluations, etc. for evidence that the employee was on notice of performance problems and had a chance to improve (except in summary dismissal type cases).

Review the reasons the employee is being discharged:

- Is the reason for discharge full and impartial?
- Are there clear reasons; does just cause exist?
- Is the termination consistent with past practices?
- What are the strengths of the witnesses who will testify as to the propriety of the termination?

- Have the reasons for termination been adequately documented?

- Does the person recommending discharge have a hidden agenda or improper motive for terminating the employee?

- What is the record and judgment of the person recommending the discharge?

- Has the employee been given a chance to tell his or her side of the story? Consider legal bases for the employee to challenge the termination and evaluate their risks and costs.

- Is the employee in a protected class: age, race, sex, disability, national origin, etc.? Consider the status of the employee's replacement, if known.

- Were all company policies and procedures followed (including any promises of specific treatment in specific situations)?

- Were any oral or written promises (offer letters, etc.) not met?

- Can the employee claim that his or her discharge violates public policy? Can he or she claim that termination resulted from asserting a legal right, refusing to engage in illegal conduct, or for whistle-blowing?

- Can the employee claim the discharge is in retaliation for some protected activity, such as complaining about discrimination or engaging in protected activity under the National Labor Relations Act?

- The "smell test": consider such factors as the employee's tenure with the company, the timing of the termination (close to retirement or vesting of benefits), any unusual circumstances of the employee (illness or personal problems), and the appearance of unfairness. How would this look to a jury?

Consider alternatives to discharge: demotion, transfer, suspension, etc. If it is a troublesome case, consider offering to allow the employee to resign and/or an incentive package in exchange for a release of all claims.

Terminating the Employee

Ensure in advance that the employment termination decision is justified and that you are able to articulate the reasons for the decision.

Set forth the reasons for termination in writing. It may or may not be appropriate to give the employee a copy during the termination interview, but documentation to the file is important in the event of litigation. Washington law also requires an employer, upon written request, to furnish to an employee within 10 working days of the request a signed written statement setting forth the reasons for termination and the effective date for the discharge.

Conduct a termination interview

- Be firm and unemotional, and present the termination decision as irrevocable.

- Be considerate. If possible terminate the employee at the end of the day to avoid an embarrassing and awkward situation for the employee. Do not allow the employee to leave the premises in an emotionally distraught state.

- Give honest and specific reasons for the termination, and make sure they are the same reasons you would give to a jury or administrative agency.

- State at the beginning of the interview that the employee is being terminated.

- Keep the termination factual, and avoid accusations or personal comments.

- Do not terminate the employee in front of other employees. If necessary, have another management person who is involved in the decision present as a witness, but no co-workers. Try to arrange a time after hours for the employee to retrieve personal belongings under the supervision of Human Resources. Do not have the employee clean out his or her desk when or where other employees will see him or her.

- Avoid arguing with the employee in an attempt to convince him or her that the employer is right and he or she is wrong. However, do allow the employee to vent frustration or feelings about the discharge.

- Take responsibility for the decision to terminate, and do not blame someone else.

- Avoid loose ends by arranging for the return of company and personal property at the time of termination. Advise the employee when and where he or she can get the last paycheck and make available information about how the employer will handle references and benefit matters such as COBRA.

Post termination communications

Communications with or about a former employee can lead to a defamation suit. Tell only those within the company who have a need to know of the reasons for the employee's termination.

Handle references according to the employer's policies, and stick to the facts when sharing information with prospective employers. Any false information disclosed with malice may be the basis of liability for a defamation lawsuit. It is usually best if all reference requests are referred to a central source, usually Human Resources.

Before giving detailed reference responses, an employer should ask or require the former employee for a release of possible claims. If the employee has resigned pursuant to a separation agreement, it is critical to follow the procedure outlined in that agreement as to how references will be handled.

17.4 Assessing Potential Liability
For Employee Termination

—by Mary Drobka and Robert A. Blackstone
Davis Wright Tremaine LLP

The following checklist is designed to give employers a *rough* basis for evaluating their potential legal liability arising out of the discharge of an employee. It is best used *prior* to any discharge as a checklist for the kinds of factors which will likely be reviewed should the discharge subsequently be challenged. Review of the checklist may suggest additional steps the employer should take or additional information which should be evaluated prior to making the final decision to discharge.

The weight assigned to particular factors is somewhat arbitrary. Especially bad facts or circumstances involving one item or another on the checklist could take on much more significance than the listed weighting, particularly in the eyes of a judge or a jury.

If you complete this checklist, remember the objective is to have as few points as possible.

Remember that this checklist is necessarily general and cannot be used as a substitute for specific legal advice regarding any particular fact situation. The checklist has not been scientifically validated. Wrongful discharge and discrimination laws vary from state to state and undergo constant change. Consultation with an experienced employment or labor lawyer is strongly recommended *prior* to filling out the checklist, so that the completed checklist would not be subject to pretrial discovery under the attorney-client or work product privilege doctrines should employment litigation arise. Unless protected by the attorney-client or work product privileges, completed checklists should be destroyed.

Employee

1. Can the employee claim membership in any of these protected classes? (If employee is a member of more than one protected class, add 5 points for each additional class after one.)
   - Female – 10 points
   - African-American – 10 points
   - Hispanic – 10 points
   - Asian – 10 points
   - Native American – 10 points

- Over 40 years of age – 10 points
- Gay or Lesbian – 10 points
- Disabled – 10 points
- Distinctive national origin – 10 points

2. How long has the employee worked for the company?
   - Less than 1 year – 0 points
   - One to 5 years – 5 points
   - Five to 10 years – 10 points
   - Ten to 20 years – 15 points
   - Over 20 years – 20 points
   - Over 25 years – 25 points

3. Is the employee now particularly vulnerable to emotional distress because of personal problems (marital or family problems, personal illness, etc.)?
   - If yes, add 15 points

4. What is the salary level of the employee?
   - 0 to $25,000 – 1 point
   - $25,000 to $50,000 – 3 points
   - $50,000 to $100,000 – 6 points
   - More than $100,000 – 10 points

5. Has employee previously filed internal or external grievances or complaints, either inside the company or with government agencies?
   - If yes, add 25 points

6. Has employee ever complained to anyone that the company was acting illegally or improperly?
   - If yes, add 25 points

7. Is the employee close to vesting of pension rights, stock options or other substantial benefits?
   - Will vest within six months – 10 points
   - Will vest within one year – 6 points
   - Will vest within two years – 3 points
   - Will not vest for at least two years – 0 points

Reasons for Discharge

1. What is the reason for the employee's discharge?
   - Repeated violation of company rule or policy – 1 point
   - Clear single violation of company rule or policy – 2 points
   - Probable violation of company rule or policy – 3 points
   - Lack of work/downsizing – 4 points
   - Poor performance based on an objective evaluation – 7 points

- Insubordination – 10 points
- Poor performance based on subjective evaluation – 15 points

2. Have other persons been discharged for the same reasons as this employee within the past year?
   - Yes – 0 points
   - No – 5 points

3. Have other persons been discharged for the same reason within the past year by the same person who decided to discharge this employee?
   - Yes – 0 points
   - No – 5 points
     If yes, were the other persons discharged members of the same protected-class(es), if any, as this employee?
     - Yes – 20 points
     - No – 0 points

4. Are there other employees who have engaged in similar conduct who have not been terminated?
   - Yes – 20 points
   - No – 0 points
     a. Were the other employees who were not terminated in the same protected class(es) as this employee (e.g., race, sex, national origin)?
        - Yes – 0 points
        - No – 20 points
     b. In a protected class, but not the same class as this employee
        - Yes – 10 points
        - No – 0 points

Circumstances of Discharge

1. What kind of notice of discharge will be given to the employee?
   - Oral only – 5 points
   - Written only – 10 points
   - Both oral and written – 0 points

2. If notice of discharge is oral, will it be done in a private location without any co-workers present?
   - Yes – 0 points
   - No – 10 points

3. If notice will be oral, will there be a witness to the discussion of the reasons for discharge?
   - Yes – 0 points
   - No – 10 points

4. Will any notice or explanation of the termination of this employee be given to the employee's coworkers?
   - Yes – 10 points
   - No – 0 points

5. Will the decision to discharge be carefully reviewed by managerial personnel other than the initiating supervisor before it will be implemented?
   - Yes – 0 points
   - No – 20 points

6. Does the company have a formal internal grievance procedure?
   - Yes – 0 points
   - No – 10 points
        Do you think it likely that the employee will use the procedure?
        - Yes – 0 points
        - No – 5 points

Warnings and Employee Performance Record

1. Was the employee previously counseled about the problems which form the basis for the discharge?
   - Yes, orally – 10 points
   - Yes, in writing – 5 points
   - Yes, in writing more than once – 0 points
   - No – 25 points

2. How much time has elapsed between the last time the employee was counseled about this problem and the discharge?
   - Less than two weeks – 10 points
   - Less than one month – 5 points
   - Less than three months – 3 points

3. Did any counseling or warning specifically inform the employee that he or she could or would be discharged if the problem was not corrected?
   - Yes – 0 points
   - No – 15 points
        Is the warning in writing, and a copy in the employee's file?
        - Yes – 0 points
        - No – 5 points

4. If the reason for discharge involves performance problems, was the employee provided with training or a meaningful opportunity to improve which could have alleviated the problem?
   - Yes – 0 points
   - No – 10 points

5. If the reason for discharge is a violation of company policy, is that company policy in writing?
   - Yes – 0 points
   - No – 10 points
       Is there any writing by which the employee acknowledged receipt or an awareness of that company policy?
       - Yes – 0 points
       - No – 5 points
6. Does the company have a policy of written performance evaluations?
   - Yes – 0 points
   - No – 15 points
7. If the company has a policy of written performance evaluations, was the reason for discharge discussed in the employee's most recent performance evaluation?
   - Yes – 0 points
   - No – 15 points
8. Was the performance evaluation reviewed with the employee and did he or she acknowledge receiving it?
   - Yes – 0 points
   - No – 10 points
9. Is the discharge consistent with the company's written personnel policies generally?
   - Yes – 0 points
   - No – 25 points
10. Was the performance evaluation given to the employee when it was supposed to be?
    - Yes – 0 points
    - No – 5 points

Evaluation of Person Making Discharge Decision

1. Is the person who made the decision to terminate the employee a member of any of the same protected classes as the employee? (If age is a relevant protected class, was the supervisor within four years of the age of the employee?)
   - Yes – 0 points
   - No – 5 points
2. What is the supervisory experience of the person making the decision to discharge?
   - Less than one year – 5 points
   - One to three years – 3 points
   - Three to five years – 1 point
   - More than five years – 0 points
3. How long was the person making the decision to discharge acting as the employee's supervisor?

- Less than one year — 5 points
- One to three years — 2 points
- More than three years — 0 points

Damages and Mitigation

1. Will the employee be provided any severance pay?
   - Zero to one month salary — 10 points
   - One to three months — 8 points
   - Four to six months — 5 points
   - Six to 12 months — 3 points
   - More than 12 months — 0 points
2. Will the employee be provided any out placement counseling?
   - Yes — 0 points
   - No — 10 points
3. Will the employee be provided any continuation of benefits (other than pursuant to COBRA)?
   - Yes — 0 points
   - No — 10 points
4. If discharge has already occurred, has the employee found another job?
   - Yes, probably at same salary — 0 points
   - Yes, probably at lower salary — 10 points
   - No — 20 points
5. How soon is the employee likely to find another comparable job?
   - Within one month — 0 points
   - Within three months — 3 points
   - Within six months — 5 points
   - Within one year — 10 points

Nature of Employer

1. Does the employer have?
   - Fewer than 50 employees — 3 points
   - Between 50 and 500 employees — 5 points
   - More than 500 employees — 10 points
   - More than 1,000 employees — 15 points
2. Is the employer?
   - Locally-owned — 0 points
   - Part of a large U.S. company — 5 points
   - Owned by a foreign company — 10 points

TOTAL POINTS: _____

SCORING:

Points	Liability Assessment
20 – 150 points	Low risk—probably in good shape[12]
150 – 250 points	Moderate risk—any steps you can still take to lower your score
250 – 450 points	High risk—call your employment lawyer
450 – 600 points	Substantial increase in litigation budget required!

---

[12] A low overall score doesn't guarantee that you won't be sued. However, if you are, your chances of prevailing may be better than most.

■ Chapter 18 ■

Human Relations Issues

18.1 Group Health Insurance

—by John M. Beveridge
AH&T Technology Brokers

Introduction

In the United States, the majority of the populace receives medical insurance coverage through employer-sponsored health plans. According to the Bureau of Labor Statistics, 75% of full-time employees in medium and large private industry establishments participate in employer-sponsored health plans. In small private industry establishments, the percentage drops to 66 2/3%, in contrast to most other countries with highly developed economies, where the government is the primary provider of medical coverage to citizens.

The percentage of employees covered by employer-sponsored health plans is markedly higher in the software and telecommunications industries, where employers must compete for a valuable resource—skilled workers who can help these firms accomplish their business objectives. Although these employers offer a combination of cash and noncash benefits to attract and retain talented workers, medical insurance is one benefit that touches almost all employees (and their families). Medical insurance is highly visible to employees because it protects the employee's physical as well as financial well-being.

Types of Medical Insurance Plans

There are four major types of medical insurance plans provided to employees:

Health maintenance organizations (HMOs)

HMOs offer a comprehensive range of medical coverage, including preventive benefits, for a set monthly fee.

In an HMO, employees can receive care only from medical providers that participate in the HMO network. Most HMOs require employees and their dependents to choose a Primary Care Physician (PCP) to manage their medical care. Employees can typically choose from pediatricians, family practice doctors, and internal medicine practitioners to be their PCP. Most HMOs require that employees get a referral from their PCP before they can receive care from a specialist such as a dermatologist.

Most HMOs cover the majority of services provided at a minor co-payment of $5, $10, or $15. They may require more extensive co-payments for services such as inpatient hospitalization or mental health coverage.

There are two primary types of HMOs:

Staff Model HMO. In a staff model HMO, doctors are typically employees of the HMO and employees go to the HMO facility to receive care. Kaiser Permanente is an example of a staff model HMO.

Independent Practice Association (IPA). In an IPA, the doctors are private practitioners who agree to participate in the network and to practice medicine out of their primary offices for subscribers of the HMO.

Point-of-Service Plans (POS Plans). Many HMOs offer an option in which employees can receive care from medical providers that don't participate in the HMO network. Point-of-service plans (POS) allow employees to choose their providers for each encounter with the health care system. Most POS plans offer HMO-type benefits if one receives care from a network provider; most POS plans require significant deductibles and coinsurance if one receives care from a provider not participating in the network. (Coinsurance is the portion of the charge for which the employee is responsible under the plan. For example, if a plan provided 20% coinsurance, an employee would be responsible for 20% of the doctor's charge after any deductible amounts had been satisfied.)

Preferred Provider Organizations (PPOs). The form of managed care closest to a fee-for-service indemnity plan, the PPO arranges for discounted services from a network of doctors, hospitals, and other providers of care. They pass these discounted charges along to employees. Most PPOs allow employees to seek medical care directly from specialists within the network.

Like a POS plan, PPOs provide a higher level of coverage if one receives care from a contracted network providers. A typical PPO arrangement might cover doctor visits:

- at 100% after a $10 co-payment within the network
- at 30% coinsurance after a $500 deductible for doctor visits provided by physicians outside of the network.

Most other services would be provided at 10% coinsurance after a $100 deductible within the network and at 30% coinsurance after a $500 deductible outside of the network.

Fee for service indemnity plans

Indemnity plans reimburse employees a set percentage of the cost of their covered medical expenses after a deductible. For example, medical services could be covered at 80% (20% coinsurance) after a $250 deductible. Most indemnity plans require employees to have their care approved by a third-party organization for surgery and inpatient hospital admissions. Because of the high cost of these plans, they are becoming rarer every day.

Providers of employer-sponsored health care plans

There are four primary providers of health care plans to American employers:

Commercial Insurance Carriers. Typically insurance companies and managed care organizations provide insurance policies to employers that cover medical costs incurred by their employers. Commercial carriers offer policies under HMO, POS, PPO, and Indemnity formats.

Most commercial carriers provide premium arrangements designed to cover the cost of medical claims, administrative costs, state premium taxes, risk charges, and profit on a prospective basis. Many commercial carriers provide retrospective and other cash-flow arrangements to employers with more than 100 employees.

Blue Cross/Blue Shield Plans. In most states, Blue Cross and Blue Shield plans operate as a combined organization. However, some states (e.g., Washington and California) have competing Blue Cross and Blue Shield plans. Each Blue Cross and Blue Shield plan operates in a specific geographic area and may offer different benefit plans. Most plans participate in the national Blue Card program. The Blue Card unites the local Blue plans and provides a seamless network throughout the United States. This network allows employees who are travelling or living outside of the local Blue plans service area to receive comprehensive benefits from a comprehensive network of medical providers.

Both organizations contract with both doctors and hospitals for their services. Participating doctors and hospitals agree to accept a negotiated fee for their services from the local Blue plan. If an employee visits a doctor or a hospital that is not participating with the Blue plan, they are responsible for paying any charges in excess of the negotiated fee. Most doctors and hospitals participate in the Blue plans.

Self-Funded Plans. Many employers self-fund their medical insurance programs. Most hire Third Party Administrators (TPAs) to administer the plans and purchase stop-loss insurance to protect them from the financial impact of catastrophic claims. Specific Stop Loss limits an employer's exposure for the medical costs of any one employee in a given time period (e.g., $50,000 per year). Aggregate Stop Loss limits an employer's total liability for medical costs in a given time period (e.g., 125% of a predetermined expected claims figure).

Employers elect to self-fund their programs because:

- Self-funded plans have an ERISA exemption from state insurance laws.

- Self-funded plans offer cash-flow advantages over an arrangement in which insurance premiums are pre-paid.

- Most self-funded plans are not liable for state premium taxes.

- Self-funded plans generally have lower administrative costs than insured plans.

Self-funded plans: higher level of risk?

It is important to evaluate the financial scenarios of self-insurance before undertaking a plan.

Association/Cooperative Plans.   Many employers pool their resources to purchase insurance through a group association or cooperative plan. This approach allows smaller employers to band together with similar employers from the same industry to increase their purchasing power. This approach allows small employers to negotiate pricing and benefit levels that allow them to compete with larger employers for talented employees.

Legislation of Health Care Plans

Health care plans are legislated by two sources: state and federal government.

State Law. State governments legislate insurance coverage provided within the state. Most insurance laws are governed by the state in which the policy is sited. In most situations, this is the state in which the company's headquarters resides. Other state insurance laws are extraterritorial: extraterritorial laws apply to all employees residing in a state, regardless of where the policy is sited. In most cases, the burden for complying with state insurance law rests with the insurance company that is providing the policy. As stated above, most self-insured plans are exempt from state insurance legislation.

Federal Law. The primary federal legislation that governs employee benefit plans is ERISA (the Employee Retirement and Income Security Act of 1972). ERISA dictates how employee benefit plans are provided to employees. Although ERISA is too complex to fully explain here, it requires that employers communicate certain information to employees and to the IRS and provides safeguards for assets set aside to provide benefits for employees. As with most federal laws that govern employee benefit plans, ERISA is an employer law. The burden of complying with the law rests with the employers.

Other common federal laws include:

COBRA. COBRA requires most employers with insurance plans to offer continued access to the plans after an employee terminates coverage and/or employment. Most employers with fewer than 20 employees are exempt from COBRA.

HIPAA. HIPAA increases the ability of employees who are changing jobs to keep their health coverage intact. One of the provisions of HIPAA allows employees to use periods of coverage with the previous employer to satisfy preexisting conditions under the new employers program.

These are capsule descriptions of some of the common federal laws covering employee benefits. Please seek a qualified legal opinion if you have any specific questions on how these laws impact your individual organization.

Summary

Employers need to offer a creative mix of cash and non-cash compensation to meet their recruiting and retention goals in today's environment of low unemployment and stiff competition for talented employees. Group health insurance is a critical component of an employee's total compensation package. There are many ways to offer group health insurance. With some research and the assistance of a qualified professional, you can put together the proper package for your organization.

For more information, contact:

The Health Insurance Association of America (HIAA)

http://www.hiaa.org

Employee Benefit Research Institute

http://www.ebri.org

18.2 Stock-based Compensation

—by Paul Brajcich
KPMG Peat Marwick

The issuance of stock, stock options, or other stock compensation arrangements to employees and nonemployees is a common practice for many emerging companies. The practice allows the company to retain its scarce cash resources and provides a significant incentive for employees and outside contractors to focus on the economic performance of the company.

Accounting for Stock-based Compensation

The accounting for stock-based compensation is extremely complex. The structure of the arrangements must give adequate consideration of the financial statement impact of the arrangements. These arrangements, if not properly structured, can have a significant negative impact not only on current period earnings but also negatively on future earnings.

Statement 123

Statement of Financial Accounting Standard No. 123 (Statement 123) provides guidance as to how all stock-based compensation arrangements, other than employer stock ownership plans, should be accounted for under generally accepted accounting principles. This statement covers stock and stock option grants to employees and nonemployees, stock purchase plans, restricted stock plans, and stock appreciation rights.

A key element of Statement 123, companies may elect to account for stock option grants to employees in a manner different from how they are required to account for stock option grants to nonemployees. These two methods are known as the *intrinsic value method* and the *fair value method*. An employer may elect to account for stock option grants to employees using the intrinsic value method while grants to nonemployees must be accounted for using fair value method. The following example shows the financial statement impact of these two methods:

Assume:

Total stock options included in the grant, all are assumed to vest	1,000 shares
Fair value per share of stock at date of grant	$9.00
Exercise price for stock option	$9.00
Intrinsic value of stock options at grant date[1]	0
Fair value of each stock option at date of grant [2]	$5.00
Vesting period 5 years	

[1] Intrinsic value is the difference between the exercise price and the fair value of the shares.
[2] Fair value calculated using an acceptable pricing model.

Intrinsic Value Method	Fair Value Method
Option intrinsic value $0	Fair value of each option $5
Compensation cost for grant $0	Compensation cost for grant $5000

Thus, if no performance criteria are attached to an option grant, there is no compensation expense under the intrinsic value method while there would be $5,000 of expense under the fair value method. This expense would be charged to earnings over the vesting period.

It should be noted that a company that uses the intrinsic value method to account for stock option grants to employees must include proforma disclosure in the footnotes to its financial statements as if it had used the fair value method.

Performance Milestones

A significant accounting issue arises if stock option grants to employees include vesting provisions that are contingent upon the achievement of performance milestones. If the company uses the intrinsic value method to account for its employee stock option grants, it will delay the date at which the intrinsic value is determined until the performance milestone is achieved. This delay can result in a significant charge to current and future period earnings if the value of the company's stock has dramatically appreciated during this time: the intrinsic value of the stock options is the difference between the exercise price of the option and the value of the stock when the performance milestone is met.

The structuring of stock compensation arrangements to nonemployees requires considering the impact of these grants on the financial statement. If no performance milestones are required to vest, the value is generally determined at the date of the grant using the fair value method. The fair value of the grant, as determined by an acceptable valuation methodology, would be recognized over the vesting period. If performance-based conditions exist, the grant will need to be analyzed to determine how it should be accounted for. The final measurement of the compensation cost of the grant would likely be delayed until the performance criteria are resolved.

The accounting for stock-based compensation is extremely complex and, therefore, it is critical that you consult a CPA with extensive experience in this area in structuring these arrangements. Such advice will help you prevent unwanted and unexpected charges to earnings.

18.3 A Basic Overview of Employee Stock Grants and Options

(prepared from a legal perspective)

—By Stuart Harris and Wendy C. Rossiter
David Wright Tremaine, LLP

Stock ownership offers an excellent way to enhance employee compensation without cash outlays. Giving employees a direct stake in the company's performance, moreover, will increase their incentive to produce positive results. Employers can convey stock ownership through stock grants or stock options. (Tax qualified retirement plans—such as ESOPs and 401(k) plans—can also convey stock to employees, but those arrangements are beyond the scope of these materials.) What follows is an overview of basic stock compensation methods. Note that tax ramifications can be complex, and employers and employees should seek individual tax advice.

Stock Grants

Stock may be granted outright to employees as bonus compensation or granted with contingencies such as a requirement to remain employed for a given number of years. Failure to satisfy the "vesting schedule" means the employee forfeits the stock upon termination of employment, and the stock returns to the company. A vesting schedule may take an all-or-nothing approach and require a specific period of employment (five years, for example), at which point the employee becomes fully vested in all the stock. In contrast, a vesting schedule may operate gradually (20% a year for five years, for example).

Stock granted to an employee constitutes taxable compensation and is taxable at ordinary income rates (as opposed to capital gains rates). The taxable amount is equal to the fair market value of the stock. An exception exists for stock subject to a vesting schedule. Since an employee may leave prior to becoming fully vested, no tax is imposed until the stock vests, unless the employee accelerates the tax by filing an election with the IRS within 30 days of the initial stock grant. This election is pursuant to section 83(b) of the Internal Revenue Code. One potential reason for electing to accelerate the tax is to trigger ordinary income tax rates early on, before the stock climbs in value.

Stock Options

Unlike stock grants, stock options allow employees to choose the time of transfer and the corresponding tax consequences. There are generally three types of stock options:

(1) a non-qualified (sometimes referred to as "non-statutory") stock option (NSO); (2) an incentive stock option (ISO); and (3) an option under an employee stock purchase plan (ESPP). The terms of an NSO are governed solely by the agreement between the employer and employee. ISOs and options under an ESPP provide employees with special tax treatment and, correspondingly, are subject to specific provisions of the Internal Revenue Code. Failure to meet Code requirements results in an option being treated (for tax purposes) as an NSO.

Non-qualified stock options

An NSO is an agreement enabling an employee to purchase a specific number of shares of an employer's stock at a specified price. An NSO can be an individual agreement between an employer and employee or part of a broader plan that anticipates option grants to multiple employees. Generally, the grant of an NSO imposes no tax liability on the employee. When the employee exercises the option (i.e., pays the specified purchase price in exchange for the stock), the employee will have taxable income equal to the fair market value of the stock (measured at the time of exercise), minus the amount the employee paid. (This taxable amount is often referred to as the "spread.") This amount, representing compensation, is taxed at ordinary income rates. Correspondingly, the employer can claim a tax deduction for this amount.

As with stock grants, employers can use a vesting schedule to limit the number of shares that can be exercised over a given period.

Incentive stock options

Statutory requirements for ISOs include: (1) only employees, and their death beneficiaries, can hold ISOs (i.e., no outside director, independent contractor or former employee); (2) ISOs must be issued pursuant to a written plan document that designates the number of shares available under the plan; (3) shareholders must approve the plan within 12 months before or after the plan is adopted; (4) there must be a maximum 10-year term for granting the option after the plan is adopted; (5) there must be a maximum 10-year term for exercising the option after it is granted; (6) there must be an exercise price equal to or greater than the fair market value of the stock (measured at the time of grant); and (7) employers must send annual notices to employees who exercised ISOs during the year. Any modification to an outstanding ISO that extends a new benefit to the employee is deemed a new ISO grant, subject to a fresh application of the statutory requirements.

An ISO offers a good alternative for employees anticipating a significant appreciation in stock value. Like the NSO, generally no tax is associated with the grant of an ISO. Unlike an NSO, no income tax is collected when the employee exercises the ISO, as long as the employee holds the stock for at least one year from the exercise date and two years from the date the option was granted. After satisfying the holding periods, any gain upon a sale of the stock is taxed as long-term capital gain income. Additional rules apply if the optionee is a 10% shareholder.

Employee stock purchase plan

An ESPP typically provides for stock purchases via automatic payroll withholding, as elected by the employee. The purchase price may be discounted as much as 15% below the fair market value, measured on either the date of the grant or exercise.

Like an ISO plan, an ESPP must designate the aggregate number of shares available, and shareholders must approve the plan within 12 months before or after the date the plan was adopted. Similarly, only employees (not outside directors, independent contractors or former employees) may hold options under an ESPP, and an amendment extending a new benefit to the employee constitutes a new grant subject to the statutory requirements. Additional statutory provisions governing ESPPs include: (1) all full-time employees must be eligible to participate in the plan; and (2) the amount of stock (based on fair market value) an employee can purchase annually may not exceed $25,000.

The tax treatment of an ESPP option resembles that of an ISO. Like an ISO, the grant or exercise of an option under an ESPP generally does not trigger taxable income, as long as the employee holds the stock for one year from the date of exercise and two years from the date of grant. (As an exception, the IRS asserts that FICA and FUTA payroll taxes, but not income tax withholding, apply to any spread at the time of exercise of an ESPP option.) After satisfying the holding periods, the sale of stock acquired through an ESPP is taxed at the capital gains rate, except for the spread at the time of exercise, which is taxed as ordinary income.

Analysis of key stock option characteristics

	Employee Concerns	Employer Concerns
NSO	▪ Income tax imposed at exercise date.	▪ Paid compensation deduction available at exercise date. ▪ Requirement to withhold income and employment taxes. ▪ Flexibility to choose who receives options.
ISO	▪ No tax at exercise date. ▪ Capital gains tax treatment (if holding periods met). ▪ Alternative minimum tax implications.	▪ No deduction for paid compensation. ▪ No withholding requirement. ▪ Need to distribute annual notice. ▪ Flexibility to choose who receives options.
ESPP	▪ No tax at exercise date (except for payroll taxes on spread). ▪ All full-time employees eligible. ▪ Primarily capital gains tax treatment (if holding periods met).	▪ No deduction for paid compensation. ▪ No withholding requirement (except for minor FICA and FUTA obligation). ▪ No flexibility to favor key employees.

18.4 Stock Options: A Compensation Tool for Entrepreneurs
(prepared from an accounting perspective)

—by Marilynn S. Turner
KPMG LLP

When creators move their brain child from the garage to the street, the first thing they need is capital. The second—a very close second—is development talent. They needs marketing wizards to develop market strategy, identify distribution channels, or court strategic partners. They need finance wizards to develop the business plan that will attract angel investors or venture capitalists and move the company toward an IPO. They need talented engineers or programmers to keep up with expanding demand.

In order to attract the best talent, start-ups with good ideas, but little cash, often turn to stock options to close the gap between what it takes to sign on a talented executive or employee and what the start-up is able to pay in cash compensation. Executives and employees who believe in their own talents and have a little of the entrepreneurial spirit themselves are often willing to take less cash today coupled with great expectations for the future. Portland venture capitalist Ralph Shaw observes, "It enables you to attract talent you might not otherwise attract." He concludes that "in today's world, it's the only way."

This section addresses what employee stock options are, provides a general overview of how they are treated for tax and accounting purposes, and discusses the cost of stock options and what entrepreneurs hope to buy with them.

Stock Options—the Employee's Side[13]

An option is simply a right to buy stock at a fixed price over a given period of time. In an employment context, the issuing company usually reserves a set number of shares for compensating employees, drafts an option plan and, over time, grants to specific employees rights to purchase shares. For example, in Year 1, XYZ Company grants Joe an option to purchase 10 shares of XYZ stock at $5 per share when XYZ stock is valued at $5 per share. The option may be exercised at any time until Year 10 when the right expires. Joe exercises the option in Year 5, when XYZ stock is valued at $10 per share, by notifying XYZ

---

[13] The information contained in this section is general in nature and based on authorities that are subject to change. Applicability to specific situations is to be determined through consultation with your tax advisor.

Company of his intention to exercise and by paying to XYZ Company the $50 exercise price. If he sells the 10 shares immediately, Joe has an instant 100% return on his investment. If he does not sell the 10 shares, Joe joins the other shareholders of XYZ Company in the risks and rewards of equity participation. The tax treatment of stock options for Joe and for XYZ Company depends on whether the options are nonstatutory stock options or incentive stock options.

Nonstatutory stock options

A nonstatutory stock option is any option that does not qualify under Internal Revenue Code section 421 as an incentive stock option. In most of the cases we see in our practice, the granting of a nonstatutory stock option is a nonevent for tax purposes.[14] The exercise, however, is a significant tax event if the underlying stock does well. When the employee exercises his options, the amount of income he must recognize is equal to the difference between the fair market value of the acquired stock and the exercise price.[15] In Joe's case (above), he must recognize income of $50 (FMV $10 x 10 minus Cost $5 x 10).

The income recognition event would not be triggered by the option exercise if the acquired stock is not transferable or is subject to a substantial risk of forfeiture.[16] For example, Joe's rights in the stock itself might be tied to the performance of future services under a vesting schedule. In that event, Joe would be subject to income tax on compensation income in the year or years he becomes vested in the acquired shares unless he decides to accelerate the recognition of income by making a 403(b) election.[17]

The compensation income recognized at exercise (or later if the acquired shares are subject to a substantial risk of forfeiture) is subject to payroll tax withholding, including federal income tax, state income tax, if applicable, and FICA.[18] Employers handle the withholding obligation in various ways, including requiring optionees to pay over withholding taxes at the same time as they pay the exercise price.

Joe's basis in his XYZ Company stock equals the exercise price paid plus the compensation income he recognizes, or $100. If he sells his 10 shares in two years when XYZ Company stock is selling for $20 per share, he will recognize $100 in capital gain. (Selling Price of $200 minus Basis of $100.)

Incentive stock options (ISOs)[19]

These statutory options are accorded favorable tax treatment to encourage the employee to hold onto the acquired stock. The employee must not dispose of the optioned stock until

---

14 The exception is an option with a readily ascertainable fair market value, such as an option that is actively traded on an established market, in which case the granting of the option results in compensation income to the employee. Treas. Reg. sec. 1.83-7(a)

15 Treas. Reg. sec. 1.83-7(a)

16 IRC section 83(a)

17 IRC section 83(b)

18 Rev. Rul. 67-257, 1967-2 CB 359; Rev. Rul. 79-305, 1979-2 CB 350; Rev. Rul. 78-185, 1978-1 CB 304; Reg. Sec. 1.83-6 and Reg. Sec. 1.83-7

19 IRC section 421(a)

the later of two years after the option is granted or one year after exercising the option.[20]

If these and certain other requirements are met, regular tax on the compensation may be deferred until the optioned stock is eventually sold. At that time, all of the income, even the compensation element, is taxed at capital gains rates. Exercise of the ISOs may, however, give rise to alternative minimum tax (AMT) at the time of the exercise depending on the individual's particular tax situation. If Joe's options for XYZ Company stock were ISOs (and assuming that he is not subject AMT), he would have no income recognition and no withholding in the year of exercise but $150 of capital gain when he sold his ISO stock.

If the employee disposes of his or her ISO shares before the required holding period expires, this so-called "disqualifying disposition of ISO Stock" causes the options to be treated, for tax purposes, like nonstatutory stock options.[21] The year of income recognition, however, is the year of the disqualifying disposition rather than the year of exercise. No payroll tax withholding is required on a disqualifying disposition.[22]

One of the disadvantages of stock options from the employee's point of view is the cash requirements of exercise and, with nonstatutory stock options, the cash requirements for withholding. Employers have several techniques available for so-called "cashless exercise," including brokered exercise, pyramiding, and tandem option and cash awards. The techniques reduce the required cash outlay for the employee but may also reduce the employee's acquired stock. In addition, for book purposes, these techniques may give rise to compensation expense.

Stock Options—the Employer's Side

All of the tax advantages of Incentive Stock Options come with a price, and the price is paid by the employer. An employer is not entitled to a deduction for compensation expense with ISOs.[23] Moreover, the employer clearly has less flexibility in plan design with ISOs. For example, the ISO exercise price must be at least 100% of the fair market value at the date of grant.[24] Nonstatutory stock options, on the other hand, may be offered at a discount. Extensions, modifications, or renewals of ISOs are usually treated as granting of a new option (i.e., must be 100% of FMV at the grant date and a new holding period starts).[25] In contrast, changes in nonstatutory stock options are generally nonevents for tax purposes. The changes for both may require recognition of expense for book purposes.

---

[20] IRC section 422(a)
[21] Prop. Treas. Reg. Sec. 1.422A-1(b)
[22] Rev. Rul. 71-52, 1971-1 C. B. 278; IRS Notice 87-49, 1987-2 C.B. 355.
[23] IRC section 421(a)(2)
[24] IRC section 422(b)(4)
[25] IRC section 424(h)

On the exercise of nonstatutory stock options, and on disqualifying dispositions of ISO stock, the employer is entitled to an income tax deduction for compensation expense to the extent the employee is required to recognize ordinary income.

Compensation expense

Although it sometimes escapes notice, the granting of stock options, whether they are nonstatutory stock options or ISOs, creates a potential compensation expense for the employer which must be disclosed, at least in the footnotes, in its financial statements.[26] In addition, granting stock options to employees often dilutes earnings per share. Just how these effects should be disclosed has been a subject of some controversy for well over a decade.[27]

In recording compensation expense, the objective is (1) to determine the amount of the total compensation expense for financial reporting purposes and (2) to determine the period or periods over which the compensation expense should be allocated. Historically, authoritative accounting literature has required that compensation cost for stock options be measured, as of the "measurement date," by the quoted market price of the stock (or, if that's unavailable, the best estimate of the market value of the stock) less the amount, if any, that the employee is required to pay. The "measurement date" is the first date on which are known both (1) the number of shares that an individual employee is entitled to receive, and (2) the option or purchase price, if any.[28] If the option grant is a so-called "fixed award," both of these elements are known at the grant date, in which case total compensation cost is measured at the grant date. If either element is not known at the grant date, the option grant is a so-called "variable award." In the case of a "variable award," the employer estimates the compensation cost each period from the date of grant to the measurement date (e.g., exercise date), using quoted market prices or estimates of fair market value for each period, and compares these prices to the exercise price.

Fixed award plan

When XYZ Company granted options to Joe, both the number of shares (10) and the purchase price ($5) were known. Therefore, this is a "fixed award" and the grant date is the "measurement date." For book purposes, compensation expense for XYZ Company's option grant to Joe is $0 because on the grant date the market price of XYZ Company stock, $5, was equal to the exercise price of $5. XYZ Company must disclose the economic substance of the transaction in the notes to its financial statements. The bottom line for the XYZ Company Stock Option Plan is this: the company compensated Joe handsomely for his services and did so with no cash outlay and no charge to earnings. What's more, the employer gets a tax deduction for compensation expense. Could this be the elusive "free lunch?"

---

26 FASB Statement No. 123
27 For a full discussion of this subject see John R. Deming, Scott L. Dekker and Perter T. Chingos, "Accounting for Stock-Based Compensation" *Paying for Performance,* John Wiley & Sons, Inc. New York, 1997.
28 APB Opinion No. 25, para 10.

Variable award plan

Let's suppose, instead, that the XYZ Company option plan increases the number of shares covered by the option by five for each year Joe reaches his target revenue goals, thus converting the plan from a "fixed award" to a "variable award" plan. XYZ Company must, under current accounting standards, report a liability for the cost of compensation for each period until the measurement date. Under this modification to the plan, XYZ Company still makes no cash outlay and still gets a tax deduction, but the plan is a drag on financial statement earnings. One could argue that, as an incentive for high-performance, this plan is superior to the "fixed award" but, for most start-up companies and growth-oriented small employers, creating attractive compensation without a cash outlay or financial statement expense has a certain irresistible charm.

The last decade has seen mounting criticism of this financial accounting treatment of stock options for overstating earnings and earnings per share. Attempts by the Financial Accounting Standards Board (FASB) to address the issue have met with fierce resistance from employers who rely on options to compete for management and employees. In a compromise reached in 1995, the FASB issued a statement allowing companies to retain the current approach to accounting for options if they expand footnotes to disclose the results which would have been reported under a fair-value method of reporting.[29]

How Much to Give Away?

There can be no doubt that a real cost attaches to offering stock options even if the only sign of a liability is buried in the footnotes to the financial statements. For start-up companies, the price is paid by the companies' founders who, at the end of the game, will not wind up with all the marbles. Sharing some of the marbles with management and employees (among others) may well have been a necessary cost of starting a high tech business in the 90s, but the question is how much sharing is enough?

Writing in *Journal of Business Strategy*, Pearl Meyer of Pearl Meyer & Partners, a New York based executive compensation consulting firm, reports "unprecedented growth in the number of shares reserved for outstanding and future grants under equity programs." Her comments are based on the results of a 1998 annual survey of the 200 largest public U.S. industrial and service corporations. More than half of the companies surveyed have allocated over 10 percent of outstanding shares to management and employee equity incentives. The survey reported that 14 companies allocated more than 25 percent of outstanding shares to equity incentives.[30]

---

[29] For a full discussion of this subject see John R. Deming, Scott L. Dekker and Perter T. Chingos, "Accounting for Stock-based Compensation" *Paying for Performance*, John Wiley & Sons, Inc. New York, 1997.

[30] Pearl Meyer, "Stock is No Longer Optional," *Journal of Business Strategy*, (March/April, 1998)

Among high technology companies in the Pearl Meyer survey, the average allocation of outstanding shares to equity incentive plans was over 19 percent, considerably higher than the overall average of 13.2 percent.[31] The 1998 Oregon Technology Benchmarks survey found that, in Oregon, over half of the companies that offered stock options to employees allocated 18 percent of their outstanding shares to the option plans. Even among the smallest firms surveyed, those with revenues of less than $1 million, the allocation was 16 percent of outstanding shares.[32]

Is Granting Stock Options Really Giving Away the Company?

Although granting stock options to employees is often thought to make "owners" of employees, the truth is that it rarely does. Whether because of cash flow problems or risk aversion, most employees exercise and sell on the same day. One survey found that more than 90 percent of the shares received through option exercise are immediately sold.[33] Commenting that this statistic matches his observations, Ralph Shaw says, "This is what I've seen people typically do. [Employees] don't exercise their options until they are ready to sell. They exercise when, in their judgment, the stock is fully priced."

For a privately held company, this tactic, of course, assumes a market for the shares. Where the employer's stock is not publicly traded, employee ownership may become a reality but most often terminates if employment terminates. This presents a cost of stock option plans that is occasionally an issue, but rarely considered in up-front planning. The situation is most likely to occur for a privately held company whose owners intend to take it public and have used stock options as part of the company's compensation strategy. The company may find itself using its scarce cash to buy back shares from terminating employees—if the company has prospered—at a higher price than the employees paid for the shares. Consequently, an option plan purported to be cashless compensation may become a net cash drain while the company is still a privately held company. Moreover, the sale can create compensation expense for financial statement reporting if the stock was held by the terminating employee for less than six months.

What Do the Company's Founders Buy With Options?

The conventional wisdom says that stock options, unlike cash compensation, align the interests of the company's management and employees with those of the shareholders. In other words, option plans motivate management and employees to act like owners. Best yet, options do this without costing any "real money." To this Michelle Elarier says,

---

31 Meyer.

32 *The 1998 Oregon Technology Benchmarks*, published by American Electronics Association, Oregon Council, and KPMG LLP.

33 Michelle Elarier, "To Have and to have Not; Analysis of Economic Effects of Stock Options," *CFO, The Magazine for Senior Financial Executives* (March 1998).

"Welcome to fantasyland . . . . The combination of overstated earnings and dilution from currently exercisable options distorts actual earnings per share." In addition, she says, they may not, in fact, motivate management to act like shareholders. Unlike shareholders, the executive with stock options faces no downside risk (and a potentially huge return) because the executive has put none of his own money on the line until he exercises. Writing in *CFO*, Ms. Elarier cites some evidence that options, in fact, motivate executives to pursue more aggressive and riskier activities than would shareholders who have some of their own "hard earned" money at stake.[34]

Is there no downside in aggressive, even risky, activities? "But that's true for young entrepreneurial companies, in general," says investment banker Gayle Veber, general partner of Veber & Partners. "They're always swinging for the fences. They want to hit the home run. If you are not aggressive and quick, you won't make it anyway." He has observed that entrepreneurs, as a group, don't focus on the downside. "They are not oriented that way." Start-up technology companies may well find that, if stock options encourage recruited talent to focus only on the upside—to engage in aggressive risk-taking behavior—then options do indeed align the interest of the recruited talent with the entrepreneur shareholder. Similarly, dilution of earnings per share is a nonissue for most start-up technology companies, many of whom would be delighted to have earnings to dilute.

Fact Is, Everybody's Doing It

The pool of executives and employees from which high tech start-ups must draw is accustomed to stock options as a standard part of the compensation mix. Even if stock options are not a good idea for all companies, "it may be too late to put the stock-option genie back in the bottle," says Michelle Elarier, writing in CFO.[35] Long-term incentives have come to dominate the compensation mix for senior executives of the nations' leading companies and stock options make up the cornerstone of these long-term incentive programs. In a survey of 133 public and privately held companies, KPMG LLP found that 78% of executives receive nonqualified stock options and 23 percent receive incentive stock options (ISOs). In fact, on average, long-term incentives (primarily stock options) make up just short of half of the compensation packages of CFOs and COOs, and 54% for CEOs.[36] And stock options are by no means exclusive to the executive suite, particularly in technology companies. Indeed, companies like Microsoft and Mentor Graphics have helped create a climate in the Pacific Northwest that makes stock options an expectation at all levels of employment in the technology industry. Ralph Shaw, whose venture funds have launched the likes of Costco, Sequent, and Protocol, sees broad participation as a definite

[34] Elarier.
[35] Elarier.
[36] KPMG Surveys Companies on Long-Term Incentive Compensation, Issues in Performance & Compensation Management, February 1998

plus. "You don't want to create a split within the organization between those who are rewarded [by the company's success] and those who are not. I'm a strong advocate that everyone in the company should participate—that everyone throughout the business is benefiting from its success."

Over the past decade, stock options have become an important and, in some industries, essential tool in the effort to attract, retain, and motivate employees. The boom in option plans, and particularly certain widely-published option windfalls, has caused some investors and lawmakers to join the FASB in looking askance at stock option plans, convinced that unwary shareholders or taxpayers are actually paying for somebody's free lunch. Certainly the favorable tax and accounting treatment explains much of the growth of stock option plans—and much of the attractiveness of this type of compensation for start-up technology companies. Moreover, for widely held, publicly traded companies, the criticism of stock option plans may have some merit. For the entrepreneur, however, the criticism is wide of the mark. If the founders understand the real costs to themselves, and nevertheless wish to attract a team that shares their vision, a stock option plan is the right way to go.

18.5   Immigration As a Source for Employees

—by Christopher R. Helm and Paul S. Taylor
Davis Wright Tremaine LLP

Introduction

The globalization of the labor market and the rapid growth of certain industries have led to increasing labor shortages for many key occupations in major employment centers. As a result, all U.S. executives and managers have had to gain some familiarity with the basics of U.S. immigration law. Since all non-U.S. citizens entering the United States must comply with U.S. immigration laws and regulations, the employer seeking to hire a foreign worker must be aware of the options and limitations presented by these laws and regulations. The following information is intended as a guide to the basic types of visas available to U.S. employers of foreign workers. You may wish to consult with an immigration lawyer regarding the application of the immigration laws to a specific individual you are considering for employment.

Foreigners may enter and remain in the U.S. under two basic categories of visas: nonimmigrant and immigrant visas. Nonimmigrant visas allow non-U.S. citizens and non-U.S.

permanent residents to reside in the U.S. on a temporary basis. Immigrant visas, commonly referred to as "green cards," grant non-U.S. citizens "permanent residency" (the right to reside and work indefinitely in the U.S.).

Although the term "visas" applies in both the nonimmigrant and immigrant visa context, the actual "visa" is only a stamp in a passport which permits entry to the United States in a certain immigrant or nonimmigrant status. The Immigration and Naturalization Service (INS) inspector at the port of entry will determine the authorized period of stay for nonimmigrants by issuing an I-94 (Departure Record) card stamped with the date of entry, the status in which the nonimmigrant has entered, and the expiration date of the period of stay. In some cases, such as with F-1 Student Visas and J-1 International Exchange Visitors' Visas, the INS inspector will stamp the letters "D/S" (for duration of status) rather than a date, indicating that the person may remain in the U.S. as long as he maintains that status.

After entry, the I-94 status and authorized period of stay indicated on the card are important, while the visa has no further significance until such time as the foreign worker seeks to depart and reenter the U.S. at some later date.

Single entry

Some visas, marked "Single Entry," are "used up" once that single entry is accomplished.

Multiple entry

Other visas, marked "Multiple Entry," permit multiple departures from and reentry into the U.S. during their period of validity, with each entry again subject to the determination of the immigration inspector, at his or her sole discretion, that the applicant is entering the U.S. for purposes consistent with the status he or she is seeking. Once the visa expires, the foreign worker can remain in the U.S. for the period of stay authorized on the I-94. However, once she leaves the U.S., she cannot reenter the U.S. without obtaining a new visa.

Of the many types of immigrant and nonimmigrant visas, this section discusses only those that are most relevant to a U.S. employer of foreign workers.

Nonimmigrant Visas

The nonimmigrant visa categories serve to bring in foreign workers for a temporary stay, including for evaluation purposes. Some employers who may need the permanent services of a worker but are unable to fill the position in the U.S., may choose to bring in a foreign worker under a nonimmigrant visa while they evaluate her suitability for permanent employment.

Discussed below are the Visa Waiver Program and the B, E, H, L visas, and other temporary visas.

Visa waiver program

Under the Visa Waiver Program, visitors to the U.S. from certain designated countries may now enter the U.S. on a temporary basis without first obtaining a visa stamp from a U.S. consulate. To qualify for this status, the visitor must be a citizen of a country designated for this program, which currently includes most countries in western Europe and Japan. Under this program, the visitor is admitted to the U.S. for a period not to exceed 90 days, during which time the visitor may not be employed by or receive compensation from any U.S. business or individual, other than reimbursement of expenses. Temporary visitors for business, as well as for tourism or pleasure, may avail themselves of this program.

Your prospective employee may be able to enter the U.S. as a temporary visitor, pursuant to this program, for the purposes of an interview, or prior to relocating to the U.S., to make certain arrangements such as locating housing or finding schools for his children.

Other business visitors who qualify for the visa waiver program may enter on a visa waiver to engage in the same activities permitted to B-1 temporary visitors for business, and which are described below.

B visas

Visitors wishing to enter the U.S. for less than six months for either business or pleasure purposes may obtain a B visa from any overseas U.S. embassy or consulate. The B-1 visa is for business visitors, and the B-2 visa is for tourists and other visitors for pleasure. To qualify for a B visa, the visitor must have a permanent residence outside of the U.S. to which the visitor intends to return. Further, while B-1 visitors are permitted to engage in commercial activities in the U.S., they may not be employed by or receive compensation from U.S. businesses, although reimbursement of expenses is generally permitted.

The foreign visitor may be able to obtain a B-1 visa in order to enter the U.S. for a short visit to arrange employment and preemployment matters. However, unlike the visa waiver situation, the foreign visitor can enter the U.S. with a B-1 visa to be interviewed, and then, if she accepts the position, change status to another nonimmigrant visa status which permits employment. The applicant should disclose this possibility to the visa consul when applying for the visa.

In addition, employees or executives from your overseas business partners, customers, subsidiaries and affiliates may obtain B-1 visas to enter the U.S. to conduct certain business with you.

While local employment is not permitted, business activities which are permitted pursuant to visa waiver or B-1 visa status may include: litigation support; business consultation; sales and marketing activities; market research; attendance at business conferences and trade fairs; limited attendance in an established training program; foreign directors of U.S. corporations entering to attend board meetings; certain professional activities on behalf of a foreign employer for a limited period of time when the employee continues to receive a salary from abroad; limited activities while setting up a business in order to qualify for an E or L visa. Please note that special rules under the NAFTA may permit additional activities to those entering from Canada or Mexico.

E visas

If your company is majority owned by nationals of a foreign country, you may be able to utilize a special class of visas to bring managers and executives, and certain employees with specialized skills, from that country, to manage and operate the U.S. company. Approximately 40 countries have entered into treaties with the U.S. to allow their citizens to enter the U.S. to facilitate business between their country and the U.S. Two types of E visas have been established for these visitors: the E-1 visa for "treaty traders" who need to come to the U.S. to facilitate trade between the U.S. and the foreign country; the E-2 visa, for "treaty investors" who make a substantial investment in the U.S. In either case, E visas are available for managers or executives of the foreign businesses who need to come to the U.S. on a temporary basis on behalf of the foreign trader or investor. These visas are also available for employees with specialized skills that are essential to the efficient operation of the enterprise.

To obtain an E visa, the applicant must first submit a detailed application to the appropriate U.S. consular office in the country in which the applicant resides. If the individual is already in the U.S. in another status which permits change of status (most, but not visa waiver), he first files a detailed petition with the Immigration and Naturalization Service regional service center in the U.S. The application/petition must include a variety of information regarding the treaty trader or investor and the employees who wish to enter the U.S. Those in the U.S. may remain in the new status, after approval, but must obtain another visa from a U.S. consulate to reenter the U.S., if they depart. These visas, normally issued for an initial period of three to five years, can be renewed indefinitely as needed by the treaty trader or investor.

H visas

Several types of H visas are available for temporary workers in the U.S. The H-1B visa is of significant interest to U.S. employers in the many high tech industries in the U.S. who wish to employ a foreign worker on a temporary basis in a specialty occupation. Unlike E visas (or L visas discussed below), the holder of an H-1B visa may work for a U.S. business even if the business is not connected to any overseas activity. To qualify for an H-1B visa, the applicant must be a professional with the equivalent of a U.S. bachelor's degree and must enter the U.S. to fill a position for which a bachelor's degree is typically the minimum requirement. In some situations, education and specialized training or professional work experience overseas, or some combination of education, training, and experience may qualify in lieu of a bachelor's degree.

To obtain an H-1B visa, the employer must first submit an application to the U.S. Department of Labor certifying that the wages to be paid are at least as high (not less than 95%) as the prevailing wage for that job for the particular locale in the U.S. and not less than that paid by the employer to U.S. workers in similar positions. Then, the employer must submit a detailed petition to the appropriate INS regional service center for adjudication. Once the application is approved, the employee must either obtain an H-1B visa from a U.S. consulate overseas or change status in the U.S., if eligible. H-1B visas are normally granted for an initial period of three years, but can be extended for up to six years if required by the U.S. employer.

The employer should be aware that the INS may issue only 65,000 new H-1Bs each fiscal year ending September 30. For the past few years, this number has been reached well before the October 1 starting date for the new fiscal year. Therefore, it is important to consider these numbers in your visa planning if you seek to hire any H-1B temporary workers. Please review this issue carefully with your immigration counsel.

If you have an established training program in your company, or are willing to set up such a program, you may be able to bring foreigners to the U.S. to train in your program under H-3 visas. To qualify, you must be able to show that you have established an appropriate training program, that the foreigner cannot obtain such training in his own country, and that upon completion, he or she will be able to make use of the training in his own country.

L visas

L visas are useful to transfer—between foreign and U.S. affiliated companies—executives, managers, and certain employees with specialized knowledge. It does not matter which is the parent company. To qualify for an L visa, the employee must have worked for at least one of the previous three years outside of the U.S. for a company that is affiliated with the prospective U.S. employer in either an executive position, managerial position, or a position that requires specialized knowledge and must be coming to the U.S. to occupy an executive, managerial, or specialized knowledge position with the U.S. affiliate.

To obtain an L visa, the applicant must first submit a detailed petition to the appropriate INS regional service center in the U.S. with information about the foreign employer, the U.S. affiliate, and the individual applicant's qualifications. Once approved by the INS, the applicant must either obtain the visa from a U.S. consulate overseas or change status in the U.S., if eligible. L visas, normally granted for an initial period of three years (one year for new U.S. businesses), can be extended for up to seven years (up to five years for specialized knowledge workers) if required by the affiliated U.S. employer.

Other temporary visas

Many other temporary visas may be used to bring foreigners to the U.S. These include F visas for students, H-2B visas for certain temporary workers, and J visas for exchange visitors. Each of these visas has its own requirements and procedures, which you should review with your immigration counsel.

Immigrant Visas

Immigrant visas fall into three basic categories: employment-based, family-sponsored, and political (asylum). Each category further divides according to preference groups. Generally, the higher the preference, the shorter the waiting time to obtain the immigrant visa. Although the focus here is on employment-based immigrant visas, you may be able to bring in a foreign worker in a permanent resident status if he or she is able to gain such a benefit by virtue of a family relationship, such as a U.S. citizen spouse, parent or sibling, or a permanent resident spouse or parent. There are five categories of employment-based immigrant visas:

1. First preference: priority workers

Certain individuals may qualify for "First Preference: Priority Worker" immigrant visas. Of particular relevance to companies with foreign affiliates such as parents, subsidiaries, branch or representative offices, is the First Preference visa for multinational executives or managers who are transferred to the U.S. to work for an affiliate company. This visa category resembles the L visas discussed above. To qualify for this visa, the worker must have worked for at least one of the previous three years for a foreign company that is affiliated with the prospective U.S. employer. Further, the worker must be an executive or a manager with substantial responsibilities within the company. Finally, the U.S. entity must have existed for at least one year prior to the date of application. This immigrant visa is not available for workers who are not executives or managers and who have specialized knowledge and thus qualify for the L visa.

This first preference is also available for certain individuals of extraordinary ability in science, arts, education, business, or athletics and for certain outstanding professors and researchers.

Obtaining a green card in this manner requires a two-step process. First, the applicant must submit a detailed petition to the appropriate INS regional service center in the U.S. with information about the individual and, where applicable, the applicant's employer overseas and in the U.S. Once approved, the applicant must then either obtain the visa from a U.S. consulate overseas or adjust status through the appropriate INS regional service center if in the U.S. In either case, the applicant will be required to submit a variety of additional documents and information before the actual visa is granted. The number of visas issued in this category is subject to quotas set by the U.S. Congress. Until recently, those qualifying for first preference visas had been able to apply for their visas or adjust their status immediately upon approval of their petitions; however, waiting periods currently apply to applicants from the Peoples' Republic of China.

2. Second preference: exceptional ability/advanced degree

Second Preference immigrant visas are available for foreigners of exceptional ability or for professionals who hold advanced degrees. To qualify for this visa, the applicant must either have exceptional ability in some specialized area or hold an advanced degree, which includes any degree beyond the equivalent of a U.S. bachelor's degree.

Obtaining this visa includes a three-step process. First, the applicant must obtain certification from the U.S. Department of Labor. This lengthy process requires the prospective U.S. employer to first attempt to recruit a qualified U.S. worker to fill the position. Recruitment activities must be coordinated with the local state employment agency. If the U.S. employer can successfully demonstrate that he has been unable to recruit a qualified U.S. worker, the U.S. Department of Labor will issue an Alien Employment Certification.

Second, the U.S. employer submits a petition to the appropriate regional INS service center in the U.S.

Third, once the petition is approved, the applicant must either obtain a visa from a U.S. consulate overseas or apply to the appropriate regional INS service center to adjust status in the U.S. In either case, the applicant will be required to submit a variety of additional documents and information before the actual visa status is granted. Further, the existence of quotas may delay visa processing for holders of approved Second Preference visa petitions.

In certain instances, the INS can waive required labor certification if the activity engaged in or to be engaged in by the foreigner can be shown to promote the national interest in one or more of number of areas, including promoting education, health, the environment, and the economy.

3. Third preference: professional/skilled worker/other workers

Workers who do not qualify for First or Second Preference visas may qualify for a Third Preference visa. These visas are available to professionals without advanced degrees, to skilled workers, or to other workers. To qualify as a professional without an advanced degree, the individual must be a member of a profession and hold the equivalent of a U.S. bachelor's degree. To qualify as a skilled worker, the individual must have at least two years of training or experience in a specific job.

The application process for Third Preference visas resembles that for the Second Preference. First, the applicant must obtain certification from the U.S. Department of Labor after recruitment efforts have been made. Second, the applicant must apply to the appropriate INS regional service center. Third, the applicant must obtain a visa from a U.S. consulate, or if in the U.S., apply to the regional INS service center to adjust status.

Quotas have been set for Third Preference visas. Applicants from India and China and applicants who do not qualify as professionals or skilled workers often must wait for significant lengths of time before their visa can be issued.

4. Other immigrant visas

Other business-related immigrant visas are available, as well, such as the Fifth Preference: Investor Visa. This visa is available for any individual or business that invests at least $1 million (or $500,000 in certain economically depressed geographic regions) in a new or existing enterprise in the U.S. and creates at least 10 additional jobs for U.S. workers.

For the many options available to the U.S. employer who is considering bringing in a foreign employee or worker to work in the United States, the simpler the duties or the more basic the type of job, the more difficult it will be to obtain any type of visa that permits the individual to seek employment in the U.S. Conversely, the more qualified the individual, and the more advanced the requirements of the employer for the position, the more opportunities exist to obtain a visa, either immigrant or nonimmigrant, for the employee. If you have any questions about the visa options available to you when you are considering hiring a foreign worker, you should probably discuss them with your visa counsel **prior** to extending an offer of employment.

18.6 Safety Issues and Ergonomics

—by Anne E. Denecke
Davis Wright Tremaine LLP

Note: This article references certain statutory requirements, using the State of Washington as an example. It is recommended that you check your own state's laws regarding the issues discussed herein.

Many nonmanufacturing employers, unaware of their safety-related responsibilities, are surprised to learn that they have similar obligations. To begin with, Washington law imposes an obligation on *all* employers to **provide a "safe and healthful environment."** In addition, all employers are responsible for implementing a program to prevent accidents and for implementing training programs in such areas as the safe use of power equipment to handle materials and the safe use of toxic materials. (WAC 296-240-020).[37] Most of

---

[37] References to "WAC" refer to the 1997 Washington Administrative Code

these obligations are combined with record-keeping responsibilities.

Records

For example, all employers are required to maintain in each workplace a "system for **maintaining records of occupational illnesses and injuries**." The definition of recordable cases includes (a) occupational death; (b) occupational illness; and (c) occupational injury that involves *one* of the following:

- unconsciousness
- inability to perform all phases of the employee's regular job
- inability to work full-time on the employee's regular job
- temporary assignment to another job
- medical treatment beyond first aid

Employers with 11 or more employees must record these occupational illnesses and injuries on federal Occupational Safety and Health Administration (OSHA) forms OSHA 101 and OSHA 200. Federal OSHA laws require that each employer annually post a completed OSHA 200 form at each of its work sites between February 1 and March 1.

All employers also must **post a notice** prepared by the Washington Industrial Safety and Health Act administration (WISHA)—form F416-081-000—informing employees of the protections and obligations under the Safety and Health Act.

Businesses employing 11 or more employees must **designate a safety committee** composed of employer-selected and employee-selected members (WAC 296-24-045). The purpose of the committee is to assist in the correction of identified unsafe conditions and practices, to evaluate the sufficiency of accident investigations, and to evaluate the sufficiency of the employer's accident and illness prevention program.

First Aid

In addition, the Safety and Health Act obligates all employers to ensure that, at all times, at least one available employee is **first aid certified**. Additionally, all forepersons, supervisors, or persons in direct charge of an off-site crew of two or more employees, or in direct charge of a group or groups of employees are required to have a valid first aid certificate (WAC 296-24-060). Employers also must provide a "readily accessible" first aid kit to employees.

These are merely a few of the safety-related requirements imposed on Washington employers. To determine whether an employer has additional obligations, the employer should contact WISHA, their workers' compensation insurance carrier, or employment counsel.

Ergonomics

A relatively new safety-related term has received considerable publicity in the past several years: **"ergonomics."** Ergonomics is the study of the physiological and anatomical capabilities and limitations of individuals relating to their work tasks, equipment, and job environment. In other words, ergonomics is the science of trying to match the abilities of the worker with the physical and mental requirements of the job. In general, the purpose of ergonomic considerations is to reduce the number of injuries caused by repeated motions and tasks, including cumulative trauma disorders and repetitive motion injuries such as carpal tunnel syndrome, tendonitis, and muscle strain. Federal OSHA has reported that an employer's failure to consider ergonomic factors in the design of workstations and job procedures results in stress and injuries.

No regulations

Although OSHA has discussed implementation of ergonomic regulations, the agency has not yet adopted a specific safety standard governing workplace ergonomics. Nevertheless, OSHA investigators pursue ergonomic hazards through the OSHA "general duty" clause. This standard requires employers to provide a work environment "free from recognized hazards that are causing or are likely to cause death or serious physical harm" (similar to the WISHA requirement for Washington employers).[38]

Citations possible

Through the use of the general duty and/or WAC 296-240-020, state and federal field compliance investigators can and do **issue citations** for ergonomics violations. Such citations typically require employers to eliminate or mitigate the hazard by:

- evaluating the hazardous ergonomic conditions in their workplace
- developing a detailed abatement plan that includes training
- developing a plan to ensure that injured workers receive necessary medical care
- developing a schedule for implementing engineering or administrative controls

Employers should consider **addressing ergonomic issues** prior to passage of a specific safety standard governing workplace ergonomics. Both WISHA and an employer's carrier for workers' compensation are good information sources for developing strategies for improving workplace ergonomics.

---

[38] The Washington Administrative Code specifically notes that state safety and health rules are intended to be "at least as effective" as those adopted by federal OSHA, and that many state rules incorporate existing federal safety rules.

18.7   Documenting the Employment Relationship

—by Bob Blackstone
Davis Wright Tremaine LLP

As is the case with many topics that raise legal issues, having good, clear documentation of the key aspects of the relationship between an employer and its workers can go a long way toward preventing problems and minimizing liabilities. In addition, increasingly a company's most valuable asset is its intellectual property, whether it be software code, technical data and plans, or customer data. Protection of that intellectual property is a very important objective for most companies.

Written Agreements

Written agreements between an employer and its workers can address these issues. A number of options govern how extensive and detailed such employment documentation should be and which workers should be required to sign what types of agreements. These most common issues should be addressed in some kind of written agreement:

- Recognition that the worker will have access to confidential information of the employer and an agreement by the worker not to disclose it outside the company or use it improperly, either during or for some period of time after the end of the worker's relationship with the employer.

- The extent of the rights that both the employer and the worker have in inventions or other creative work product which the worker develops during his or her relationship with the employer.

- The extent, if any, to which the worker will be precluded from competing with the employer after the relationship ends, and/or from soliciting the employer's customers or other employees.

The regulation of agreements between employers and workers rests primarily in state law. For example, in some states noncompetition agreements are essentially unenforceable, while many other states will enforce such agreements to the extent they are reasonable. Some states limit the extent to which employers can require employees to assign inventions over to the employer. Many states have adopted a law called the Uniform Trade Secrets Act that protects an employer's trade secrets, but even this law is not exactly the same in all states.

(**Note:** This discussion refers both to "employees" and to "workers," a designation which may include both employees as well as persons who are independent contractors. For these purposes, different considerations may apply to each category, depending on the issue. For example, independent contractors may refuse to agree not to work with competitors once they have completed an assignment (or conceivably even during an assignment) and may refuse to assign their rights to inventions to the employer. Having a clear written agreement which carefully spells out the individual's rights and obligations is thus particularly important.)

Like any documents with legal consequences, these agreements should be drafted or at least reviewed by a lawyer familiar with the employment laws of the states in which the company will be operating.

Confidentiality and Nondisclosure Agreements

Typically, employers will require *all* employees and independent contractors to sign a confidentiality and nondisclosure agreement before they begin employment. These agreements commonly contain language that requires employees to disclose and assign the rights to the employer of any inventions or other creative work product developed in the course of employment.

Although employers have certain legal protections for their trade secrets under both state and federal law, written confidentiality and nondisclosure agreements can significantly enhance the protections available to employers. Such confidentiality and nondisclosure agreements typically address the following types of issues:

- The kinds of information which the employer considers to be confidential

- A specific promise by the employee to maintain the confidentiality of the information

- Recognition that the employee may receive confidential information from third parties, such as customers or suppliers, and an agreement also to maintain the confidentiality of such information

- An agreement to return any confidential information upon the termination of employment

- Recognition that the company can be irreparably damaged by the release of confidential information and agreement by the employee that injunctive relief may be appropriate

- Acknowledgement by employees that they will not be using confidential information belonging to others in the course of their work

- Disclosure of any other confidentiality or similar agreements with other employers that the employee may still be subject to

Assignment of Rights Agreements

These provisions, frequently included in confidentiality and nondisclosure agreements, require the worker to disclose and assign the rights to the employer, of any inventions or other creative work product developed in the course of employment. Typical provisions in these kinds of agreements include the following:

- Recognition of employer ownership of inventions, improvements, processes, discoveries, and other types of work product developed by the worker while employed by the employer

- Assignment by the employee to the employer of any of employee's rights in such inventions

- Agreement by employee to disclose any inventions or other work product that they make while employed

- Agreement by the employee to sign any necessary documents which will allow the employer to secure legal protections for such inventions and other original work, such as patents and copyrights

Some states restrict these kinds of provisions by not allowing employers to require employees to assign rights to inventions that do not relate to the business of the employer and did not involve use of the employer's time, equipment, facilities, or equipment.

Noncompetition/Nonsolicitation Agreements

Given both the relative importance of confidential information to many businesses and the growing mobility of workers, many employers find themselves increasingly interested in restricting the ability of workers to go to work for competitors and/or to solicit customers or other employees after they leave. Employers are concerned that they will train employees and give them access to important business data and customers only to see them quit and go into competition, either working for themselves or for a competing company. On the other hand, American law recognizes the general desirability of competition, and courts are reluctant to restrict a person's ability to earn a living or to enforce a restraint of trade. Written noncompetition and nonsolicitation agreements with employees can provide employers with some protection against these risks.

As noted above, the enforceability of noncompetition agreements, a matter of state law, has to be assessed on a state-by-state basis. Although they are generally disfavored by the courts, most states are willing to enforce noncompetition agreements if they are supported by consideration (i.e., the employee received something of value in return for giving up their right to compete) and if they are "reasonable." Whether a particular agreement is "reasonable" typically depends on the duration of the restriction, the scope of the restriction in terms of the lines of business and geographic area covered, and the extent to which the employer can demonstrate a legitimate basis for imposing the restriction (such as protecting trade secrets, realizing the value of training provided the employee, or protecting the customer relationships and goodwill of the employer).

Generally speaking, agreements which prohibit solicitation of clients or customers are more likely to be enforced than blanket restrictions on competition. Most restrictions last for between six months and three years after employment. The shorter the restriction, the more likely it is to be enforced. Counsel, familiar with the laws of the states in which the company will have employees, should carefully draft and review noncompetition agreements.

Employment Agreements

A number of employers are expanding the use of comprehensive employment agreements to document all of the significant aspects of the employment relationship, and not just with their most senior executives where they have traditionally been used. These agreements typically include confidentiality, assignment of inventions, and noncompetition provisions, but they also deal with issues such as job descriptions, salary, benefits, stock options, termination, severance pay, and alternative dispute resolution procedures. Although in most states employment is still "at will," the courts have increasingly found a variety of exceptions to the general "at will" rule based on documents such as employee handbooks, supervisory manuals, and offer letters. Rather than face the uncertainty of what a court might interpret as constituting a term of the employment relationship, employers and employees see value in spelling out the essential terms in one document which they both sign. Having an employment agreement can reduce employer flexibility in making changes to the employment relationship, but careful drafting can minimize this problem.

There has been a significant increase in employment litigation throughout the United States over the last 20 years. One of the most compelling reasons for many employers to consider written employment agreements is to be able to include a provision by which the employee and employer agree to arbitrate any disputes concerning the employment relationship rather than traditional court litigation. Many employers would prefer that disputes with their employees be decided by an arbitrator with experience in employment law issues rather than put their fate in the hands of a jury.

- Chapter 19 -

Marketing Your Products

19.1 Revenue Forecasting

—by Barry Briggs
Barry Briggs & Company

Forecasting simply means predicting the revenue you expect your products and services to generate over a fixed period of time. Used to prepare operating budgets for the same period, forecasts are typically prepared several months prior to the start of a fiscal year. A revenue forecast and the resulting budget form essential parts of a yearly business plan.

Because the technology marketplace changes very quickly, forecasts are moving targets, at best. It's smart to do a formal forecast; it's also smart to review and revise it halfway through a fiscal year, if necessary.

Forecasting revenue is not rocket science. In the best of circumstances, it constitutes an educated guess. In less rosy circumstances, it's simply a guess. This section defines some of the important variables you should consider as you develop a forecast.

Developing a Baseline

A forecast is typically based on previous performance. If your product or service has been in the market for one or more years, you should have a good idea of what you can expect in the coming year. In this situation, your forecast should reflect revenue growth similar to that which you've experienced in previous years. Of course, one or more important variables may have changed, and these changes should be reflected. Important variables can include:

- new versions of your product
- changes in the competitive environment
- changes in the markeplace
- changes in your organization

If your product or service is new, you'll need to rely on estimates and research in the performance of similar competitive products. When you created the business plan for your venture, if you did not perform this research, you'll need to understand the overall size of the market, the number of competitors, and their market share and revenue. Then, you'll be in a position to estimate the impact your product will have on the market.

Market Conditions

Whether or not your product has a market history, you'll have to factor changing market conditions into the forecast. This will vary widely by category. Two common factors are these:

Competition

Are significant changes in the competitive environment anticipated in the next year? Such changes could range from new product entries to product/company acquisitions.

Technology Shifts

Is your category likely to experience a major shift in technology in the next year? If so, what does that imply for your revenue opportunity? The rapid acceptance of Microsoft Windows opened new revenue opportunities for some companies and reduced opportunities for others. The integration of utilities and networking capabilities into operating systems impacts revenue opportunities for some companies. The introduction of advanced hardware platforms can create opportunities for new product ideas.

Organizational Commitment

Your ability to generate revenue will be determined, in part, by the company's willingness to make this a priority. A company and its structure can impact revenue in several ways.

Marketing Budget. By increasing marketing expenditures, a company can reasonably expect improved business performance, at least in the short-term. Of course, an increase in the marketing budget may come at the expense of the research and development budget. Or, perhaps your company will have received a new round of investment that can be put toward marketing programs.

Size and Structure. In addition to increasing the marketing budget, organizational size and structure can impact forecasts. For example, increased staffing or quality in the sales organization can mean increased sales to corporate accounts. New marketing or communications managers can mean greater market awareness of your product. This awareness can translate into revenue.

In every case, it will be important to obtain the commitment of your sales organization to your forecast. After all, it's the sales department you will hold responsible for delivering the revenue.

Building a Forecast

Once you've clarified the unique assumptions that will affect your business performance, you'll need to create a spreadsheet that projects revenue by product, by month and quarter, and by channel. By forecasting at this level of specificity, you'll not only examine all aspects of your anticipated revenue stream but you'll be able to measure actual results on a monthly, quarterly, and yearly basis. These performance measures will enable you to adjust programs, spending, staffing, or other parts of your business plan, as needed.

Successful companies usually are conservative when it comes to forecasting, yet aggressive when it comes to marketing and sales. Since company operating and marketing budgets are based on the forecast, a conservative forecast can reduce the impact of rude surprises halfway through a fiscal year. Such surprises can come when products don't ship on time, when the competitive environment changes unexpectedly, or when expected investment doesn't occur. At the same time, a forecast can be too conservative: since budgets are based on forecasts, the small budgets that result from ultraconservative forecasting could make it difficult for the company to compete successfully.

19.2 Creating a Marketing Budget

—by Barry Briggs
Barry Briggs & Company

Once a fiscal year forecast has been developed, operations and marketing budgets can be developed. Creating a marketing budget for a multiple product company ultimately will depend on your unique situation—your product, your target market, your distribution channels, and your financial health.

Once a marketing budget has been created and the fiscal year begins, make every effort to adhere to the budget. Six months into the fiscal year, review marketing against the original marketing budget and against actual revenue. If necessary, make adjustments to planned marketing activities.

All company budgets begin with the company's profitability model that determines the basic operational assumptions for the business.

Profit Model

The profitability model you've created for your company constitutes the single biggest influence on a marketing budget. A typical software company profitability model looks like this:

Net Revenues	$1,000,000	100.00%
Cost of Sales	$ 180,000	18.00%
Gross Margin	$ 820,000	82.00%
Operating Expenses		
Research & Development	$ 160,000	16.00%
Sales & Marketing	$ 380,000	38.00%
General & Administrative	$ 100,000	10.00%
Total Operating Expenses	$ 640,000	64.00%
Operating Income	$ 180,000	18.00%

As you can see from this model, Sales and Marketing represent 38% percent of the total planned expenditure for this company. Sales expenses translate into head count. Marketing expenses translate into both head count and program expenses, reflected in the marketing budget.

The Marketing Budget

There are three steps in creating a marketing budget.

- Create a marketing pool. This pool shows the source of each product's budget and the general areas of allocation (e.g., corporate trade shows, individual product activities).

- Create individual product marketing budgets, showing planned spending by program (e.g., advertising, direct marketing).

- Spread the budget across the fiscal year—the marketing budget spread

The average software marketing budget represents 10% to 15% of revenue. For retail products, the budget is typically 10% to 12% of revenue; for products you sell directly, the budget may represent 12% to 15% of revenue.

Marketing Pool

Multiproduct companies usually have "above the line" expenses, like trade shows, catalogs, and other company-wide activities that benefit all products. Each revenue-producing product will be asked to contribute to these activities "above the line." The budgeting of marketing dollars across these programs is reflected in the marketing pool spreadsheet.

"Above the line" expenditures are usually budgeted into a separate corporate marketing budget.

Product Marketing Budget

"Below the line" activities benefit one product only. The funds left after the "above the line" contribution represent the actual product marketing budget available.

The "below the line" budget for retail products typically spreads across several categories of marketing activities, including advertising, public relations, direct marketing, promotions. While no hard-and-fast rules govern spending in these categories, some general guidelines apply.

Advertising	50% of budget
Public Relations	15% of budget
Collateral	10% of budget
Direct Marketing	15% of budget
Promotion	5% of budget
Research/Other	5% of budget

It's important to remember that these are general guidelines. The actual division of your marketing budget must reflect your product's unique market situation.

Marketing Budget Spread

Once a product's marketing budget has been determined, it's useful to spread the planned expenditures across the fiscal year. By placing planned expenditures in the months in which you expect them to occur, it will be easier to monitor actual spending versus planned spending.

19.3   Marketing Communications

—by Barry Briggs
Barry Briggs & Company

Communications Strategies: Getting the Most Out of Your Marketing Dollar

This section is designed to help you determine how and when to employ the various communications strategies, such as advertising, public relations, collateral. After this discussion, you will know what to expect from each strategy. This section does not discuss tactical implementation, that is, how to do it. For implementation, you should seek professional communications expertise.

Definitions

Advertising, direct marketing, point-of-sale displays, public relations, and sales materials are known as communications strategies. These strategies can be employed to build awareness, consideration, trial, and/or purchase of your company's products.

A successful communications program uses two or more of these strategies to accomplish the following objectives:

- Create initial consumer awareness of your product
- Place your product in the "consideration set" (the set of two or three products that are likely candidates for purchase)
- Obtain product trial (where relevant—some products will be purchased without trial)
- Generate product purchase
- Stimulate purchase of additional products, either new versions or other products in your company's line

No single communications strategy can achieve all these objectives. Each strategy plays a unique role in the process of creating product sales. The following chart illustrates this.

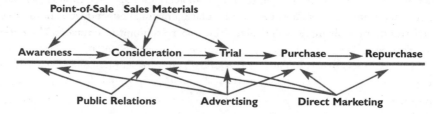

Getting Results

Communications strategies vary in their ability to successfully influence your audiences. The ability of a communications strategy to drive sales depends, in part, on the level of message control it offers. Advertising, for example, is a highly controlled medium; point-of-sale offers a lesser degree of control. The following discussion evaluates your ability to control consumer behavior—get results—with each of these strategies.

- *Advertising* is the purchase of media space or time (magazines, radio, television, newspapers, etc.) to deliver a message about your product, service, or company to the readers or listeners of that media. Of the various communications strategies, advertising offers a very high-level of control—you completely control the content and timing of your message; and by carefully selecting media, you can control who reads your message. The impact of advertising can range from building initial product awareness through purchase of your product.

- **Direct Marketing** is the process of selecting a well-defined target audience and then delivering a message directly and personally to each member of that audience. Common strategies for directly delivering a message are direct mail and telemarketing. Successful design and implementation of a direct marketing program gives the highest level of control of any communications strategy. Direct marketing, not very effective at building product awareness, can be extremely effective at creating product trial, purchase, or repurchase.

- **Point-of-Sale** displays provide a means of attracting attention to a product within a retail selling environment. Point-of-sale materials include product packaging, posters, shelf-talkers, counter-cards, and free-standing product displays. Except for packaging, getting the materials placed in-store and keeping them up in the store can be challenging. Successful deployment of a point-of-sale program usually requires an active field sales program. Point-of-sale materials offer a moderate-level of control: you control the message and how it's delivered; you have little control over the placement of the message or who sees it. As a result, point-of-sale programs are usually secondary for most developers.

- **Public Relations** is a means of delivering a message through third-party activities such as press relations, trade shows, conferences, or other events. Press relations relies on editors of selected magazines to deliver appropriate messages about a product. As a result, press relations offers a moderate amount of control (message content, timing, and whether the message is delivered at all can be difficult to control). The trade-off for this lower-level of control is a high degree of credibility for the message (which is great if the message is good, not so great if the editor doesn't like your product). Trade shows and other events offer a way to speak directly to potential buyers of your product. At these events, you completely control the message and its delivery; you typically have moderate or little control over who is exposed to your message.

- **Sales Materials** are printed materials—collateral—used to encourage purchase of your product. Data sheets, white papers, and brochures are examples of sales materials. While sales materials offer a high-level of control, research has shown that they play a relatively minor role in the purchase of software products. Prospects will already be aware of your product before they look at collateral and the collateral will, at best, encourage prospects to find out more about the product by reading reviews or, perhaps, by purchasing a trial version.

A General Approach to Communications

The communications strategies defined above work best when two or more are used to cover all aspects of the purchase process, from initial awareness through purchase; in fact, synergy is created when two or more strategies are deployed together. Research has shown that when advertising and public relations are used in tandem, you'll get more than twice the sales volume you'd expect from advertising or public relations alone.

The next section will help you think about which communications strategies can best achieve your marketing objectives.

Evaluating Communications Strategies

To determine which communications strategies need to be employed, identify what you need to accomplish.

Introducing new product

Are you introducing a new product or a new version of an existing product?

- If yes, then your primary marketing objective will be to create initial awareness of the product. Advertising and public relations are the two most effective strategies for creating initial awareness. Point-of-sale displays can create in-store awareness, but your company will probably need to have an established retail presence before a retailer will accept point-of-sale materials for a new product. Direct marketing will be very important if you have an installed base of product owners; however, direct marketing is not a cost-efficient means of generating initial product awareness.

- If no, then the market should already be aware of the product and you'll need to move the market toward product trial and/or purchase.

Narrowing consideration

When prospects evaluate products in your category, is your product generally one of the two or three products they consider?

- If yes, then your advertising and public relations have been effective. Direct marketing techniques can be used to stimulate customer predisposition toward your product and can even stimulate a sale. Advertising and sales materials can be used to properly position your product vis-a-vis the competition, thereby helping to place your product within the consideration set. It's harder to use public relations to position your product against competing products since editors steer away from overtly competitive claims.

- If no, you may have a problem with customer awareness (your product isn't considered because the prospect isn't aware of it), your product may not meet the technical requirements (you may need a new version of the product), or the customer may think that your product won't meet his/her needs. In this last case, you can modify consumer awareness of your product by changing your communications messages (maybe your product is mispositioned), by changing your communications media (maybe you're advertising in the wrong places), or by increasing your advertising, public relations, direct marketing, or other communications budgets.

- If you don't know, then you'll need to do some market research. This can be informal. Your sales staff can query prospects for information about other products the customer is considering and a survey of retail salespeople can be useful if your product is distributed through the channel. More formal research, like focus groups, can help you understand the market's perceptions of your product.

Evaluating products

Do products in your category typically go through extensive evaluation and trial before purchase?

- If yes, then you can use direct marketing techniques to monitor the trial process and insure customer satisfaction. In addition, if you can identify the job titles and/or functions of the individuals responsible for product evaluation, then you can use direct marketing to promote a trial version of your product. Advertising can also be used to promote a trial version. Public relations, sales materials, and point-of-sale materials are relatively inefficient at stimulating product trial.

- If no, then you should use communications strategies like advertising and direct marketing to create the impulse to purchase, either directly from you or through the channel.

- If you don't know, then you'll need to perform either formal or informal research to understand better the purchase process for products like yours.

Selling direct

Can you sell your product directly to the customer or must the customer go through the channel?

- If yes, then both direct marketing and advertising can be profitably used to create product sales. These strategies can be applied whether or not the product must first go through an evaluation phase.

- If no, then advertising and direct marketing will need to refer customers to a reseller in their area. You should still prompt calls to come to you since you can refer customers directly to one of your resellers and you can build a database of interested prospects. It will be difficult to measure the results of the effort since the sale will go through a retailer.

- If yes, then there are probably a wide variety of mailing lists available for purchase. You can use these lists for both direct mail and telemarketing. In addition, advertising and public relations can be especially cost-effective in vertical market publications.

- If no, then direct marketing techniques can be employed, but it will be more difficult to develop appropriate lists. This means that the return on the investment will be lower.

- If you don't know, see the section entitled "Identifying Markets."

Summary

The following chart summarizes the roles, impacts, and costs associated with the various communications strategies.

Strategy	Expected Results	Level of Control	Cost
Advertising	Awareness Consideration Trial Purchase	High-levels of control	Expensive out-of-pocket cost Efficient on a cost-per-thousand basis
Direct Marketing	Consideration Trial Purchase Repurchase	Very high-levels of control	Moderate to expensive in cost Highly effecient cost-per-thousand
Point-of-Sale	Awareness Consideration (Purchase)	Low-level of control	Moderate to expensive cost Inefficient
Public Relations	Awareness Consideration (Trial)	Moderate, but varying levels of control	Inexpensive to moderate cost Moderately efficient
Sales Materials	Consideration Trial	Moderate-levels of control	Moderate cost Highly efficient

Effective communications programs usually employ two or more of these strategies. In the current competitive environment, most developers are employing at least four of the five strategies we've discussed. Consumers naturally resist commercial messages. For this reason, when multiple strategies are employed in a synchronized fashion instead of using only one strategy, the campaign has a much greater overall impact. The consumer may consciously resist an advertising message, but a few days later, the subliminal effect of that message will cause the consumer to respond to a direct mail solicitation.

19.4 Horizontal vs. Vertical Marketing

—by Russ Mann
Onyx Software, Inc.

Vertical marketing seems to be quite a fad these days, from Geoffrey Moore's *Crossing the Chasm* to the premium valuations that certain E-commerce and ERP vendors are receiving for their vertical focus. Yet, hearing reporters talk about the "Internet tools vertical" or entrepreneurs focusing on the "cellular phone vertical" clearly indicates a misunderstanding of the concept. Since, however, no standard definition exists to guide us, this section attempts to differentiate between horizontals and verticals and to describe how and why to use vertical marketing. At the end of the day, however, it is important to remember that these concepts simply provide a method for listening to and creating compelling solutions for your customers.

Horizontal vs. Vertical Marketing

Imagine that you have a new software product for human resources professionals:

You actually have two prospects you are talking to. One is the VP of HR for a manufacturing company, and one is the Director of Personnel for an HMO. You already have a customer who works at a hospital. What is similar about these two prospects and what is different? Which will be easier to talk to?

When you are marketing or selling, you are speaking to people's issues, trying to solve a problem they have. Solve the problem and you get the sale. Yet, buyers will have different issues depending on what hat they are wearing. In the example above, you are selling to HR executives. They have an affinity based on their skills and competencies. These skills and competencies will be similar across a wide variety of companies. Thus, the HR activity cuts horizontally across many industries.

You might have guessed (from the example above) that HMO executives will be more interested in your software than will manufacturing executives. Why? Because they have an affinity with your current hospital customer based on their vertical industry. It will be easier for you to demonstrate use in a similar situation. By vertical industry, I mean "the integrated supply chain of raw materials, production and services to deliver a whole product to an end consumer." Hospital and HMO executives, though they work in different segments of the same industry, will still understand each other better than they would understand the manufacturing prospect.

It is important to note that vertical and horizontal marketing apply primarily in business-to-business products, based on this affinity. Thus, it helps to have a set of customers or reference base for your sales and marketing activities to leverage, enabling you to show similar sets of prospects live solutions to their issues.

Some recognized questions surround the definition above. For example, are pharmaceuticals part of the health care vertical or are they a stand alone? The same might go for bandages: are they part of the end user whole product called health care? If so, why not electricity and construction of hospitals as well?

How and Why

Don't get caught up in these details. Marketing and sales are about defining your targets and speaking to them appropriately, where and how they want to listen. With a new product, you need to understand the issues that it solves and for whom.

In the example above, assume you are at a Start-up with limited funds, people, and time. Will it be better for you to go to the Human Resources Software trade show and advertise in HR magazine or better to go to a Health Care trade show and advertise in health care magazines? Most new software companies opt for the former, trying to cover everyone possible. Both Geoffrey Moore and Ries and Trout in their *Positioning: The Battle for your Mind* will tell you that what you give up you get back tenfold. They mean you will do better by focusing than by trying to go after everyone. In this way, you can better speak to prospects. You have a horizontal product, but you market it and focus it vertically. Most ERP and core product developers like Microsoft and Oracle are taking this approach.

What About the Opposite?

When might you have a vertical product that you want to market horizontally? Pegasystems (PEGA) provides an interesting example. Pegasystems designed an excellent application for the financial services industry which covered sales, service, accounting, and other customer-related functions. Retail banks, trusts, transfer agents: they all used PEGA in some form. While similar sales force automation (SFA) and customer service and support (CSS) vendors like Vantive and Siebel scooped up any customer they could get, PEGA stayed steadfastly focused on its one vertical. They actually became known as an industry-specific product and were almost never even compared to the horizontal competitors. PEGA was known to dominate the financial services space.

Recently, however, they have begun to extend into other verticals like health care and utilities. As they enter these markets, their reputation for thoroughly understanding customer needs precedes them. The competition has recently attempted to take a more focused approach, but it may be too late. The valuations of all but one have tanked, with many of the analysts saying that the little vertical focus they have is propping up their hopes for future growth. PEGA's opportunities remain bright.

Companies normally use horizontal marketing to extend their reach once they have dominated a vertical. Usually, they will take the most value-adding piece of their application, in PEGA's case the sales and service functionality, and market it to affinity or activity-based targets in other industries.

A Final Note

Remember, at the heart of vertical and horizontal marketing lie the questions:

- What problem are you solving for your customer?
- How do they want to find out about your solution?
- Who do they most compare themselves to?
- How can you use this knowledge to most efficiently and effectively leverage your limited resources?

Don't just market a technology and look for a problem to solve with it. Listen to the market closely, fill its needs appropriately, and you will be rewarded.

19.5 Positioning

—by Joe LePla
Parker LePla

What Is Positioning?

Positioning is: that which distinguishes you in your customers', prospects', and other audiences' minds in relation to your competition. Your goal is to create a defensible position around differentiators that are not easily copied by the competition—at least not until you've built a huge market share lead or moved on to new differentiators.

A position is short-term in nature and will change as market demand, technology, competition, and products change. Depending on how dynamic a market is, your positioning may need to change in three months or three years. You can position both your company and individual product lines. Company positioning tends to change less often and is more based on a response to broader market or technology trends than product positioning. Xerox Corporation used to position itself around copiers; now it positions itself around documents. This positioning expands its peers to include desktop printer companies such as Hewlett-Packard and Tektronix.

A position is used as the structure, like the steel rebar in a building, for all other messaging. Typically companies don't use positioning word for word, but use the concepts to focus and prioritize their communications.

A simple way to critique a positioning statement is the "3 Bs test." Does the position:

- State your *Business*?

Answers the question of what business you are in from a customer/prospect point of view.

- State your primary *Benefit*?

States your primary benefit from the customer/prospect point of view. Primary means the overriding reason people will buy your product right now.

- State why you are *Better*?

While the reason people buy you right now may change, your differentiator will tend to be more defensible and more closely tied to your underlying brand strengths.

Like other message building blocks such as the mission and the brand principle, a position needs to be stated as clearly and concisely as possible. Because of this, companies or product management teams typically go through an iterative process for developing and refining their positions.

Sample positioning statement

Company X develops Internet-based business solutions that automate legal billing, resulting in faster revenue capture. In this statement:

business = Internet-based business solutions
benefit = automate legal billing
better   = faster revenue capture

All companies are tempted to add multiple benefits and differentiators to this statement. In the case of positioning, "less is more." Think of your position as the one message you always need to communicate to any audience.

Positioning in a new software category

In a new category, positions focus more on selling the category than on unique product benefits. This focus can be a trap. As the category matures, a company may find that is has not communicated its uniqueness to its customers, which may allow other companies to steal market share or force the company to discount its pricing because its product has become a commodity. It's important to build company-specific benefits and differentiators into the equation as early as possible in the market cycle in order to gain awareness and preference and a defensible position. If you want more detail on positioning, read Jack Trout's *The New Positioning: The Latest on the World's #1 Business Strategy.*

Product Features, Benefits and Differentiators

When you are creating positioning and positioning-based messages around your product, one of the first things that you need to do is distinguish between features, benefits, and differentiators. By doing this exercise, you will have a better idea of what your prospective customer will respond to positively.

- *Features.* Features are aspects of the product useful to the customer. They help the customer do the job your product was designed for.
- *Benefits.* Benefits are how doing the job translates into an advantage for the customer.
- *Differentiators.* Differentiators are features or benefits that make your product stand out from its competitors.

When you haven't marketed a product before, it's easy to assume that prospective customers will be much more interested in your product than they really will be. But because you've poured your heart and soul into the product, you do not have the objectivity to determine to what degree things are important to the marketplace. Also, unless you match the description of a typical user of the product, you will not have the same responses to it as the marketplace will.

Conduct research

The first step in understanding what features your market values, what benefits they are looking for, and what differentiates your product in a way that will increase the number of people who buy it, is to conduct research with potential customers. The most effective research for this purpose is in real-time—either over the phone, one-on-one in-person interviews or through focus groups where you get a number of potential customers in a room and a moderator walks them through a product demo.

If features help your customer to do their job—such as the spell checker in a word processing program—then the benefit would be how the spell checker improves the job: such as a more professional finished document. Your spell checker could also differentiate your word processing product if it was the only spell checker that automatically corrected misspelled words as you typed. The benefit of the automatic function would be faster, professional documents.

The most saleable features are simple, obvious ones. Again, because you spend so much time with your product, you will assume that everyone will want to understand its abilities to the same depth that you do. The truth is that most users of software learn only what they need to know to do the work that is right in front of them, and no more. Because features that impact everyday activities are most valued, the benefits of those features is where you should focus your messaging.

The same is true with benefits. Highly specific benefits, like those making it easier to create professional documents, are most valued. If you have to go into a detailed explanation of a benefit, you will lose the attention of the market—and the sale. Therefore, benefits like cost of ownership and productivity in most cases aren't good sales motivators. These benefits are typically too general and hard to understand or to prove.

Sell the sizzle

"Sell the sizzle and not the steak" is a concept as effective in software marketing as it is in most other fields. You need to get your potential customers, whether they are in business-to-business or consumer markets, to get excited about the promise of your product, even more than what the product actually does. Your vision in creating the product: get prospects excited about it through communications that are upbeat, colorful, and concise. Always return to the customer's point of view when creating messages. Use the customer's language, and you will have a much stronger story to tell.

Differentiating Your Product

In marketing, there are two types of differentiation. One is differentiating by creating a new category and the other is differentiation of a product. When possible, you should consider using both.

As software become more complex, new categories emerge to help classify and define product types. Personal computers started out with operating systems, a word processing application, and a spreadsheet application. Now categories exist for desktop publishing, personal information management, scheduling, e-mail, personal firewalls, browsers, gophers, and presentation software, just to name a few.

Category differentiation

If your software has applications across several existing product lines, or is a totally new application, or is a subset of an existing application, you should consider creating a new category or conduct online research to see if a category that fits your application's functionality already exists.

If you do decide to lead the market into a new category, the upside is that you can be viewed as the expert or leader in a new market. A leader's obligation is to educate audiences—very few categories take off on their own. You will need to support the category with educational pieces, speeches, and analyst and editor meetings until it reaches a critical mass.

The downside to category creation is the money, time and focus it takes to accomplish. Creating a category means becoming the name that is synonymous with a hot-selling market. Aldus found itself in this position with desktop publishing. So by differentiating your product into a new category, you will differentiate your product as a market leader. You can then build on this differentiation to cement your lead over the competition.

Product differentiation

Differentiation is also possible at the product level. Even if you are in a field where a category exists, product differentiation can generate market interest and sales in a very powerful way. There are two ways to differentiate a product: around its features and around the support you provide for it.

Differentiating Criteria. When you begin the process of positioning based on a differentiator, ask the following questions:

- Is this a differentiator from the customer's point of view? "A better quality product" is not a customer differentiator; neither is "leading technology."
- Is the differentiator something you can defend for as long as possible? Focus your messaging on differentiators that are closest to the purchase decision and that are the most defensible.
- Is the way you distribute the product a differentiator? If you distribute through more outlets or in a way that allows for automatic upgrades or pay-as you need, you should consider these as possible positions.
- Is your support different from the competition's in quality or cost? Free support may be a strong differentiator in a support-heavy category.

Differentiating In a Mature Market. Longtime users of a particular software product, particularly on the business side, are typically unwilling to switch products without a very good reason. Especially true with large enterprises, their switching means changing and training thousands of users and the resulting disruption to company-wide productivity—not to mention the headache this gives the information technology department. Mature market users will not switch without either a major product or service misstep from their current vendor or a significant technology breakthrough in the marketplace.

If you are going into a mature market, you must bring a differentiator that adds a whole new twist to the technology if you expect to gain significant market share. One example of this was the change from DOS to Windows operating systems, which allowed new companies to field products in mature spaces as older companies with established products failed to move quickly to the Windows environment.

Key Messages and the Positioning Statement

As a software vendor, you are faced with a complex task: telling prospective customers why they should invest money, time, and energy in your product. Your challenge is even greater if you don't sell face-to-face: you are also forced to rely on a few words, a box, or a Web site to sell your product. So it is important to focus your communications through positioning and very carefully selected messages.

Positioning

A typical positioning statement explains what business you are in, what benefits your product provides, and why you are better. We call this the three Bs test, as discussed in "What is Positioning?" Here's an example. Company X develops Internet-based business solutions that automate legal billings resulting in faster revenue capture. In this statement:

- *Business* = Internet-based business solutions
- *Benefit* = automate legal billings
- *Better*   = faster revenue capture

A position is used as the structure, like the steel rebar in a building, for all other messaging. Companies typically don't use positioning word for word but use the concepts to focus and prioritize their communications.

Positioning statement

As you go through the process of developing the positioning statement, you will come across supporting messages that become the building that the statement supports. You should be communicating enough messages to complete the building. Put another way, you need to tell the primary story of why a prospective customer should buy the product, rarely involving more than three supporting messages. If you supply your markets with too many messages, they will become confused and probably not remember any of them.

Three messages to support our hypothetical positioning statement might be:

- Time spent on legal billings has quadrupled since 1995 and now accounts for 40% of a law firm's administrative load.
- Over 50% of all legal bills are either disputed by the client or are sent 7 to 10 days late because of billing complexity.
- By automating billings, Product Y has reduced bill disputes by 80% and eliminated tardiness.

These messages tell the story of why you would want to buy Product Y. Notice what isn't in the primary messages: we haven't mentioned operating systems, databases, code or specific features. None of those questions is immediately relevant to the target customer— office managers or administrators. (The questions are important to the IT person or department who will be installing it, and you need to have technical materials to support your messages.) So here's the rule: unless you are selling directly to IT, or you are positioning based on a hot technology, your technology will always take a back seat to solving the customer's problem.

Talking your messages

The same messages that you use in written materials need to be leveraged in conversation. Many companies fail to consistently use their positioning and messaging in direct sales, in speeches, or in talking to the press. We recommend creating a one-page message cheat sheet to be used for all occasions. Also we suggest conducting training sessions where you role-play your key messages prior to speaking engagements or talking to the press.

19.6 Creating Successful and Loyal Users

—by Peg Cheirrett
WASSER, Inc.

Successful users become loyal users. They tell their friends and coworkers about products that work for them, and they are likely to try the next product released by the company that helped make them successful. Furthermore, successful users are less costly than confused and dissatisfied users—they don't clog tech support lines night and day!

To create successful and loyal users of *your* product, first and foremost you need to understand who your users are and what they are trying to do. Before you can design a product and documentation that will actually help them do something better or faster, you must understand their current challenges.

Get to Know Your Users

- In her article "Start With the End in Mind" (in this section), Tami Goodall describes two tools that can help you get a picture of your user base before you begin building code.

Once you know who your users are and what they are trying to do, you need to ensure that you keep them in focus during the hectic development process. In Goodall's second article, "User Advocates on the Design Team," you will get some ideas about who in your company can be designated User Advocate and what that person needs to do to ensure that the product is a hit rather than a miss with your users.

Once the product is designed and the User Advocate has helped you determine what information your customers will need to help them master the product and become successful users of your product, you need to turn your attention to documentation. You need to create information products that accomplish one major purpose: helping users find exactly the information they need when they need it. In his article "Give the User a Break," Robert DeFord offers time-tested suggestions for designing documentation that will really work for your users.

Ensuring Usability

Ensuring the usability of the product and the documentation is critical. (See Chapter 23.2— "Beta Test the Documentation, Too!") By beta testing the documentation with the product, you discover whether or not the documentation has achieved its purpose of providing the information that users need when they need it.

The final test of a "user-focused product" is what you choose to do about shipping product outside the United States. Do you ship English-language product and documentation only, or do you "localize" for your different target markets? The article "When and Where to Localize?" (Chapter 25.3) presents some of the pros and cons of localization and suggests a two-phase approach to becoming a globally sophisticated software provider.

If you carry away one thought from this chapter, I hope it is a new conviction to become more focused on helping the people who buy your product become successful users of your technology. It will save you money in tech support costs and it will create a cadre of loyal customers!

19.7 Helping Your Users Succeed

—by Tami Goodall
Mosaix, Inc.

Start With the End in Mind: What Do Your Users Need to Succeed?

To develop useful products, you must understand your users and be able to interpret and anticipate their needs. With a clear understanding of your users, you can make smarter choices if it becomes necessary to cut features or reduce scope to meet critical schedule dates. It is also very important to communicate knowledge of your users as broadly as possible among your marketing and development teams. A common vision of your users will enable all members of the project team to stay focused on the primary objectives for your product. All team members can communicate more effectively if they have common terms to use when discussing users and their needs.

User profiling and *task analysis* are two processes that can help you understand your users' needs and enable you to define product requirements that ensure you will address the users' needs and desires.

User Profile

Creating a *user profile* is a critical first step to identifying realistic ideas and priorities for a new software product. A good user profile describes your users' personal characteristics and work environments. You can collect the data you need through work site visits, interviews, and surveys. (An excellent resource for conducting site visits is *Field Methods Casebook for Software Design* by Dennis Wixon and Judy Ramey.) Obviously, the more data you can collect, the more accurate your user profile will be. You should plan to validate your user profiles periodically to keep up with the fast-changing high-technology market.

You can begin the user profile process by selecting a few potential user groups and using observation, surveys, and interviews to collect the following personal characteristics:

- How many years of **experience** do the users have with the company and in the industry? How long have they been in their position and are they full- or part-time?
- What is each person's age, gender, nationality, primary language, and secondary language? What are other key *demographics?*
- What **mental models** or analogies do they use in accomplishing their tasks?
- What **skills** do they have that qualify them for their position? Include computer skills, education (highest grade or training), and special business skills.
- How do they **learn** best—by doing, by direction, through formal training, or by on-the-job training?

The other important data you need to collect are descriptions of the users' work environments and the types of business problems they encounter while doing their jobs.

- How do they solve problems when they encounter them?
- What is the typical workday schedule and work flow?
- What is their working attitude or mode?
- What constraints exist in their physical environment?
- What objectives must they accomplish and how do they get them done?
- How do they define success and what do they have to do to get it?

Refer to your user profiles often during the development cycle, particularly when you must make project decisions.

Task analysis

The next tool you can use to understand your users' success factors is the *task analysis* process. An effective method of collecting the information you need for task analysis, the focus group is a technique often used by marketing organizations to ask potential users what they are looking for in a product. During these sessions, one person facilitates the verbal exchange of ideas while someone else records every idea that is suggested or discussed. Often marketing and/or product development personnel watch the sessions behind two-way mirrors.

A second focus group session with the same group is sometimes used to combine ideas, identify and eliminate redundancies, and categorize or classify the ideas. It is advisable to conduct sessions with more than one group, including different user types to get a broad list of tasks and critical success factors.

Once you have an accurate picture of the problems your users want to solve and the tasks they need to perform, you can determine which tasks should be automated with software and systems and how to proceed to your next step: translating the requirements into a software design.

Through task analysis, you can create user scenarios that help developers visualize their users and make better design decisions. Task analysis also helps identify a complete set of product requirements at the beginning of the project. It prevents vague and hidden requirements from surfacing late in the project, when adding requirements might jeopardize the schedule.

Learning what your users need to succeed offers far-reaching benefits within an organization. You can make educated decisions regarding feature design and changes, reduce implementation time, create a higher potential for user satisfaction, win more sales, and decrease customer support costs.

User Advocates on the Design Team

User-centered design, a software development methodology, has proven benefits for increased sales and reduced customer support costs. By putting *user advocates* on your software design team, you can ensure that your design delivers the features that your users want.

User advocates act as a sounding board for design decisions. Their primary responsibilities include validating design decisions from a user's perspective, conducting high-level task analysis, verifying feature requirements, helping to set benchmarks for usability testing, and providing guidance for user assistance and training. Companies that include a user advocate on the design team understand that the product is more than the lines of code that make the software work; it's everything that goes "in the box."

Who makes a good user advocate?

The best user advocate is an individual who understands user needs from a broad perspective. Technical writers, training curriculum developers, customer support representatives, test engineers, and marketing people all make good user advocates. You can find them inside your development organization as well as inside your support, marketing, and sales groups. In simple terms, a user advocate understands and can communicate what it's like to walk in the user's shoes.

Some companies ask actual users to participate on the design team, but this approach poses risks. McConnell (1996) points out that end-user feedback can improve software usability but can sometimes reduce overall user satisfaction. He states that involving users can "clarify requirements, improve the match between the software and the users' needs, and improve your product's overall usability. However, unless you control the users' access to prototypes, you could see unrealistic schedule and budget expectations, diminished project control, unrealistic performance expectations, feature creep, and a design geared toward a small user group's unique needs."

The best approach: find user advocates who can represent your target user profile when design decisions and performance metrics are required. After you create a user profile based on market research, interviews, and customer surveys (see article "Start with the End in Mind"), you can choose a user advocate who best matches or understands that profile.

Technical writers often make excellent user advocates and provide a number of benefits to the development team. Although in the past the technical writer typically became involved with a project only after the product specifications were complete, today that is no longer the case. Technical writers are becoming user interface designers, human factors specialists, and usability engineers. Technical writers must have a firm understanding of the user to write their part of the code that addresses the human part of the system design. They are familiar with both the underlying technology and the basic needs of the user. They can also assist in determining which parts of the users' jobs need extensive automation and which parts need to allow for human analytical functions.

What does a user advocate do?

Like other participants on the design team, the user advocate must be a good communicator. He or she should be able to translate in two directions: between the users' language of job functions and critical success factors and the software developers' language of coding tools, controls, and metrics.

A user advocate who can define user interface requirements is especially helpful. This input can reduce design time and alleviate the burden on software developers who may be unfamiliar with the target user community and be designing the user interface in a vacuum. A user advocate can also take on the responsibility for defining elements such as:

- work-flow diagrams and descriptions
- user scenarios for test planning
- screen layouts and reports
- functionality that requires wizards
- user assistance requirements
- training requirements

User advocates play a critical role in the user-centered design. They constantly ask and help answer the questions:

- Does this feature help users do their job more effectively?
- Have we included this feature simply because we can or does our user really need it to succeed?

▪ Chapter 20 ▪

Branding Your Company

20.1 What Is Integrated Branding?

—by Joe LePla
Parker LePla

Integrated branding is the development of a brand-driven company, where all company actions and messages are based on the value the company brings to its business.

By integrating actions and messages around company and product strengths, a company can create a deep, long-lasting relationship with its customers.

A strong, integrated brand also provides these other benefits:

- the ability to charge a 15–20% price premium above the market average
- company-wide focus for consistent product development and messaging
- a shorter customer purchase decision cycle
- high-levels of customer loyalty
- customer evangelists

Integrated Branding

Of the two definitions of integrated branding, one is general: an underlying concept that serves as a rudder for a company's long-term vision. The other is specific to a company or product and becomes the point of reference for branding activities and processes that company must go through to reveal the brand.

Long Term Vision. The general definition is this: "Brand is the promise that you keep." This says that at the heart of any company is a promise that it makes to its customers. The basis of a brand is understanding the promise and doing everything in the company's power to make it happen because it is the basis for building strong customer relationships. That promise is carried out by people at all levels of the company—from the CEO to the receptionist—so that brand is much more than a communications strategy or set of messages. It is the way the company makes decisions, the types of actions it takes, and the way it expresses itself.

Conscious Brand Management. When executed properly, brand can be transformational—permanently changing the way each employee represents a company and its products. This is called conscious brand management. When a brand is managed consciously, it becomes integrated with every decision and every process in a company. Ultimately, an integrated brand, managed judiciously, communicates with a company's best customers, leading to market leadership in that niche.

Point of Reference

The second definition is the starting point for the integrated branding process: "Brand is the intersection between core company (or product, or service) strengths and what customers value." Company strengths are what the company does well. What customers value goes beyond the benefits of a product's or service's features to speak to what people see as the ongoing worth of a relationship with the company. A caveat to this definition is that these strengths must also be ownable over the life of the brand. In other words, a company has to be able to walk the talk, as well as define the path it is walking that distinguishes it from all others.

Because a strong brand is much more than image, brand development needs to be part of the job description of practically everyone—the CEO, sales associates, product or service development team, human resources, and marketing executives.

To begin your integrated branding process, determine what is driving your brand right now, what is at the intersection of company strengths, and what customers value. Poll your internal team and clients to discover this. Then, determine a method for putting this information into practice—revealing your brand.

Revealing Brand Components

While all companies have brands, most do not consciously manage them. We have developed three brand drivers that will allow you to bring your brand to consciousness and then *drive* its development. These are concepts and activities that apply to how employees focus, how they act, and how they communicate externally.

They are:

- the *principle*, the basis for all actions and messages—the compass for decision making. If your mission is what business you are in, the principle is your unique approach to that business. Volvo's mission is "to make automobiles," its principle is "safety."

- the *personality*, the voice of the brand used in communications. The tone used in writing. Many brand personalities have a one-word summary for ease of implementation.

- *associations*, concepts (usually visuals) that are mental shortcuts to brand value and holders of brand meaning; they can include component brands such as Intel Inside. They answer the question of "What do you think of when I say (brand name)?" While companies' logos are often one of their strongest associations, companies usually require an additional visual to create a stronger brand.

Identify the Core

To reveal these brand drivers, find out what your employees believe the core of the company is, in combination with what your customers value about the company. You can do this through a combination of research processes including telephone interviews, focus groups, and Internet interviews. The following are criteria for effective brand drivers:

Principle

The principle—the basis for all actions and messages—remains the same for the life of the brand; so it is very important to spend the time and energy to get it right the first time. The principle must be stated in a way that is benefits-oriented, and meaningful to employees and customers. It is a compass for employee decision making.

Employees need to be able to ask, "Is this decision in line with our brand principle?" and be able to come up with an answer quickly. At the same time, if a principle is *too* narrow, your company or product brand won't be able to grow with the needs of the market. So a principle that says, "Exceeding global safety standards" might be too narrow whereas a principle that says "high quality" might be too broad.

The principle must inspire; it must encapsulate part of your vision. It must get people excited about your company's or product's approach to your business.

It must also be brief. If it is to be used, people must be able to remember it without having to refer to a written version. Finally, it must be ownable by your company or product group. This does not mean that it has to be unique. In the case of Volvo, many companies claim that their cars are safe, but Volvo owns "safety" in the minds of consumers.

Personality

Personality—the voice of the brand—is the second brand driver. The personality must reflect the way that the company truly acts in a way that customers can relate to. During your research phase, ask your customers questions regarding business style and corporate personality.

The personality must reinforce how customers experience your products and services. Customers expect an organization to deal with them in a consistent manner, particularly important in service-based companies.

The personality should also help guide your actions. For instance, if the basis of your personality is respect, you can use this trait to define how you will work with business alliances. Because it helps define actions, it must also be consistent with the principle. If you have a principle of "collaboration," you should have a personality trait—like "open"—that will not conflict.

Associations

Associations—mental shortcuts to brand—are the third brand driver. They help deepen the customer relationship with the brand by engaging the customer on a different (usually visual) level. The meaning of an association must be easily grasped and remembered by your audience.

Since most companies don't have the dollars to do heavy promotions to build associations in customers' minds, when you have determined what association you are going to use, apply the following test. Imagine that your association is a billboard and your customer is passing by in a fast car. Will they notice it? Will they understand it? An example of an obvious association is the RCA dog, listening to his master's voice, denoting sound fidelity.

If you use visual associations in communications, chances are that they will be sharing a limited amount of real estate with other messages that you need to convey. This means they need to tie back to the company or product in a way that promotes the buying decision. The bunny used in the commercials for Energizer batteries was very memorable in tests, but people couldn't remember what product it represented. The bunny is now referred to as the Energizer bunny and has a picture of an Energizer battery on its drum to enhance product awareness.

"You can grow a company by: increasing brand power; extending the product line; or geographically expanding the reach of your products and their life cycles and adoption rates."
—Jeremy A. Jaech, *Chief Executive Officer; President; Chairman of the Board, Visio Corporation*

20.2 Capturing and Maintaining Market Leadership Through Brand

—by Joe LePla
Parker LePla

Using Brand to Create Long-Term Customer Relationships

One of the most important things to understand about brand is that it serves as a model for building the most important asset any company has—its *relationship* with each of its customers. Brand studies have demonstrated that strong brands enjoy significantly higher customer loyalty numbers than weak ones. If you understand that your best customer is the one you keep, then creating a rationale for solidifying and deepening your company/product relationships with customers will be of great value to you. If you believe that selling products is not part of a larger, long-term continuum of relationship building, then you don't need to read further in this section.

Building long-term customer relationships and all that goes along with them (including loyalty and positive word-of-mouth) takes place through giving your customers opportunities to relate to your company or product in as many ways as possible.

- What is the rational basis for a customer's relationship with your company or product?
- Can they tell what your goals are?
- How do your actions promote an emotional relationship?
- Do you help them learn more or deepen the relationship through visual or other sense-related communications?

Think of a company that you have had multiple interactions with. Did you come away from those experiences with a positive feeling, with more loyalty towards the company? If so, why do you think that happened?

Brand recognizes consistent company actions, business style, and other distinctions like memorable visuals as all critical to selling and retaining loyal customers. Put another way, a company that lacks a consistent plan for actions based on their core strengths, a defined business style, and a strong visual style appears two-dimensional to potential customers. This lack of depth translates into a lack of customer loyalty and differentiation that indicates a commodity product. Even product sales based on unique products or benefits ultimately result in decreasing market share. Price wars also result as formerly unique benefits disappear.

In the branding model, you create long-term customer relationships by treating your company or product as if it were *a person*. If you do what this book recommends, you will develop a corporate and/or product persona that customers can build relationships with. Those aspects that define the company/product persona—its beliefs, goals, business style, and unique attributes—will set your brand apart from the competition. They will also be difficult or impossible to duplicate because you have many years' head start or because a competitor's actions don't square with your style. The more consistent your company/product actions and communications are, the more customers will recognize your brand as an ally, associate, or friend and choose you over all competitors.

Capturing and Maintaining Market Leadership Through Brand

You can use brand to build market share and retain the market share. The following set of brand-related actions can define and build market leadership.

Market leaders have several things in common:

- Leaders have the clarity of purpose to be first or second in a new market category. If they were originally second, they understood how to deliver most of the things the market valued at a reasonable price. Leaders are clear about the business goals of their brand.
- Leaders are willing to spend time and money educating the market on their product. They look at the education process as a critical part of setting their brand apart and are willing to put time and money into activities that do not directly generate revenue.
- Leaders have a point of view about their product category. Leaders use brand to differentiate their products and focus their messages. Leaders look at what they can own in the market, rather than trying to appeal to all market segments equally.
- Leaders have a vision for the future. Customers want to know where you are going tomorrow and why. This vision will help them determine whether to buy in today. Leaders assure continuity between their brand and their vision.
- Customers expect their business dealings with you to be consistent. They give you extra points for a real personality. Leaders develop a consistent brand personality that provides a basis for a relationship not based exclusively on product.
- Leaders understand where their strengths are and never stray from those strengths. They use brand research and appoint a brand manager and brand team to evaluate strengths, and they focus only on those that are highly valued by customers.
- Leaders create a brand structure and brand components that organize and drive future brand development. These components are based on strengths, but are more defensible than product features. A brand structure ensures that a leader's products or brands never break the original promise.

■ Chapter 21 ■

Gathering Information

21.1 Intelligence Gathering: Making Information a Tool

—by Randy Fisher
Randy Fisher Communications

Watching the frenzied rush to jump aboard the Internet bandwagon, high tech entrepreneurs might be forgiven if that's where they start their initial reconnaissance. But if that's the last stop on their due diligence journey, then the response from their competitors and potential entrants may not be so forgiving.

It takes a great deal of ingenuity, imagination and *chutzpah* to investigate traditional and Internet information sources—to ferret out juicy tidbits of valuable information often buried in a local newspaper, resting on the tip of a supplier's tongue, or contained in a dusty legal document that hasn't seen daylight in years.

It also takes top-level commitment and a well thought-out corporate intelligence plan to identify areas for scrutiny and analysis and to create and maintain a bank of accessible corporate and tacit knowledge that can help managers and executives consistently make better and more informed decisions.

> I keep six honest serving-men (and women)
> Their names are What and Why and When
> And How and Where and Who
> —Rudyard Kipling

The key to developing a timely and relevant corporate intelligence plan lies in first aligning the effort with the firm's business strategy, objectives, and timelines. Ask where your company is going, what you are trying to achieve, why and how you are expecting to reap the benefits, and when will it take place and by what means. Asking these questions up-front will give indications of what kind of information you need to gather, who to speak to, and where to get it.

Consider for a moment the questions you might have for a partnership or acquisition project:

■ How serious is the interest of the acquisition candidate's management?

- What is management's track record?

- Do they own all of their intellectual property?

- Are there significant changes expected in the technology in the next two to three years?

- Is your target firm in discussions with other companies?

- How serious are they?

- What are the perceived strengths and weaknesses of your company and theirs?

In a project focused on a competitor's product and sales, one might be interested in finding information on the sales objectives and volume of a given product. Or, one might want to know about specifics behind the corporate, marketing, and production strategy, and areas of potential vulnerability/opportunity.

- What about timelines for product upgrades and new features and benefits?

- Does the competitor have any serious challenges to its distribution channels, cost structure and staff retention? Clearly, the right mix of information and intelligence around these questions could have significant implications on whether a company stands pat or moves forward.

Knowing Is Understanding

Now that you know what you want to know, remember that successful information searches start with your imagination, experience, and gut instincts—as well as some outside help to verify your knowledge and give you perspective, insight, and speedy access to fresh sources of intelligence (you didn't even know existed).

Understand too, the value of the information search. If you recognize the hidden costs of an alliance early, then you could develop a comprehensive integration strategy, thereby saving millions of dollars in potential market share, keeping programmers happy and productive, and saving face (in a different cultural milieu).

Or, the effort could be scrapped, saving a lot of time, money, and aggravation.

Similarly, a payoff scenario for investing in intelligence gathering or market research could mean benefits of a cycle time reduction of 30% and of leapfrogging the competition: a pretty significant advantage in a $50 million market with a 12-month window of opportunity.

Remember to sketch out an initial plan/strategy with cost budget and deadlines for gathering the information you need. Make sure to allow adequate time for analysis, interpretation, and bouncing ideas off people you trust. Know who's doing what so you don't reinvent the wheel, sap scarce resources, or tip off your competitors or your acquisition target.

Seek and Ye Shall Find

In the preface to *Empire*, a 687-page tome on Howard Hughes' business goliath written by award-winning *Philadelphia Inquirer* reporters Donald L. Bartlett and James B. Steele, the authors referred to:

> thousands of Hughes' handwritten and dictated memoranda, family letters, CIA memoranda, FBI reports, contracts with nearly a dozen departments and agencies of the federal governments, loan agreements, corporate charters, census reports, college records, federal income-tax returns, Oral History transcripts, partnership agreements, autopsy reports, birth and death records, marriage license applications, divorce records, naturalization petitions, bankruptcy records, corporation annual reports, stock offering circulars, real estate assessment records, notary public commissions, applications for pilot certificates, powers of attorney, minutes of board meetings of Hughes' companies, police records, transcripts of Securities and Exchange Commission proceedings, annual assessment work affidavits, transcripts of Civil Aeronautics board proceedings, the daily logs of Hughes' activities, hearings and reports of Federal Communication Commission proceedings, wills, estates, records, grand jury testimony, trial transcripts, civil and criminal court records.

"The good news is that there is an incredible amount of information in the public record," said Steele (as quoted in *The Reporter's Handbook: An Investigator's Guide to Documents and Techniques*, second edition, edited by John Ullman and Jan Colbert of *Investigative Reporters and Editors Inc.*, p. 210). "The bad news is, that it's not all in one place," he said.

That was before the Internet whirlwind really took hold,

It's a Small, Small World

The Internet provides a vast wealth of information on numerous topics contributed by people around the globe. Users can access a wide variety of services at their fingertips: electronic mail, file transfer, vast information resources, interest group membership and discussion, interactive collaboration, multimedia displays, and much more. The Internet consists primarily of a variety of access protocols which include e-mail, FTP, HTTP, Telnet, and Usenet news—many of which have programs that allow users to search for and retrieve information made available by the protocol. An excellent primer on Internet use resides at the University of Albany Library site **http://www.albany.edu/library/Internet/search.html**.

To begin searching, the basic general search engines (such as Infoseek, Excite, Hotbot, Yahoo!, Magellan, and AltaVista) ask for your search terms and then look for them in various Web sites; they provide a bevy of data, some of it meaningful, much of it irrelevant. Still, Hotbot (**www.hotbot.com**) is the rave of many professionals because of its ability to search by media type (video, audio, GIF), URL, geography, and personal names. Megasearch engines such as MetaCrawler, Profusion (**profusion.ittc.ukans.edu/**) and Dogpile are more useful but somewhat slower, because they search all the other search engines, and then give the first, most highly-rated items from each list.

Additional resources abound, from Scott Nicholson, who bills himself as the Virtual Reference Librarian **www.askscott.com**; Open Text's Livelink, Pinstripe's Business Knowledge engine **http://pinstripe.opentext.com/**, and Northern Light's extremely useful site **www.northernlight.com**. Visitors to this site are prompted for entries into categories such as: "words anywhere" or "words in title" or "words in URL." All WWW sites and Northern Light's 4500-title Special Collection are searched, and the results are grouped into concepts and site folders. A modest fee is charged to retrieve documents from the Special Collection.

Other useful sites include:

http://www.nttc.edu/gov/other.html:	The National Technology Transfer Consortium site
http://www.nttc.edu/gov_res.html:	an extensive list of government resources
http://lcweb.loc.gov/rr/tools.html:	The Library of Congress with 110 million-plus items
http://www.odci.gov/cia/publications/factbook/index.html:	the CIA World Factbook
http://www.nasdaq.com	Nasdaq

When using these search engines, it's important to remember that as a self-publishing medium, nothing personifies change more than the Internet; there will always be new information available, Web sites that disappear replaced by the dreaded 404 Error code, and new technology to help you get it. Also, in some search engines there are invisible defaults. For example, a space between terms will automatically default to "and" or "or". Put phrases in quotation marks if you want to find words next to each other. Field searches to can also bring about impressive results [marketing vs. hi-tech:marketing]. For best results, three caveats are worth remembering:

1. Multiple searches invariably yield more information than one attempt

2. Search within a search

3. Invest time in learning advanced search techniques

Your Friendly, Helpful Librarian

Whether on staff, at a university, community college, or government library, librarians (or information specialists as they're now known) are usually the most underrated, cost-effective, and supportive sources known. They can help you navigate through uncharted waters, electronic and otherwise, saving countless hours to find the quintessential book, report, white paper, or statistic that you need. They can search a host of government resources, and fee-for-service trade and business-oriented databases like NEXIS and come up with qualified leads and critical, substantive information.

An information specialist can also help enormously in getting background information and stories from daily newspapers (e.g., *New York Times*, *Wall Street Journal*, *Seattle Times*, *San Jose Mercury*); wire services and business networks; radio and TV programs; business magazines (e.g. *Forbes*, *Fortune*, *Time*, *Business Week*, and a host of trade publications (via the Business Periodical Index and the F&S Index of Corporations and Industries). *Red Herring* is an excellent publication for the hi-tech investment community.

The specialist can also help point you to information about inter-corporate linkages, board membership, and biographies (e.g., Who's Who publications). Newsletters can be found in the *Newsletter Yearbook Directory*, and you can locate the requisite vertical and horizontal trade and professional associations via Internet search, in the *Encyclopedia of Associations*, or in the National Trade and Professional Associations of the United States. High tech associations which have excellent schmoozing and learning events are the Washington Software Alliance, the Software Publishers Association, the American Electronics Association, and the Institute of Electrical & Electronics Engineers.

The best sources of corporate information are regularly updated reports from Standard & Poor's, Moody's, and Dun & Bradstreet. Detailed analysis of companies and industries issued by securities analysts cover specific sectors (e.g., E-commerce, aerospace, advanced manufacturing) for large brokerage houses, investment firms, and venture capitalists. The annual Price Waterhouse Technology Forecast (and other publications) also provide excellent information, pointing to new industry trends, market forecasts, companies on the move, and technology development. The Gartner Group and Forrester Research Inc., are also excellent, but often pricey, sources of "inside-track" briefings and information.

Basic corporate data is available from publications such as Dun & Bradstreet's *Million Dollar Directory* and *Middle Market Directory* and from Standard & Poor's *Register of Corporations, Directors and Executives*. The voluminous *Thomas Register of American Manufacturers* and Thomas Register Catalog File are more comprehensive than the other two, advises *The Handbook*.

The Securities & Exchange Commission **http://www.sec.gov**, a useful repository of corporate information, contains public documents (provided by companies) so that shareholders can make informed decisions about management performance. (If companies are unwilling to provide these documents, they are available for a fee through private firms, such as Disclosure Inc.)

These public documents include the preliminary prospectus, the annual report, the 10-K Form (which discloses significant litigation involving the corporation), the proxy statement, and other relevant filings. The 13-D, 14-D1, and 14-D9 have also been invaluable for business reporters seeking business, financial, and investment information about corporate takeovers. Annual report footnotes often bury important and relevant information in language such as "other matters, legal proceedings, additional information," or "one-time write-down," or "unusual exceptions." It is precisely these details that need scrutiny: they are clues to the health and wealth of the company and its major shareholders.

Other information also on the public record includes tax proceedings, bankruptcy information, and hearings and reports to state and federal committees. In addition to SEC filings and the court system, companies must file documents with other government agencies, such as the Federal Communications Commission, the Interstate Commerce Commission, the Labor Department, and many state agencies, and even through U.S. embassies around the world.

Most of these documents are public and free. But if you're fixed on the Fedex "just-got-to-have-it-overnight" slogan, then you might want to engage the services of a corporate intelligence/counter-intelligence expert. Eerily reminiscent of a John Le Carré novel, these cloak-and-dagger types are secretive, surreptitious—and expensive. Usually ex-military types, they have access to information that *is* probably off-limits through a far-reaching global contact network. But they do deliver, and it may be the edge you need in a very competitive international marketplace.

Books: An Old-fashioned Resource

As a former business journalist, my favorite search engine is a single book: *The Reporters' Handbook*, referred to earlier. It's a fabulous primer to the ins and outs of investigative reporting (easily transferred to the business world) and for sifting through well-concealed but juicy nuggets of corporate and human sources of information to shed light on everything from complex financing, new product developments and enhancements, and a CEO's leadership style, to insight as why the Fed might be considering an interest rate hike or even why a contract might be awarded to one bidder over another.

For guidance through the maze of documents, directories and source books, several books are particularly valuable, advises *The Reporter's Handbook*. They are *Business Information Sources*, by Lorna M. Daniells (University of California Press); *Where to Find Business Information*, by David M. Brownstone and Gorton Carruth (John Wiley & Sons); *Encyclopedia of Business Information Sources* (Gale Research Co.); and *Building Corporate Profiles: Sources and Strategies for Investigative Reporters*, by Alan Gugenheim (Salem Press).

Other standbys include: information maestro Matthew Lesko and his beefy *Information USA* compendium to wade through the bureaucratic maze; and *Instant Information* by Joel Makower & Alan Green (Tilden Press). For international business, consult The Economist series of country guides and Hoover's Business Publications; *Sources of Information for Canadian Business*, by Brian Land (Canadian Chamber of Commerce); and the irreverent, comprehensive, and often hilarious Fielding guide, *The World's Most Dangerous Places*, by Robert Young Pelton et. al., and its companion Dangerfinder® Web site: **http://www.fieldingtravel.com/df/index.htm**. For informative insights into global adaptation and cross-cultural issues, don't miss *Communication Between Cultures*, and *Cultural Communication*, both by Larry Samovar and Richard Porter (Wadsworth Publishing).

The Art of Conversation

All the technological wizardry and electronic communication in the world can't replace the simple and elegant act of talking to another person—sensing the nuances of a conversation, or the feeling of "where there's smoke, there's fire." Indeed, entrepreneurs might well be surprised how much information—and intelligence—they can get for the price of lunch; time spent touring a plant, cultivating a relationship with a journalist or academic expert, or having a tête-à-tête with a brokerage analyst.

Some important human sources of information include off-the-cuff discussions with company officials at industry meetings, SIGs, and user groups, although senior officials will generally be wary of giving anything but the party line. Middle management, and even administrative staff, can be more forthcoming. Still, look for executive profiles and quotes in local papers and magazines: these can often tip you off to news and precious gems of intelligence. Former employees also afford an excellent source of information about corporate culture and direction, key players, and work practices, although many have axes to grind; there may, moreover, be legal implications to approaching or even hiring them. Some of the information they provide might be gossip or hearsay, so make sure to check your impressions and their anecdotes with other sources, or there may be significant competitive or legal implications.

Before you engage in costly reverse engineering activities, be sure to have a chat with a company's customers, suppliers, and competitors; they can provide an incredible wealth of information and insight into competitive missteps and marketplace gaps. Informally ask loading dock workers, or Friday afternoon revelers at the local brew pub, and most will tell you (off the record) about issues ranging from your competitor's product quality, service responsiveness, and overall customer satisfaction. If they've had trouble getting paid on time, you can glean insights about a competitor's cash flow, organizational culture, staff morale, compensation schemes—you name it.

"Using a wide variety of sources should reduce the chances of being fooled," cautioned *Business Week* reporter Chris Welles in *The Reporter's Handbook*. "I never feel comfortable in accepting what the person (source) tells me unless I've been able to confirm it with at least two other sources with different interests to protect."

That's great advice, and a key ingredient in the recipe for a successful information search. Certainly, it's worth heeding.

21.2 A Condensed Guide To Market Research

—by Jim Young
Market Trends

Areas of Investigation

Here are seven common areas of investigation for software companies:

1. **Market Analysis—New Products**
   1.1 What features and attributes do prospective customers want in a new product area?
   1.2 What will be the most effective message to communicate about the product?
   1.3 What will be the primary and secondary market segments for the product?
   1.4 What will be the optimum distribution channels for the product?
   1.5 What will be the optimum price for the product?

2. **Market/Customer Analysis—Current Products**
   2.1 What new features or attributes do customers or prospective customers want from the product?
   2.2 What do customers want to see in the next upgrade/version of the product?
   2.3 Who are our primary and secondary customers?
   2.4 Are we missing a market we should be targeting?
   2.5 Are we using the proper distribution channels and in the most effective way?
   2.6 Are we pricing the product optimally?
   2.7 Are we pricing our upgrades optimally?

3. **Customer Satisfaction Analysis**
   3.1 What features and attributes of our products are customers satisfied/dissatisfied with?
   3.2 What needs to be done to improve these features/attributes?
   3.3 What aspects of our service are our customers satisfied/dissatisfied with?
   3.4 What needs to be done to improve our service?
   3.5 What new features or attributes need to be included in our products to increase customer satisfaction?

3.6 What new products or services do we need to add to increase customer satisfaction?

4. Company Image/Positioning Analysis

4.1 How is our company perceived? • Innovative? • High quality? • High-end or low-end products?

4.2 Is the image consistent with our marketing emphasis?

4.3 Does the image vary by market segment?

4.4 What is our image vis-a-vis the competition?

4.5 What image should we have, given our strengths and products?

5. Competitive Analysis

5.1 Who are our primary and secondary competitors?

5.2 How are they positioning themselves against us? • Price? • Image? • Specific product attributes?

5.3 What are the strengths and weaknesses of the competition?

5.4 Is the competition targeting selected market segments? · Which ones?

5.5 What channels of distribution are our competitors using?

5.6 Is the competition's distribution mix giving them an advantage?

5.7 What media are the competition using?

5.8 Is the competition's media mix and message giving them an advantage?

5.9 What is the market share among the competitors?

5.10 How is market share changing among the competitors?

5.11 How is market share changing in specific product market segments?

5.12 Why is market share changing in these market segments?

6. Advertising Analysis

6.1 What is the awareness level of our advertising?

6.2 What message is being received from our advertising?

6.3 How does the effectiveness of our advertising differ among market segments?

6.4 Which media are most/least effective in raising awareness or delivering the message?

6.5 What should the media mix be?

6.6 What message should be communicated for a new product?

6.7 What will be the most effective way to communicate the message for the new product?

6.8 What should the media mix be for the new product?

7. Channels of Distribution Analysis

7.1 How effective are our current channels of distribution?

7.2 Are our channels of distribution in conflict with our marketing emphasis/our desired company or product image?

7.3　What is the level of dealer satisfaction with our products, our pricing, our promotions?

7.4　How are our products being "bundled"?

7.5　Are dealer retailing practices in conflict with our desired image/marketing strategies?

7.6　Should we consider other channels of distribution?

7.7　What is the best way to market our products in an alternative channel?

When to Conduct Research

The correct timing of a study can be critical to the value of the results. Studies conducted right after a price increase, for example, can distort people's attitudes and opinions from their "norm." Likewise, studies conducted in "good times" will understate the negative feelings held by customers.

In addition, management must be ready and willing to accept the research and make decisions, or the research has no value. The following table can help in answering the "to research or not to research" questions.

When not to consider marketing research

- When you honestly know (not just think you know) what you need to know to make a decision.
- When relevant secondary information already exists.
- When time is short for a decision (less than one week).
- When the cost of research exceeds the payoff if your unresearched decision produces negative results.
- When the purpose and objectives for the study are unclear.

When to consider marketing research

- When you lack all the information you need to make a decision.
- When you are weighing alternatives.
- When there is conflict in the organization as to the direction to take.
- When you detect symptoms of problems from your customer base.
- When you embark on something different (i.e., new products or new advertising campaigns).
- When time will allow (more than one week).
- When there is a clear understanding as to the purpose and objectives of the study.

The Research Process

The key research steps include developing an understanding of the research objective, developing a research plan, implementing the research, developing a report designed to answer management's questions, and providing sound marketing recommendations.

Things you need to do:

Pre-Research Planning
1. Clearly define the overall marketing objective the research should address.
2. Develop a specific research purpose and wish list of research objectives.
3. Prioritize the research objectives and determine possible management action based on different data results.

Technical Specifications for the Proposed Research
1. Set measurable objectives that relate to a specific marketing objective.
2. Specify methodology, as well as sampling procedures and quotas.
3. Determine how the data will be processed and what cross tabulations will be run.
4. Set up the statistical analysis methods and how the data will be reported.
5. Establish the cost/time parameters.

Things to make sure the research firm does:
Questionnaire Development
1. Design the questionnaire based on the objectives.
2. Review for biasing and leading questions, and for biasing question order.
3. Pretest a draft of the questionnaire among respondents from the target market.
4. Review the pretest results to see if the questions are clearly understood and that the proper types of responses are being gathered.

Data Collection
1. Set interviewing and quota control standards.
2. Establish quality control measures. Randomly monitor telephone calls to review interviewer question presentation. Verify 10% of all calls for accuracy. Edit 100% of all surveys for completeness.
3. Establish a coding plan for preparing the surveys for data processing.

Data Processing
1. Conduct the data entry and 10% verification.
2. Conduct the first computer run. Provide a quick top-line report of the data and develop final computer report. Prioritize tabulation plan.
3. Make the final computer run and conduct the appropriate statistical routines.

Reporting Results
1. Analyze data and draft the executive summary report.
2. Develop recommendations and action plans based on research findings.

Overview of Available Research Methodologies

Quantitative and qualitative research are the two major types of market research. Quantitative research is used to determine and predict the attitudes, opinions, and behavior of the market based on a scientific sampling. Telephone, mail, and in-person interviews fall into this category. Each may be appropriate for certain research objectives.

Qualitative research, on the other hand, is used to determine why people feel the way they do about certain issues; the primary qualitative technique is focus group research.

Quantitative Research

Below is a summary of each quantitative method's strengths and weaknesses.

Overall Evaluation of the Three Major Quantitative Survey Methods

Criterion	Mail	Telephone	Personal
Ability to handle complex questions	Poor	Good	Excellent
Ability to collect large amounts of data per respondent	Fair	Good	Excellent
Accuracy on "sensitive" questions	Good	Fair	Fair
Control of interviewer effects	Good	Good	Poor
Degree of sample control	Poor	Good	Excellent
Time required	Poor	Excellent	Fair
Probable response rate	Fair	Good	Fair
Cost	Good	Good	Poor

Telephone Research

Advantages	Disadvantages
Fast way of obtaining data	Questions must be shorter and somewhat less complex than personal interviews
Ability to control sample size and establish quota groups of respondents	Interviews must be short (less than 30 minutes)
Easier to monitor and control interviewers	No visuals can be used
Interviewer can probe for and clarify responses of complex or ambiguous areas	
Callbacks are easy to make	
No large off-site staff required	

Personal Interview Research

Advantages	Disadvantages
Sample is more controllable	Expensive per interview
You can see respondent face-to-face, allowing for more interactive interview	Interview bias (e.g., personal appearance or interviewer effects)

Personal Interview Research (cont.)

Visuals may be used	Cannot reach everyone; out-of-the-way locations are cost prohibitive
Permits deeper probes of questions	
More flexibility (can interview up to one hour)	

Mail Research

Advantages	Disadvantages
Wider sample distribution possible (can send to thousands)	List may be outdated; inaccurate (high sample error)
Visuals may be used	Addressee may not be the one who actually responds (can't control who is interviewed)
No interviewer fees	Slowest method of all (takes up to three months)
Less respondent "prestige bias"	No probing of complex questions
Equal cost per interview as telephone	Only those interested may reply (response bias)
More frankness likely on personal issues	Bias due to nonresponse difficult to measure

Once again, the particular nature of your research objectives will dictate the optimum methodology to employ.

Qualitative Research

Focus groups are the most common method of gathering qualitative research information. One-on-one and one-on-three interviewing are also becoming increasingly popular. The section below summarizes focus group research.

Focus groups

A focus group is a group discussion among eight to twelve individuals, typically lasting 1½ to 2 hours. Focus groups are designed to uncover the "why" of customer behavior through the candid discussion of opinions, attitudes, and perceptions. Properly designed and conducted focus groups can generate a wealth of ideas, hypotheses, and information on the topic at hand.

Groups generally contain a homogeneous selection of participants, screened to have one or more characteristics in common, such as job description, education level, product purchase patterns, age category, or type of buying behavior. Participants usually receive a "cooperation fee" to compensate for their time and mileage, as well as to increase their likelihood of attendance.

Typically, focus groups are conducted in facilities equipped with a one-way mirror or video equipment allowing clients direct observation of the group. Clients then have the opportunity to send in questions on the spot, as the discussion progresses. In addition, clients can gain better insight into issues by directly observing nonverbal behavior such as nodding heads, smiles, or frowns.

When should you use a focus group or one-on-one/one-on-three methodologies?

Qualitative research, including focus groups, can be used wisely or unwisely. As previously mentioned, focus groups are designed to get at the "why" of customer behavior. In a focus group, one might ask probing questions such as, "Why would you vote for candidate Jones?" "Why does brand X differ from brand Y?" and "What changes would have to be made to brand Y for you to prefer it?"

These probing questions can lead to useful data which may:
- Evaluate new product concepts and features
- Test your communication's effectiveness, clarity, and perceived message
- Assess your firm's existing image and position in the marketplace
- Generate hypotheses and new product/service ideas

Focus groups and one-on-one/one-on-three interviews are especially valuable for the evaluation of visuals, such as product packaging or advertising layouts, or of products requiring sensory feedback, as in taste testing or new product demonstrations.

Uses Of Focus Groups	Misuses Of Focus Groups
When you are unfamiliar with decision makers' opinions and want to get a broad idea of them quickly	In place of larger-scale quantitative study
Need fresh ideas and revitalization	Assuming responses are representative, quantifiable and projectable
Want to raise awareness and begin brainstorming process for new solutions to problems	To select a "winning" new product idea or concept
Need to check a communications concept to determine if anything is confusing, misleading or negative	As a final step in decision-making, instead of a first, exploratory step (although there are a few exceptions)
Need to learn people's level of understanding as well as psychological "levers"	Need diagnostics to add dimension to data and/or to design quantitative research
To listen to customers' languages in describing their use or misuses of your product(s)	

Research You Can Perform In-house

Companies can do much in-house in the area of market and marketing research. Much of what you need to know may be as close as your company's filing cabinet. Any information, presuming it is accurate and objective, is better than none; systematic means of accumulating and disseminating market information and intelligence, in some cases, offer an adequate alternative to retaining an outside research firm.

Information You May Have In-house

Customer information

What type of information have you systematically collected and kept on the decision makers and companies who buy your product or visit your establishment? Do you know their past purchases, occupation, household income, geographic location, media habits, buying preferences, etc.? (If not, you may want to create a questionnaire form to address these issues.)

Registration forms

If you require customers to register your product with you, what common, repetitive types of information are you receiving from them? Do these bits of information form any patterns? What would you like to know about your customers that you could have them provide to you on warranty forms?

Product information

If you keep records of calls to technical support for your products, do any patterns emerge in problems or questions?

Information You Can Collect Yourself

If, once you have exhausted your internal information sources, you decide you need more or other types of information, you might consider conducting a short customer survey with key clients. Write down the most important issues you would like to know from your customers: how they use your products, why they like your products, how yours compare to those of your competitors, etc.

Formulate these issues into simple, unambiguous questions and then make the calls yourself. Customers are flattered to get a call asking for feedback and you'll cement good relationships while getting the information you want.

You may want to extend this idea and create an evaluation card that can be inserted along with your billing or is available at the point of purchase to allow your customers to provide you with feedback on the products and/or services you provide.

Other Secondary Sources

Also, take advantage of your public library or university business library. Consult the *Business Periodicals Index* for the latest year. Under the appropriate heading you will find magazine and journal articles written on that subject. It represents an extremely simple way to brush up on market developments in your industry. Other sources include government census data, the *Survey of Current Business*, and the *Survey of Buying Power*.

Whether you choose to do your own market research, part of it, or hire most of it out to trained, experienced researchers, gathering readily available information is one of the first steps in the market research process.

Suggestions For Research Proposals

Once you have decided to go outside to a professional research organization, you may wish to review proposals from several firms. A good research proposal submitted to you should cover, in detail, a number of elements; if specific enough, it can serve as the body of the Agreement for Services. If you are writing a request for proposal (RFP) for research, the more elements you request be covered in a proposal, the more likely you will be able to compare apples and apples when reviewing proposals. As a minimum, you should include the following elements:

Research Purpose / Objectives
Your RFP should provide some background information, as well as the decisions to be made as a result of the research. The proposals submitted to you should reflect an understanding of these needs.

Methodology
Telephone surveys vs. personal interviews vs. mail surveys vs. focus groups. In some cases, a quantitative study might follow from focus group research.

Sample Size
The number of completed interviews/surveys in each area. Example: 100 completed telephone interviews in each of the three market areas.

Target Respondents / Quota Groups
Who qualifies to complete a survey (e.g., executive in organization most responsible for purchasing decisions)? Also, should quotas be established to ensure enough interviews are conducted with various subgroups? Quotas might be established by region, household size, purchasing patterns, customer status (e.g., past, present, prospective), public vs. private sector, etc.

Relevant Universe of Respondents
Invariably, when surveying customers and prospective customers, a list of relevant firms or people must be obtained from which to sample. The lists may be derived from professional association directories, area phone directories, lists arranged by SIC code, purchased mailing lists, lists already assembled by you, etc. Specify in the RFP what you already have available; if you do have lists, how many people or organizations are on the list, do they have working phone numbers, current addresses? Proposals you receive should detail what lists will be used, and any associated costs.

Analysis and Reporting

How will the information be analyzed, summarized, and reported? Do you or your organization have any preferred means of formats of reporting? Should graphics be provided to facilitate understanding? Should reports contain recommendations based on the findings? Should the research supplier be available to make presentations to interested parties in your organization?

Time Frame

By what date will you require the findings of the research? Will the research supplier require four weeks or four months to complete the work? Will top-line findings be available prior to detailed analysis and reporting?

Budget

To simplify your task of evaluating proposals, you may want to request a line item budget with the following breakdowns:

Professional Fees:	Materials Fees:
Research Design/Questionnaire Design	Long Distance
Data Collection	Printing
Coding/Content Analysis	Shipping/Postage
Programming/Data Processing	Travel/Per Diem
Analysis/Reporting/Presentation	Miscellaneous

Should budgets be firm, +/- 10%, or cost plus? What payment terms/schedule do you require or prefer? It will help the proposers, as well as the evaluators of proposals, if you state some general budget parameters in your RFP.

Confidentiality

Can the research supplier commit with you that all discussions, materials, and findings will be held in confidence? This is especially critical in cases of new product feasibility studies, particularly in the industrial sector with long product development/introduction cycles.

Past Experience of Project Team

Request information on who specifically will be involved in your project. What relevant experience and credentials do they have?

References

Relevant references provide the most valuable input in evaluating any professional service, including market research firms. Request references not only for the firm but for the individuals to be working on your project. Ask the references about their satisfaction with the working relationship, as well as with the final product.

Some Specifics for Quantitative Research

If a research study under consideration is quantitative in nature, you may want proposals you receive to detail specific assumptions made that lead to the time frame and budget estimates. Again, this will simplify your comparison of proposals.

The following items are especially relevant to telephone surveys:

- **Data Collection Facilities / Personnel**
  Will the telephone interviews be conducted from an in-house facility or subcontracted? This question has implications for quality control measures and scheduling. What related experience do the interviewers have?

- **Completed Surveys Per Interviewer Hour**
  The data collection arm of a research firm, in simple terms, is an information factory. The costs of data collection depend largely on the number of surveys that can be completed in a labor hour. A short, executive level survey with accurate lists might be completed at a rate of 1.0 to 1.2 completed surveys per hour (CPH). Knowing the proposer's assumptions will again allow for "apples to apples" comparisons.

- **Pretesting**
  Will the draft questionnaire be pretested to evaluate clarity, question wording, and its ability to generate relevant information? Will you be given the opportunity to personally monitor these interviews?

- **Coding / Content Analysis**
  Coding is the process of reviewing open-ended responses to questions, categorizing them, and assigning them code numbers for computerization. The budgeted number of open-ended questions will explain the coding budget in the proposal. Also, how many open-ended responses will be typed and included in the report. This may involve extra typing costs, but will provide dramatic insight into the "state of mind" of respondents.

- **Data Processing**
  You may wish to request an example of raw data output to evaluate its readability and usefulness to management. Depending on the proposer's computer system, the output may be highly useful in its raw form or in a rather esoteric form, requiring extensive analysis. How many breakouts (cross tabulations) of the data are associated with the budget?

21.3 Sales And Market Feedback

—by Mark Ursino
Marketing Consultant

Aside from moving product, perhaps the most valuable service a sales organization provides to the company is real-life, timely market feedback. The more in touch the marketing team is with the market itself, the more responsive they can be in providing sales with the product, services, and materials they need to address changing market conditions. Sales is one of marketing's most important sources for this kind of information. In this section, we'll take a brief look at three basic forms of communication a company needs from the sales group: market intelligence, competitive intelligence, and management reporting. "Heads up" selling—aware of the need to be constantly feeding this kind of information back into the company—can make the difference between selling one's brain out and never being successful and making the right adjustments at the right time, thereby overcoming the sales challenges every company faces from time to time.

Market Intelligence

Market intelligence consists of things like customer feedback on the product itself, the packaging, documentation, support, pricing, and policies. Also of great value is feedback on how people are using the product, what other products complement your product, and what customers need to do that ought to be added to the product (or taken care of by a companion product). Feedback on the channel and how they are dealing with the product also needs to be provided as a part of sales's feedback.

Sales is also in a good position to provide feedback on how the company itself is being perceived by customers and the channel. Finally, sales needs to provide feedback on any resistance they may be running across in selling the product, and specific input on the kind of sales support materials they need to help them overcome that resistance. "Resistance" in this case means anything that is seriously slowing the sales process, from a lack of collateral, to a need for channel training, to changes in the packaging to improve store visibility.

Competitive Intelligence

Companies can get intelligence on their competitors in many ways, but one of the most timely and valuable is information gained from your own salespeople. When sales reps run across the competition, they should be alert to what they're doing to the product, how they are selling it, how they position it compared with your product, how they demonstrate it.

If you send people to a trade show, you should make sure that they have assignments to scout out the competition and report on their participation.

You'd be amazed at what they can find out just listening to your competitors' reps as they talk to customers and prospects in their booths. Sales reps should cultivate within the channel to keep posted on the business practices, pricing, and merchandising programs being offered by the competition.

Management Reporting

It's no big secret that salespeople hate reporting and paperwork—always have, always will. If they were the kind of people who enjoyed such administrivia, they wouldn't make very good sales reps. On the other hand, since most reps have to operate quite independently, you have to depend on them to provide management with the information they need to do their jobs. Management, then, should ask for what they need, but only for what they really need, and refrain from asking for whatever seems interesting and/or possibly useful.

Here are some principles to keep in mind.

A good rule to keep in mind is to test the value of what you are asking for by asking the question, "What will the rep see happen as a result of the information I'm requesting?" Ninety percent of the time, if you really need the information you're requesting, then there should be some way to use that information in a way that will show the contributor the value of your having that information or will provide some direct benefit to the contributor.

Another principle to keep in mind is to see how you can help your reps integrate the information gathering/disseminating into their normal sales processes so that they are spending less "dedicated" time to paperwork. Adopt standardized formats and processes that allow them to concentrate on content rather than form and mechanics.

Last, remember that reporting is a two-way street. Don't expect reps to be very forthcoming with their reports if they can't get the reports they need to do their jobs. Nothing kills a rep's productivity faster than having managers pester reps for reports or data sheets. It's not justifiable, but it's a fact of life—they will spend more time grousing about the situation than it would take them to do the report—doubling the productivity loss.

• Chapter 22 •

Selling the Product

22.1 Why Do People Buy?

—by Ron Angerame
Autodesk

One appropriate way to open a sales section is to discuss why people buy. Fundamentally, people buy things because they need them. This answer, as simple as it may seem, is all too often missed by many companies trying to market their goods. For example, a software company has developed something that is fast, easy to use, simple, and has lots of different file formats; however, it is not something that people need, or else the buyer is not convinced that it is something that he or she needs.

When reviewing the typical need/satisfaction sales program, most salespeople will first earn the right to talk. To do this, they develop a dialogue that convinces the prospect that they have something of value. Next, they should ask questions to better understand what the prospect's specific needs are. At this point, many salespeople immediately launch into presenting their solution. They feel they have an excellent understanding of the customer's needs and it is time to convey the benefits their product brings. They then summarize the benefits into some sort of a close.

Missing from this picture is a key step that salespeople often miss: "upsetting the homostasis." Though salespeople are keen on presenting a solution to the customer, the customer may not believe he has a problem. No matter how elegant, fast, user-friendly, and sophisticated a program is, if the customer doesn't see it as a need, the value of the solution greatly diminishes.

This means the salesperson's presentation to the customer must convince the customer of the need. The better convinced that this need exists, the more attractive the solution will be. Let me explain further. A new wonder drug that comes on the market could be the fastest, most effective, easiest-to-take medicine in the world, but if you are not sick, you are not going to buy it. In our industry, software companies push specifics of the product without really showing the customer's need to buy it. Remember, people hate to be sold, but people love to buy.

Subsequent sections of this guide discuss different elements of a sales program: individuals best suited for sales, how they should be paid, developing forecasts, prospecting, managing territory, communicating, sales meetings, trade shows, and alternative sales channels.

22.2   Selling Through Channels

—by Sheri Marion-Hoff
Cohesion, Inc.

When asking if selling through channels is appropriate, your answer is an unwavering "yes." But the real question is "*which* channel is the most appropriate to sell my product or service?" To answer this question requires a strong blend of sales and marketing understanding and expertise. You can have a top-notch outbound corporate sales organization, but if you have a product best sold through catalog, retail store, or e-commerce, you may not be realizing the full sales potential of your product. Great products and hot salespeople don't always add up to sales if you're moving your products through the wrong channel.

Sales Channels

During the early 60s to 70s, sales models for high tech products were fairly straightforward. Business products were sold direct through a company's sales team. Consumer products were generally sold through the retail channel. But today offers a fairly complex model for distributing high tech products and services. You can sell directly, use two-tiered distribution, or sell your products over the Internet directly to your customer. The primary reasons for this shift in channel strategy are the cost of sales and technical complexity associated with selling high tech products. In identifying your channel choices, you must first understand what options are available and the pros and cons of each. Listed below are the channel segments used today to distribute hightech products and services.

- Direct Sales
- Distributors
- OEM
- VARs
- Retail
- Outside Rep Firms
- Direct Mail and Advertising
- E-Commerce

The flow of product through these channels may look something like this:

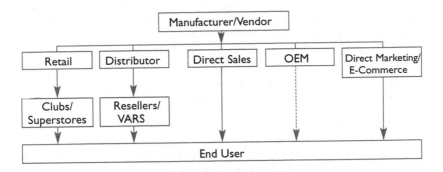

Each offers a number of distribution options, characteristics, risks, and advantages. Of course these generalizations will only give you a good place to start in exploring the channel for yourself.

Sales Channel Definitions

Direct sales (outbound sales force)

An Outbound Sales Force may be effective when you have a complex product or a complex and extended sales cycle. It is also effective when your product is early in its lifecycle and is targeted toward large corporate customers as opposed to the consumer masses. Because an outside sales force is also expensive, your product should have enough built-in margin to support the expense and significant sales potential per corporate customer.

Distributors

Unless a vendor sells direct or has a single-tier relationship with large VARs, OEMs, or retailers, its product will typically move through another level of distribution, namely the distributor. Distributors such as Ingram Micro, Tech Data, and Merisel typically link the vendor with the reseller. The movement of products from a manufacturer to a distributor to a reseller is referred to as two-tiered distribution. Distributors purchase large volumes of product from the vendor at a discounted price and provide inventory management, marketing, and immediate access to thousands of resellers and/or retailers that resell the vendor's products throughout the country. Distributors may be multinational companies or regional players.

OEM

The term "Original Equipment Manufacturer" typically refers to a hardware company that integrates components from other sources and produces complete systems, usually under their own brand name, such as Compaq or Hewlett-Packard. Large OEMs will also resell standard retail software products, or manufacture the software and documentation under license and bundle the software with their branded systems. If your product is software and has a broad market appeal, the OEM channel may be a good one for you to pursue. If your software needs some unique hardware or can take advantage of some unique features of the OEM's system, then the OEM channel is particularly valuable since the OEM has all the more reason to demonstrate and sell your product. Large OEMs typically have a single-tier relationship with the vendor since they are purchasing product in very large quantities.

Smaller OEMs, known as System Builders or White Box Builders, offer vendors another distribution opportunity if their products are hardware components or software that can be hard-disk-loaded. Smaller OEMs utilize the branded components of other vendors to integrate and build nonbranded systems that are sold to both business and consumer customers. Smaller OEMs traditionally purchase through two-tiered distribution.

VARs

VARs, or Value-Added Resellers, are "full-service" outbound sales organizations that offer a complete solution—hardware, software, service, training, and support. Typically they service the corporate customer within some vertical segment of the market. If your product requires an outbound sales approach and can complement some type of vertical offering, then the VAR channel may be a winner. VARs are geared to deal in longer, more involved sales cycles and to provide quality ongoing support as opposed to the retail sales channel.

Resellers

Resellers typically work through a two-tiered distribution model and sell to both corporate and consumer end customers. Resellers may focus more on volume sales of product and less on the service, training, and support components than a VAR. If your product is an easy add-on or peripheral, or requires a less sophisticated sales approach, the reseller channel may provide a viable option.

Retail

The Retail sales channel tends to be the most visible and well-known channel of distribution. This channel offers a number of different segments, such as independent retailers, large chains, and superstores. Each is traditionally serviced by large national distributors that offer quick shipment of the hot titles and a wider array of titles than an individual store might want to keep in inventory. The retail channel is appropriate for products that have mass appeal such as computer games, productivity applications, and hardware peripherals. (Products that typically appeal to a vertical market such as financial, legal, or health care, are better served by the VAR, reseller, or direct model.) Because shelf space is at a premium even within large superstores such as a CompUSA, your product, if accepted, may get lost in the clutter. To draw attention to your products, support the retailer with marketing materials such as Point of Purchase (POP) displays, banners, and counter cards. If you sell through the retail sales channel, remember, you must spend dollars on building brand and advertising your products to the end user. Since customers must go into the retail store to purchase the product, your marketing messages must drive that customer to the store.

Outside rep firms

If your product requires "industrial-strength" selling, and you can't afford to build an industrial strength sales group, you may want to explore sales through an outside rep firm or "manufacturers' reps." These small firms typically comprise experienced salespeople who pick up a select number of products to represent within a specified geographic area.

Direct marketing

You can sell directly to your customers through direct marketing using direct mail or telemarketing as the communications medium. Selling direct offers you the best margin on your products, the best opportunity to make aggressive promotional offers, and the opportunity to target a particular segment or vertical market. However, your cost of sales may be higher through this channel than through other channel options.

Direct Mail. Direct mail can be effective if you have a strong, straightforward offer and a source of qualified prospects. Many companies make the mistake of assuming that a one-time direct mail communication will yield a strong return-on-investment since the actual cost of a direct mail piece can be fairly low ($.75–$1.00 each). But statistics show that any direct sale requires multiple contacts to generate any type of significant results. Do not measure success by response rates alone but by return-on-investment. For a high-margin product, a response rate of .05% may provide a high return-on-investment, where a lower margin product even with a response rate of 5%-6% (which is above average) may not offer the return-on-investment you require.

A database of qualified prospects is essential for effective direct marketing. Leads may come from your own user base, trade show lists, publication subscriber files, or trade lists with noncompetitive companies. Tracking response, list, offer, seasonality, price point, and creative execution will allow you to improve on your direct mail efforts over time. If you don't have the expertise in-house to develop a strong direct mail program, seeking outside help will pay you in the long run.

Telemarketing. Telemarketing may be done with well-trained in-house staff or with an outside telemarketing company. Using many of the same techniques as direct mail, telemarketing requires a source of good prospects, multiple contacts, and an effective script with a strong offer. The script, a key component, may require outside services to fine-tune. Telemarketing is especially effective when combined with direct mail. A follow-up phone call after the recipient receives the direct mail piece increases the chance of a positive response to your offer.

Direct marketing must be used cautiously and with consideration. Consumer privacy, a highly publicized concern, should not be disregarded. Companies that do not use direct marketing intelligently open themselves up to damage to their reputations and even lawsuits. In cooperation with The Direct Marketing Association, most mail production houses will run your mail list against the DMA no-mail file, a list of individuals who have requested not to receive direct mail solicitations. A similar list exists for telemarketing. Remember, most people regard direct mail that is of no interest to them as "junk mail." On the other hand, they consider communication that is timely and pertinent to them a benefit.

E-Commerce. While E-Commerce currently falls under the category of direct marketing, it is being adopted at such a rapid pace as to becoming its own category. Most progressive companies, if they are not currently offering an e-commerce option, are considering e-commerce as a viable sales channel. The Internet offers customers the opportunity to purchase product online 24-hours a day, 7 days a week and provides one of the most cost-effective sales channels available today. Products that do not require a hands-on, consultative sales experience may do well on the Web.

Channel Interaction

When you use multiple sales channels, "channel conflict" is likely to occur if you do not put precautionary measures in place. In other words, multiple sales channels typically mean competing sales channels. For example, for maximum distribution a company that uses a direct sales force to sell products into corporations may also use a VAR channel for selling the same products into the same companies. Competition amongst the VAR channel is difficult enough without adding competition from the vendor as well. To minimize the amount of "channel conflict," clearly outline the role of each sales channel and devise a compensation plan that encourages teamwork between the various sales channels. The direct sales force may be much more inclined to work with the VAR channel if they know they will receive credit for the sales made by the VARs within their territory. Other forms of creative compensation may be investigated to minimize channel conflict and realize the full potential of selling through multiple channels.

Developing a Channel Strategy

Many companies that introduce technologically advanced or perfectly engineered products cannot understand why their products are not selling as rapidly as anticipated. Building a better mousetrap does not always guarantee success, but understanding what sales channel to use may increase your chance of success. To develop an effective channel strategy, you need answers to some important questions:

- What does it take for someone to *buy* my product?
- What does it take for someone to *sell* my product?
- What is the margin potential of my product?
- Is the product complex?

- Can the product be integrated easily into a solution?
- Where is the product in its life cycle?
- What is the breadth of the target audience?

In addition, you must consider these:

- How does my product match up to the competition?
- What channel(s) is my competition using?
- What are the overall strategic objectives for the product?

Let's investigate the answers to some of these questions.

What does it take for someone to buy my product?
If the buyer requires a large amount of information to make a purchasing decision, the retail channel that typically makes many quick sales may not be the best channel for your product. More appropriate may be a direct sales force, if there is enough margin built into your product to support the expense, or a VAR channel where sales personnel are trained on technical products.

Is the price point such that a buyer can make a spontaneous decision or does it require the signature of a vice president for purchasing?
Lower price point products may move well through a retail or in some cases a direct marketing channel. A product that has a high price point or requires a presentation to the purchasing committee may once again be better suited for a direct sales force or a VAR channel.

Is my product an add-on or peripheral to another system that is purchased through a specific channel?
If you are selling desktop printers that easily connect with personal computers, it probably makes sense to sell the printers through the same channel being utilized by the PC manufacturers.

What does it take for someone to sell my product?
It is vital that you understand how business "happens" in the channel. This typically means talking directly to the various players and finding out how they actually do business and what tools they need to sell your product. Understand from the channel what product, instead of your product, they are currently selling. The answer can greatly affect your assessment of potential success in selling through the channel. You'll also gain a better perspective of how they will accept your product, what support they are expecting from you, and what you can expect from them.

To answer the remaining questions, the following simplified chart may be useful as a guideline in determining the appropriate channel(s) for your products or services:

Channel Sales Models

Model	Life cycle Stage	Product Complexity	Margin	Breadth of Target Audience
Sales	Early	High	High	Top 5000 Revenue Producing Accounts
Single-Tier	Early-Mid	Moderate-Low	Moderate	Moderately-Broad
Two-Tier*	Mid-End	Moderately-Low	Moderately-Low	Vertical Application
Direct Marketing	Mid-End	Low	Low	Broad-Based Consumer-Oriented

*Two-tier distribution may be affected by volume sold through the single-tier.

Gathering the answers to the questions above will help you narrow your options, but considering your broader strategic objectives will guide you to make the best choices.

If you have plans for rapid growth around a diversifying product line, broader strategic concerns may impact your channel strategies.

- Are you simply looking to maximize profit in the short-term, or are you looking for market penetration?
- Are there likely add-ons or follow-ons to sell, or is this a stand alone product?
- Do you have other products in your line that should be considered when positioning your product?

If you are hoping to establish a new category of product and secure an overwhelming market advantage in the category, then market penetration is important. That usually means broad distribution at an aggressive price. OEM bundling (if your product is appropriate for this strategy) offers a great way of gaining market penetration.

If you are looking to go head-to-head with an established competitor in an existing category, penetration is once again the key.

To sell add-on or follow-on products, you will want to consider how you will gain a database of 100% of your best prospects, your user base. Direct marketing or e-commerce will be the best method for obtaining this information, since typically through two-tiered distribution, obtaining end user information can be difficult.

Establishing an effective channel strategy is not an easy process but certainly one required to achieve business success. Gain knowledge and experience by working with professional channel marketing experts and by putting your "feet on the street" to understand what the channel needs and what they can provide to you. In addition, by understanding what your potential customers want and how they want to buy it, you can establish a channel strategy that will reap many rewards.

22.3 Sales Recruiting

—by Joe Verschueren
Image X.com

Developing a Profile of the Person You Want to Hire

Attracting the right people to your organization is important to its success. In a large, established company, making the wrong hiring choice can have unfortunate consequences. When your company is small, however, and just starting to grow, every hire you make is critical. Making a "bad hire" at this stage can have disastrous results.

Recruiting good people begins long before you have someone sitting in front of you for an interview. Consider what you need in a salesperson— —not just your immediate needs but your mid-term and long-term requirements.

Understanding your long-term goals and needs as a company will help you to develop a profile of the individual you would like to attract to your company. Knowing your long-term needs will assist you in describing what your expectations are of this new individual. Finally, understanding your company's business goals will also help you in recruiting key people to your organization.

With a clear definition of your goals, you can communicate where it is you want your new team member to help you take the company and what the future holds for that person within your company.

So, for example, let's assume that you know that you want your company of annual revenues of $300,000 to grow to a $10 million to $50 million venture within the next 10 years. You have a good idea that your product will continue to be distributed both through direct and indirect channels. Your company is growing and you fret that you need to spend increasing time managing the business and less time selling. You need somebody to take over the sales responsibilities that you have been doing "part-time."

Forget the stereotypes that you have come to know about salespeople as the quick talkers who perform magic as they tell jokes and slap the client on the back. Today's salesperson

"After three years of operation, we reached a turning point where the company was about to go out of business. I decided to invest in a person. I hired a sales and marketing whiz who said the first thing that Active Voice needed was money in the bank. He said 'we had to be profitable.' Then he hit the streets running. We found this guy —and it paid off." —Bard Richmond, Founder and Chairman of Active Voice

is a professional. Selling, not unlike programming skill, improves with experience. Many qualified people in the marketplace have worked hard to refine their skills as professional salespeople. The art of selling comprises many tangible and intangible skills, skills which few people have fully developed. Your goal is to find someone with as many of them as possible.

You will want to look for these basic things in a salesperson:

Sales experience

You don't have time (and maybe not the expertise) to train someone in sales. But in determining what kind of sales experience a candidate should have, don't limit your requirements to software sales. If you think that the indirect channels will be a large part of your business, look for someone with dealer or VAR experience. If international sales is important, look for that. If your product is a low price, high volume product that appeals to consumers, look for someone with a consumer products background.

Candidates don't have to have exact experience; similar experience will go a long way in making them successful. As you evaluate candidates' backgrounds and compare them to the list of requirements of your ideal candidate, you will have to compromise somewhere. Rarely will you find a candidate who both fits your profile exactly and is also available and affordable.

Product vs. people experience

Since this person that you hire is probably going to be the person who develops and implements your distribution strategy, you will want someone who has some experience managing people. Many great salespeople, when asked to move into management positions over other salespeople, fail miserably.

The dynamite salespeople you hire have to be able to grow eventually into roles where they hire, train, and motivate your outside and inside sales force and your indirect channel of distribution.

You will want to place special emphasis on these "people skills" because they are an absolute imperative in a young, tightly knit entrepreneurial environment where every team member has to work closely with one another across vaguely defined areas of responsibility. Every successful salesperson does not possess flexibility. Your new team member must have a lot of it.

Strategic selling

Many salespeople who work hard are good at selling high volume high demand products. Being successful at this kind of selling seldom requires any strategic skills. When looking for someone to help you create a selling strategy, look for someone who has sold a new technology, a high ticket item, or an intangible/concept product. This salesperson not only knows how to sell but also has experience developing a strategy.

The Recruiting Process

You know you need a salesperson, and you know the type of salesperson you are looking for. Now you face the difficult task of trying to get people to join your team who are at the top of your qualification matrix and at the bottom of the job's salary range. Nor do you want to bankrupt the company trying to recruit them.

You can't afford to hire a recruiting agency, but you can get someone to introduce you to someone in the recruiting business. Offer to buy lunch and allow the recruiting professional to give you a few free tips on recruiting. Let the recruiter know that you are looking for someone but can't afford a recruiter's services right now. Be sure to tell them that the person you are looking for will be responsible for hiring many people as the company grows. The recruiter might consider it a future investment to refer someone to you.

Additionally, tell anyone invested in your company—your banker, your advertising agency—that you are looking for new members for your team. Finally, place an advertisement in the Sunday paper or in the local business paper, or if you have had a good month of sales, go for the *Wall Street Journal*.

Don't let anyone tell you that you won't get quality people from placing a newspaper ad. (Didn't you ever look in the paper for a job?) When placing the ad, don't let the newspaper or any other third party write the copy for you.

This simple formula for creating an advertisement has yielded a large number of responses, a minimum of unqualified respondents:

- Use your company logo in the ad. If you don't have one, then put your company name in large black type at the top or the bottom of the ad.

- Put a brief one-sentence description of what your company does. "High tech," "Start up," "entrepreneurial environment," and "fast growing" are all overworked clichés, but use them anyway so people know that they aren't applying for a job at the local utility company.

- Spend the bulk of your words describing the position you are trying to fill. To minimize the number of unqualified résumés you will receive, be specific and firm in your language: "minimum five years experience in high tech sales"; "proven experience in indirect channel development"; "willing to work in fast-paced environment." (You will still receive résumés from unqualified people. We will discuss résumé filtering next.)

- Be sure to put some description of what the candidate can expect in terms of compensation, both short-term and long-term: "base salary with attractive incentive package"; "equity participation based on attainment of sales goals." Don't give any specific numbers for compensation. Leave that for discussion with the candidate when you meet.

- Put "no phone calls please" in the ad. Be sure, however, to interview anyone who calls. They have the assertiveness and resourcefulness you want in a good salesperson.

- In the local paper you can expect to spend anywhere from $500 to $1,000 for the ad, including the cost of development. If you need to run the ad again, the cost will be less. You can also use this first ad as a template that will reduce the cost of future ads which you place as your company grows.

Filtering the Résumés

Now the résumés come pouring in. On Monday, you will receive one or two résumés that will come in overnight express mail. Take a close look at these candidates; they are well schooled in job seeking, they are usually hungry, and they are almost always immediately available.

On Wednesday, the bulk of your résumés will arrive. On Thursday and Friday, you will receive a few stragglers. Anyone who responds after this you will want to relegate to another pile for later consideration, if all of your primary candidates are disqualified. People who respond any later than Friday to your ad aren't hungry enough and aren't aggressive enough to fit into the fast pace of a Start up environment. You won't have time to meet with them.

Depending on how many responses you get, you will need to employ various criteria for eliminating respondents. You are trying to work down the pile to a manageable size. Realistically, you won't have the time to interview more than 10 to 15 candidates per position. Remember you have all of the day-to-day responsibilities to manage, the reason you are looking to hire someone in the first place. You can't put the business on hold while you spend two weeks interviewing everyone who responded. Keep in mind that you will involve other people in the interview process: how much of their time can you afford to take?

You begin eliminating respondents using the criteria that you outlined for the job. Sounds simple, but what you will find is that no one has done exactly what it is that you are asking them to do (if they have, you probably can't afford them). So you must interpret the vague descriptions that everyone has on their résumé to see if they closely approximate what you are looking for.

There are some other subtleties that you should use to screen résumés. Here are examples:

- The look and feel of the résumé says a lot about the person. Even if you like the content of their résumé, if you don't like the way the candidate comes across in writing, don't waste your time filling up one of your valuable interview slots. You probably won't like how they present themselves in person.

- Like everyone else, you probably like to work with people who share your values. Look at the personal interests of the candidates. Do they sound like people who will fit into your young company's culture?

- You can learn a great deal about reading résumés by looking at one of the books that help people write résumés.

Interviewing

When scheduling interviews, try to line up everyone else that you want the candidates to meet. Let the candidates know that they will spend time with you and anyone else you would like them to meet. If you don't think that you have a good feel judging a candidate's "sales" qualifications, include someone who does in the interview process. You could have the sales manager at your friend's software company meet with the final candidates. Or ask your neighbor who is in sales to have breakfast with your final choice.

Although most books written on interview techniques address the interviewee's benefit, you—as an interviewer—can learn much from reading these resources.

(See also Chapter 15.)

?? 4 The Sales Process

—by Joe Verschueren
Image X.com

Having recruited sales professionals to manage the sales effort for you, you can leave to them the day-to-day tasks of forecasting, prospecting, managing the sales funnel, and conducting sales meetings.

The magical things that sales management does (like forecasting and prospecting) are things that you don't have time to do. But for a number of reasons you want to understand these tricks of the trade:

- it will help you in the interview process to be able to discuss them with your candidates

- it will help you to empathize with your salespeople when they come to tell you that the forecast is off

- it will help you to understand that selling, not unlike computer programming, isn't all science—it is also an art

Forecasts

As you read in the finance section and in the marketing section of this work, forecasting is not scientific. Enviably, the scientist can with certitude predict that for every action there is an opposite and equal reaction. Sales forecasts attempt to tell management that if we perform the action of selling, the reaction of the consumer will be a quantifiable "X."

Unfortunately, nothing in selling is certain. The best barometer for building a forecasting model is history, history about how your product has sold in the past. Your salespeople's challenge is to extrapolate that limited data to project future sales.

Presuming that you offer a software-based product, you could determine the systems that your product can run on, determine how many products that compete with yours exist in the marketplace, or determine what kind of market share you think you can carve out of the marketplace.

Using these factors and many other techniques, marketing research can determine how big the market is. Sales can attempt to develop a forecast by first taking the historical data of how your product has been selling and what resources were being used to push it through the existing channels.

Next, sales and marketing determine what resources will be used to attempt to penetrate the existing market further.

- If you have been doing all the selling in the past, how much more can be sold with your new salesperson and two others?

- If you have only two VARs today, what if your new salesperson added 10 VARs?

- If you are the highest priced product today, what if you reduced your prices by 10%?

- If you don't do any advertising today, what if you ran an ad in *PC Week*?

After you sit down with your sales and marketing people and make these strategic decisions, then sales can begin to develop a forecast. Forecasts are developed by month and by years, not unlike the discussion in the marketing section.

Prospecting

In the marketing section you read about identifying your target market. Prospecting or lead generation is the process of looking within your target market to identify those candidates who are most likely to buy your product. Sometimes they are people who will beat a path to your door once they hear about your new mousetrap. More often they are people whom you need to identify and go sell. They are people who are going to buy a product like yours from your competitor unless your salespeople are successful in demonstrating to them why your product is a superior value.

Marketing's step of identifying candidates is followed by the sales department's step of contacting "suspects," that is, prospecting. With the explosion in databases and database management tools, identifying your suspects has become easier, but it is also easier for your competition.

In some cases this prospecting process may simply consist of trying to identify candidates within the indirect marketplace to distribute your product. Identifying channels of distribution is often one of the most challenging things a salesperson has to do.

Sales Funnel

The sales funnel is not unlike the project management timeline which is used in product development. The main purpose of the funnel is to track the progress you are making in the sales cycle with each of your prospects.

There are a number of ways to structure a funnel, but the general idea is to identify and label the stages in your products particular sales cycle. For example, the first stage might be "suspect account"; after some research that account could move down the funnel to "identified opportunity"; after an initial presentation and some information gathering, the account might move further down the funnel to "application/need defined." The number of stages and the names of the labels will be unique with your product. Most funnels will contain stages which include "proposal given" and "sale made."

Set criteria to determine if an account is qualified to be moved to the next stage in the funnel. And make the dollar amount of each opportunity part of the funnel.

An individual funnel is maintained by the salespeople for each of their accounts. Sales management compiles the funnels and provides a master sales funnel report for upper management and operations.

Sales Meetings

As we discussed before, the person whom you hired to manage the sales responsibilities can plan and conduct your company's sales meetings. However, we will discuss sales meetings at some length here because we want to take the mystery out of them for you, and we encourage you to have sales meetings on a regular basis beginning right now, if you are not already doing it today.

The term "sales meetings" is really a misnomer. You want to have two types of meetings with your salespeople, or at the very least you want to address two key areas in a meeting with your salespeople.

The properly conducted sales meeting can greatly improve the effectiveness of all of your team members. Since your company is in business to sell its product, then any meeting your have is a sales meeting. The sales meeting is a great time to improve the communication among the team members. Start having a meeting on a weekly basis. The best sales meetings will include more than just the salespeople. Be sure to include someone from the development team, someone from production/shipping/engineering (whoever is responsible for getting your product out), and people from any other key departments (like finance).

In this type of a sales meeting, go over the funnel reports together. Let engineering know what you expect to be shipped over the next month/quarter. Finance can see what kind of cash flows they can anticipate in the weeks/months ahead. It also gives finance a chance to impress upon the salespeople how much revenue you need to make payroll next week.

As your company grows even beyond four or five people, communication tends to break down. A meeting like this on a regular basis can go a long way in making the team work closely together toward your common goal.

The other type of sales meeting should focus on recognition of your people's successful sales efforts. This touches on the issue which we discussed earlier regarding what motivates salespeople. A motivational sales meeting is an opportunity to announce a sales contest, pass out awards, or in any number of ways recognize and reward your salespeople with something other than money. When you are interviewing candidates to be your sales leader, ask them about their experience with developing these type of programs.

22.5   Planning Compensation for Sales

—by Joe Verschueren
Image X.com

There is certainly no more complex and sensitive issue in recruiting, motivating, and retaining quality employees than compensation. Many companies are penny-wise and pound-foolish when it comes to compensating their employees. Salespeople are reputed to be greedy, motivated only by money. The fact is, as several studies have shown, salespeople may differ from other employees in the amount of risk they are willing to take, but they are like every other type of employee in wanting more than just dollars as a reward for hard work.

Compensation takes many forms and has many different ways of being calculated. How you structure the compensation for a salesperson will be largely dictated by the type of job performance and behavior you are looking for. Keep in mind that this salesperson you are hiring, a key addition to your team, generates new revenues: the lifeblood of your company's survival.

If you plan that these people will develop and implement your sales strategy, you may want to have them take a cut at developing their own compensation program. If you determine that it is a win/win situation for them and your company, then they have already begun to do what they were hired for—relieve you of having to manage the sales area and free you to get back to where you should be spending your time in strategic planning, raising capital, or new product development.

As a general rule any sales compensation package should have four elements: a base salary, a performance package, equity participation, and benefits. How much weight you put into each of these will depend on what your company can afford, what you are trying to motivate this person to do on a day-to-day basis, and what long-term goals you and this person have set for them within the company.

We won't attempt to be too specific, but here are a few comments on each element:

- Base salary will be based in large measure on a person's experience and how the performance package is structured. Most salespeople look at their targeted yearly earnings. They will take a low base if the upside potential looks good.

- The amount of weight placed on a performance package is driven by the way you want to motivate your salesperson, the economics of your business, the length of your sales cycle, and the amount of experience your company has in selling your product. Performance packages, in the form of commissions or bonuses vary greatly in how they are calculated and how often they are paid varies: the closest thing to "rocket science" in American business. The uniqueness of your business will almost certainly assure that you can't use someone else's formula.

- Equity participation can have many forms. If this salesperson is going to help you grow the sales organization in your company, consider making growth a strong part of the compensation package, helping you to recruit someone with the type of experience you need but can't afford. For salespeople whose main responsibility it is to sell, equity will be less of a motivator.

- Benefits mean as much to salespeople as they do to you. Benefits may mean more if you are trying to attract a mature candidate than it will for attracting younger candidates who have no family responsibilities. Don't overlook the attractiveness of alternative work styles: telecommuting; flex hours; flexible workweeks. Many salespeople are more productive in a less structured environment.

Don't be misled by myths about salespeople who spend time playing golf instead of working. If you structure the compensation package that bases the weight of salespeople's income on revenue generation, you don't have to worry about how much they apply themselves. You can add additional motivation with an unconventional work environment, making your company a fun place to work. No employees like to work for a company where they are made to feel that they have to punch the clock.

22.6 Using Manufacturers' Representatives as Sales Vehicles

—by Suzanne Capener
Northwest Marketing Group

Using a manufacturers' representative can be an extremely quick and cost efficient way to get your product into the hands of dealers and customers. Or it can prove to be a waste of time and resources. The difference lies in having a realistic understanding of your product, your market, your expectations of what a manufacturers' rep can do for you, how to interview and select a firm which fits your needs, and finally how to manage the relationship so everybody wins.

What Is a Manufacturers' Representative?

Technically a rep is an independent entity contracted to represent a manufacturer's product in a specific territory. The best way to think of a rep is as the outside sales extension of your company's sales force. Manufacturer representatives generally represent several manufacturers at the same time and often will have a particular product focus such as network products or a customer focus such as mass merchants or storefront retail dealers. The most important thing a rep can bring to your company is established relationships. It stands to reason that the reps with the best customer relationships are the ones who put their customers needs first.

Representatives are paid on a commission basis that can range from 2% up to 20% depending on the product, price point, and market. Representatives pay for all expenses incurred in the operation of their business such as office space, personnel, and travel. Representative firms range from very small to relatively large, and both structures have associated advantages and disadvantages. For example, a large firm may offer more extensive dealer coverage but have less time and mind share to devote to your product. A small firm may be more restricted in their market coverage but offer much more time and energy.

In addition to the obvious sales functions performed, many reps offer a range of services that may include:

- Marketing feedback to keep you informed of current regional market conditions and opportunities
- Development and implementation of marketing support programs to include advertising and sales promotion programs
- Sales forecasting, sales analysis, lead follow-up, and reporting
- Informational mailings to customer base, disseminating new product information and sales promotions
- Customer sales training and performance incentive programs
- Regional and national tradeshow representation
- Representation into major end-user accounts to ensure product visibility and mind share

How to Select the Representative Who's Right for You

The key to having a positive and profitable relationship with your rep company is choosing one that fits your company's products, channels, goals, strategies, strengths, and weaknesses. Each territory will have several firms to choose from. A good way to start is by talking to another company who has used reps in the past and who can give you some names to start with. Call the rep company and request a copy of their résumé and line listing. This should give you an overview of the company, its size, focus, and products currently represented. Consider a few things when interviewing prospective rep companies:

Who do they call on and is this your target customer base?

For example, if you have a VAR-oriented product, a rep company whose main lines sell in mail order or superstore accounts would not be your best choice. Choose a rep firm whose main focus is calling on your best customer prospects.

Do they have complementary or conflicting product lines?

You should look for a firm that carries other product lines that will complement your product, not conflict with it.

Thorough product education.

Choose a firm that has a staff with enough industry experience to have a comprehensive understanding of your product, its category and positioning within the marketplace.

Check customer references.

Your best reps will believe that they work for the customer first. Good customer relationships are the single most important advantage a rep has to offer a manufacturer. Thoroughly check the customer references listed on the rep firm résumé. If you have an account that is important to you and they were not listed as a reference, ask the rep for the name of a reference at that account or call and ask to speak to the sales or purchasing manager at that account.

Check manufacturer references.

Manufacturer references should also be listed in the rep firm's resume. This is an excellent way to find out how effective the rep firm has been from the manufacturer's viewpoint. Always look for a firm that is proactive in representing you: presents ideas for marketing in their territory; follows up on product shipments; and asks for product information and training.

Ask for recommendations in the territory.

Reps who have a line conflict and cannot take on your line will generally refer you to another rep firm in the territory. Be proactive and ask whom they would recommend anyway even though they want your line. This will tell you a little about whom they respect as their competition and how they present themselves in a sales situation. Let them give you a sales presentation on themselves.

Managing the Rep Relationship: What You Gain and What You Lose

Although you employ reps to represent your products, successful reps feel that they work for the customer. Where manufacturers tend to come and go, the customers remain. Since good customer relationships are the most important thing a rep can bring to you, this works to your advantage. You can expect a rep to resign a manufacturer product line rather than to do anything to strain customer relationships.

What you will gain in instant market coverage and built-in relationships you will lose in control. A rep is an independent entity, not an employee. You will have no control over how much time is devoted to your product, to whom it is presented, and when. Since reps are paid on commission, they generally devote the most time to the products that make them the most money. Be realistic in your timeline expectations. You may not get all the time you may hope for, but you will certainly benefit from the relationships.

Utilizing reps is a variable cost structure that adds no fixed costs to your overhead. Because you pay them only when they sell your product, to a company watching expenses, reps provide one of the most cost-effective ways to get your product to market. You should expect to support your reps with inside sales and technical support. They will also need an inside contact to place orders, follow up on shipments, check pricing, and generally disseminate information.

Good representatives interview their manufacturers just as you interview them. They look for manufacturers who have quality products well positioned in the marketplace with either a technology or price advantage, preferably both:

- manufacturers who will support them with inside staff, communicate regularly, and provide sales aids in the form of literature, point of sale displays, co-op or MDF funds for their customers

- manufacturers who have reputations for being loyal: after they have championed your product and they start to make money, they like to know you are not going to fire them and take the business in-house

- manufacturers who pay rep commissions promptly after the product sale has taken place

Final Thoughts

Your rep firm can be a major asset in helping your company realize its sales potential. The best relationships come about when both parties are active participants in reaching mutually agreed upon goals and objectives and conduct business in an atmosphere of respect and cooperation.

22.7 Using Temporary Sales Representatives

—by Jill Orman
Autodesk

Using an outside organization to perform sales calls can often serve as an effective and affordable way to present information to dealers. Several agencies that provide this service work with the vendor to provide a cost-effective solution. Typically, one or more vendors participate in a "tour" in which vendors train the temporary representatives who in turn visit dealers to discuss and/or give demonstrations of the vendor's products. While several vendors can present their products on the same tour and share the costs, vendors with several products may find more benefit in an exclusive tour. Parameters for the tour such as the number of dealers visited in a tour, the length of a tour, and the duration of each dealer visit vary and can often be specified by the vendor.

The many advantages of using temporary representatives include reaching numerous dealers quickly and with greater effect than by direct mail, expanding the sales force temporarily without tying up office resources, and eliminating guesswork in budgeting travel and expenses by using predefined fees. Most importantly, these agencies represent an excellent way to develop relationships with dealers; dealers appreciate receiving a personal visit and demonstration.

Using any outside organization, however, can pose management problems. To obtain maximum results from an outside sales organization, identify areas of concern up front and write provisions into the contract to handle these issues. These provisions should address a wide range of problematic issues, including these:

Starting with the contract, make sure that the agency is identified as an independent contractor and will not attempt to create any obligation or enter into any agreement on behalf of the vendor. This clause addresses false promises conveyed by the temporary representatives to the dealers. Specify how any deposit will be allocated, a deposit that may be used to cover travel and training expenses as well as a portion of the dealer visits. (This allotment should occur in the middle of the tour.) Review the termination clause to ensure that any unused portion of the deposit and all unused vendor materials return to the vendor.

Detail the parameters for the tour such as:

- the number of stores to visit
- the length of time to spend with the dealer
- the number of dealer staff to attend the presentation
- the quantities and types of literature or materials to leave with each dealer
- the time frame for completion of the tour

Because a salesperson's worst enemy is time, make every minute count.

If the duration/completion date of the tour is time critical, include contractual provisions for untimely completion of the tour. Also, itemize hardware requirements, what materials you will provide as the vendor, and what software or hardware the agency provides the temporary representatives prior to training by the vendor.

Enumerate which dealers will be visited on the tour. Determine whether the agency will visit dealers solely from an agency list, exclusively from a vendor list, or both. The vendor should review the agency's list to assess the range and breadth of the dealers and to determine the percentage of those dealers that are appropriate for the vendor's product. If some combination of the agency and vendor lists is used, itemize how many of the total visits must come from the vendor list and—if needed—the number per geographic region.

Agencies may provide the vendor with reports or responses to dealer surveys during the tour. Outline the format of this feedback, what statistics should be tabulated, and how often the vendor will receive this information. This material is invaluable for follow-up campaigns (both mailing and phone) and for assessing the effectiveness of the program.

Research what, if any training the representatives receive from the agency (sales, computer, etc.); how many previous agency tours the representatives have participated in; and which products they have presented. If the representatives range in background, consider variable compensation commensurate with experience.

The vendor should address these issues when considering using an outside agency to perform sales calls. The personal visit and presentation to dealers is unparalleled for their positive reception. Utilizing temporary representatives is often the ideal way to maximize product awareness and promote dealer relationships in a cost-effective manner.

22.8 Managing Territories

—by Ron Angerame
Autodesk

Today's increasing travel costs require that sales representatives have territory management skills which cost-effectively work a geographic area. It's least effective for a salesperson to become a "star" salesperson, one who when plotting travel is all over the like a constellation, covering an enormous amount of ground but yielding few contacts.

The value of the people you are seeing is one of the critical issues to effectively work a territory. To maximize the number of contacts without needlessly becoming an executive premiere member with every airline, follow a few basic rules:

Rule One: Area of Focus

For people who have to cover large multistate or national regions (like everything east of the Mississippi), it is better to focus on a couple of small, select geographical areas than to try to cover the whole territory. If a territory includes everything west of Colorado, for example, it may be best not to worry about the Pacific Northwest and Denver until hitting every piece of business in Los Angeles and Southern California.

Rule Two: Develop an Overall Circuit

Once every three months, go to Los Angeles. This way, when appointments in Los Angeles come up, they can be scheduled into those repetitive time blocks since you know once a quarter you will be in Los Angeles. As interest or inquiries come up, you schedule them into your preplanned trips rather than haphazardly responding to individual customer requests for visitation or demos.

Rule Three: Multiple Meetings

To maximize travel efficiency, have customers come to you. When you go into a major metropolitan city, see if it is possible to get a hotel suite and schedule a number of people to come to see you. In this way, instead of consuming time driving about to see each customer, you could make three to four appointments in one day.

Rule Four: Get Prospects to Prospect for You

If your visit requires you to give a demonstration (and it is not cost effective to make a trip to visit one person), a prospect can help. If the prospect knows anyone else who would be interested in your products and demonstration, see if it's possible for them to attend the same demonstration and present to both. In this way, you can respond faster to their request to see you.

Rule Five: Travel With Your Prospect List

Make sure you have a copy of all prospects in the particular territory you are traveling in. Inevitably, cancellations and shortened appointments occur, leaving you with empty blocks of time. Keeping your prospect list with you enables you to squeeze in some last-minute appointments.

Rule Six: Manage Appointment Cancellations

If key appointments cancel after you put a trip together but you still have others scheduled, take a critical look at those remaining appointments. Ask yourself if you should still see those people based on the reduced number of contacts or should you reschedule the trip for a later time.

In territory management, "plans change." To avoid plan changes, confirm and reconfirm all appointments. Contact management software today typically includes automated follow-up; you should try to immediately confirm an appointment in writing and then reconfirm later by fax or phone just before your trip. People are less likely to cancel when confirmations are made in writing.

Rule Seven: Have a Set Agenda

Be sure the prospect knows why you are meeting. Is it mutually understood that if conditions are met, an order will be signed this trip? Remind the prospect that you are unable to fly out on a moment's notice to meet with the other managers or further discuss items: your goal is to accomplish as much as possible while you are there. Is that their goal as well?

22.9   Selling Through Telemarketing

—By Barbara M. Marvin

Rapidly shrinking profit margins caused by slower sales cycles, increased travel expenses, and stiffer competition have forced sales and marketing executives to take a closer look at increasing sales while lowering their sales costs. However, telemarketing can remedy these critical issues without having to spend more money in advertising or hire additional sales people.

The Sales Solution

Most companies have the raw materials, the tools, and the skills to shape technology to make their company unique. But more and more companies are beginning to ask themselves how they can support and manage salespeople to sell more effectively and efficiently, better track and manage advertising efforts, devise an internal process that will provide online communication between all departments?

An effective sales automation system can provide a company with the means to manage all aspects of the sales cycle. For example, the software system should provide complete integration for lead qualification, literature fulfillment, field sales, remote updating, quote preparation, forecasting and customer service. Once this is in place you can begin to supply your system with marketing intelligence, qualified prospects, and customers.

Traditionally, sales managers believe salespeople identify and qualify new sales leads, schedule field visits, close new business, and manage customer accounts. These highly specialized salespeople spend their time cold-calling many prospects to identify a few hot leads. They will respond to trade show leads, response cards, or other advertising methods and find that they are spending 70% of their time chasing down unqualified leads and only 30% of their time selling, resulting in expensive selling costs and unpredictable sales.

Instead, refer your lead identification/qualification to telemarketing experts. Less expensive personnel can survey your market and pass qualified prospects to your salespeople. They focus efforts so that sales expertise can be applied where it is most needed, ultimately using your resources more efficiently. Now your salespeople can take a "proactive" approach to selling that will result in increased sales opportunities and a significant reduction in selling costs.

Why You Can Expect Higher Sales Efficiency With Telemarketing

When salespeople try to reach the elusive decision maker, they often have to make 10 or more calls to reach one prospect. They have neither the time nor the patience to handle the usual obstacles like bypassing the call screener, dealing with voice mail, or calling at odd hours during the day. Telemarketing professionals are expert at getting to the decision maker.

Salespeople who do not canvass their territories systematically will not be able to take advantage of new sales opportunities. Telemarketing companies identify and qualify every potential customer in their marketplace. Salespeople will receive better and faster qualified leads as well as a database of information.

Telemarketing In-house vs. Outsourcing to Professionals

Setting up an in-house telemarketing department requires many considerations: space, equipment, overhead expenditures, and costs associated with employee management. Most businesses underestimate the management intensive nature of this process. It is normally difficult for a telemarketer to work alone. Nor can you expect a high-level of productivity for more than six hours, including a number of breaks and a variety of projects. So start your first telemarketing endeavor with a professional telemarketing organization with the resources established and the dedication to telemarketing.

Choosing a Telemarketing Company That Will Best Fit Your Needs

Choosing the right telemarketing company of the hundreds across the country, ask the telemarketing organization to determine whether or not they meet your standards:

- How long has the company been in business?
- Does it own its own equipment?
- What is the telemarketing professional's background and education?
- What is its remover percentage?
- Will it allow testing the quality of its services before an agreement to do business?
- What is the set up charge and what does this include?
- Is there a charge for miscellaneous calls such as wrong numbers?
- Does it charge by a completed contact basis or by the hour?
- Will it supply at least three references?
- Does it have remote updating capabilities?
- Does it specialize in business-to-business calling?

Once you have gathered this information, ask them if you may visit their facility. During a tour, listen to several telemarketers and have them show you how their calling process works. If you have not left with good feeling, chances are this firm is not right for you.

What to Avoid

- Start-up telemarketing companies
- Those that do not specialize in business-to business calling
- Companies that charge hourly rates
- Companies that conduct telephone surveys with a manual script
- Companies that are not automated with interactive sales technology
- Those that do not have report writing capabilities
- Those that do not allow you to test their services first before doing business
- High remover among telemarketers
- Those that provide no detailed proposal
- Those who lack three references

Proposal Evaluation

Each telemarketing firm will have a unique presentation. Be sure to look for those firms that offer an evaluation or test phase. Ask them to test 50 to 60 calls for you and then provide a complete proposal. If done correctly, the proposal should contain the following information:

- Company introduction
- A list of your short-term and long-term goals and objectives
- A detailed description of your telemarketing project, which should include total list size, number of calls to perform per month, specific criteria to determine a qualified

lead, and the final script
- Test results, sample calling reports, and any qualified leads uncovered from the test.
- Pricing
- Cash flow analysis
- References

When evaluating the proposal, ask them to walk you through each section for explanation. Because each telemarketing firm prices differently, look for some price on a per-completed contact basis, hourly, or bundled. Most require half up-front while others require a deposit. Evaluate the cash flow analysis carefully to determine your long-term return on investment.

Services and Procedures

Most telemarketing organizations offer the following services:
- Market research
- Prospect qualifying
- Appointment scheduling
- Follow-up reinforcement
- Literature fulfillment
- Phone sales
- Inbound inquiry handling

Normally three criteria are required to begin a successful telemarketing project:

The Script

The script, the most important aspect in generating a quality call, should take a great deal of forethought to determine which questions are the most important to ask. The purpose of each telephone call is to identify a qualified buyer. Normally, a qualifying call will comprise 8 to 10 qualifying questions. Usually these questions are the same 8 to 10 questions salespeople ask when they first talk to a prospect.

Always be sure to test the script several times before calling your entire marketplace. You may find you can ask more questions, or the questions asked may provide your salespeople with too little information.

Prospect Names

When choosing a good list, first identify your target market. If you are unsure, you may want to call several prospects yourself just to confirm you are calling into the right market. Several places can yield list acquisition: list brokers, associations, publications. When ordering your list, be specific about your market criteria and make sure all information is current. Your broker should provide you with these key criteria:

- Key decision makers
- Title
- Company size
- Updated telephone numbers
- A total count of all prospects in your market

Once you have received the prospect names, your telemarketing firm will request a copy for calling.

Training and Brochure Information

Spend at least one hour with the telemarketing professionals to explain what you are looking for and the functions your product and/or service provides. In addition, supply them with several brochures to refer to should they need to.

Once the script, names, and training have been delivered, the telemarketing firm should be ready to start the first set of calls. The telemarketer should average five/six completed calls per hour. One telemarketer working on your project with six hours of calling a day should contact 36 prospects a day, with a qualifying average of 30 to 40%. This means you should receive an average of 10 qualified leads per day.

You may request your leads to be furnished to you daily, biweekly or monthly. On a monthly data transfer to your sales system, your salespeople should receive 250 qualified leads per month. If your sales rep has a 10% closing ratio, they should be able to close two new sales per month.

Communication and Reporting

To maximize the use of the information gathered by the telemarketers, determine how the data will be transferred to your sales system. Data transfer through a Message Handling System (MI-IS) or e-mail provides immediate update to your sales system for literature fulfillment and rep contact.

When your telemarketing project is complete, you will be left with a valuable database of prospects, including correct contact, decision maker, purchase intent, purchase time frames, budget information, specific features needed and wanted, and competitive information: the means to determine where your immediate business is and to make your future marketing and sales decisions.

22.10 Supporting Sales

—By Russ Mann
Onyx Software

Sales support is a loosely-used term that encompasses many activities. Generally, pre-sales support includes a variety of tools and services provided to the field force to make them more successful in closing deals. Post-sales support deals more with customer service and technical support. This article will focus on presales support.

In many companies, a certain tension exists between sales and marketing. Sales says that Marketing isn't doing enough to bring them good leads and isn't providing the tools to help close them. Marketing tends to say that Sales doesn't appreciate all they are doing and that they have to work with the Development team as well. In many organizations, I have seen a group formed to ease this tension, normally called Sales Support.

Sales Support

When Sales complains about Marketing, they are usually saying that some or all four of the levers to increased sales are not being pulled:

- increase the number of leads
- increase the size and quality of the deals
- improve the close ratio of opportunities
- shorten the sales cycle (thus making time for more deals)

Your marketing communications team is normally tasked with the first bullet, implementing various aspects of the marketing mix like trade shows, advertising, and direct marketing to generate leads. Product marketing is often delegated the second bullet: identifying the best markets to pursue to maximize the targeting of MarCom's lead generation activities. In most marketing organizations, however, the second two bullets are normally not addressed. This is where a sales support organization can play.

Three Categories

There are three general categories of activities normally found within a Sales Support organization:

- Business/Operational

- Technical
- Deal-specific

Any one or a combination of these may be the focus of your sales support group, depending on how these activities are covered in the rest of your organization.

Business services

The business services of sales support tend to be items like competitive analysis, maintenance of RFP response libraries, reference coordination, site visit coordination, and sales tool provision. Sales tools include online databases for prospecting and prospect research, ROI templates, field sales CDs of corporate information, and any other item that falls through the cracks of a communications or product marketing team.

Sales support business services also tend to include a heavy sales training component. Sales process education and market-specific education are two areas often covered in this group, when not addressed by sales management.

Technical services

In smaller companies, sales support is often built around technical services, primarily systems engineers. This team is generally responsible for gathering prospect requirements and building demos for sales presentations. systems engineers often end up acting as a field-based help-desk for account executives as well.

Corporate-based technical services may work with other teams to deliver technical white papers and analysis of new technologies affecting the field, and they may act as a precursor to a more formal ISV (independent software vendor) program. An inside technical sales support team also can be the one-stop-shop for technical questions from the field, triaging queries to tech support, product management, or fevelopment resources as required.

Deal-specific

Finally, sales support can be oriented toward a more deal-specific approach, where a "tiger team" is assembled for larger deals. This sometimes overlaps with sales management but sometimes adds different perspectives or added resources to stretched sales managers. Deal-specific sales support often gets involved in deal strategizing, RFP response coordination, cross-functional communication point, and occasional quick-hit collateral generator.

Many of these activities can be addressed in other ways. Competitive analysis can be the province of product management. Reference coordination and site visits can be handled by a sales administrator. Technical services can be taken care of by hiring more technical sales people or from within a designated group in sales. Deal-specific activities are more normally directed by sales management.

In almost every organization, however, many of these activities are not adequately addressed. The close ratio and sales cycle levers of sales success are then not maximized and line sales people become frustrated with corporate divisions. A sales support group is often a good way to remedy these issues and to build better communication between the field and home teams.

22.11 Trade Shows

—By Mark Ursino
Marketing Consultant

Trade shows can be either a valuable sales tool or an incredible drain on a company's resources. How successful a show can be for you doesn't entirely depend on how much money you have to spend. Many companies do well on a limited budget.

Because how you deal with trade shows depends on your particular circumstances, we can't get too specific here on "dos and don'ts," but we can present some general guidelines.

Developing a Trade Show Strategy

Trade shows should be viewed as a sales channel and receive the same careful thought and planning. Don't just go to whatever shows your competitors choose and set up shop. Certainly, if your competitor is committed to participate in a certain show, you should consider it, but trade show promoters are well practiced at playing competitors against each other in order to goad them all to attend. If the will waste time and money, you are much better off letting your competitors waste their time and money while you look for more useful ways to apply your sales resources.

Look for alternative ways of getting exposure through shows, like participating in someone else's booth or getting onto panels. You needn't have your own space to make an impact. But if you do have your own space, make sure you also look to these techniques to increase your presence at these shows.

Participation Strategy—Which Shows to Do

Do some research on the shows you might attend to find out who attends and in what numbers.

- Are these people your prime prospects?
- How many of these people can you get into your booth?
- How many of those will ultimately buy?

You are going to have to make a lot of educated guesses based on a little data, but if you do attend the show, you can collect data that will tell you how well you did at guessing so you can do a more accurate job next time.

Reasonability Analysis. Here is one shorthand test of the advisability of participating in a show: figure out the total cost of participation and determine how much of your product you'd have to sell to pay for it and what percentage of the attendees that represents. Unless you are talking about an extremely well-focused show, if that percentage isn't something less than one, you probably aren't being realistic.

If we're talking about a dealer show, things get a bit fuzzier because dealers aren't direct buyers. On the other hand, getting a dealer to represent your product could lead to multiple sales. If your aim in participating in the show is to land dealers, then figure out how many you need to get signed up to meet your goals for the show, and use that in doing your reasonability analysis.

Strategic Reasons. Even if you don't think the direct sales results will pay for participation, sometimes you have strategic reasons to participate in a show. You should make that decision only after making the reasonability analysis. You can invest only so much money in "presence" and "credibility," money that may better be spent in other ways.

So develop specific objectives for participation in a show and then look to see if you can really meet those objectives by being in that particular show at this particular time.

Sales Strategy

Once you developed your objectives for the show, you need to plan how you are going to meet those objectives. Simply showing up with these objectives in mind doesn't mean you've set yourself up with the best opportunity to meet those objectives. You have to map out how the transaction will occur on the show floor and to make sure your people are trained to facilitate those transactions and have the tools they need to support themselves. Don't assume your salespeople will know how to do this instinctively. Only a few trade show professionals really know how to work a show.

Train all your people in weeding through the people that come by your booth and identifying the real prospects. Far too many good prospects get away because people let themselves get bogged down or waste time talking to unqualified prospects. Develop a multi-layered sales strategy. Coach people on what questions to ask to quickly identify prospects. If they aren't prospects, then employ many polite ways to demonstrate to them that they are talking to the wrong company and move them along. If they are prospects, get their contact information and some additional particulars and tell them someone will follow up with information and a phone call (if appropriate) after the show. Reserve "talking turkey" on the floor only for those very best prospects, since time to deal with people one-to-one will undoubtedly be limited. Even with these, you are probably better off scheduling a time away from the booth (if you can't leave right then) to meet. Unless you have a larger booth with a private conference area, it's not a good idea to get into serious conversation with top prospects in the booth. You never know who is loitering around "gathering intelligence."

If you are planning some direct sales promotions in the booth, then do the same trans-action analysis on those promotions. Work through with your staff how the transaction is to take place—in detail. They should know who you want involved in the promotion, how they are supposed to become aware of the promotion, what they are getting, how to go about getting it, and when they can expect to get it.

Fine-Tuning the Strategy

You should meet with the entire booth staff after the first day (and maybe at the end of every day) to debrief on how effective your strategies have been. If they are specific in the first place, your people will know what's working as expected and what isn't, so you can make intelligent adjustments "on the fly." Too many companies muddle through a show, doing no assessment until it's all over. Your most professional show teams constantly assess how they are doing at meeting their show objectives and look to see what changes they can make midstream to improve their results. You shouldnt also get the staff together to de-brief afterwards to integrate everyone's experience so that you can apply what you've learned in subsequent shows.

Demonstration Strategies

A good presenter will never walk into a presentation unprepared and start talking about whatever they know about their subjects; yet that is exactly the way a lot of smaller compa-nies approach demonstrations at trade shows (and some are not even that knowledgeable about their product). You should have some specific messages that you want to get across. The features of the product are how you make your point but—contrary to instinct—are not the point of the demonstration. Communicate key features not for themselves but in the broader context of the sales message you want to deliver.

As with any presentation, a good demonstration will have a logical flow, with a begin-ning, a middle, and an end. Even though you don't want your presenters to sound like they are working from a script, the demonstration should be scripted. Good demonstrators will deviate from the script, doing it their way, but if they have a script to start with—even if they don't consciously work with it—their demonstrations won't come off as being nearly as ad hoc as if they had no guidelines at all. Inexperienced demonstrators may need to follow the script verbatim. They may sound stiff and wooden, but that is far better than sounding clumsy—or worse.

Try to keep the demonstrations simple but complete. Avoid getting sucked too deeply into the product details. Remember, people are filtering by your booth all the time. You have at best a few seconds to capture their interest. While your demonstrator is involved in some deep detail of the system, you will lose the people who will walk up and find themselves immediately lost. A layered strategy works best. Depending on booth size and layout, find some way to have multiple demo stations, with the most "public" stations for the real broad appeal selling demos, and set aside a station or two with your more technical people to get into deep detail with good prospects who want more than they can get from the demo "out front." A theater (even a small one) offers a good place to conduct more detailed information. While your demonstration on the "outside" sends people who want that level of detail to the theater, the demonstrators can keep up their primary job: getting your total sales message out to as many people as possible.

If you prepare a flexible demonstration, you can tailor it on the fly to the specific interests of the people standing at the booth. Ask specific questions to qualify their interest. Don't ask open-ended questions such as, "What can I show you about . . . ?" Because most people don't know how to respond, they'll feel uncomfortable because they don't know enough to ask an intelligent question. Ask them about what they do and then show them how your product fills their bill. Getting them talking about what they know best—themselves—keeps you in control of the demonstration and lets you show off what you know to put your product in the best possible light.

Booth Strategies

Although bigger may be better, bigger doesn't guarantee results. Our best advice is to talk to a trade show professional to work out the best booth plan for you and your budget. You need to be able to contribute some things to the design process.

Sales Strategies. First, you need to have your sales strategies worked out. The booth should be designed to support how you intend to sell—not simply according to the "style" that someone prefers. If your booth is something more than 10' x 10' or even 20' x 10' space, then you will want to plan for the traffic flow through your booth. That flow needs to correlate with the sales strategies you've chosen to employ.

Obvious Messages. You also need to know what messages have to be obvious at a glance. Booth designers are good at helping you make your messages visible, but you need to figure out what those messages need to be. You could stand and stare for minutes at many small booths and not figure out what these people do. Trade show attendees often won't take the time to figure it out: they have to know at a glance the relevance of what you have. You benefit by greatly improving the quality of people who stop at your booth.

Collateral

Use literature or product collateral at a trade show as bait. People will pick up vast quantities of collateral at shows—much of it doesn't make it beyond their hotel rooms. You can waste money putting your standard sales brochures out as fodder. Instead, develop an inexpensive piece designed not to educate but to entice. When people ask for more information, you get the opportunity to qualify them. By using the inexpensive piece to get people interested, you can keep your costs lower, you can capture contact information for your direct mail and telemarketing efforts, and then you can offer to send them more detailed information.

You will want on hand a small quantity of everything you have for the really hot prospects. But sending information to people after the show guarantees that it actually gets to their place of business and at a time when they are probably more likely to take some time considering it. It also tells you how many of what kind of people you worked with at the show so you can better evaluate your results.

Staffing Strategies

A few last words on staffing your booth: do it.

If you are going to go to the expense of participating in a show, make sure you have enough of the right people there to do a good job on it. In a busy 10' x 10' booth, it isn't overkill to have three people there; yet you commonly see booths staffed with only one or two harried people. It neither looks professional nor allows you to capitalize on your presence there. If things are slow, the third person can give the other two more breaks or can do some additional intelligence gathering.

Don't expect the people to work the whole day with limited breaks. Working a show— even a slow one—is hard work. To keep a good attitude and deal effectively with the masses for hours on end, ideally your people should work no more than half-day shifts, with several break opportunities during their shift. If you can't bring enough people to accommodate half-day schedules, then at least make sure you bring enough so that everyone gets several long breaks during the day.

Finally, make sure the people you bring are trained to carry out the role they are assigned and know who to refer people to if they get a question they can't field. To make themselves not only available to passers-by but inviting to them, they should not visit with each other.

Leave wall flowers at home. Also, since appearance counts, everyone needs to be neat, clean, and uniformly dressed, whatever your philosophy on dress (suits, sport coats, polo shirts).

Trade shows can be fun, but they aren't a game. Even the fun events need to be taken seriously and conducted professionally. A fine line is drawn between casual, friendly or festive atmosphere, and merely tacky. However much or little you have to spend, spend your trade show dollars wisely and professionally to achieve a specific purpose.

22.12 Web-based Sales Strategies

—by Richard J. Lancaster
President & CEO CobWeb, Inc.

Fundamentally, creating a sales strategy for the Web involves nothing uniquely different from any other type of distribution medium or channel. The planning, ambition, focus, discipline, and determination needed are comparable to those required for print media, television, billboard, or radio campaigns.

The essential ingredients remain the same: a vision of what you are attempting to achieve, backed by a solid understanding of the medium, your target marketplace, the size of your budget, and the amount of resource you can bring to bear on your project. In our dealings with companies large and small, and their perception of a strategy for Web distribution, a large gap typically exists between what a company thinks it can achieve on the Web and the amount of resource they are planning to dedicate to the effort—either the opportunity is perceived to be far greater or smaller than reality.

Companies all too often mistakenly assign junior managers to the task of building the company store/catalog online. These individuals, not empowered to move the initiative ahead in a timely fashion, are often so under-funded that they have to continually try to reposition their management in order to acquire adequate funding.

Of course, we also hear numerous stories of over-bloated budgets spent frivolously on hair-brained e-commerce implementations that were doomed from the get-go! We seem to lack a happy middle ground where management understands the medium—its potential, and true value to the corporation—and can therefore craft a successful sales strategy.

So, we believe a company should undertake as its first major initiative the assessment of the value of the online sales effort to the company, and as its second the adoption of the commensurate level of management resource. In other words, if your electronic storefront is capable of producing as much revenue as a physical store location, then your company should be prepared to empower the human resource (the Webmaster) assigned to building it with the same level of financial and managerial empowerment as a physical store manager.

Whether you are building an electronic storefront (e-storefront) or some other form of Web sales entity, try to ensure your Webmaster is given access to the heads of finance and accounting, legal, marketing, sales, information systems, and operations. In turn make those functional heads aware that the Webmaster is in a position that requires their attention and support because profitability is on the line. After your company has provided adequate support to its Webmaster, it can then begin the process of creating an appropriate sales strategy.

There follows a brief introduction and overview of recognized methods for marketing an e-storefront, or for selling directly on the Web.

Location, Location, Location

Location is a direct analog from the: if you build your store on the bayou, when the traffic is on Interstate 10 passing through New Orleans, you are going to fail (investors may feed you to the alligators!). Similarly in the Web world, if you pick a counterintuitive domain name for your store, then you have violated a fundamental principle of good Web marketing—and relegated your sales effort to some stagnant, mosquito-ridden backwater of the Web. However, if you wisely place your store in the center of the mind's eye of the customer, then you are a genius destined for promotion.

As an example of a good strategy, my company decided to get into electronic commerce product development early on; so we acquired some "virtual real estate" in order to secure our position. We registered at the Internic the following domain names, for future products and services:

www.e-supplier.com

www.e-wholesaler.com

www.e-retailer.com

www.e-storefront.com

We actually grabbed more than just these four, but you get the point. Not only did we secure our ability to have a great piece of real estate for ourselves but we actually created a brand strategy for a series of products and services that we could only just begin to imagine! So, start with a usable, recognizable, repeatable, spell-able, extensible, naming paradigm.

Trafficking In Eyeballs!

Primary to the goal of any commercial site is the attraction of traffic (or as we say, "eyeballs")—and typically not just any traffic but traffic that is going to purchase your product or service and, you hope, be so thrilled that they will return again and again. To attract Web surfers of the most appropriate kind requires some knowledge of the demographics of the consumers of your product.

Assuming you have sufficient knowledge of the type of individuals or organizations you are trying to attract, you then need to know what attracts them to the Web and then what makes them purchase. In other words, you need to know what you can do to locate these users and then what kind of incentives you can provide them to come to your site and purchase your product.

These are some of the most obvious methods for attracting eyeballs:

Search Engine Voodoo! Now that you have the store name, you need to begin the process of telling the search engines you are open for business. Currently, Yahoo! and Excite dominate that landscape, with Lycos trailing along in a close third place. Yahoo! is by far the dominant player here (50% + of current users); so you should focus your efforts accordingly. Actually registering your new site is relatively easy, but getting the search engines to correctly and accurately position you in their databases is where the voodoo spell casting needs to occur!

To succeed at this complex undertaking, what you really need is the help of an expert who can correctly determine the "keyword" strategy you should adopt. For instance, if your company sells electronic commerce solutions to businesses then you may choose to use the keyword "e-commerce." Once you have decided on the keyword strategy, you then need to determine who is currently being listed in the top 10 positions on the top three search engines under "e-commerce." Then you need to analyze those sites to see how their content is structured to determine how they were so highly ranked in the search engines!! To do this you need an understanding of page structures, HTML, and "meta tags": now you know why I said that this can only be done by an expert!

The good news is there actually is a way to massively increase your Web site's chances of rising up to near the top of the search engines.

Banner Advertising Magic. One of the most accepted forms of driving traffic to a site is the banner ad, where the merchant purchases a small piece of interactive real estate on a well traveled site (like on one of those "portal" sites, Netscape's NetCenter, Yahoo! Excite, etc.). This little animated billboard serves to tease purchasers and gets them to "click" on the ad, automatically sending them via a hyperlink to your Web site—where you hope they will make a purchase. This is perhaps the most recognized form of Web-based selling. Ad purchasers are buying space based on CPM ("cost per thousand," a metric for measuring the thousands of eyeballs checking out the pages where the ads reside). Until recently very little data was available for measuring effectiveness; that is starting to change, and with it the perception of banner ads as the best approach to attracting eyeballs.

A recent derivative of the more traditional banner ad is the less obtrusive "private label" approach. Basically, the portal company badges pages of content with small logo'd images inviting surfers to visit a merchant's site and purchase an offering. (In this visible approach on Yahoo! Amazon.com appears on almost every search result! CDNow is also buying this type of space to drive traffic.)

In our experience, Microsoft has done the most effective banner ad campaigns in the history of the Web. They have the ability—and the cash—to afford the best analysis of an ad's effectiveness, resulting in a better return on investment—or a better CPM.

Link Trading. A simple approach to driving traffic is to identify sites that you believe attract potential buyers of your product and then trade links with that site's Webmaster. This can be particularly effective if thought through properly. Of course this activity requires good salesmanship and communication skills: after all you are going to have to get the Webmaster to clutter up his site with your link and then convince him that the links will be reciprocal, that traffic will go both ways.

Clearly, you don't want to hemorrhage traffic from your site: having eyeballs arrive on your Homepage to be greeted by an opportunity to immediately exit to a much tastier site! So you need to balance your approach by trying to push traded links as far down into your site as possible, and then have the other site come up inside your own site if possible (this can be done using "frames"). Another method is to open the linked site in a new browser window (generally a simple programming option), which keeps your own site from getting lost in the transition.

A subset of link trading is the "Award Site": this site exists to heap kudos and praise on new sites that tickle the Award Sites proprietor. Even though I don't rate them as a great means of driving eyeballs to a site, but every little bit helps. Trading links is quite easy to do, but doing it creatively and efficiently takes practice.

Legitimate E-mail Programs

A more acceptable way to communicate a sales promotion or opportunity to a prospective client is through a controlled e-mail list that has been created through a voluntary program on your Web site. The Microsoft SiteBuilder Network, a classic example of such a program, has approached a million online members.

Here is how it works: on your Web site you create a program that offers some valuable content available only to prospects who voluntarily fill in a form that captures the information you are looking for into a database. After you have collected enough data from interested parties, you create follow-on up-sell/cross-sell messages that you send out to the prospects that have already shown interest in your products.

When our company built the first two versions of the SiteBuilder Network for Microsoft, the goal was to capture 500,000 Web developers into a database within a six-month period. Of course, this needed a great offer to succeed. Microsoft budgeted millions of dollars to create that pull. They put together a combination of free downloads of valuable software, programming tips, competitions, and sweepstakes to attract Web folks en masse. In addition they spent more millions on banner ads and direct mail programs. The result, an unbelievable success, cost far less than the value of the database over time. By the time CobWeb handed management of the program off to internal Microsoft staff, we had nearly exceeded 500,000 members on the system in just over seven months! Microsoft now uses this database of qualified, enthusiastic prospects to routinely e-mail messages of more offers.

Now that we have touched on most of the *viable* forms of selling on the Web, let's look at some of the more esoteric and exotic:

Personalization. Technology can tell you who is coming into your site (usually cookies) and then produce content personalized for them. Obviously the personalization of the message is based on a clear understanding of the prospect, and a cross-sell/up-sell opportunity that is meaningful.

Avatars. These cute little genies appear on a Web site and hold a text based dialogue with you, which probably would be based on a personalization program! While Avatars have a limited scope now, in the future—with the advent of better speech recognition capabilities on the Web (like ConversaWeb by Conversa)—an Avatar will be able to have a full two-way conversation with you!

Configurations. In certain businesses, customers' abilities to configure their purchased items online and to customize them on the fly, provides a key differentiation. Dell Computers for instance has a beautiful means for configuration on their Web site. When we need a new machine, we go to their Web site and configure the system to our specifications. We can then track the manufacturing and shipment of our new machine through their Web site: a cool and valuable functionality. We feel satisfied when buying through this Web site! Such means of configuration make an excellent use of Web technology.

Online Auctioneering. A hot space on the Web now, the ability to sell your product to the highest bidder in the market has been a viable sales strategy for a few millennia now! A cursory look around the Web today will show you a rapidly growing number of auction-based sites, from airline tickets and cruises to Beanie Babies!

Media Streaming. Audio and video media streaming can offer a viable way to attract eyeballs, disseminate content, and hook consumers. If you are a radio station in Seattle, you have a limited market reach if you rely on your transmitter as the sole means of signal distribution—pretty much as far as your signal can travel clearly through the air. However, you can achieve global reach if you transmit your signal on the Internet real-time, using something like RealAudio. Although the reason for doing this might not be immediately clear, when you consider that the station may be a leader in, say, the alternative rock field, then perhaps folks in Britain and beyond may be interested in tuning in on the Web to listen to the latest local bands who are breaking on to the scene.

Streaming media may have a rosy future, especially with the advent of broadband connections to the home (like xDSL from USWest). If you are in a business with some unique content to offer, then this is a viable medium for experimentation.

Community Building. Your selling strategy may best be crafted around the building of a community of like-minded individuals on your Web site. A number of successful business models out on the Web in this space (GeoCities for instance) attract folks to their sites on a repetitive basis, by means of some absolutely unique content or functionality. In the past, communities have been built around the offer of free e-mail services, free Web sites, free content, etc. If you have something to pull in the masses and if the pull is strong enough, you can almost rely on word-of-mouth to get the message out. Once you have your community established, you can begin to leverage the power of the people to draw advertising revenue, to charge membership fees for enhanced content/service, or to sell mailing lists.

In Conclusion

You have to have the right level of commitment to succeed, and you have to be prepared to try and fail, and keep trying and failing until you get it right. But don't forget to integrate your sales strategy on the Web into all of your traditional media. Wherever it is appropriate, be sure to brand your site on other corporate material, from business cards to radio ads to billboards.

· Chapter 23 ·

Documenting Products

23.1 Give the User a Break: Documentation That Works

—by Robert DeFord
The Write Stuff

People aren't going to buy your product because they want to use it. Sorry, that's not the way it works. Only one thing will motivate human beings to become users of your product: they believe that your product will help them accomplish something that is important to them. As a result, creating documentation that works is straightforward. Just help them use your product to accomplish whatever it was they bought it for. Sounds simple doesn't it? It's not. Most documentation merely tells the user how to operate the product, and does a poor job of it. You can do a lot better.

The first step is to design your documentation so that it fits the needs of each type of user. Keep in mind that there are *many* ways to actually carry out your design. These approaches include simple black and white printed sheets, color fold-out cards, video tapes, interactive CDs, Web-based HTML documents, voice recognition and response, and just about anything else you can imagine. It is easy to get carried away and get lost among the bells and whistles. So, do not start your design by trying to decide which approach you are going to use. Instead, start by considering the needs of your users. It is not that hard. You need to take into consideration only four types of users: first-time users, regular users, intermittent users, and gurus.

First-time Users

First-time users are trying to accomplish just one thing: get results fast. They probably had to struggle hard to justify the purchase of your product to their bosses, and those bosses will be coming around to see some results. If you give these users an obvious way to get your product up and running quickly, you will be their friend for life.

To create a positive experience from the very beginning, position a Quick Start Guide so it is the first thing they see when they open the box. Then, give them Tutorials that accomplish real-world tasks. To the extent it is possible, make each tutorial a stand-alone module. Give each tutorial an obvious title so the first-time user can scan the titles quickly and chose the right tutorial to begin with. If one tutorial uses material from another tutorial as a basis, make that fact obvious so the user does not flounder. Remember that the boss will be coming around to see some results. Make use of "canned" material along with step-by-step instructions to teach the basic principles of operation and help these users get results quickly.

Regular Users

Regular users are best served with a task-oriented User Guide—a manual consisting of a series of sections or modules, each telling the user how to accomplish a particular task. Writing a task-oriented manual forces you to walk a mile in the shoes of the user. It requires you to focus on how the user will be using your product and what he or she wants to accomplish.

Since you are probably the designer of the product, you have an advantage over the typical technical writer. You are privy to all the needs-analysis material that the product design is based on. That material is a good place to begin. Map those needs into a set of tasks that match the workflow of the user. Then map those tasks against the product's features, functions, controls, and commands. Define a standard template for the task modules. For example, your task modules might all look something like this:

- *Introduction*—what the task is, what it accomplishes
- *Preparation*—the previous required or logical task(s) if any
- *Step-by-step instructions*—how to carry out the task
- *Short cuts*—how to do things rapidly
- *Where to go next*—the next required or logical task(s) if any

Start your User Guide with a good overview of the product that ties all the tasks together. Sometimes the overview also includes the product specifications. Besides the overview and the task modules, there will be a few loose ends to cover. These loose ends include tasks such as site preparation, initial set up, maintenance, and troubleshooting.

Intermittent Users

Intermittent users have already mastered the tutorials and used as much of the task-oriented User Guide as they needed. But it may have been several months ago and they have forgotten a few of the details. Typically, these users just dive in, start trying to do something, and get stuck. To get unstuck, they need a Reference Manual, which typically includes elements such as a command reference, a description of the controls and indicators, and a glossary. Typically, it is a dictionary-style manual, which means that you organize the material alphabetically. As with the task modules in the User Guide, you need to define a standard template for each command definition or description.

A good index is mandatory. It is the first place intermittent users go when they are in trouble. Yes, on the one hand it duplicates the alphabetical listing of the command names in the main body of the manual. But, on the other hand, it includes *lots* of other ways to access the information. For example, it could group the command names into related sets; give alternate, user-oriented names for the commands; and so forth. Creating a good index is a nontrivial task, and many companies find it worthwhile to hire the services of a professional indexer. If you decide to do the index yourself, study the good ones from other manuals you are personally familiar with. Pirate all the good ideas.

Gurus

Gurus already know everything significant provided in the other manuals. What they want are short cuts and ideas for how to program or modify the product to do things outside the normal usage. The documentation you provide for the gurus can take many different forms. It can range from a Programming Guide, to a set of Application Notes on your Web site, to a subscriber-only mailing list. Depending on the depth of information you provide at this level, you may or may not want the regular user to have access to it. You may, for example, want to tie it to a certification program or provide other special training prior to giving it to a customer.

Documentation That Works for Your Users

By ensuring that your product documentation meets the unique needs of your different user groups, you have created a set of related documents that include: a Quick Start Guide, some Tutorials, a User Guide, a Reference Manual, and a Programming Guide or other material to support the advanced user. This information can be packaged in one manual, but it is usually packaged as a set of manuals or booklets. It can be integrated into the product as online material, or it can take shape as other non-paper components. What's important is that you make things obvious and consistent:

- *Obvious* The users must be able to scan the titles and know which documentation component contains the information they need.

- *Consistent* Once into any given piece of documentation, the users must find that you have used words and terms consistently, and that you have used common templates and formats for all your documentation components.

23.2 Beta Test the Documentation, Too!

—by Robert DeFord
The Write Stuff

In our polite culture, nobody will tell you that your baby is ugly. Yet, if your baby is a high tech product, you need to know the truth before you release it. That's why it is worth your while to do a beta test.

During beta testing, real users, in the real world, attempt to get real work done with your product. There is no substitute for this type of testing. No matter how rigorous your internal final test process is, it cannot hold a candle to the demands of the real world. Users will try things you never anticipated. Your product may be up to the challenge, or it may not. Either way, you win. If your baby is beautiful, you rest easy as you go to market. If your baby is ugly, you find out up front when you can do something about it before real customers vote with their dollars. However, if you rush off to beta without the product documentation, you will get only half the picture. Not only will you miss the chance to find out if your documentation is working, but you may also get an incomplete beta test of the product because documentation helps users discover product features.

After all, in the real world, product documentation is your first line of support for customers who are trying to use your product. Of course, they can always call or e-mail technical support to get help, but is that what you want? Many organizations have found that good documentation is a lot cheaper than extra support staff.

Planning the Beta Test

Product documentation's ultimate purpose is to help users be successful by providing them with the information they need at the time they need it. A good beta test program will find out if the documentation accomplishes this mission. Of course this information varies greatly depending on the type of user, so try to set up your beta test accordingly.

Here are some basic guidelines:

- Novice, less-technical users need to get your product installed quickly and become familiar with it as rapidly as possible.

- Users who are comfortable with technology need to learn how to use your product to accomplish the various tasks that make up their workday.

- Software gurus need to learn how to customize or program the product to do things beyond the ordinary tasks.

As you can see from this list, setting up a good beta test for the documentation will take some thought and up-front planning. Depending on the type of product, and product introduction deadlines, it may be difficult to get all users to test the documentation according to their needs. However, most beta test customers are willing to help you set up and plan the testing once you explain what you want to do.

Gathering the Information

A critical part of your beta test plan is deciding how to gather the documentation test results. There are several approaches, each with strengths and weaknesses. The most common approaches are *documentation evaluation forms* and *on-site observation and reporting*.

Documentation evaluation form

The simplest approach is to have the customer fill out a documentation evaluation form at the end of the test period. With this approach, one challenge is to structure the questions on the form to address all three types of users described above and to determine whether or not they are able to access the information they need when they need it. The other challenge is to persuade the users to take the time to fill out the form. Furthermore, no form is as effective as on-site observation and reporting.

On-site observation and reporting

On-site observation is fairly easy to accomplish if your product requires a technical support staff to install the product on the customer's site. You can assign them the extra task of observing the customer and taking notes. However, it is important to give them a little training up front on what they need to do to ensure accurate results. For example, it is very important to let the users flounder a little and watch to see how well the documentation works. This restraint will be difficult for support people. They earn their living trying to prevent that sort of thing by jumping in and explaining how to operate the product.

Another approach is to send someone involved in writing the documentation to the customer's site. Heathkit found this approach very successful in the 80s. They paid housewives to beta test their "Build-Your-Own TV" kits and had technical writers watching and noting when the individuals couldn't follow the documentation. As is the case with support staff, it will be difficult for writers to hold themselves back when the users have difficulty understanding the documentation. The temptation will be to explain and defend the documentation.

Ideally, no matter who is doing the on-site observation, the process should be one of passive observation. The conditions for this observation can range from a special room with one-way mirrors and hidden microphones to a simple bar stool set up behind the user at a workstation. The goal is to identify all instances in which the documentation does not provide the right information at the right time.

One of the most important things you will find out by beta testing the documentation is whether customers even bother to use it. If they don't, you may be able to find out why. That information could be worth its weight in gold, if you are wise enough to act on it and fix the problem.

23.3   Print or Online Documentation?

—by Peg Cheirrett
WASSER, Inc.

There's no getting around the fact that online documentation can lower your costs—but not as much as you'd like to think. Once the documentation is researched, written, edited, illustrated, designed, produced, and declared ready for either the printer or the CD-ROM duplication service, the costs associated with online delivery are much cheaper. And if you combine CD-ROM delivery with the ability to deliver updates via your Web site, you will save real dollars compared to the cost of printing, binding, and revising manuals.

But please note that the actual costs of developing the documentation content—whether print or online—are not much different. It's the *delivery* of that information that can make a difference in your costs.

It's smart to base your decision as much as possible on the needs of your users. If your users are working in an environment that favors print manuals, find a way to deliver print manuals. On the other hand, if your product is being delivered to the end-users over a network, most users will not have access to a print manual and will rely heavily on accurate and thorough online documentation.

The prevailing trend today is to provide thorough procedural information (with excellent indexes) via online help, provide installation and troubleshooting information in a Getting Started leaflet, and minimize the print documentation shipped in the box.

Other common trends:

- Minimal documentation—often called "task-based" documentation—that describes the 10 or 15 tasks most commonly performed with the product. An example of this trend is the print documentation shipped with Windows 95. The Microsoft User Assistance team reduced the number of pages shipped with the product by a factor of 10—from 1,100 pages shipped with Windows 3.1 to 110 pages shipped with Windows 95.

- Online documentation files that the customers can print out for themselves. Some companies distribute copies of their manuals in PDF format on a CD-ROM included with the product.

- Print documentation provided only on customer demand. Some companies provide an order form for print documentation in the box. The only way for a customer to get a manual is to buy one.

- Reference material provided by a third-party publisher or by an in-house publishing company. If your customers can purchase a big, meaty, detailed book containing everything they want to know about your product, they will be more accepting of slim-to-none documentation shipped with the product.

■ Chapter 24 ■

Corporate Giving

Leading the Way Back to the Community:

Personal Observations About Why the Software Industry Can and Must Remake Corporate Giving

—by Patty Stonesifer
Co-chair and President, Bill and Melinda Gates Foundation

"Our direct u...
our software ...
our talents to ...
something goo...
was so meanir...
It's the right t...
to do. We have...
nice structure ...
this country to...
make money, a...
we have a resp...
bility to give b...
to the commu...
—*Richard Rich...*
Founder and
Chairman of Ac...
Voice

I recently read an article on philanthropy in *Worth Magazine*, in which the writer described in glowing terms the unique generosity of the American spirit. He even went so far as to characterize philanthropy as America's "most distinctive virtue." Now, I am sure if you asked a dozen social critics to expound on that statement you would get a dozen different opinions, but the point for me is that personal and corporate giving is a unique part of our democratic heritage and something we can be very proud of as Americans.

Yet, with only a few notable exceptions, the software industry is just beginning to take on corporate giving in a serious way. According to a February 1997 *Corporate Philanthropy Report*, the high tech industry contributes less than one-half of one percent of pretax earnings to charitable causes. This is ironic for a number of reasons, not the least of which is that our industry has been on the very forefront of so many human resource issues over the years: whether that includes embracing new forms of employee ownership, sharing equity in corporate success, abolishing the old business hierarchy, even getting rid of dress codes—high tech hasn't done anything the old-fashioned way. And thank goodness for that!

So why then are we still stuck in the past when it comes to practicing corporate philanthropy? Outrageous as Ted Turner sometimes is, I think he's got a point about one thing: hasn't this marketplace been good to us over these past two decades? And isn't it time to take that success and use it to build up communities and causes we care about? Isn't that the legacy we'd like to leave for future generations, in addition to the new technologies and capabilities we're creating every day?

Remake the model

I think it's time technology employees and leadership wake up and remake the corporate giving model in the same way we so radically remade the corporate ownership model. I would hope—in fact, I'm sure of it—that as the industry and its denizens mature, we will take on this challenge with our typical gusto.

Why am I so confident our industry will step up to corporate philanthropy? For two simple reasons: it's the right thing to do, and it makes sense from a business perspective. Let me talk about the business rationale first: why does a fast-moving and ever-changing high tech business need a philanthropy strategy and program? I believe successful, long-term players need to think about giving as they would any other business investment, just like R & D. A thoughtful, well-communicated giving plan says much about a company: it signals to all your key stakeholders an important message of who you really are and what you care about beyond the typical key business metrics. It builds goodwill with all your constituents, sends a strong message about an organization's leadership, and says to your community that you've made a commitment to give back and be a part of the bigger picture.

Crossing the gulf

So, let's talk about the rightness of giving. And allow me to elaborate here, because I firmly believe—and have seen with my own eyes—that our industry has something unique and important to offer that I'm passionately concerned about: access to technology for the undeserved in our community. It would be a shame if all Americans couldn't share in the computer revolution; yet only 14 percent of families earning under $30,000 have computers in their homes, compared to 73 percent with incomes over $50,000. Pundits have dubbed this "the digital divide," and those of us in the technology business are perfectly poised to help build a bridge across this gulf.

At the Gates Library Foundation we see ourselves as catalysts, helping America's public libraries in the neediest communities get critical access to computers and the Internet, We want to be able to say in the years to come that "if you can reach a public library, you can reach the Internet." As we travel across the U.S. working with librarians, we've seen some amazing things that continue to leave me both aghast at the needs in this country and very hopeful that working together we can affect meaningful change.

Especially as government funding shrinks for programs that assist at-risk children and older Americans, we will have to rely more and more on the private sector for help. Non-profits and social agencies can use all the help they can get, whether it is in the form of cash or product. Simply put, more is better when it comes to helping people on the margins. Companies should evaluate all of their resources for giving, whether it's product, cash, manpower, or all of the above! Otherwise, how will people who cannot afford access get it?

Leave no one behind

We have a huge task at hand making sure that in today's world—driven by rapid advances in technology—no one is left behind in the explosion of opportunity being made available via the Internet. When I talk to Becky Nichols, the head librarian in Selma, Alabama—a city that knows first hand about the high costs of leaving groups of people behind—she tells me amazing stories of how access to technology has made her library a more vibrant place among everyone in that very historic town.

The library has become the de facto community center for the marginally educated and low-income citizens of Selma. High school dropouts are turning to the library to learn basic computer skills and are finding their appetites whetted for further learning as they taste the grand banquet of the Internet. Becky told me, "I have one young fellow who has never been out of Selma Dallas County. When he first sat down to take his turn on the computer, I said to him 'Let's go somewhere!' and he looked at me like I was crazy. So I took him to the White House's Web site, and, the next day, to Yellowstone Park. The Internet is without question expanding his boundaries. Hopefully this poor kid from Alabama will find he can grow and learn and reach his full potential thanks in part to the excitement of these visits we make together on the Internet."

"I'm seeing adults who for the first time in their lives are gaining the desire to excel," said Becky, which is amazing to me. That drive is so basic in my professional peers, I have a hard time remembering it's a behavior instilled by the environment: by teachers, parents, people who care. It's difficult to imagine not having that. But what a thrill to think the simple gift of a computer and Internet access can act as the match to start a fire burning within an adult for the love of learning. That is an amazing accomplishment!

We're seeing kids—and adults too—gaining self-confidence, problem-solving skills, logical deduction processing, typing, but most importantly, curiosity about learning and improved literacy at all levels. Because while technology is great, it's not an end in itself.

The Internet, I'm sure we all agree, is not the be-all and end-all, but a powerful tool for literacy. Books remain our favorite tool for learning. So I'm happy when librarians all across the country tell us that they see computers actually bringing more young people into the library than ever before, and that when people use the library, book circulation increases. And when circulation rises, books are being read and enjoyed. It's a wonderful, satisfying circle. People are reading for pleasure, reading to their kids, enjoying literature together, or reading to improve their lot in life. This is something we're particularly excited about and hope to track in the months and years to come.

While individual companies must think about their giving priorities, I would like to see all of us make technology access to all Americans a natural extension of our corporate programs. That's my unabashed bias, and one I think makes sense for the industry to get behind and embrace. Imagine putting our competitive differences behind us and rallying around a single cause.

Start a program

So, now what? Above and beyond my thoughts about access, how can a company take those first exciting baby steps toward building a true philanthropy program? Why not start with an employee matching program? It's a very practical, elegant solution, requiring minimal administration, while reaping a bountiful harvest.

Microsoft has an amazing program, and it's one that can easily be emulated by other companies. Employees target personal gifts into the community and the company matches, dollar for dollar. It's a generous way to tell your employees that you care about what they care about. But the best thing about this plan is that it gives employees the opportunity to make a human connection with their causes: Connections which can last for years, and act as catalysts for individuals to write not only bigger checks, but share time and talent as well. This kind of corporate activism at the employee level is the equivalent of sending thousands of goodwill ambassadors out into the community on behalf of the company.

While I also believe that corporations need to step up and write checks to selected charities and causes that reflect their own values and markets, an employee matching program is a very straightforward first step. So is in-kind giving. There has been criticism about in-kind giving in our industry, which is unjustified. Give product; be it software or hardware, consulting time, or other expertise. To buy your company's product on the open market is prohibitively expensive to many nonprofits, yet the marginal cost of goods makes it a relatively easy way to enter the world of corporate philanthropy.

And, the funny thing of it is, all this giving is contagious can turn into a way of life. As Winston Churchill said, "We make our living by what we *get*, we make a life by what we *give*." In an industry as young, successful and—most importantly—-as innovative as ours, I believe we can make a living while giving . . . all at the same time.

• Chapter 25 •

Global Marketing

25.1 Global Markets for Software

—by Lynn Jensen
Global Results

International markets can offer big opportunities for software developers. A software company with a well-established international presence may earn over half of its annual revenues from international sales. But when, how, and where should a company begin pursuing international opportunities? Should a company wait until it has a certain revenue level or until it has successfully penetrated the U.S. market before addressing international markets?

In the past, before venturing overseas, getting a strong foothold in the U.S. market may have been a feasible strategy. But today, with the widespread use of the World Wide Web by software customers everywhere, it is nearly impossible to contain sales within the U.S. borders. As soon as a software developer puts up a Web page describing a great new product, international inquiries will begin to flow in. Therefore, even small Start up companies can and should begin addressing international market issues as soon as they begin their approach to the U.S. market.

Some of the most frequently asked questions about selling internationally are:

Q. *What are the most basic requirements for our company to begin doing business internationally?*

A. A company must have a corporate-level commitment to selling internationally; a strong product; a good, easy-to-navigate Web site; and a few resources to dedicate to international markets. It need not have a big budget. But some international expertise is critical and can be hired in-house, or provided by an experienced consultant. One small, rapidly growing software company selling a technical server product reaped over 45% of its revenues from international markets simply by having a good Web site and one experienced international person who was able to sign up some strong distributors.

Q. *How should we prioritize the international markets?*

A. Market prioritization partly depends on the type of product and the amount of localization you have done, but most software companies address the European market first. Europe as a whole represents a market roughly equal to the U.S. market; however, it is important to remember that within the European Union, 15 separate countries speak at least nine major languages. Germany is the biggest market for most software products, followed by the U.K., France, and Italy. Because they are often comfortable with English-language products and because they tend to adopt new technology rapidly, the Benelux and Scandinavia tend to be early international markets for many U.S. software companies. Japan, the second largest PC market in the world after the U.S., can offer a very lucrative market for software companies. Although Japan usually requires localized product, it is often possible to find a Japanese partner who will take care of localizing and promoting your products. By contrast, Australia/New Zealand is a relatively easy market to address from a language and culture standpoint. Countries in S.E. Asia such as Singapore and Malaysia can use English product, as well. Software markets are growing in Latin American countries such as Brazil, Mexico, Chile, Colombia, and Argentina; here localized products are important.

Q. *Do I need to wait until I have localized versions of my products before going after international markets?*

A. In most cases, no. You can almost certainly begin selling your American English product in at least some international markets, such as the U.K., Australia, New Zealand, Singapore, India, and Malaysia. The Benelux and Scandinavian countries are often comfortable with English-language products as well. Remember, though, that you may need to *internationalize* your product, even if you have not yet localized, in order to sell it in foreign markets. Internationalizing includes such things as the ability to handle European date format, nonstandard quantities of digits in telephone numbers, extra lines in address fields (including "country"), and other currency signs.

With most products, you will maximize your sales by making them available in local language versions. However, for highly technical applications or programmers' tools, users may actually prefer the English to a translated version. Beginning to launch your products internationally before they are fully localized offers the advantage of valuable feedback from customers and distributors regarding the level of localization needed in their country. In some markets, such as Japan, it is very difficult to sell a nonlocalized product of any sort; in other markets such as The Netherlands, some users may actually prefer English product.

Q. *How can we use the Internet in our international sales and marketing?*

A. The Web can be a great tool for marketing your products internationally, but do not assume that it can act as your only marketing means, any more than it can in the U.S. One big advantage of the Web for international marketing is that you can allow your potential customers to view information or try your product easily, without the time and money required to send a demo or information internationally. However, you still need more conventional marketing to make them aware of your company and your product.

Selling over the Internet with a credit card may appear to have a lot of appeal internationally, since it is possible to avoid customs and shipping issues and the problem of other currencies. There are, however, quite a few pitfalls. First, only relatively inexpensive products will be purchased this way. Secondly, consider how your international customers will obtain support on the product if they require it. Is your tech support line open 7 x 24 to accommodate international time differences? Thirdly, you may be undermining local pricing and the ability of distributors to sell your product profitably in local markets.

Q. *What kind of control can we have over local pricing in international markets?*

A. Control of pricing depends on several factors, but the most important is the level of presence your company has in these markets. If you are selling directly, you will be able to control price levels, even if you also use distributors. If you are paying for and implementing all the local marketing programs, you can also control the pricing by including it in your promotions (some countries prohibit this). But if distributors represent your company, you may not legally dictate the price at which they resell your product. Having either strong competitors or more than one distributor per market will ensure that competition keeps prices reasonable.

Keep in mind that it is more expensive to do business in international markets, so a price 10% to 20% higher than U.S. list may be justified, depending on the discounts you are offering. Economies of scale which apply to the U.S. market are not available in a small country, and costs of staffing, selling, and marketing tend to be higher overseas.

Q. *What impact will the new Euro currency have on selling software in Europe?*

A. Eleven European Union countries initially adopted the Euro as their currency at the beginning of 1999: Austria, Belgium, Finland, France, Germany, Ireland, Italy, Luxembourg, The Netherlands, Portugal, and Spain. The U.K., Sweden, and Denmark opted not to join the currency initiative at that time.

The Euro simplifies some issues for American companies doing business in the E.U., including eliminating currency exchange transaction costs, reducing price differences between EU markets, and dealing with a single currency which will be close in value to the U.S. dollar. The Euro is also likely to force companies to reexamine many strategic issues in Europe, such as pricing, cross-border competition, and even distribution arrangements.

25.2 International Distribution

—by Lynn Jensen
Global Results

Most software companies use a network of international distributors to sell their products internationally, whether or not they are using direct sales in the U.S. market. The cost-efficiency and effectiveness of having local distributors in each country make this method an especially good choice for companies who do not have a lot of up-front resources to commit to selling internationally.

Selecting qualified, reputable partners in each country is critical to the success of your international business. If you make a poor choice, changing distributors can cost you six months' sales and can even cost your company its reputation in a particular market. Companies who have been successful internationally usually have developed long-term partnerships with the distributors who sell their products. Distributors can give you important feedback on product features and direction, as well as investing to build market position for your product. Strong two-way communication is essential in order to get maximum benefit from your distributors.

Frequently asked questions about establishing and working with an international distribution channel include these:

Q. *Will I find international distributors comparable to the U.S. distributors I've been working with?*

A. That depends on which channels you are using in the U.S., but generally speaking, international distributors will be smaller in scope than the big distribution houses in the U.S. It is also more difficult to find highly specialized distributors internationally since the economies of scale in most markets do not allow them to carry a very narrow product line. Exceptions are distributors who have maintained a narrow product focus by expanding across geographical boundaries.

Many international distributors have strong technical staff on board to help provide product support since their customers cannot rely on technical support from the U.S.-based software vendor. In many international markets, you may also find good Value-Added Resellers who focus on a particular type of product and/or vertical market.

Q. *How do I go about locating qualified international partners?*

A. Some sources that you can explore without venturing far include trade show exhibitor lists; trade publication ads and articles; competitors' distributors; and distributors of complementary products. Of course, if possible it would be worthwhile to attend a local trade show or conference in order to see firsthand who the key players are. Contact any interesting companies with your product and company information to determine their interest level.

The U.S. Department of Commerce's Foreign Commercial Service in many countries offers a distributor search program for a minimal fee. In this outbound search program, your marketing materials are sent to a large database of distributors, and meetings are set with interested responders. In some cases, this search can and does result in good matches. A possible drawback to this approach is that the really good companies may have plenty of products chasing them and thus may not be the ones who respond to such a query. Consultants who specialize in international sales and distribution issues can also offer a targeted selection process for distributors who focus on products like yours, resulting within a few weeks in a short list.

Once you have a short list of qualified distributor candidates, it cannot be stressed too highly that you should if at all possible try to visit them before making a selection. Seeing a distributor's premises and meeting with a few customers or resellers will give you information that you would never get on paper. Because you are looking for a long-term partner, selecting the wrong one can be extremely costly in time, lost resources, and lost sales. A trip now may save you several later when you must undo problems that have cropped up.

Q. *What should I look for in distributors, and what can I expect from them?*

A. Write down the criteria you would ideally like your distributors to meet; they will likely all fall short in some area, but your list will give you a standard to work toward. If you find distributors who meet most, but not all, of your criteria, you can negotiate with them to make up where they are lacking. Your criteria list might include such items as these:

- whether dedicated sales and technical support resources are available
- whether localization assistance is available
- whether a realistic marketing plan is in place with resources to implement it
- whether they have been established in business for X years
- whether they carry complementary products
- whether they provide market coverage: geographic and vertical
- whether they are resellers and/or do enduser sales (as relevant)
- whether they make a reasonable forecast/quota commitment

Just about anything can be negotiated with your distributors, but get a commitment as a condition of signing them. You may want to base discount levels on their achievement of certain agreed-upon criteria within a specific time period.

Q. *Do I need a contract with my distributors? If so, should I agree to an exclusive arrangement in order to get their commitment?*

A. It is always a good idea to get commitments in writing, and signing up an international distributor is no exception. Since one or more of the people discussing terms and commitments will likely be speaking a language not his native tongue, having written documentation will help ensure that the understanding is mutual. Use an attorney familiar with the contract law in that particular market; if you include language that isn't valid in that market, you may not secure the protection you expect. You may want to discuss with your attorney the idea of forgoing a lengthy, standard American legal contract in favor of a shorter contract in plain English. Europeans are often amused at the length and unreadability of American contracts; business people outside the U.S. often find signing them intimidating. Clearly stating the intentions and commitments of the parties should be your goal.

As for exclusivity, avoid it if at all possible. Distributors will always ask for this, but if you are firm that your company does not offer this option, they will often acquiesce. If you have found a distributor that you believe will fully develop and invest in the market for your product, it may be worth agreeing to a short-term (6 to 12 months) exclusive if that appears to be the only way they will agree to carry your product. In this case, though, be sure your contract allows you to get out of the agreement if the distributor isn't performing.

Q. *How should I price product to my distributors, and how will they price it in the market?*

A. The discount you offer your distributors should reflect the services you have agreed that they will provide. If you expect them to localize product or marketing materials, do beta testing, recruit and train resellers, and provide technical support, it won't be adequate to offer them U.S. dealer pricing (unless your U.S. dealers are providing all these services!).

Typical discounts to international distributors range from 30% to 50%, or up to 70% in the case of some republishers. Discounts are usually based off either U.S. list pricing or an international list price that includes an uplift. The uplift is meant to cover additional product expenses the software developer faces, such as localization, local-language technical support, local sales support staff and offices, and localized marketing materials.

Usually, your distributors will set prices at whatever level the local market will bear. If you are selling directly, you will be able to control price levels, even if you also use distributors. If you are paying for and implementing all the local marketing programs, you can also control the pricing by including it in your promotions (some countries prohibit this). But if your company is represented by distributors, you may not legally dictate the price at which they resell your product. Having either strong competitors, or more than one distributor per market will ensure that reasonable prices are maintained.

Q. *How can I help these distributors be successful once they're signed up?*

A. Responsiveness on the part of the software vendor is essential to the distributor's success. Surprisingly many software vendors don't respond in a timely manner to technical or sales inquiries from their international distributors. To allow for time differences, responses should be sent within 24 hours. Even a response to simply say, "We're working on it" allows your distributor to get back to the customer and portray you as a responsive, professional software company.

Good two-way communication is another key to success. Your distributors need to know exactly the same information as your best U.S. salesperson. Provide them with Web sites, regular fax updates, reference manuals, and sales tools that you update on a regular basis. Going the other way, your international distributors can contribute excellent customer feedback, product and feature suggestions, and even marketing tactics that have worked well in their markets. Seek their opinions frequently, and listen to their input. Travel regularly to visit them, and encourage them to visit your company as well.

25.3 When and Where to Localize

—by Peg Cheirrett
WASSER, Inc.

At some point in the development of your company, you will ask yourself if you should be marketing your product outside the United States. At that time, you should also ask yourself if you should be localizing your products for those additional markets.

What is Localization?

What exactly is localization and how does it differ from translation? Why should you care about localization?

In a guidebook called *Customers Guide to Translation and Localization*, Lingo Systems defines localization as "the process of customizing a product for consumers in a target market so, when they use it, they form the impression that it was designed by a native of their country." They make the point that *translation* is a subset of localization.

Many U.S. software development companies are getting more than 50% of their sales from international markets. Some localize their products into 26 or more languages while others ship only in English. Localization is a big expense, and it can be a logistical nightmare. If you are developing global markets, what are your localization options?

To Localize or Not to Localize?

The first decision you need to make is "Do we localize or do we ship our product and documentation in English?" If you decide to localize, you'll also need to consider:

- How many languages do we need to tackle?
- Do we do the work in-house or do we outsource?
- If we outsource, do we use U.S. vendors or vendors in target markets?
- Can we stage product releases or must we release in all languages simultaneously?

Can you afford not to localize?

As international markets become more vital to a company's growth and profitability, the pressure intensifies to satisfy international consumers with products customized for their use. If two products are relatively equal, users will most likely prefer the product that is customized to their language and culture.

How many languages are enough?

Depending on where you target your international sales, you could localize in many languages, or you could pick a few languages that will get you the biggest mileage. Many companies entering the European market begin by localizing in French, German, Spanish, and Italian.

Do we do it ourselves or outsource? In the U.S. or abroad?

Few companies employ staff translators and localizers because the work is so periodic. Instead, they rely heavily on contract translation/localization service providers. Some companies use vendors headquartered in the U.S.; others go abroad. Those that go abroad either set up shop in a couple of centralized locations (often Ireland for Europe and Japan for Asia), or contract with a series of different vendors in the target countries.

Gradual or simultaneous release?

Those companies that do localize are experiencing increasing pressure to release their full spectrum of localized versions simultaneously. In some sense, the tail begins to wag the dog. Companies find the product and documentation development cycles increasingly driven by the need to "release to localization."

If you become convinced that localization is the right thing for your company to do, you might think about implementation in a couple of phases.

Phase I: Internationalization

While you're getting started and don't have the extra capital to spend on localization, you can prepare for localization by mastering *internationalization*, the process of engineering a product and its documentation so that it can be easily and efficiently localized. The following are generally-accepted practices for preparing a product for localization:

1. In all components of the product's User Interface (screen buttons, dialog boxes, taskbars, etc.), imagine that you are designing in the German language, which expands anything written in English by 30%. Use visual icons whenever possible. When you use text, use it sparingly.

2. In the product documentation—online or print—follow a few simple rules:

    - Be watchful of culture bias. Avoid metaphors and euphemisms that might not be understood outside the U.S., or that might be offensive to non-U.S. readers. (There are many humorous examples of mistakes made by companies attempting to market their products to cultures they don't understand.)

    - Write simply and concisely. This will simplify the translation process. Some very heavy users of localization go so far as to use a subset of the English language—a minimal vocabulary and grammar called Controlled English—to streamline the translation/ localization process. One example of Controlled English is Caterpillar Technical English.

    - Allow plenty of "white space"—make sure that the text on a page or a screen written in English could be expanded by 30% and still fit. When the time comes to localize, this will ensure that you can reuse the English-version page or screen layout.

    - Avoid imbedding text in graphics. One technique is to substitute numbers for text call-outs, and cross-reference the text to the numbers in a caption adjoining the graphics.

    - Begin building a glossary or terminology list. The more consistant you are in the words that you use to document your product, the easier it will be to translate those words when the time is right for localization.

Phase II: Localization

Getting serious about localization will require you to first develop a localization strategy and plan. The good and bad news is that your competitors have probably already begun localizing their products, so you can benefit from their experience and mistakes.

Before you begin the localization process, you will need to:

- Decide which markets require localization.

- Determine the cost of the localization effort and your funding strategy. There may be financing options you've never considered. (See Lingo Systems' *Customer's Guide*.)
- Designate or hire a localization coordinator or manager to serve in a project manager capacity.

Decide whether to implement the translation and localization effort in-house or contract with an outsourced translation/localization service. A few facts to consider when making this decision:

- In either event, you will need a home team consisting of a localization coordinator, a technical expert to answer the translator/localizer's questions about the product, and an in-country reviewer to confirm the accuracy of the translation.
- A typical software product localization project can involve as many as 20 steps.
- If a software-related product is localized in 10 languages, the translation process alone could involve 30 specialists (translators, editors, engineers, project managers).
- If you decide to handle the localization process in-house, the choice of tools is a critical element, especially for complex online documentation products such as tutorials. Tools called "machine translation software" exist to streamline the translation process. They are not foolproof, however, and require careful editing. They also do not take the place of full localization.
- If you decide to contract with a translation/localization service, you must be very careful in negotiating actual deliverables such as files, templates, art, style guides, glossaries, and project summary information.

Localization is a complex and expensive process and requires careful research and planning before jumping in. It is, however, a logical strategy for any company seeking to expand into global markets, and can be approached in phases.

Resources

Hoft, Nancy, **www.world-ready.com.** (A Web site dedicated to international technical communication and cross-cultural communication.)

Lingo Systems, *Customer's Guide to Translation and Localization*, Portland, OR, 1998. **www.lingosys.com.** (A translation/localization vendor.)

Homnack, Mark, SimulTrans, L.L.C., Mountain View, CA. **www.simultrans.com.** (A translation/localization vendor.)

25.4 Export Sales: Tax Issues

—by Monica Gianni
Davis Wright Tremaine

Export sales into a foreign country by a U.S. person may be subject to foreign income taxes (FIT).

Foreign Income Taxes

In order to determine if export sales will be subject to FIT, your U.S. tax advisor should consult with local tax experts. The form used for doing business in the foreign country will often determine whether FIT is due.

The following are alternative structures for export sales into foreign countries:

- *No presence in foreign country.* A U.S. company that makes export sales directly to independent parties abroad and has no representative or office abroad will not, under the tax laws of most countries, be subject to liability for FIT.

- *Foreign subsidiary.* If the U.S. firm sells its products through a foreign subsidiary, the foreign subsidiary will generally be subject to FIT. The U.S. parent may also be subject to FIT, depending on the nature of the subsidiary's business activities and its relationship to the U.S. parent.

- *Branch office in foreign country.* If the U.S. company sets up a branch office in the foreign country, it may face substantial exposure to FIT. The nature of the U.S. firm's relationship with the foreign representative or office will generally be an important factor in determining if there will be FIT. If there is an income tax treaty between the U.S. and the foreign country, the exposure to FIT may be reduced. If a treaty is in effect, a greater degree of activity in the foreign country by the U.S. firm is generally required before FIT is imposed.

Under most income tax treaties, only income attributable to a "permanent establishment" is subject to tax in the foreign country. Permanent establishment is defined differently under each treaty, but in general includes (1) a place of management; (2) a factory or workshop; (3) an office used for activities other than storage, display, delivering goods, or information collection; or (4) a dependent agent in the foreign country who has and habitually exercises contracting authority.

Foreign Tax Credit

A U.S. exporter can generally credit FIT paid against the exporter's U.S. income tax. The amount of FIT creditable against U.S. income tax is subject to limitations, including that FIT is creditable only to the extent it does not exceed the U.S. income tax due on the same income. For example, if a U.S. corporation pays U.S. income tax at the rate of 35% and a foreign country imposes a 60% tax on export income, only FIT equal to 35% of the export income would generally be eligible for the U.S. foreign tax credit.

This limitation for the foreign tax credit is computed on "foreign-source" income. For sales of inventory, foreign-source income is generated in whole or in part based on the place where title passes. For example, if an exporter sells products it has purchased in the U.S. for use in a foreign country, it may offer an advantage if the exporter passes title outside the U.S. in order to generate foreign-source income. If title passes in the U.S., the source of the income will be U.S., with no opportunity to credit any FIT due from the sale. If property is produced in the U.S. and title passes outside the U.S., the source of the income must be split between U.S. and foreign. For export sales, a U.S. firm thus can increase its foreign tax credit limitation by having title to the goods pass in a foreign country.

If the U.S. exporter operates abroad through a foreign subsidiary corporation, FIT paid by the subsidiary is not normally creditable against the U.S. parent corporation's U.S. income taxes. Through proper tax planning, the FIT could be a creditable tax through the use of a different type of foreign or U.S. entity. Exporters should work with their tax advisors to develop the most advantageous structure for operating overseas such that overall tax liability is reduced.

Licensing Arrangements

A U.S. corporation that licenses rights to a business in a foreign country is not normally considered as doing business in the foreign country. Payments under a licensing agreement from a foreign person to the U.S. company may, however, be subject to a flat foreign withholding tax on the gross amount of the royalty. The rate of the withholding tax is often reduced under an applicable income tax treaty.

Intercompany Transfer Pricing

The Internal Revenue Service has the power to reallocate income, deductions, or credits between two trades or businesses owned or controlled by the same interest. If the price charged between the related entities is an "arm's-length" price (i.e., the price that unrelated parties would pay), no reallocation will be made. If the price is not at arm's length, the company can be subject to severe penalties. In addition, specific documentation must be maintained to support the arm's-length price. Other countries also have transfer-pricing requirements that require compliance.

Foreign Sales Corporations

For taxation of "foreign sales corporations" or "FSCs," the U.S. tax laws provide for a special regime that gives tax incentives for exports of goods produced in the U.S. If a foreign corporation qualifies for and elects FSC status, the tax benefit accorded the FSC exempts the corporation from the U.S. corporate income tax for a portion of its export-related income. This portion can be distributed tax-free to the U.S. parent since the distribution qualifies for a 100% dividends-received deduction.

In general, the use of an FSC results in tax benefits if gross export sales exceed $1 million. FSCs are usually organized in U.S. possessions or foreign countries that impose low or no corporate tax, such as Barbados and the U.S. Virgin Islands. Beginning in 1997, computer software licensed for reproduction abroad can qualify as export property eligible for FSC benefits.

Customs Tax

Goods exported to foreign countries will generally be subject to customs tax in the country of import. Customs planning in conjunction with local tax advisors may permit customs duties to be reduced and unnecessary customs duties avoided.

Indirect Taxes

In addition to FIT, the U.S. exporter could be subject to other types of foreign taxes on its export sales, such as value-added tax, sales tax, or capital tax.

25.5 International Tax Considerations

—by Greg Alwood
KPMG LLP

Because successful software applications are in demand around the world, it is not unusual for a relatively new company to move into international distribution very early in the company's life cycle. International sales introduce a number of tax issues that the company must deal with. It is not unusual for three tax regimes to apply to a software company's international transactions: U.S. tax laws and regulations, foreign country tax laws and, typically, an income tax treaty between the U.S. and foreign country that overrides a number of each country's domestic rules.

Stages of International Development

One of the first tax issues facing a company entering the international marketplace is whether sales or other activities in a foreign country will create a tax presence. Most countries with which the U.S. enjoys significant trade have entered into income tax treaties with the U.S. These treaties generally adjust the two countries' domestic tax laws to create a more favorable tax environment for trade. An important concept in each treaty is the "permanent establishment." The treaties generally provide that business profits will be subject to income tax in neither country unless a minimum physical presence is created: a permanent establishment, broadly defined to include a branch, office, factory, or workshop. An installation project lasting more than six or twelve months (depending on the treaty) or a local agent with contracting authority in the country can also be viewed as creating a permanent establishment. If care is taken to avoid the creation of a permanent establishment, for example by making sales through independent agents or distributors, a company could make significant foreign sales without creating an income tax liability in the foreign market.

Most software companies generating significant foreign sales do eventually require a presence in their primary foreign markets to support sales and service activities. This presence generally creates a tax presence or permanent establishment in these foreign markets. A decision then needs to be made regarding the legal form of that presence. The usual choices are a representative (rep) office or a branch or a subsidiary corporation incorporated in the foreign jurisdiction. The appropriate choice depends on the nature of the activities required in the foreign location. If direct involvement in sales activities is not required, a rep office may suffice and can usually be set up under an agreed-to taxation regime that creates a deemed taxable profit based on expenditures. These arrangements are relatively easy to manage and the taxation levels are generally low in the foreign jurisdiction. However, direct involvement in sales and support in the foreign jurisdiction usually requires either a fully taxable branch or subsidiary. Of the numerous factors to consider in making the choice, the usual choice is a subsidiary corporation incorporated in the foreign country. One common non-tax reason is the perception that customers in foreign markets prefer to deal with local country companies rather than nonresidents.

When a company moves to the level of creating foreign subsidiaries, the initial—and many times permanent—operations of the subsidiaries usually consist of direct sales activities and after-sales support. From a tax and legal perspective, decisions must be made regarding the business relationship of the U.S. parent company with its foreign subsidiaries. The traditional relationship is commonly referred to as a "buy/sell" arrangement; the subsidiary buys product from the U.S. company and sells it in its country of incorporation. However, a number of alternatives to this traditional relationship have evolved, including an increasing use of "commissionaire" arrangements, under which the U.S. parent company is usually an undisclosed principal making direct sales to customers in the country in which the subsidiary is incorporated, with the subsidiary soliciting the sales on behalf of the parent company under a commission arrangement.

Some companies eventually move beyond the status of U.S. companies engaging in foreign sales activities with or without the assistance of foreign sales subsidiaries. They evolve into truly global companies. The characteristics of these companies include foreign direct and contract manufacturing, duplication activities, software development and other R&D activities conducted outside the U.S., and a mobile international workforce. Generally, these companies decide on the location of their activities, driven by the location of resources, logistics and tax, and legal considerations, rather than the location of the "home office."

Each of these stages of a software company's life poses international and domestic tax issues unique to that stage. Management should not only focus on the critical tax issues associated with the company's current stage of development but also anticipate the next stage in order to lay the groundwork for the transition.

International Tax Issues

A number of tax issues are associated with the international operations of software companies.

Source of income rules

The tax consequences of an international transaction depend on the source and nature of the income from the particular transaction. Most countries, including the U.S., have fairly sophisticated rules for determining the source location of income. These rules were generally created with tangible products and services in mind, not software. The unique nature of software has created difficulties in many tax jurisdictions in applying traditional rules to the sale of software across borders. Depending on the nature of the software transaction and the jurisdiction, software sales have been treated as product sales, the provision of services, or the license of an intangible: these differing transactions create dramatic differences in the tax consequences. Fortunately, in the U.S., the Internal Revenue Service has recently issued final regulations setting out rules for classifying transactions involving the transfer of computer programs. These rules, focusing on the copyrights associated with most commercial software, have brought much needed clarity to this area; we hope our significant trading partners will follow with similar rules. Software companies must consider the implications posed by certain countries where the sale of software is still deemed to create royalty income, which is subject to withholding taxes. In this way, Japan and Korea continue to be problematic jurisdictions.

Transfer pricing

The transactions between the U.S. company and the subsidiary, when they are dealing with a controlled subsidiary in a foreign jurisdiction, are subject to a special set of rules in both countries setting out the acceptable methods for determining the "arm's-length" prices required to properly reflect the financial result of the transactions. The pricing methods can be complex and, if significant income is associated with these transactions, the assistance of specially trained economists is generally advisable to arrive at the correct methodology and to meet documentation requirements in each country. Transfer pricing issues tend to be the most contentious cross-border tax area. They generate some of the largest litigated tax cases due to the large amounts of income and potential tax liabilities that can be involved. Obviously, this is an important area for international software companies.

Foreign sales corporation (FSC)

In order to provide a tax incentive to U.S. companies to export products "manufactured" in the U.S., special rules provide for a very favorable tax regime applicable to FSCs. An FSC is, very broadly, a wholly-owned foreign subsidiary set up by a U.S. company to assist with the export of its products. If the subsidiary and the transactions it assists with comply with the FSC rules, approximately 15% of the export income associated with the FSC is exempt from U.S. income tax. The rules are not particularly difficult to deal with and the tax benefit is generous. Fortunately, recent tax legislation has cleared up a controversy and confirmed that software sales can qualify for FSC benefits. Most U.S.-based software companies with significant export sales now avail themselves of the benefits of the FSC legislation.

Cross-border acquisitions and technology transfers

Because software companies are operating in a dynamic environment, it is not unusual for a software company operating internationally to either acquire or be the target in an acquisition involving foreign companies. These transactions typically present opportunities to capture current or future tax benefits if care is taken in planning the cross-border aspects of the deal. On the other hand, tax traps are awaiting the unwary. These transactions can also present an opportunity to restructure an international organization to a more appropriate legal and tax structure for future operations.

Software companies also need to be particularly careful when transferring or licensing their intellectual property outside the U.S. Special anti-avoidance rules apply to these transactions and, if care is not taken, the company can incur an unfortunate U.S. tax cost.

Expatriate tax issues

Moving nationals of one country to another on behalf of the company (e.g., a U.S. citizen transferred to a foreign country to work for the company's subsidiary in that country) creates significant tax issues for the individual. The employee, if a U.S. citizen, remains subject to U.S. taxation on worldwide income and, of course, will typically also be subject to the income tax laws of the foreign jurisdiction. A U.S. citizen or resident can qualify for a "foreign earned income" exclusion, allowing the individual to exclude up to $72,000 a year of income earned outside the U.S. (increasing to $80,000 in 2002), if certain foreign residency requirements are met by the individual. In spite of this exclusion, it is not unusual for an individual on such an assignment to suffer increased taxation and, of course, other significant costs associated with the assignment. Usually the employer covers employees on these assignments with a special plan that provides for the reimbursement of excess costs and other allowances to financially assist the employee with the assignment. The costs, including taxation, can be significant; therefore the prudent company seeks the assistance of specialists to assist with the appropriate planning of these assignments and reimbursement/allowance plans.

Electronic commerce

As mentioned earlier, most tax laws and regulations created in an earlier environment focus on the sale of tangible products and services. Such laws generally did not contemplate software transactions and certainly did not anticipate transactions over the Internet, including the delivery of software. The rapid increase in the use of the Internet has created a dilemma for tax authorities. A broad consensus agrees that taxation should not encumber the use of the Internet by individuals and commercial enterprises. However, tax authorities are concerned about their tax base, which could erode significantly as transactions migrate to the Internet if, in their view, appropriate tax rules are not put in place. The Internet Tax Freedom Act, signed into law on October 21, 1998, will be in effect until October 21, 2001. This is clearly a developing area of tax law in the U.S. and most other foreign countries. Companies engaged in electronic commerce must continue to monitor developments in this area.

Indirect taxation

This discussion has focused on direct income taxation at the national level. Significant indirect taxation issues are also usually encountered as well. Value added taxes (VAT) and various import duties in foreign jurisdictions can impact a software company's foreign sales activities significantly. It is important to seek local country professional assistance in this area to assure compliance with these rules. A cost that should be borne by the company's customers, if care is not taken, can become the company's liability.

Generous rewards await software companies that successfully enter the international marketplace with their products. However, tax issues unique to international business exist. While this short article touches on some of the most significant issues, please note that the information is general in nature and based on authorities that are subject to change. Determine applicability to specific situations through consultation with your tax advisor. Any company facing these issues should seek the advice of experienced international tax practitioners.

25.6 Preparing to Open an International Office

—by Lynn Jensen
Global Results

After selling product internationally for some period of time, companies may consider opening one or more offices overseas. This prospect raises a number of questions, and thoroughly exploring these issues prior to making decisions will save your company substantial time and money over the long haul.

Key Questions

What is the purpose of the office? Wanting to be closer to some key customers in a specific country may be the case if your software is primarily sold, for example, to big OEM customers in Japan. Or you may want a regional office which can serve the needs of multiple countries. If you are selling through distributors in multiple countries in a region, this may be your focus. Or perhaps you want your office to meet both objectives.

What type of functions/services do we want to provide from this office? If it will primarily support sales for your distribution channel, you may initially or eventually want to do direct selling, also. Try to picture the requirements not only for the first year, but for the next five years or so: whether you will need technical staff in the office; whether you will need to keep stock and fill orders from this location. Of course you can move your office if unexpected needs arise which can't be met in your initial location, but thinking ahead will help you avoid this expensive and disruptive situation.

Defining your goals for the office will help in answering this question:

Where should we locate our office? Prepare a "pros and cons" sheet for each country under consideration to begin clarifying the trade-offs. Categories include: market, staffing, logistic cost, and financial, tax and structural considerations.

Market Considerations

Customers: Will local laws put you at an advantage selling to some customers if you have a local presence?

Ascertain the location of your current and potential customers. For example, if your key customers are government or military organizations, you may gain substantially from locating in a country such as Australia, where preference is given to purchasing from companies with a local presence.

Product: Do you have product localized for this market? Ascertain other special requirements that your product meets (or does not yet meet).

Competition: Will you be facing tough local competition or is the market open for products such as yours?

Staffing Considerations

Employee Availability: What kind of staff will you need to fulfill the goals you've defined for the office? Talk to recruiters in the countries you're considering to determine if trained technical staff are available. If you want to establish a regional HQ, you'll need a multi-lingual staff readily available. That English is widely spoken can also be helpful.

Labor Laws: What are the labor laws? Some countries have very restrictive labor laws that make it difficult and/or expensive to get out of employee contracts once you have entered them. Although it is critical to understand these laws, they often sound worse than they are in actual practice. Ask questions of local companies about how the laws actually work. Some countries, like The Netherlands, offer a "trial period" of six months, during which time the employee can be terminated at the employer's discretion. Also, take advantage of any special offers, such as training stipends, which may be available in countries which are trying to attract foreign employers. Again, local recruiters will be a good source.

Cultural/Lifestyle Issues: How different is the lifestyle from that in the U.S.? Will your U.S. HQ employees be able to establish rapport with the new staff? If you plan to send expatriate employees, will it be difficult to convince them to take on the assignment because of local living conditions? Is it possible to find adequate schools, housing, English-speaking medical personnel, etc.?

Logistic Considerations

Transportation: Especially if you are setting up a regional HQ, what is the accessibility from all key countries in the region, as well as from your U.S. headquarters? It may seem like a minor issue, but it will be day-to-day reality for many of your employees. Flight costs and schedules may vary tremendously among neighboring countries.

Telecom: For the software industry it is particularly critical to select a country where the telecommunications structure is relatively stable and mature, if possible. You will want to have good communications links between your U.S. HQ and your new foreign office, preferably at a reasonable cost.

Real Estate: Office rental costs and availability vary tremendously from country to country, as well as between cities in the same country. Accessibility is a key criteria, as is intended office function. If you primarily want to meet (and impress) your customers, look at the key hightech or city-center locations. If you will need to do distribution and stocking at your location, then an industrial park location may be more appropriate. Ask about any special government incentives. The attached spreadsheet, "International Office Setup Cost," outlines what costs, in addition to rent, you may be faced with. Local realtors or Chambers of Commerce are good resources for this information.

Cost Considerations

A thorough preliminary budget for the countries under consideration may help to clarify your choice of office location, since costs for setting up an office differ substantially even between neighboring countries. The attached spreadsheet, "International Office Setup Cost" provides sample budget categories to work through.

Financial, Tax and Structural Considerations

Financial: Are there any restrictions on foreign investment or currency movement that may hinder you from doing business the way you would like? What is the climate like to borrow locally if you expect to do that? Are capital requirements reasonable?

Tax: What is the local tax rate for the type of business you are proposing? Does the country have a tax treaty with the U.S. to avoid double taxation? Are there structures available under which your tax liabilities can be limited during the initial year(s)? For example, in some countries it is possible to negotiate with local tax officials for a tax based on costs, rather than on revenues, for some initial period. If you will be sending expatriates, what will it cost to equalize their personal taxes? The tax section of any big international accounting firm can advise you. Ask for an introduction from your local accounting firm.

Once you have completed and reviewed your "pros and cons" list for the various countries, you may see a very clear choice of location, or you may see that trade-offs exist between several good candidate countries. For example, you may be attracted to lower-cost locations, but the logistics are not so favorable. How do you make the final choice? First, understand your own priorities. If you are currently and for the foreseeable future short on resources, you may be willing to put up with less-than-perfect telecom and transportation infrastructure to save on costs.

Secondly, it would be very valuable to visit your top candidate countries. Meet with local officials to see how much assistance they seem willing and able to provide a foreign company planning to locate in their country. Check out the available real estate. Meet with a few foreign companies who have located there. This is another instance where spending the money for a trip now will pay for itself many times over by helping you make the right decision on where to locate your office.

25.7 Global Trade Resources

The Washington State Department of Community Trade and Economic Development has assembled a set of tables that display resources and contact information for a number of countries and areas:

- Africa
- Asia—China, India, Japan, Republic of China, Malaysia, Singapore
- Canada
- Europe—Austria, Czech Republic, France, Germany, Hungary, Russia
- Middle East—Arab nations, Iran, Israel
- South America—Brazil, Ecuador

(See Appendix B for contact details)

• Chapter 26 •

Liquidating

26.1 Exit Strategies

—by Byron B. McCann and Theodore Feierstein
Ascent Partners, Inc.

No entrepreneur should enter a business without considering how to exit it.

Introduction

The two key exit outcomes are selling the company or taking it public through an initial public offering (IPO). As the extended bull market of the 1990s continues around the publication of this text, the ratio of company acquisitions to IPOs is increasing, and for several reasons. Public company valuations keep increasing to create more valuable "currency" (company stock to issue) for acquisitions; competitive forces and consolidations are accelerating so companies are actively buying competitors or complementary product lines; acquisitions offer more immediate liquidity to sellers; and valuation spreads between IPOs and acquisitions have narrowed. In essence, demand for acquisitions has increased along with the supply.

Distinctions between Sale, Merger, Acquisition, and IPO

A sale, merger, acquisition, and IPO have in common the shifting of the risk of future successful outcomes to parties other than only founders and original investors. These transactions provide liquidity ranging from immediate to deferred. In all cases, it marks a critical milestone reflecting your company's ability to convince others that your value is attractive relative to other entities and has the potential for growth.

	Sale/Acquisition (purchase)	Merger (pooling)	IPO
Liquidity	High if for cash; lower if with earnout	High if pooled for stock and stock is registered with SEC to trade	Medium. Rule 144 restricts amount of stock principals can sell
Valuation	Medium to High	Higher	Highest

| Flexibility | High | Deal structure is limited to meet pooling requirements.[38] Can't have "contingent" arrangements | Limited. Must meet market conditions, underwriter's require-ments |
| Key Benefit | Customized deal structure to meet special demands of buyer and seller | Good valuations and reasonable liquidity | Raise cash; build publicly traded value to make acquisitions, etc |

Other Liquidation Events

Sometimes full acquisitions are "disguised" as different types of transactions for different purposes but amount to virtually the same outcome. Some of the alternative events are:

- OEM deals which are *exclusive* for long periods of time with significant up-front payments

- Technology licenses which are *exclusive* for long periods of time

- *Exclusive* distribution contracts

The common theme is exclusivity. With an acquisition, everything is by definition exclusive. The three deals (above) approach the endgame contractually while maintaining two distinct corporate entities instead of combining them. This approach permits you to keep your company running and perhaps to expand it in another direction. Raising funds in exchange for exclusivity rights to technology or products could be a simple solution. Just remember exclusivity is valuable: do not grant it without knowing the capabilities and intentions of your partner; and make sure you can get it back if they do not perform. The only exception perhaps is the case of one large up-front payment in which the future outcome is unimportant economically. Nevertheless, there could be a case where even if you have been paid, you might benefit from a return of the products or technology rights to sell to another party.

"Don't try to it all yourself. Don't bring in wrong leaders to replace you There's corpo DNA and the person is the leader and the company is aff by the leader." —CharlesCryst Founder, CTO c Chairman of th Board, Chili!Sof

[38] Pooling of Interests: this is a form of merger that, when complete, assumes that the entities have been one forever. Thus, all historical financial statements are added together without revaluing assets and avoiding the intangible asset called "goodwill." This eliminates the need to amortize (write off) goodwill, which does not reduce earnings.

26.2 Shareholder Liquidity:
A Primer on Mergers & Acquisitions

—by Peter Parsons
Davis Wright Tremaine LLP

In theory, the owners of a company will choose to sell just before the profits or growth curves begin to flatten out. Occasionally, theory and reality actually meet at the closing table, but this is more through fortuitous happenstance than design. Every day companies are sold for a myriad of reasons such as a deal looking too good to refuse, an investor bolting for liquidity, an entrepreneur finding himself no longer challenged or perhaps far too challenged, a seller seeking deeper pockets to distribute its product—or it just seems like the right thing to do.

IPO and M&A

As an exit strategy, the IPO has a seductively lyrical ring. Invariably going public will yield cash for the company. An IPO is a corporate "coming of age" ritual that is celebrated by the press, professional advisors, and management. It is a great vehicle for raising cash and putting real meaning behind employee stock options. It will not necessarily put a dime in the pockets of the shareholders. If the goal is shareholder liquidity, IPOs are vastly over-rated. If the company's offering is not met by an enthusiastic market, it may be months, years—or never—before the existing shareholders can dispose of their stock.

While an IPO remains the Holy Grail of many entrepreneurs in the world of technology-based businesses, M&A transactions are far more prevalent than IPOs as a means of achieving an exit strategy and shareholder liquidity. By way of contrast, M&A transactions are far more private in nature but usually result in shareholder liquidity in the near term.

This chapter will acquaint you with aspects of M&A transactions that are common to most deals. No two transactions are alike. Some entrepreneurs are veterans of several M&A transactions. However, the vast majority of entrepreneurs come to the event with little knowledge and a fair amount of trepidation. After all, the hopes and expectations of the employees and shareholders rest upon a successful transaction. (The fact that the employees and shareholders usually do not know that a transaction is in the offing makes the entrepreneur's burden heavier.) But, we are getting a little ahead of ourselves.

The decision to sell

Let us back up to the point where the board of directors decide it is time to consider the sale of the company. The directors may be reacting to market forces, shareholder demands, or a chance inquiry by a third party. However they reach their decision, they are committing to a process that may adversely affect the company. By way of example, competitors may use the knowledge that the company "is on the block" to discredit it in the marketplace, employees may become unsettled, or management members may start floating their résumés. Further, selling a company means a lot of work for management and others; if the board is committed to a sale, a CEO may not make the same types of strategic or tactical decisions.

Impact on management

In deciding to sell, a board should first look to its management team. Will they commit to staying onboard until the transaction is complete? What are their incentives to do so? What would happen if they walked? Very often an incentive package for existing management is the first order of business in deciding to sell.

Impact on employees

What about the employees? Will they start defecting to greener pastures? The answer to this question is usually unknowable. Certainly most employees will focus first on whether their jobs are endangered before they begin to marvel at the potential for global corporate synergies. Knowledge that a company might be sold should be kept on an absolute need-to-know basis, as most boards wisely decide. Often M&A transactions are given cover names. The most successful cover names are those that suggest a logical strategic relationship such as the "Microsoft Alliance." In this example, visits by senior Microsoft executives are less likely to set off the rumor mill.

Buyers and Bankers

The logical buyers for most companies can generally be lumped into two categories. Strategic buyers are those that would have a natural interest in the company to extend or complement their existing product lines or to provide a quicker time to market in a new area. Financial buyers are interested in purchasing a company based upon its current performance or anticipated future performance. Financial buyers may also have strategic goals, such as the acquisition of several similar or complementary companies to acquire a greater market share. Likewise the strategic buyer is unlikely to be insensitive to a very profitable company that may immediately increase its earnings per share. While the calculus is rarely clear, strategic buyers will invariably pay more for a company than their financially driven counterparts. As buyers are often public companies, a preview of the types of transaction that may be offered by a suitor can often be gleaned by reviewing their public filings with the SEC.

Identifying the ideal buyer

If markets were perfect and all persons acted rationally, a company would merely have to knock on the door of the strategic buyer that needed them the most. Identifying the ideal buyer, however, is not a perfect science. Often, the board and management have a fairly accurate view of potential acquirers in their industry but rarely cast their eyes over the broader range of companies that should be in their industry or—better yet—must be in their industry to survive. Occasionally, a promising buyer will have been ardently pursuing the company at every trade event. Even more difficult to identify are the financial buyers who may have interest in several industries but will be driven more by financial promise than marketplace synergies.

Identifying prospective acquirers is not the type of analysis that most CEOs are trained to do. Even if the CEO (or a board member) has the experience, it may not be wise to have him or her knocking on a competitor's door. Enter the investment banker.

Selecting an investment banker

Investment banker, one of those wonderfully elastic terms, includes all manner of beings. There are respected investment bankers that work out of their homes in one-person operations; others that are associated with institutional firms may not be worth their salt. Fortunately for most industries, investment bankers with known reputations can readily be checked out. While an institutional firm may be multi-faceted, the individual investment banker who can take you public may not be the person to handle an M&A deal. Checking references of investment bankers is essential. It is also essential that you obtain the services of the person you hired. There is nothing wrong with training younger colleagues, but there is an essential difference between training youngsters and being shunted off to the "C Team." In most industries such as software, there are investment bankers that work different parts of the market. The appropriate banker for a $500 million company may not be the best choice for a $25 million company.

Interfacing between buyer and seller

I have digressed to talking about the merits of an investment banker—who is probably going cost your company a bundle—because investment bankers earn their substantial fees by providing the essential interface between buyer and seller. A good banker will have the "pulse" of the market and will make sure the buyer pays a fair price for your company. As a part of his service, the banker will prepare a professional "book" on your company and counsel you about its probable worth. The banker will be able to confidentially contact strategic and financial buyers on the company's behalf without compromising the likely seller.

When a suitor (or suitors) is identified, it is the banker who works with both buyer and seller to reach mutually agreeable terms. While they are amply compensated, studies consistently show that investment bankers obtain more value for shareholders than companies that attempt to negotiate their own deals. Remarkably, this is also true when the company has already identified (and had initial discussions with) the most appropriate acquirer.

Closing is objective

Beyond their initial retainers, investment bankers are paid when a deal closes. Most are conscientious and work to assure that the ultimate transaction meets the objectives of the selling company and its shareholders. Good bankers are too concerned about their long-term reputation to compromise it in a single transaction. Undeniably, however, their sole objective is a closing. No closing—no pay. Good bankers will not make introductions and hope something happens. They will drive buyers, sellers, accountants, and attorneys to make sure that the process gets on track and stays on track and that the track ends at the closing table.

Discussing "fairness opinion"

Companies will find it desirable to discuss a "fairness opinion" with the investment banker at the time of retention. Fairness opinions are formal opinions of the investment banker that the proposed transaction is "fair" to the shareholders and that the company's directors have obtained a reasonable price for the company. Essentially, fairness opinions are a form of insurance for the directors and acquiring company. Like insurance, fairness opinions come at a premium—often a hefty one: because the issuance of the fairness opinion is coupled with a modicum of liability, it is not an opinion freely given. If the company waits to discuss fairness opinions until the final stages of the deal, the investment banker will be in a strong position to demand a large fee for the opinion. At this juncture, the company is in the difficult position of paying the banker's exorbitant fee or hiring another investment banker/valuation expert unfamiliar with the transaction whose fees are likely to be far greater. On the other hand, if the fairness opinion is discussed while the company is being courted, the investment banker is more likely to include the opinion within its proposed fee structure to cement the relationship.

Control of the Experience

If you are the CEO/entrepreneur charged by the board with spearheading this process, take caution. Most entrepreneurs go through this experience only once. If you are the person at the center of the process, it is essential that you control it—rather than being controlled by it. Some deals should not be done. As the process picks up steam and experienced professional advisers surround you with excellent advice, remember: it is your deal, not theirs. Always consider the bias of the advisor. An investment banker, shareholder, or key employee may each have valuable but different perspectives and motivations.

Backing out of a deal

If an element of the transaction cannot be explained to your satisfaction, something is wrong. You, your board, and shareholders are the beneficiaries of this transaction. Never become so committed to a deal that you cannot back out if something is amiss. Deals fail regularly for good and bad reasons. It is always personally and financially painful to back away from the table. Nonetheless, almost always no deal is better than the wrong deal.

Selecting an attorney

Selection of experienced legal counsel is of the utmost importance. In most transactions, the investment banker and the attorney are the only people that have had the benefit of having consummated several transactions. The motivation of the investment banker is to close the transaction—period. The M&A attorney is focused on getting the deal done in a manner that achieves the seller's objectives while affording the seller reasonable protection against later liability. Because these are not necessarily compatible objectives, tensions will often exist between the banker and legal counsel. Unless referred by legal counsel, investment bankers will often seek assurance that the company's counsel is experienced in M&A transactions. Often the investment banker will offer recommendations to counsel that have represented them or client companies in past transactions. The banker's nightmare is a lawyer's inexperience standing in the path of a closing (and payment of a fee).

Scrutinizing legal counsel

Scrutiny of legal counsel for the M&A transaction by the board is entirely appropriate regardless of the concerns of the investment banker. The best law firm is often the one that has been representing the company in other matters. If that law firm has experienced M&A attorneys and the board is comfortable with the M&A partners, it should stick with the incumbent law firm and ignore advice to the contrary by the investment bankers.

If not, accept the recommendations of the investment banker and gather suggestions from the board or from colleagues. Interview partners from at least three law firms. You should like this person. He or she is going to be working intensely with you for a period of weeks or months. While there is some convenience in having local counsel, neither hourly rates nor proximity should determine your selection.

Choosing an individual

Make sure that your choice will commit personally to the transaction (versus getting you in the door and handing it off to another partner). While it is entirely appropriate to delegate work to younger partners and associates and to use specialized attorneys (e.g., tax, anti-trust) in their areas of expertise, you are choosing to entrust your legal matters in this critical transaction to a specific partner—not to a law firm. Check with the CEOs that have worked with this partner in other transactions. When hard choices are to be made in the midst of a transaction, it is often the attorney that provides the dispassionate "reality check" on a proposed course of action. Upon selecting M&A counsel make sure that person has an ample chance to "breathe the air" in your company.

Orienting the attorney

Any person experienced with M&A transactions will attest that "culture is king" in a successful deal. Even the most experienced counsel cannot be parachuted into final stages of negotiations and be expected to suddenly be expected to intuitively know the myriad aspects of company culture that have been carefully nurtured since incorporation. In the final analysis, time invested in bringing counsel up to speed on the nuances of company culture, decision processes, biases, and motivations is time and money well spent. In short, you are hiring a skilled transactional advocate, not a mind reader. That counsel cannot be fully effective in advocating your position unless they understand company culture.

Anatomy of a Transaction

The anatomy of a M&A transaction generally follows a set pattern. Suitors are approached or approach; upon signing a confidentially agreement, they are provided with information regarding the company (the investment banker's book, business plan, and minimal due diligence). The suitor prepares a draft letter of intent ("LOI"). Through negotiations, the parties begin to improve and refine the LOI to a form acceptable to the company and its shareholders. Due diligence then begins in earnest and continues until closing by the parties, their accountants, attorneys and consultants. Immediately prior to or after signing the LOI, legal counsel begins the preparation of definitive agreements to document the "handshake" reflected in the LOI. When the definitive agreements are acceptable, signing occurs. In most transactions, shareholder approval of the transactions follows three weeks to a few months after signing. Closing immediately follows shareholder approval.

Offering LOI

Let us begin with a discussion of the letter of intent. A prospective suitor may offer an LOI after simply reading the investment banker's book or may require extensive meetings and due diligence review. Regardless of its genesis, the letter of intent is the point at which matters become serious. While LOIs are rarely binding (except as to matters like confidentiality, non-shop provisions, and break-up fees), they invariably recite deal terms that are difficult to change or modify in the definitive agreements. By this time, M&A legal counsel should be fully engaged and involved in the LOI process. Sellers should also be aware of a common variation on the LOI. Fearing a possible need to publicly disclose an acquisition, public companies will sometimes follow the practice of not signing a letter of intent, but will agree with the seller on its terms while the parties usually rush to prepare definitive agreements. Unsettling as this arrangement may appear, the seller with a solid confidentiality agreement in place is usually at no great disadvantage.

Depending on the parameters of the transactions and the predilection of the parties for detail, LOIs often run from three to ten pages in length. The LOI often includes critical deal elements cloaked in such jargon as "the selling shareholders will provide the representations and warranties customary to transactions of this nature." Veterans of M&A transactions know that "customary" is a relative term that changes from one transaction to the next. By way of example, the foregoing language puts the company's shareholders on the hook for some level of liability—which is not necessarily "customary." While the seller may be focused on valuation, the attorneys will be concerned with language that alludes to matters such as personal indemnification by shareholders, escrows, provisions that may trigger tax liabilities, and securities registration.

Most buyers will expect that the LOI stage should be completed within a few days. It must not be rushed. The company should understand each line of the LOI and its implications before the LOI is signed. The LOI is the handshake that reflects a meeting of the minds. While it may be non-binding, neither party will be pleased by substantial changes requested or demanded by the other.

Doing due diligence

Due diligence is the process of managerial and documentary scrutiny and analysis that determines whether either party will wish to complete the transaction. Usually some level of due diligence is accomplished by the time the LOI is signed. This initial scrutiny is often a screening process for both parties to determine if it makes sense to expend the necessary resources to work toward consummation of a transaction. If the buyer has done other acquisitions, the seller is well advised to talk with those earlier sellers before accepting an LOI.

Unless the purchase price is to be paid in cash, it is equally important for the seller to perform a due diligence review of the buyer. Due diligence may involve managerial review of the party's business and marketing plans, audits of books and records, review of the status of intellectual property, and analysis of every material contractual relationship. In every instance, the level of due diligence is governed by the comfort level of the party. We have been involved in transactions where the buyer virtually ignored due diligence on the basis that the CEO trusted the management team and could "afford to spill $20 million." In other transactions, no document is left unexamined regardless of the representations, warranties and indemnification offered by the other party.

It is the responsibility of both parties to determine what level of due diligence suits their needs. The most valuable scrutiny is that performed by the decision-makers of the parties. The subsequent post-LOI financial, legal, and accounting due diligence is most often designed to assure that the definitive agreements accurately reflect the intentions of the parties as refined by review of the target company's records. Delay often kills deals. One very simple (and inexpensive) way to expedite a transaction is to organize all likely due diligence documents before the transaction starts. Properly cataloged and indexed documents can usually be prepared in a few days or weeks with the assistance of temporary help (far cheaper than by a paralegal) and made available (often offsite) to a suitor.

Admitting to blemishes

Every selling company has "warts" that they would prefer to avoid disclosing. Warts may range from a major lawsuit to a mere blemish such as a state inquiring whether it is owed sales tax. Obviously, no buyer is going to be pleased with surprises at any stage in the transaction. Most sellers will probably avoid leading a sales pitch with a description of a major lawsuit, but such disclosure early in the process will avoid considerable expense and embarrassment. The seller should view due diligence as an inoculation against future claims. If the buyer is informed of each and every wart (and it is appropriately reflected in the definitive agreements), the problematic issues will likely be considered "part of the deal." If withheld information is discovered during the transaction, it may well sour the relationship by casting a pall on the trustworthiness of a party. Withheld information discovered after closing will likely trigger indemnification provisions or claims of fraud. It is not enough to say that the buyer had a chance to look at the offending document or event. To be safe, a seller has to virtually rub his buyer's nose in the offending matter by making sure that issue is covered in the definitive agreements.

Insuring against risk

Occasionally an issue arises in due diligence that is viewed by the buyer as a horrendous risk and by the seller as inconsequential. On occasion, the parties are brought together by the opinions of objective experts on the risk event. By way of example, patent litigation is expensive—very expensive. Even seemingly frivolous cases with virtually no possibility of success may be viewed as showstoppers by a buyer. Conversely, the seller may not wish to offer indemnification that will satisfy the buyer. In recent years, specialized insurance has been created to bridge the buyer-seller risk chasm. In these instances, the insurance company will step in the middle, assess the risk, charge a premium and assume the risk. With the major impediment reduced to the cost of an insurance premium, the parties can now close their deal.

Providing supporting agreements

"Definitive agreements" is a generic term that refers to the mass of transactional agreements that document a deal. Those agreements are variously characterized as "Merger Agreement," "Asset Purchase Agreement," "Reorganization Agreements," or other similar titles. They are supplemented by other agreements such as escrow, shareholder, and employment agreements. These are supported by such documents as accounting, tax, legal, and fairness opinions, Hart-Scott-Rodino and SEC filings, exchange applications, and corporate consents. The names, number and content of the definitive agreements and their supporting schedules are dictated by goals and objectives of the parties. Typical transaction agreements when bound are four to eight inches thick! No volume could cover the infinite permutations of transactional documents. To give the reader a passing familiarity with some of the fundamental elements of a merger document, we will discuss some highlights.

Agreeing on acquisition terms

Acquisition agreements invariably begin with sections of keenest interest to share-holders: the recitation of the amount and form of consideration and the manner of its exchange or delivery. Cash is easily understood. Exchanges of shares are also reasonably straightforward and (with public companies) usually predicated upon relative stock values in the days preceding closing. The stock of public companies received in a transaction is usually registered (freely traded) either at closing or within a short period thereafter (subject to statutory, SEC, IRS, and pooling of interests restrictions). Transaction closings are often predicated upon the merger qualifying for treatment as a "pooling of interests" pursuant to APB Opinion 16 and as a tax-free exchange under the Internal Revenue Code. Pooling of interests is essentially an accounting concept that permits the combining of two companies without the recognition of good will. While the buyer's accountants are usually the final arbiters of whether a merger qualifies for pooling of interests, pooling rules prohibit changes in capital structures in anticipation of the transaction. In recent years, the majority of acquisitions in the high technology community by public companies have been pooling transactions. Pooling rules prohibit "earn-out" transactions. Under most circumstances, experienced counsel often discourages the creation of earn-out arrangements. Painful experience suggests that portions of a purchase price allocated to an earn-out are rarely achieved. Clients are best counseled to be content with the consideration that is exchanged at closing. If an earn-out materializes, it should be frosting on the cake—not the cake itself.

Negotiating representations

Representations and warranties are the part of the acquisition agreement where most of the inter-counsel negotiations take place. In most acquisition agreements, the seller (and to a lesser degree the buyer) are expected to represent that certain facts are true. In several pages of representations and warranties, the parties will be asked to attest to the such matters as

- the legal standing of the company
- the accuracy of financial statements
- the validity and enforceability of every material contract
- that the company is not in violation of any law, rule, or regulation of any governmental entity.

Warranting non-violations

It should be obvious that no company can ever faithfully warrant that its has "not violated any law, rule, or regulation of any governmental entity." Did the delivery driver speed today? Are the elevator inspection stickers properly posted? The representation should be restricted to "laws rules or regulations that, if violated, may have a materially adverse effect on the company." Properly qualified by counsel, each representation and warranty then becomes a verity for purposes of the agreement unless qualified by a disclosure schedule (sometimes called a schedule of exceptions). The disclosure schedules list each and every material document, event, or relationship that, if not listed, would render the representation untrue. Again using the foregoing example, notification of an IRS audit should clearly be listed on the disclosure schedules. Failure to list the audit notice, would violate the party's warranty and, if penalties were ultimately assessed, be subject to the remedies discussed below. Prior to closing, counsel will sit down with the client's executives and slowly go over each and every representation, warranty, and its associated disclosure schedule to assure nothing has been omitted.

Negotiating shareholder representations

Cynically, selling shareholders may be unconcerned with the representations and warranties *made by the company* as they no longer will be shareholders after closing. Not surprisingly, buyers are rarely content with representations and warranties made solely by the target company. After all, the shareholders will be receiving the consideration. Fairly, the buyer often will require that the selling shareholders also join the company in some or all of its representations and warranties. As might be suspected, shareholder representations and warranties are often the most hotly negotiated provisions of an acquisition agreement. In all fairness, the buyer will likely refuse to give in on some representations and warranties. By way of example, shareholders should reasonably be expected to own the shares they are selling. More difficult issues involve representations and warranties on such matters as copyright infringement or undisclosed liabilities. A guiding principle in negotiation of representations and warranties is that the buyer should be willing to shoulder the burden of business risks but should not be exposed to undisclosed liabilities that are known to the sellers.

Indemnifying the buyer

Indemnification is the dark side of the representations and warranties made by the company and its shareholders. Unlimited indemnification is virtually unheard of. Imagine selling your company and years later having a disgruntled buyer knock on the door demanding its money back. In most instances, the parties will agree to an escrow arrangement for 5% to 10% of the transaction value. Typically with an escrow arrangement, matters that violate the representations and warranties (usually exceeding a certain threshold) are debited against the escrowed consideration. At the end of the escrow period (not more than one year under pooling of interests), the balance is distributed to the shareholders.

The value of making sure that the buyer is acquainted with each and every material event, contract, or relationship (and the inclusion of those in the disclosure schedules) becomes readily apparent. In short, if the buyer accepts the disclosure schedules there can be no complaint when inventories turn obsolete or the rogue jury delivers an outrageous verdict in a whistle blower's suit. Reasonably if the selling shareholders have defrauded the buyer by a knowing misrepresentation, no limitations on representations, warranties or escrow provisions will limit their exposure.

Ascertaining compatible cultures

Virtually all transactions require that key management personnel make the transition to the merged entity as an officer, employee, or consultant. Again, ascertaining the cultural compatibility of the two entities is of paramount importance. The environment, freedom to operate, and maneuverability that has often contributed to the target company's success (and valuation) is often lacking in the acquirer's organization. The cultures of both companies may use the same vocabulary, but with different meanings.

Most entrepreneurs will not blossom in the environment of a larger company. By analogy, a command "Hard to port!" will spin a ski boat in a hundred feet but will take a super-tanker more than a mile. Deal structures that make a significant consideration of the entrepreneur's "fitting in" are often formulas for disaster. If The management team that marches to its own drummer must realize this before time to close the deal.

Conclusion

This brief tour of mergers and acquisitions necessarily focuses on the documentary portion of an M&A transaction. Great deals are not made in the attorney's offices. Nor will the most perfect documentation salvage an ill-fated deal. Like any relationship, the courting period is usually a time of optimism and enthusiasm. Infatuation with a prospective merger cannot substitute for judgment and continued scrutiny as you proceed to closing. If you remember nothing else from reading this chapter, I leave you with two M&A axioms:

- cash (or negotiable securities) at closing is King.
- if the transaction is not all cash at closing, Culture is King.

■ Appendix A ■

Washington Employment Law Deskbook

—by Sandra L. Massey
Davis Wright Tremaine LLP

The Washington Employment Law *Deskbook* is a comprehensive, easily understood explanation of the state and federal laws and regulations that Washington employers must comply with every day. It will be useful not only for human resource professionals but also for managers at all levels.

The *Deskbook* is a clearly written reference book designed to answer almost any question and to deal with almost any situation in the employment area. Although it analyzes and explains important employment laws and court decisions, this is not a law book. Written for the nonlawyer, the *Deskbook* focuses on the practical, day-to-day application of statutes, regulations, and judicial decisions. It is designed to help personnel professionals, line managers, business owners, and public employers make the right decisions at critical points in the employment relationship. The breadth of coverage and the sophistication of analysis also make the *Deskbook* of value to attorneys, consultants, and human resources managers in larger companies.

It was written by the lawyers in the Employment Law Department of Davis Wright Tremaine LLP, who drew on their experience in representing hundreds of large and small employers in every aspect of the employment relationship. The *Deskbook* comes in a convenient loose-leaf format for easy annual updating and has an index for quick reference.

The Table of Contents Includes:

1. Employee Information and Privacy
2. Health Issues—Substance Abuse, AIDS, and Smoking
3. Employment Discrimination Law
4. Immigration
5. Wrongful Discharge
6. Union Organizing
7. Wages and Hours
8. Special Public Employer Considerations

9. Unemployment Compensation Insurance

10. Workers' Compensation

11. Occupational Safety and Health

12. Garnishment and Other Wage Levies

13. Miscellaneous—NonCompetition Agreements, State Employment Standards, Employee Benefit Plans-COBRA and Plan Portability, Voting Time, Jury Duty, Family Leave Laws, Plant Closing Laws, Health Insurance for Dependent Children, Employee Rights to Inventions, Reemployment Rights, Dress Codes, Software Protection, Transportation Management, 1995 Health Care Legislation, and Service of Process on Employers

14. Complete List of Required Records and Postings

The Deskbook Has Several Unique Features

It gives a special focus on Washington State employment laws and regulations, plus federal laws of general application. It offers clear, detailed explanations of legal requirements, with emphasis on employer rights and obligations. It provides practical recommendations to help you understand and comply with each employment law. It includes full coverage for both public and private employers. It contains many sample policies and forms for quick reference. Annual updates, available for a small fee, ensure that your *Deskbook* remains current.

To Order The Washington Employment Law Deskbook

To order the Washington Employment Law *Deskbook*, please call Bill Hill at Davis Wright Tremaine LLP (206) 622-3150. Cost is $90.00 per copy, plus Washington sales tax. Because the *Deskbook* is sent via UPS, please include street address (not P.O. Box) to ensure proper delivery.

• Appendix B •

International Resource Charts

International Resources—Asia & Europe

—prepared by the Washington State Department of Community Trade
and Economic Development

Country	URL	Contact Information	Description
Brazil Brazilian-American Chamber of Commerce	**www.bacc-ga.com** tel: (404) 880-1551 fax: (404) 880-1555	1 Suntrust Plaza Suite100 LL 303 Peachtree ST NE Atlanta, GA 30308	Serves the Brazilian and American communities by fostering better relations through international trade
France American Chamber of Commerce in France	**www.amchamfr.com** tel: 01 40 73 89 92	21, avenue George V 75008 Paris France	Organization of the collective voice of Franco-American business interests
French-American Chamber of Commerce in Los Angeles	**www.faccla.org** tel: (213) 651-4741 fax: (213) 651-2547	Suite 1608, 6380 Wilshire Blvd Los Angeles, CA 90048	Nonprofit and nonpolitical organization that seeks to contribute to the development of economic, commercial, and financial relations between France and the U.S.
Promosalons	**www.promosalons. com**	Contact French-American Chamber of Commerce for information	Nonprofit organization providing information of various trades shows organized in France
Asia American Chamber of Commerce in Taipei	**www.amcham.com.tw/** tel: +886-2-581-7089 fax: +886-2-542-3376 **amcham@amcham. com.tw**	Suite 1012, China Hsin Building Annex 86 Chung Shan N Road, Sec 2, Taipei 104, ROC	Nonprofit organization that is dedicated to promote the interests of international business in the Republic of China
Ministry of International Trade and Industry (MITI) in Malaysia	tel: (603) 651-6022 tel: (603) 651-0033 tel: (603) 651-8044 fax: (603) 651-0827 **mitiweb@miti.gov.my**	Block 10, Government Offices Complex, Jalan Duta 50622 Kuala Lumpur Malaysia	Government organization that disseminates information on investment, trade and technology in Malaysia and issues trade licenses, certificates, quotas, etc.

Singapore Trade Development Board	www.tdb.gov.sg/ webmaster@tdb.gov.sg		Nonprofit organization that offers a wide range of services to help companies internationalize. By registering with them on their Home page, they will provide information and services of relevance. (free registration)
Overseas Development Council	webmaster@odc.com		Private nonprofit international policy research institutes in Washington D.C. that seeks to inform and improve the multilateral approaches and institution
Asia Washington State China Relations Council	www.eskimo.com/ ~wscrc Tel: (206) 441-4419 Fax: (206) 443-3828 wscrc@aol.com	2601 Fourth Ave. Suite 330 Seattle, WA 98121	Nonprofit organization which is committed to encouraging a favorable environment for state the of Washington's growing trade with China
Ministry of International Trade and Industry in Japan	webmail@miti.go.jp		
Asia Trade Network	www.tradeasia.com/ tradeAsia.html		Home page that contains resources of Asian trading companies and trade products
Asia-Pacific Chamber of Commerce	http://oneworld.wa. com/apcc tel: (206) 728-1108 fax: (206) 728-1109 apcc@halcyon.com	1932 1st Avenue, Suite 1010, Seattle, WA 98101	Government organization that helps promote growth and cross-cultural understanding by creating linkages that are mutually beneficial to the Asia-Pacific Community.
North American Asian Marketing Trade Corporation (NAMTC)	http://namtc.com/ tel: (615) 370-1342 fax: (615) 371-5077 namtc@namtc.com	115 Penn Warren Drive Suite 300-112 Brentwood, TN 37207	Trading company that provides sources of new or existing products from Asia for American based companies: helps small to large companies import products at the lowest cost
Asia-Pacific Economic Cooperation (APEC)	www.apecsec.org.sg/ apecnet.html info@mail.apecsec. org.sg		Home page for the organization which promote open trade and practical economic cooperation

U.S. Pan Asian American Chamber of Commerce (U.S.PAACC)	tel: (202) 296-5221 **uspaacc@his.com**	1329 18th Street, NW Washington DC 20036	Government organization that is committed to fostering new trade ties between U.S. business and Asia
U.S. Trade and Development Agency	Tel: 703-875-4357 Fax: 703-875-4009	1621 North Kent Street Arlington, VA 22209-2131	Nonprofit organization that provides technical assistance, training grants, workshops for infrastructure and industrial projects in middle-income and developing countries
Russia Russian-American Chamber of Commerce	**www.rmi.net/racc/inde xmain.html** Tel: (303)745-0757 Fax: (303)745-0776 **russia@rmi.net**	The Marketplace-Tower II 3025 South Parker Road, Suite 735 Aurora, CO 80014	Nonprivate organization which promotes America's business in Russia
American Chamber of Commerce in Russia	**www.amcham.ru/ amcham/index.htm**		Government organization represents the interests of investors in Russian Federation
Africa American Chamber of Commerce in Southern Africa	Tel: (27 11) 788-0265 Fax: (27 11) 880-1632	P.O. Box 1132 Houghton, 2041	
South African Chamber of Business	Tel: (27 11) 482-2524 Fax: (27 11) 726-1344	P.O. Box 91267 Auckland Park, 2006	
South African Foreign Trade Organization	Tel: (27 11) 883-3737 Fax: (27 11) 883-6569	P.O. Box 782706 Sandton 2146	
Canada Canadian Consulate General, Seattle	**http://www.canada-seattle.org/CS_EN. HTM** Tel: (206) 443-1777 Fax: (206) 443-9662 **seacons@consulate-seattle.org**	412 Plaza 600 Sixth & Stewart Street Seattle, WA 98101-1286	Government organization which helps American businesses lower production costs, locate new services technologies, discover new products, expand operations into Canada

U.S.A Office of Computers and Business Equipment	**http://infoserv2.ita.doc. gov/ocbe/ocbehome. nsf/** Software Division Director: Tel: (202) 482-0569 Fax: (202) 482-0952		A part of International Trade Administration at the U.S. Department of Commerce. It promotes the growth and global competitiveness of the U.S. computer and software industries. Click on "Contact List" on this Home page for various contact information
Export Finance Assistance Center of Washington	**www.trade.wa.gov/ eac.htm** Tel: (206) 553-5615 Fax: (2060 464-7230	2001 6th Avenue, Suite 650 Seattle, WA 98121	Government organization which provides access to Ex-ImBank program, which provides guarantees of working capital loans for U.S. exporters, guarantees the repayment of loans or makes loans to foreign purchasers of credit insurance against non-payment by foreign buyers for political or commercial risk. EFACW also provides guidance on export financing available through private resources
Germany German American Chamber of Commerce of the Western United States, Inc.	**http://www.gaccwest. org/** Tel: (310) 297-7979 Fax: (310) 297-7966 **gaccwest @compuserve.com**	5220 Pacific Concourse Drive, Suite 280 Los Angeles, CA 90045	Nonprofit organization which promotes trade between Western United States and Germany
Hungary Hungarian-American Chamber of Commerce of New England, Inc.	**http://www.hungary.co m/haccne/** Sophia Lengyel, D.Sc., President Tel/fax: 617-698-6335 **102746.3400@compus erve.com**	286 Congress St. Boston, MA 02210	Experts associated with the Hungarian Chamber will explore market opportunities in Europe through Hungary for products and services, or establish distribution channels or joint ventures in manufacturing on behalf of U.S. companies
Iran Iran Chamber of Commerce, Industries and Mines. Public Relations	Tel: (9821)8830064 Telex: 213382 tcim ir Fax: (9821) 882511	254, Taleghani Avenue, P.O. Box. 15875-4671 Tehran 15814	
Ecuador Ecuadorian Chamber of Commerce of Greater Miami	**www.ecuachamber.co**		

International Resources—Japan

Country	URL	Contact Information	Description
American Chamber of Commerce in Japan	www.accj.or.jp	William Swinton, Membership Manager Tel: 03-3433-7304 Fax:03-3436-1446 join@accj.or.jp	Has more than 2,800 members from over 1,000 companies, whose makeup is about 50% American, 35% Japanese, and 155 from other countries. The membership directory serves as a "telephone book" of foreign owned businesses and Japanese businesses catering to the foreign community. Puts out a monthly journal magazine which discusses bilateral trade issues and tips on living and working in Japan
American Electronics Association Japan Office	www.aea.or.jp	Sean Hackett, Director, Japan Market Development Tel: 03-3237-7195 Fax:03-3237-1237 sean_hackett @aeanet.org	Largest U.S. Trade organization serving the electronics and IT industries. The AEA mission is to represent U.S. interests in trade issues, to help members develop product marketing and distribution channels, and to increase members' business presence in Japan
American State Office Association	www.venture-web.or.jp/asoa/	ASOA Secretariat Ms. Akiko Kanayama Tel: 03-5325-3214 Fax: 03-5325-3131 COHQ2TOK @gol.com	The office in Tokyo has 33 state and local government members including Washington. The office may assist with questions related to business trips, trade shows, or office setup in Japan
Foreign Investment in Japan Development Corporation (FIND)	www.fid.com	Ms. Maki Terada Tel: 03-3224-1203 Fax: 03-3224-9871 fid@gol.com	FIND was created to provide Start up support services for foreign companies with no base in Japan and those wanting to upgrade a representative office to branch or subsidiary status. FIND also charges for it's services

Japan Development Bank (JDB)	**www.jdb.go.jp/**	Tokyo Head Office International Department Tel: 03-3244-1784 Fax: 03-3245-1938	Offers long-term, low interest yen-based loans aimed at the promotion of foreign investment in Japan, import facilities enhancement, and promotion of international joint R&D projects in Japan. Rates are currently at 2.0% to 2.6% for new loans depending upon the project
Japan Information Service Industry Association	**www.jisa.or.jp/index-e. html**	Ms. Junko Kawauchi International Affairs Department Tel: +81-3-5500-2610 Fax: +81-3-5500-2630 **info@jisa.or.jp**	JISA comprises hundreds of firms in the fields of data processing, systems integration and operation, and IT services. Its members account for over 60% of the software sales in Japan
Japan Personal Computer Software Association	**www.jpsa.or.jp/english/ index.htm**	Tel: +81-3-3253-9166 Fax: +81-3-3253-0159 **ohba@jpsa.or.jp**	JPSA is an association of about 400 small and midsize companies. Membership carries the benefits of newsletters, a directory, events, and opportunities for networking, but you'll need a Japanese subsidiary to join. Nonmembers have an opportunity to meet with a JPSA mission to COMDEX this fall
New Business Investment Co. Ltd.	**www.isif.go.jp/english/ kabue.html**	Mr. Takeshi Nakabayashi, Manager, Investment Department II Tel: 03-3231-2380 Fax: 03-3231-2380 **tnNBI@isif.go.jp/ english/kabue.html**	NBI targets technology-oriented firms at the start-up and early growth stages, and offers follow-up services beyond investment
U.S. Commercial Service	**www.csjapan.doc.gov**	Information Technology Unit Mr. Takuya Ogawa, Commercial Specialist Tel: 03-3224-5059 Fax: 03-3589-4235	CS serves as a business assistant within the U.S. Federal Government. Specialists within CS provide market research and one-on-one business counseling, match companies with Japanese partners and for a fee will arrange appointments for business travelers. CS rates computer software as one of the top three fields best poised to make large profits in Japan

International Resources

Middle East and Russias

Country	URL	Contact Information	Description
Austria Austrian Federal Economic Chamber	**www.wk.or.at/aw** Tel: +43-1-50105-0	The Austrian Federal Economic Chamber Foreign Trade Department Weidner HaupstrRe 63 P.O. Box 150 A-1045 Vienna	Assists all Austrian companies and their partners abroad and they help to minimize entrepreneurial risk, and are not allowed to do business in the name of any firm
Former Soviet Union BISNIS—Business Information Service For the Newly Independent States	**www.itaiep.doc.gov/ bisnis/bisnis.html**	**bisnis@usita.gov**	The U.S. Government's area for doing business in Russia and the other states of the former Soviet Union
Arab Nations U.S—Arab Chamber of Commerce (Pacific) Inc.	**www.usaccp.org/ chamber.htm** Tel: (415) 398-9200	U.S.—Arab Chamber of Commerce (Pacific), Inc. P.O. Box 422218 San Francisco, CA 94142-2218 arabtrade@usaccp.org	Provides the link from the 13 Western States to the 21 Arab countries of the Arab world, promoting trade and business between U.S. and Arab companies
Germany German-American Chamber of Commerce of the Western United States, Inc.	**www.gaccwest.org/ greenpgx.html** Tel: (310) 297-7979 Fax: (310) 297-7966	German-American Chamber of Commerce of the Western United States, Inc. 5220 Pacific Concourse Drive, Suite 280 Los Angeles, CA 90045	GACC conducts market research, market analysis, offers membership, and a quarterly newsletter. The newsletter examines trade leads within the U.S. and Germany
Israel Chamber of Commerce and Industry of Haifa and the North of Israel	**www.haifa121- coc.org.il/** Tel: 972-4-8626364 Fax:972-4-8645428	Chanoch Winnykamien, Director 53 Haatzmauth Road 31331 Haifa Israel	Offers the opportunity to make proposals to the Chamber, which then disseminates the offer among more than 3,500 members

Russia			
Chamber of Commerce and Industry of the Russian Federation	**www.rbcnet.ru** Tel: 7-095-9290009 Fax: 7-095-9290360	Feodor V. Loushtchik 6 Ilyinka Street 103684 Moscow Russia	CCI RF is a social organization that assists in developing the national economy
Russian-American Chamber of Commerce	**www.rmi.net** Tel: (303) 745-0757 Fax: (303) 745-0776	The Marketplace Tower II 3025 South Parker Rd. Suite 735 Aurora, CO 80014	RACC is a nonprofit, nonpartisan organization acting to promote American business in the Russian marketplace
India Indian Chamber of Commerce	**www.allindia.com/icc/** Tel: +91-33-2204790/3886/3242-44/3988/4088 Fax: +91-33-2204790	The Secretary General 4 India Exchange Place (9th Floor) Calcutta 700 001 India **icc.iccal@gems.vsnl.net.in**	ICC's mission is to facilitate a healthy and competitive business environment, resolve present economic problems, anticipate the future, spearhead the promotion of trade globally and to ensure consumer welfare
Czech Republic American Chamber of Commerce in the Czech Republic		Stacey Weston Executive Director U Boziho oka, Mala Stupartaka 7/634 110 00 Prague Czech Republic	Representing businesses in the Czech Republic and in the U.S.

Selected Bibliography

Baird, Michael L. *Engineering Your Start-Up: A Guide for the Hi-Tech Entrepreneur.* Professional Publications, Incorporated, 1993.

Bell, Gordan C., and John E. McNamara. *High Tech Ventures.* Addison-Wesley, 1991.

Berry, Tim. *Hurdle. The Book on Business Planning.* Palo Alto Software, Inc., 1998.

Bias, Randolph G. *Cost-Justifying Usability.* Academic Press, 1994.

Bodwell, Donald. *High Performance Team.* Internet Publication, 1997.

Carroll, John M. *Scenario-Based Design: Envisioning Work and Technology in System Development.* John Wiley & Sons, 1995.

Chandler, Linda. *Winning Strategies for Capital Formation.* McGraw-Hill Companies, 1996.

Collins, James C. and Jerryl Porras. *Built to Last: Successful Habits of Visionary Companies.* Harper Business, 1994.

Coe, Marlana. *Human Factors for Technical Communicators.* John Wiley & Sons, 1996.

Covey, Stephen R. *The Seven Habits of Highly Effective People: Powerful Lessons in Personal Change.* Simon and Schuster, 1990.

Dangerfinder® Web site: **http://www.fieldingtravel.com/df/index.htm.**

Daniells, Lorna M. *Business Information Sources.* University of California Press, 1994.

Davis Wright Tremaine LLP. *Washington Employment Law Deskbook.* Davis Wright Tremaine LLP, 1999.

Deming, John R., Scott L. Dekker, and Perter T. Chingos. "Accounting for Stock-Based Compensation." *Paying for Performance.* John Wiley & Sons, 1997.

Dyson, Ester. *Release 2.0: A Design for Living in the Digital Age.* Broadway Books, 1997.

Elarier, Michelle. "To Have and to Have Not: Analysis of Economic Effects of Stock Options." *CFO, The Magazine for Senior Financial Executives.* (March, 1998)

Fitter, Fawn. "Annual Training Survey." *Computerworld, Inc.* (1998)

Gale Research, Inc. *Encyclopedia of Business Information Sources.* Gale Research Co., 1998.

Guggenheim, Alan. *Building Corporate Profiles: Sources and Strategies for Investigative Reporters.* Guggenheim Research Association, 1983.

Hamel, Gary, and C.K. Pralahad. *Competing for the Future*. Harvard Business School Press, 1994.

Hoft, Nancy, **www.world-ready.com**. (A Web site dedicated to international technical communication and cross-cultural communication)

Kawasaki, Guy. *Selling the Dream*. Harper Business, 1992.

Kelly, Kevin. *Out of Control*. Addison-Wesley Publishing Company, 1994.

Lesko, Matthew. *Information U.S.A.* Viking, 1986.

Lexmundi. *Deskbook of International Intellectual Property*. Kluwwer Law International, 1998.

Lingo Systems, *Customer's Guide to Translation and Localization*. Portland, OR, 1998.

Maguire, Steve. *Debugging the Development Process*. Microsoft Press, 1994.

McConnell, Steve. *Rapid Development: Taming Wild Software Schedules*. Microsoft Press, 1996.

Meyer, Pearl. "Stock is No Longer Optional." *Journal of Business Strategy*. (March/April 1998)

Moore, Geoffrey. *Crossing the Chasm: Marketing and Selling High-Tech Products to Mainstream Customers*. Harper Business, 1995.

Moore, Geoffrey, et al. *Inside the Tornado: Marketing Strategies from Silicon Valley's Cutting Edge*. Harper Business, 1995.

Moore, Geoffrey. *The Gorilla Game: An Investor's Guide to Picking Winners in High Technology*. Harper Business, 1998.

Nagle, Thomas T. and Reed K. Holden. *The Strategy and Tactics of Pricing*. Prentice-Hall, 1994.

Nesheim, John L. *High Tech Start-Up*. Strategic, 1993.

Novicki, Christina. "Best Outreach: Homegrown Mindware." *Fast Company*. Issue 5.

O'Farrell, Neal. *Stepping into Magic: A Handbook for the High Tech Start-Up*. Pylon Books Inc., 1998.

Ogilvy, David. *Ogilvy on Advertising*. Crown, 1983.

Peppers, Don, et al. *The One to One Fieldbook: The Complete Toolkit for Implementing a 1 to 1 Marketing Program*. Doubleday Company, Incorporated, 1998.

Peppers, Don, and Martha Rogers. *Enterprise One to One: Tools for Competing In the Interactive Age*. Doubleday Company, Incorporated, 1999.

Peppers, Don, and Martha Rogers. *The One to One Future: Building Relationships One Customer At a time.* Doubleday Company, Incorporated, 1996.

Pirouz, Raymond, and Lynda Weinman. *Click Here: Web Communication Design.* MacMillan Computer Publications, 1998.

Rayner, Steven. *Recreating the Work Place: The Pathway to High Performance Work Systems.* John Wiley & Sons, 1993.

Ries, Al, and Jack Trout. *Bottom-Up Marketing.* Plume, 1990.

Robinson, Everett. *Leading the Way.* Consulting Group International, Inc., 1994.

Roman, Kenneth, and Jane Mass. *How to Advertise: A Professional Guide for the Advertiser. What Works, What Doesn't, and Why.* St. Martin's Press, 1997.

Samovar, Larry, Richard Porter, and Lisa A. Stefani. *Communication Between Cultures.* Wadsworth Publishing Company, 1997.

Samovar, Larry, and Richard Porter. *Intercultural Communication.* Wadsworth Publishing Company, 1999.

Senge, Peter, ed. *The Fifth Discipline: The Art and Practice of the Learning Organization.* Currency/Doubleday, 1994.

Siegel, David S. *Creating Killer Web Sites: The Art of Third-Generation Site Design.* Hayden, 1997.

Smith, William J. "Winning the Battle for Key Talent." *Washington CEO Magazine.* (February 1998.)

Stone, Bob. *Successful Direct Marketing Methods*, 6th ed. NTC Business Books, 1996.

Treacy, Michael, and Fred Wiersema. *The Discipline of Market Leaders: Choose Your Customers, Narrow Your Focus, Dominate Your Market.* Addison-Wesley Longman, Inc., 1996.

Trout, Jack, and Al Ries. *Positioning: The Battle for Your Mind.* Warner Books, Inc., 1981.

Weil, Elizabeth. "Every Leader Tells a Story," *Fast Company.* Issue 15.

Wixon, Dennis, and Judith Ramey. *Field Methods Casebook for Software Design.* John Wiley & Sons, 1996.

▪ Appendix D ▪

Biographies of CEO Commentators

John Ballantine—Managing Partner, Chairman & CEO, iStart Ventures

No stranger to start-ups, John Ballantine has been involved in starting more than nine ventures and has more than 11 years of senior management experience in the computer and electronic commerce industry. In 1994, as president and CEO of Online Interactive, John grew the company into a 120-person outfit.

John is also the cofounder of FreeShop.com, a powerful online direct marketing vehicle that enables companies to reach and retain millions of online shoppers. Prior to starting Online Interactive, John was a Vice President at Softdisk Publishing, where he launched the world's first download software store. John holds a BSE in Finance and International Business from the San Diego State University School of Business.

Bill Baxter—President & CEO, BSQUARE

Bill Baxter is founder, Chief Executive Officer and Chairman of the Board for BSQUARE Corporation in Bellevue, Washington. BSQUARE was founded in 1994, and through Bill's leadership has quickly grown into a multimillion dollar company. Prior to founding BSQUARE, Bill received both his Bachelor of Science and Masters of Science degrees from the University of Wyoming. His professional work experience includes senior software engineering and leadership positions at multiple companies including Digital Equipment Corporation and Intergraph Corporation.

Charles Crystle—Founder, CTO and Chairman of the Board, Chili!Soft

Charles Crystle's unique insight into the marketplace and his progressive views on the value of people and fun in a company form both the vision and the culture for Chili!Soft. A former musician and editor, Charles has refocused his energy and creativity toward leading the company's strategic mission. He has managed client/server development for manufacturing, insurance, and financial companies before founding Chili!Soft and was instrumental in the initial design and development of Chili!Soft ASP and Chili!Reports. He received his BA in English from the University of Delaware.

Jeremy A. Jaech—Chief Executive Officer, President, Chairman of the Board, Visio Corporation

Jeremy Jaech cofounded Visio Corporation in 1990. Prior to forming the company, Jeremy was a cofounder in 1984 of Seattle-based Aldus Corporation (since acquired by San Jose, California-based Adobe Systems Incorporated). At Aldus, he served as technical leader in the development of the original PageMaker software program that helped create the desktop publishing industry. Previously, Jeremy held software-engineering positions with Atex, Inc., and with Boeing Computer Services. He has also been a scientist with the Pacific Northwest National Laboratory at the Battelle Research Center.

He is holder of the 1993-94 Alumni Achievement Award presented by the College of Engineering at the University of Washington in recognition of outstanding contributions to the engineering profession. Jeremy has a bachelor's degree in mathematics and a master's in computer science, both from the University of Washington.

Peter Neupert—CEO, drugstore.com

Peter Neupert brings more than 15 years of computer industry experience to drugstore.com. In his last position at Microsoft Corporation, he was vice president of news and publishing for the Interactive Media Group-including *Slate*, and media business partnerships for MSNBC Cable and Internet, and Microsoft's joint venture with Black Entertainment Television. His responsibilities also included online ad sales and business development. At Microsoft, Peter also held the position of senior director of strategic relationships for Microsoft's Advanced Consumer Technology Group, managing a broad variety of business and marketing relationships to foster the development of the information highway. His endeavors provided the backbone for Microsoft's entry into the media, entertainment, and content worlds. Before joining Microsoft, Peter was vice president and chief operating officer of Graphic Software Systems in Portland, OR. He holds an MBA from the Amos Tuck School of Business at Dartmouth College, and a BA from Colorado College.

Robert Richmond—Chairman of the Board, Active Voice

Robert Richmond, commonly known as "Bard," comes fresh from $15 million of R&D spending, and a two and a half year birthing process.

Active Voice features computer-based call processing software and hardware systems that convert e-mail, voice mail, and faxes into voice or text.

After leaving Cambridge, Mass.-based Intermetrics, Inc., where Robert developed engineering software for NASA and The Boeing Company, and helped invent a system for detecting avionics problems on Boeing 757s and 767s, he systematically sought an answer for his next calling. Robert crisscrossed the country and bounced ideas off friends and colleagues. The result: speech recognition and its many variations. MIT-trained computer scientist and engineer, Robert teamed up with Robert Greco and set about applying the vision to a huge market poised to explode: corporate voice, fax, and voice mail.

Sponsors Company Descriptions

Ascent Partners

"Assisting Software and eCommerce Entrepreneurs to Maximize and Realize Their Shareholder Value"

Ascent Partners specializes in merger and acquisition, strategic alliance, and private equity services to the software and e-commerce entrepreneur. Ascent's mission is to assist technology company principals to maximize and realize their shareholder value. Ascent's team of professionals has consistently demonstrated the ability to get the most value and the best terms for their clients. Its principals have been lead on transactions or sales of companies to Amazon.com, Mypoints.com, EarthWeb, Manugistics, BDM International, EDS, Computer Associates, Disney, Symantec, SHL Systemhouse/MCI, Fujitsu-ICL, Safeguard Scientifics, Allen Bradley/Rockwell, GE, GT Interactive Software, Harbinger, IMNET, Landmark Graphics, CFI Proservices, Network Imaging, E-Systems, PictureTel, QC Data, Quarterdeck, SPSS, SunGard, Borland, Xerox and more.

Ascent's proven track record as successful dealmakers provides great value to the technology entrepreneur. Nothing is more important than hands-on, negotiating table experience. Importantly, Ascent's professionals have successfully started, operated, and sold software companies where they were principals. This hands-on operating experience translates to better deals for clients because it adds-up to more credibility when defending a client's valuation or when taking point on sensitive negotiations. Ascent focuses exclusively on the software and e-commerce industry so that it is on top of fast-breaking industry-specific issues such as mergers, acquisitions, financing, alliances, and other news relevant to smart deal making. It also means that Ascent knows who the buyers are, both here and abroad, and how to best position a client to get the attention of highly busy candidate acquirers. From a quality perspective, Ascent's principals do the work even after the engagement begins. As a result, Ascent's clients get the personal attention they desire and deserve. All of this adds-up to the best results for its clients; solid valuations and consummated transactions.

The Ascent process begins with a focus on understanding a potential client's sources of value such as core competencies, market positioning, technology, personnel strength, financials, customer base, alliances, and the principal's personal objectives. Next, a preliminary valuation is prepared to ensure that both Ascent and the candidate client are like-minded regarding valuation ranges and predicable terms and conditions. A list of targeted larger partners is assembled as well as an offering document and presentation for the critical face-to-face meetings with potential partners. Finally, the transaction is negotiated to successful completion.

Ascent maintains offices and affiliates in the West Coast, Mid-West, and East Coast.

www.ascentpartnersinc.com

Davis
Wright
Tremaine LLP

Davis Wright Tremaine LLP

Davis Wright Tremaine LLP is a national law firm serving technology, telecommunications, software, and media clients with a full range of services including public and private offerings, intellectual property and patent law, mergers and acquisitions, taxation, and employment advice. Our clients on the local, regional, national, and international scene range from emerging businesses to Fortune 500 companies.

DWT is a leader in the area of new technologies. With headquarters in the technology corridors of Seattle and Portland, and offices serving Silicon Valley, Northern Virginia, and New York's Silicon Alley, our lawyers work regularly with the leaders in these fields and understand the impact of technology on all our clients' intellectual property and financing needs. With our nationally recognized litigation capabilities—particularly those in the areas of intellectual property, First Amendment, and employment law—should the need arise we are prepared to protect your company's intellectual property and other interests.

Many of our lawyers are recognized as experts in their fields. Equally important, they include former senior management members, in-house counsel, editors, engineers, chemists, CPAs, and others with hands-on experience in the industries we represent. Working with company leadership as a member of your management team, we can provide practical legal solutions to your business challenges. While many firms approach intellectual property issues in a narrow, compartmentalized manner, we focus on providing our clients with an integrated approach driven by practical business needs. As a full-service law firm, in addition to providing advice on technology and content of intellectual property, we can assist you with structuring your business, financing, employment practices, marketing, and regulatory matters so necessary for you to become a productive and profitable business.

DWT's attorneys deal daily with private equity and institutional investors. Our business lawyers structure and provide support for any deal of any size – from a first round of financing, through venture and mezzanine rounds and strategic alliances. When the time is right for shareholder liquidity, we offer experienced guidance through an initial public offering or a merger or acquisition. And throughout the critical transaction, our experienced deal teams will provide you with the expertise, counsel and attention you deserve.

Davis Wright Tremaine LLP
A. Peter Parsons, Partner
2600 Century Square
1501 Fourth Avenue
Seattle, WA 98101

(206) 622-3150/Fax (206) 628-7699

www.dwt.com

- Anchorage
- Los Angeles
- Seattle
- Bellevue
- New York
- Washington, D.C.
- Charlotte
- Portland
- Shanghai
- Honolulu
- San Francisco

KPMG LLP

KPMG LLP, a U.S. partnership organized in 1897, is the member firm of KPMG (Klynveld Peat Marwick Goerdeler), one of the world's largest accounting and consulting firms with offices in over 840 cities in 155 countries. KPMG employs over 85,000 worldwide, with 20,000 U.S. employees and 1,700 U.S. partners. In the U.S., KPMG has over 100 offices representing substantially all major cities and commercial centers.

KPMG recognizes that its clients expect the services rendered by their professional accounting firm to go beyond an auditor's report. We understand the needs and expectations of our clients and welcome the opportunity to serve not only as auditors but also as trusted business advisors. As part of our commitment to excellence in client service, we have invested substantial capital and human resources in the development of a business approach to all services.

As a provider of information-based services, KPMG delivers understandable business advice—helping clients analyze their businesses with true clarity, raise their level of performance, achieve growth, and enhance shareholder value.

Albany, New York	Anchorage, Alaska	Atlanta, Georgia
(518) 427-4600	(907) 276-7401	(404) 222-3000
Albuquerque, New Mexico	Arlington, Virginia	Austin, Texas
(505) 391-6380	(703) 469-3200	(512) 320-5200

Baltimore, Maryland
(410) 783-8300

Baton Rouge, Louisiana
(225) 344-4000

Billings, Montana
(406) 252-3831

Birmingham, Alabama
(205) 324-2495

Boston, Massachusetts
(617) 988-1000

Boulder, Colorado
(303) 939-8080

Buffalo, New York
(716) 854-1830

Burlington, Vermont
(802) 864-7491

Century City
Los Angeles, California
(310) 553-1280

Charlotte, North Carolina
(704) 335-5300

Chicago, Illinois
(312) 665-1000

Cincinnati, Ohio
(216) 696-9100

Columbus, Ohio
(614) 249-2300

Dallas, Texas
(214) 840-2000

Denver, Colorado
(303) 296-2323

Des Moines, Iowa
(515) 288-7465

Detroit, Michigan
(313) 983-0200

El Paso, Texas
(9150 532-3665

Fort Lauderdale, Florida
(954) 524-6000

Fort Wayne, Indiana
(219) 423-6800

Fort Wayne, Texas
(817) 335-2655

Greensboro, North Carolina
(336) 275-3394

Greenville, South Carolina
(864) 250-2600

Long Island
Melville, New York
(516) 425-6000

Los Angeles, California
(213) 972-4000

Louisville, Kentucky
(502) 587-0535

Melvern Pennsylvania
(610) 722-2800

Memphis, Tennessee
(901) 523-3131

Miami, Florida
(305) 358-2300

Midland, Texas
(915) 682-3791

Milwaukee, Wisconsin
(414) 276-4200

Nashville, Tennessee
(615) 244-1602

New Orleans, Louisiana
(504) 523-5000

New York, New York
(212) 758-9700

Norfolk, Virginia
(757) 616-7000

Northern Virginia
McLean, Virginia
(703) 442-0030

Northern Virginia
Tyson's Tower
(703) 747-3000

Northern Virginia
Barents Group LLC
(703) 747-3000

Oakland, California
(510) 465-4663

Oklahoma City, Oklahoma
(405) 239-6411

Omaha, Nebraska
(402) 348-1450

Orange County
Costa Mesa, California
(714) 850-4300

Orlando, Florida
(407) 423-3426

Philadelphia, Pennsylvania
(215) 299-3100

Phoenix, Arizona
(602) 253-2000

Pittsburgh, Pennsylvania
(412) 391-9710

Plano, Texas
(972) 516-5800

Portland, Oregon
(503) 221-6500

Princeton, New Jersey
(609) 896-2100

Providence, Rhode Island
(401) 421-6600

Radnor, Pennsylvania
(610) 995-4400

Raleigh, North Carolina
(919) 664-7100

Rancho Cucamonga, California
(909) 980-8454

Redmond, Washington
(425) 497-1337

Richmond, Virginia
(804) 649-9091

Roanoke, Virginia
(540) 982-0505

Rochester, New York
(716) 454-1644

Sacramento, California
(916) 448-4700

Salt Lake City, Utah
(801) 333-8000

San Antonio, Texas
(210) 227-9272

San Diego, California
(619) 233-8000

San Francisco, California
(415) 951-0100

San Jose, California – OAD
(408) 437-0500

San Juan
Hato Rey, Puerto Rico
(787) 756-6020

Seattle, Washington
(206) 292-1500

Short Hills, New Jersey
(973) 467-9650

Shreveport, Louisiana
(318) 227-8800

Silicon Valley
Mountain View, California
(650) 404-5000

St. Louis, Missouri
(314) 444-1400

St. Petersburg, Florida
(727) 822-8521

St. Thomas, U.S. Virgin Islands
(340) 776-8350

Stamford, Connecticut
(203) 356-9800

State College, Pennsylvania
(814) 234-5638

Syracuse, New York
(315) 471-8167

Tampa, Florida
(813) 223-1466

Tulsa, Oklahoma
(918) 585-2551

Valencia, California
Compu-Max
(805) 284-1800

Warner Center
Woodland Hills, California
(818) 227-6900

Washington, D.C.
(202) 533-3000

West Palm Beach, Florida
(561) 832-8300

White Plains, New York
(914) 421-2100

Wichita, Kansas
(316) 267-8341

Wilmington, Delaware
(302) 425-0100

Wood Dale, Illinois
(312) 238-5900

Microsoft

Microsoft

Since its inception in 1975, Microsoft's mission has been to create software for the personal computer that empowers and enriches people in the workplace, at school and at home. Microsoft's early vision of a computer on every desk and in every home is coupled today with a strong commitment to Internet-related technologies that expand the power and reach of the PC and its users.

As the world's leading software provider, Microsoft strives to produce innovative products that meet our customers' evolving needs. At the same time, we understand that long-term success is about more than just making great products. Find out what we mean when we talk about Living Our Values.

Corporate headquarters:
One Microsoft Way
Redmond, WA 98052-6399
Telephone: (425) 882-8080

Washington
Software Alliance

Washington Software Alliance

Get connected to the "New E-conomy"

There is no better way to get connected to the technology industry in Washington State than with the Washington Software Alliance. The WSA and its more than 1,400 member companies are your connection to people and knowledge. Get connected to policy makers whose decisions influence your business everyday; peers who share your challenges and concerns; educational opportunities that keep you on top of an ever-changing industry; business resources to help you grow; top-notch talent to fuel your growth; and so much more. The Washington Software Alliance: it's the network for success in the New E-conomy.

Get Connected to the WSA

When you join the Washington Software Alliance you'll have the connections to grow your business. Nowhere else can you tap into the most comprehensive network of people, resources, and talent driving the information age. The WSA is your door to statewide, national, and international alliances, to customers and resources.

A National and International Voice

The Washington Software Alliance works with government, education, and community leaders to foster a positive climate for information technology companies and to raise the regional, national, and international profile of the technology industry. WSA's presence in Olympia, Washington and in Washington, D.C. assures that the industry's interests are heard and acted upon.

The Washington Software Alliance is a statewide organization representing technology across the state from Spokane to Seattle and Bellingham to the Tri-Cities. Join the WSA in making Washington State the Center for the New E-conomy.™ Visit our Web site today, give us a call at (206) 448-3033, or e-mail the WSA at info@wsa1.org.

www.wsa1.org